Traveling with the Saints in Italy

Also by Lucinda Vardey
(not published by HiddenSpring)

THE FLOWERING OF THE SOUL
A Book of Prayers by Women

GOD IN ALL WORDS
An Anthology of Contemporary Spiritual Writing

A SIMPLE PATH
Mother Teresa

BELONGING
A Book for the Questioning Catholic Today

BLESSED
A Novel

Traveling with the Saints in Italy

Contemporary Pilgrimages on Ancient Paths

Lucinda Vardey

HiddenSpring

Cover design by Amy King
Cover art: L'incredulita de San Tomaso, *1505 (partial image) by Luca Antonio Busati*
Text design by Lynn Else

Library of Congress Cataloging-in-Publication Data

Vardey, Lucinda.
Traveling with the saints in Italy : contemporary pilgrimages on ancient paths / Lucinda Vardey.
p. cm.
Includes bibliographical references and index.
ISBN 1-58768-024-6 (alk. paper)
1. Christian pilgrims and pilgrimages—Italy—Guidebooks. 2. Christian saints—Cult—Italy—Guidebooks. 3. Christian shrines—Italy—Guidebooks. 4. Italy—Guidebooks. I. Title.

BX2320.5.18V37 2005
263′.04245—dc22

2005005952

Published by
HiddenSpring
An imprint of Paulist Press
997 Macarthur Boulevard
Mahwah, New Jersey 07430

www.hiddenspringbooks.com

Printed and bound in the
United States of America

For Gemma (1913–96)
in honor of her faith and courage
and
for Antonietta
with gratitude for her love of saints and for Montecasale

Contents

II. PILGRIMAGES IN NORTHERN ITALY

III. A PILGRIMAGE IN ROME

IV. PILGRIMAGES IN SOUTHERN ITALY

Introduction

I was first attracted to the saints of Italy in the early 1990s when I befriended St. Francis of Assisi, or more precisely, he befriended me. The encounter began subtly. Sick in bed with the flu, I had time to peruse the books on the shelf beside me, a familiar stack of long-ago-read novels and soon-to-be-read nonfiction, and in between them a thin, yellowing paperback of *The Little Flowers of St. Francis* with an inscription from my deceased grandmother. On reading some random pages I was transported into the joyous stories of the early Franciscan friars, all strung together by the unconditional love and creativity of this young man from Assisi. And thus began our relationship. Before long I was absorbed in biographies of St. Francis, studying that marvelously simple prayer that bears his name, and feeling a certain inner freedom and excitement. St. Francis's heroic story moved something deep within me, a stirring for a fuller, simpler life, one that was more faith-filled and more pastoral, less cluttered with distractions of the city, more in the moment—living, if at all possible, like the birds of the air, the swallows that soared over the tall grasses in fields. It seemed as if my desire was heard through the stillness of my illness; it was a call to Italy, an invitation from St. Francis himself to discover what awaited me among the places of his life. A retreat house was to be one of them.

I booked my flight to Rome. My first night there, a nightingale singing outside my hotel window assured me that all was well. I rented an apartment in a southern Tuscan hill town called Anghiari and from there contacted some local real estate agents with the details of what this retreat house might look like. In a couple of days while trundling down a dusty dirt road that bordered a stream of waterfalls rushing over sandy-colored rocks, I noticed that two wood pigeons were flying ahead of the realtor's car as if leading it. The abandoned farmhouse we came to was called *Migliara,* and its pastoral peace was what first struck me. Then I saw an old tin picture of St. Francis nailed over the animal troughs. That was sign enough: this was the house. And as I stepped through its open door hanging on a broken hinge, I saw it in its transformation, what it was to become, as naturally as if I had known it forever. Its accompanying field, wrapped by the river continuously gurgling, was sprinkled with violets and primroses. A cuckoo called from a distant wood. I felt I had come home, not to something I knew but to somewhere I belonged; from encountering Migliara I had at last found bliss. And that was enough to move me to buy it. Over a year, with much help from St. Francis (in keeping the vision) and his friend St. Anthony (in finding the funds), Migliara was restored and opened to pilgrims, who came and felt the same bliss: healing, rest, and peace, their souls nourished, their bodies renewed.

A neighbor who loved to gather local histories turned up with Migliara's. Its name, he said, came from the Italian *mila* (thousand): in Etruscan times, pilgrimages were made on foot to the holy monoliths on the summit of the hill behind, and the last stop before you arrived was at Migliara, from where it was a climb of one-thousand footsteps. In Christian times, Migliara was a pilgrim's rest, a welcome to those traveling to Rome. In medieval times, it stood on the main Roman road between La Verna and Rimini, a path certainly taken by the saints, especially St. Francis as he traveled up and down the country visiting his brothers in their hermitages. It had been a mill and a farmhouse, and then left abandoned for twenty years until I found it. I told my neighbor of my plans to convert one of the barns into a chapel, and he said that was no coincidence as it had been an oratory centuries before. This man died soon afterwards, leaving me with the wonderment and awe of connection, of heritage, and of gratitude for the call of St. Francis. But like most calls, this was only the beginning. Shortly after finding *The Little Flowers of St. Francis,* I met my husband, John Dalla Costa, and from then on we have both made research and pilgrimage in the footsteps of the saints central in our lives, venturing out from Migliara with a map and a prayer, toward the unknown, the undiscovered, and a new friend always waiting somewhere on the way. The friendships are very real; the relationships with the saints overflowing with blessings and graces, revelations and gifts, lessons and guideposts, always refreshing, never disappointing, full of laughter, excitement, challenge, and adventure. Some of our greatest joys have been to find places that we did not know existed; to come across a hidden grotto, an unexpected shrine, an exquisite chapel; to encounter God in the least likely places. We wanted to share these sacred sites, wanted to make them available in a book like this for anyone who wishes to travel on these roads with these saints.

Defining Saints

Saints are not just "holier than thou" people whom the pope has recognized and who have survived the scrutiny process of canonization; they are people who have significantly touched and affected their neighbors or their communities as they met the unique challenges of their time to live in the presence of God and, as Christians, to reflect the teachings of Jesus Christ.

Some of the most perspicuous insights into the make-up of a saint have come from the saints themselves. Many of the saints in this book had a common thirst for understanding the saints that went before them, as if they were teachers to emulate, guides on the path. St. Pio (commonly known as Padre Pio, who died in 1968) wrote about the process of becoming a saint as difficult but "not impossible." He summarized that "the road to perfection" takes a lifetime, and that the common challenges were to remain balanced in physical and spiritual well-being, to be utterly surrendered and faithful to God with a clear understanding of the commitments made to the Divine, and to be prepared for ridicule, to be viewed as a fool, to be "sneered at by the world."

Blessed Pope John XXIII (1881–1963) wrote that God desires us to follow the examples of saints "by absorbing the vital sap of their virtues and turning it into our own lifeblood, adapting it to our own individual capacities and particular circumstances." In the thirteenth century, St. Anthony explained that living a Christian life exemplified by the saints required "a steady courage to face the ups and downs of life, the call to love and forgive, to be concerned for the needs of others, to deal with crises great and small, and to have our feet solidly on the ground of total, trusting love and dependence on God." St. Anthony also likened the lives of the saints to the sun "shining upon the temple, for in its rays we can see the dust of our defects." The twentieth-century English mystic Evelyn Underhill defined a saint as simply "a human being whose soul has thus grown up to its full stature," someone who lived a greater life than most common people and who had "a more wonderful contact with the mysteries of the Universe, a life of infinite possibility." This infinite possibility goaded them on to desire, and sometimes to be willing to suffer for, "unreached possibilities," which they recognized as always waiting for them. This insatiable desire was not about self-ego or gratification but was spurred solely by a pure, transcendent love of the Divine, and a dedicated discipline to give over their lives in a total surrender to the will of God.

The Legacy of Virtues

The saints understood all the parts in the process of conversion by experiencing all parts themselves. Most calls to a deepening, more real and truthful union with God require change and a stripping away to the bare essentials of the gospel of Christ. Most of the saints in this book shared an intellect of spiritual understanding and religious knowledge and were fortunate to have had an education that gave them the ability to read the scriptures they were attempting to emulate, write theological treatises, and speak and preach in a variety of languages. During the Middle Ages, this was largely due to their noble or upper-middle-class backgrounds. More recently, when education became widely available to those with less means, learning still provided a valuable platform from which to launch onto the journey to sainthood (for example Pius X, Pope John XXIII, and Padre Pio all came from poor peasant backgrounds). Most did not display anything personally peculiar or particular to their future when starting out in life, except that, as they grew up, they became eager for the challenge of Christ. Because of their religious and spiritual education and training, they were taught the necessary practice of the cardinal virtues of a saintly life: humility, obedience, patience, loving kindness, and generosity to others; a disciplined and fervent approach to prayer and the sacramental life; and the continual examination of their interior motives and habitual imperfections to prevent error in their future ministry.

Books also played their part. Biographies of St. Francis and St. Clare (one of them written by St. Bonaventure), inspired sixteen-year-old Ursula to take the veil in a Franciscan cloistered convent in a trading town in Umbria four hundred years later; books also helped her to recognize what was happening to her when she received the stigmata (the wounds of Christ in her body, which St. Francis had experienced), and to record the process in her diaries. She was later canonized St. Veronica Giuliani. Similarly, without the saints' legacy, would Padre Pio have known the significance of what happened to him when, in September 1918, he received the five bleeding wounds of Christ on *his* body? Without the heritage of stories and the details of the suffering that saints underwent in their love of Christ, the virtue of courage to stand between the darkness and light, to transform the energy of death to life, might have seemed impossible, or simply not worth taking. Because of the examples of other saints, St. Catherine of Siena (1347–80) carried on with her mission against all odds, a woman in the midst of plague and war in fourteenth-century Europe. St. Clare of Assisi (1193–1254) persevered in hope and obedience for over thirty years, while she was forced to live a papal-imposed Rule of conduct that dismissed her deepest desire for poverty. What gave Pope John XXIII the conviction to stay on course with the workings of the Holy Spirit (against a backbiting traditional curia) when he attempted to transform a medieval-style Church into modern-day Catholicism through Vatican II? How did St. Veronica and Padre Pio continue to love and respect their brothers and sisters in their communities when many of them turned suspiciously against them, believing them to be frauds? And how did St. Francis, riddled with sickness, pain, and blindness, write one of the world's most beautiful prayers in praise and glory of God and all God's creatures? The answer to all these questions is "grace," the grace received through prayer and the wisdom of the teachings and example of Christ, the grace poured out by the love God has for saints in their suffering. To be able to love more and to be loving and compassionate to others, it was necessary for the saints not only to experience suffering but to overcome it in themselves in order to embrace the sufferings of others.

The lives of the saints capture us because they are full of examples of heroism. From the beginning of their conversions, locked up in cells or dungeons, to their being stripped away from their families, to traveling far and wide (sometimes appearing in two places at the same time), to preaching to people on the way (and to birds and fishes, in the case of St. Francis and St. Anthony), to fighting for the right to live their lives as they were called (St. Clare, St. Veronica), to accepting their afflictions as God's way of loving them (Blessed Margaret, Padre Pio), and to persisting to the end, sometimes with no sign of success (St. Catherine)—in all of this, the saints can seem superhuman. But we need to remind ourselves that a saint's humanity is composed of interior and exterior valor.

Saints recognize the darkness as ways of smothering the light, and they take responsibility by looking deeply into their interior for where that darkness might live in them. They can, due to spiritual training, discern God's word in their lives; they know when to go into action and when to be still, in retreat and contemplation; they know when a decision has to be made or when not; they can deal with the emergencies of life, and they even welcome death as the ultimate embrace. They are leaders and they are lovers. They lead by their example to be the heart of God in the presence of others, and they are witnesses to eternity, seers of the "bigger picture," of the canvas of divine reality.

Underhill said of the saints that they are

> specialists in a career to which all Christians are called. They have achieved, as it were, the classic status....The difference between them and us is a difference in degree, not in kind. They possess, and we most conspicuously lack, a certain maturity and depth of soul caused by the perfect flowering in them of self-oblivious love, joy, and peace. We recognize in them a finished product, a genuine work of God. But this power and beauty of the saints is on the human side simply the result of their faithful life of prayer, and is something to which, in various degrees, every Christian worker can attain. Therefore we ought all to be a little bit like them, to have a sort of family likeness, to share the family point of view.

Meeting the Family

Following the saints on pilgrimage usually begins in the silence of ourselves. We need to hear the call to follow them, to ritualize a personal or professional challenge or responsibility, or to pray for courage to change, for clarity before offering ourselves in readiness to step into the unknown, step into what God is calling each of us to be or do. Or we may not know at all *why* we are called to travel, to move toward them, and will discover the answers only during our pilgrimage or afterwards. However, we will gain something merely by going into action in response to the call. A pilgrimage requires our physical self, a commitment to travel to reach our next destination. A pilgrimage also demands our entire being—our senses, our mind, our souls, our hearts, our readiness, our movement, our surrender, and our faith. And a pilgrimage needs accompaniment, a companion or two on the way who can guide you—and this is the role of the saints. They can be like a distant sister, brother, uncle, aunt, or cousin in your family. This is why it is worthy to learn about their lives and their times before you encounter them in places of their earthly existences. If you make the effort to travel to them, they certainly return the favor a hundredfold and enter your life with a loving fervor, staying around you, being a source of comfort, teaching you, and interceding for you.

It is more common for us to be aware of our limitations than our heroism, but by meeting a saint, by visiting the places of meaning to him or her, we are rewarded with an experience of the miraculous. We open ourselves to their heroism and feel the devotional energy that lives to this day in the stones of their homes, convents, and churches. By befriending the saints, it is as if we become messengers in the master plan of God's mystery: a more formed member of the family. Michelangelo once said that "by rekindling memories of others, long extinguished, you make both them and yourself live for eternity." Evelyn Underhill summed it up as the "mysterious interaction of energies" that provide us with the tools of a "dynamic love," a love that is purged of self-interest and made more perfect by the saints at "tremendous cost to themselves, and with tremendous effect....It is ours to use on spiritual levels: it is an engine for working with God."

Transcendent Steps

As we require a physical vacation and a rest for our bodies, so too do we need the same for our souls. Yet our souls thirst for nourishment in different ways, for example, through prayer in pastoral beauty, or surrounded by sacred symbolic imagery. They long for insight (learning of spiritual matters, experiencing God's wisdom) and growth (taking risks in faith, practicing courage in surrender). And our souls long to serve others, so it is wise to begin your soul's retreat with a purpose. This is why an intention is vital. This book offers suggestions for pilgrimage intentions, and you will surely have your own. Offering your pilgrimage for another can bear profound gifts to both yourself and the recipient. Making a pilgrimage for a sick person, for instance, can bring about healing and peace. Whatever your intention(s), keep open to change and surprises. The answers to our prayerful intentions might not be what we expect. A pilgrimage is inclined to push us into the moment, to the presence of God in the "here and now." Whatever might happen (including some disappointments—and changed plans), take it as the will of God for you, and all will be well. Grace will always be at work on any pilgrimage, however small, however great.

Marian Williamson in her book *Illuminata* defines pilgrimage as "a process by which we change what we think and transform who we are. Prayer is the pilgrim's walking stick...." Prayer is a necessary part of your pilgrimage, so much so that you must at times lean on prayer to guide you to the right path, the right decision, to enable you to hear what is being said, to recognize the signs, to be present and conscious to what is happening around you.

You may not see the rewards of all your effort immediately. Trust the process and the lasting power of pilgrimage long after you have completed it. There are always rewards for the journey, and due to the mystery of God, they will come in many ways and guises. What is guaranteed is that they will be more than you could probably expect or even imagine.

How to Journey Using This Book

The pilgrimages are divided into geographic regions to enable you to either take one as a tag-on to another trip or visit, or to take a number of pilgrimages sequentially, depending on your time and plans. Popular pilgrimages in Italy are usually to Assisi, following St. Francis, and to Rome, stepping into the heritage of the early Christian Church. You can go on a traditional pilgrimage to either place outlined in this book, and spread out from there to others. Or you could start in the north of the country and work your way south. Some of the pilgrimages described in this book are for as little as one and two days, others for up to a week or more. Give yourself extra time to absorb your travel as well as to take a day of rest and contemplation, either at the end on a shorter pilgrimage, or in the middle on a longer one.

Throughout the book there are sections flagged as "Art & Soul" that highlight the sacred arts and backgrounds of the artists of the area, although I have tried to keep information otherwise found in guidebooks to a minimum. For example, when you visit a church (which is not a museum, but a sacred place of worship), I focus on what is important to the particular pilgrimage and saint, rather than everything you can possibly see (artistically and otherwise) within its walls. Undoubtedly you will find your own way, style, and preference.

Finally, a note about the language of prayers quoted in this book. As far as possible I have attempted to keep the language and quotes in a unitive gender in reference to the Divine. In some cases this required small changes to certain words of the saints, but special care has been taken not to alter the meaning of the quotes.

Lucinda Vardey
Migliara, Tuscany

PRACTICAL TIPS

Traveling in Italy

- When renting a car, you need to specifically request "automatic" if you do not want to drive a manual gearshift.
- Major freeways *(autostrada)* charge toll fees that can become a substantial expense.
- Rely on detailed maps, not local road signs, to reach your destination. Please note: while some international maps of Italy use a single "S" for certain road numbers, in Italy the same roads are designated with an "SS."
- Follow signs saying *"Tutte Le Direzioni"* ("All Directions") to exit cities and towns.

Best Time of Year

- The best time for your pilgrimage is from late spring through fall. Avoid August, if you can, because of holiday traffic and long lines.

Visiting Hours

- Hours to visit sacred sites vary. Most are commonly open in the morning (9 a.m.–12 p.m.) and late afternoon (4 p.m.–6:30 p.m.). Many sites have extended opening hours during the summer. During lunchtime, many sites remain closed for up to three hours.

Etiquette

- Be respectful and quiet when visiting convents, monasteries, and churches.
- Dress appropriately. Shorts and tank tops are usually not permitted in sacred sites, so wear long pants or skirt, and bring a shawl to cover shoulders.

Lodgings

- These are only listed when the places of pilgrimage are remote.

Pilgrim's Essentials

- Good walking shoes and a change of socks.
- Plenty of bottled water.
- A journal for prayers and thoughts in the moment and to chart your soul's course.
- A stick for country hikes.
- Hat and sunscreen during summer months.

Nota Bene

Every effort has been made by the author, editors, and publishers to make the information in this book as accurate as possible. However, travel routes, telephone numbers, and times of availability can change because of occasional renovations, because of special feast days and prayer times, or other factors.

There's usually a spiritual reason for diversions or last-minute changes to well-laid plans. Surrender to the signs of God's will, and all shall be well.

Give me my scallop-shell of quiet,
My staff of faith to walk upon,
My scrip of joy, immortal diet,
My bottle of salvation,
My gown of Glory, hope's true gage;
And thus I'll take my pilgrimage.

Sir Walter Raleigh
(1554–1618) from "His Pilgrimage"

I

Pilgrimages in Central Italy

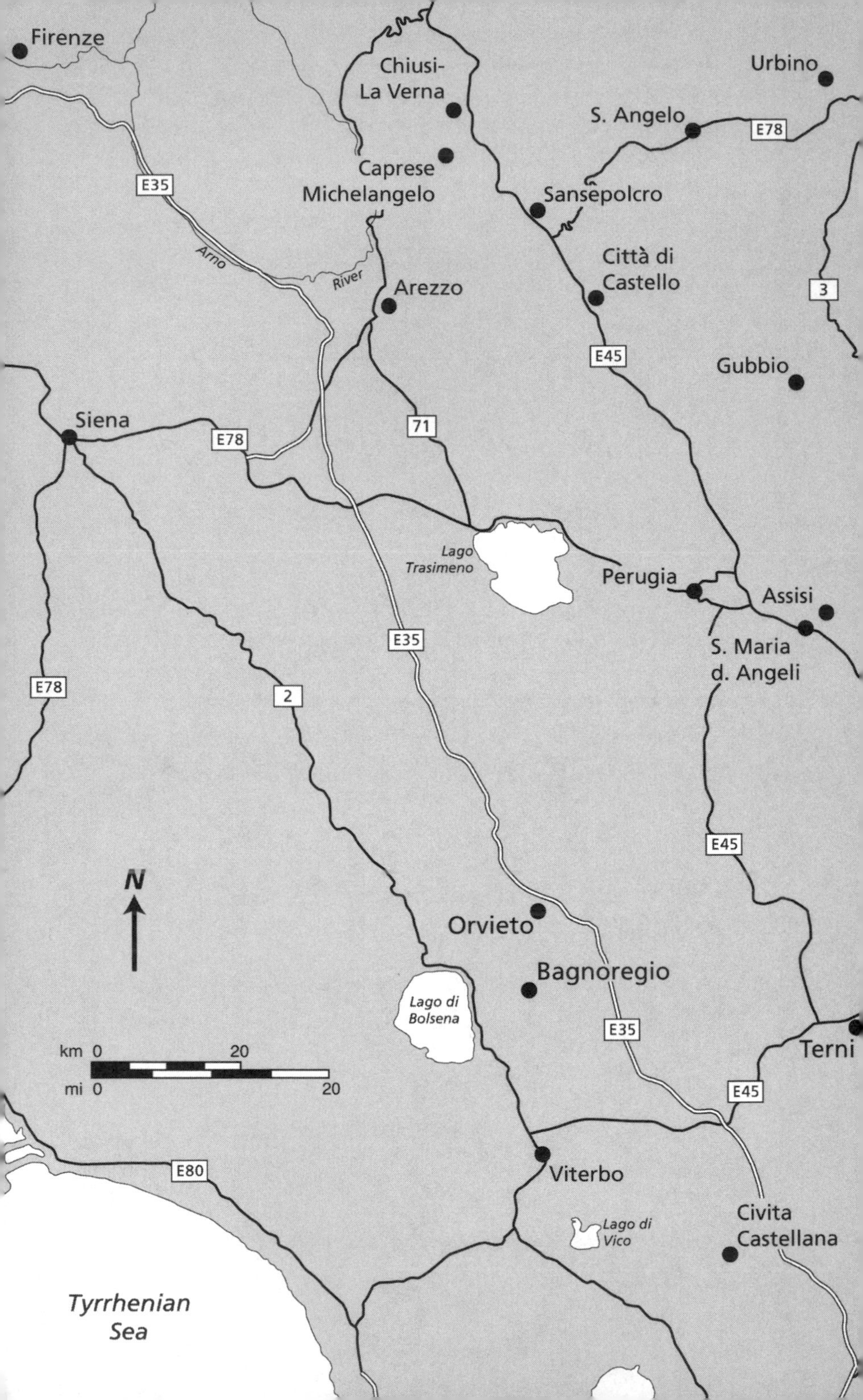

Firenze
Chiusi-
La Verna
Urbino
S. Angelo
E78
Caprese
Michelangelo
Sansepolcro
E35
Arno
River
Città di
Castello
Arezzo
3
E45
Gubbio
71
Siena
E78
Lago
Trasimeno
Perugia
Assisi
S. Maria
d. Angeli
E35
E78
2
E45
N
Orvieto
Bagnoregio
Lago di
Bolsena
E35
Terni
km 0
20
mi 0
20
E45
Viterbo
E80
Lago di
Vico
Civita
Castellana
Tyrrhenian
Sea

ST. FRANCIS OF ASSISI
Christ's Work of Art

"He was raised to God by devotion,
Transformed into Christ by compassion,
Brought near by condescension to his neighbor,
And by the love which he bore all creatures,
He attracted them to himself."
St. Bonaventure in *The Life of St. Francis*

His Life

Of all the saints of Italy, Francis is certainly the best known. His outstanding life, his teaching, his loves, his poetry, his preaching, his Franciscan Order have reached and affected the corners of the globe. His commitment to serving all for the love of God, including animals and all living things, makes him very much a saint for our times, a man who understood the underlying connectedness in ecology, a man who speaks to all of us in some way. From his time—eight hundred years ago—to today, he lives as strongly as ever as an example of loving compassion, humility, and heroic spiritual courage. Francis's legacy is that he managed to capture the elements that created his age, and combine them into the magnificent work of art that was his life. Francis's genius enabled him to successfully pluck the expressions and sentiments that typified the time in which he lived, and with spiritual alacrity, form a community that not only reflected all these parts, but radically changed the face of religion, art, and the social order. He absorbed and unified all the elements—even the expressive arts—into a theology of love. And Francis's unique talent was that, after discovering who he was, he entered into a lifelong partnership with his master, Jesus Christ, following the teachings of the Gospel to the letter. He was, perhaps, the first of Christ's disciples to exemplify how living the directions of the Gospel incurs a grace beyond one's imaginings; he illustrated how this grace can infuse a life, spread to others, and transform the future. This he managed to portray, like a theatrical masterpiece of mythic proportions, by bringing Christ's words to life through the particulars of his own actions, the originality of his words, the artistry of his ministry, the purity of his heart, and his genuine love for everyone. Francis could advise his followers to "preach by your actions" because he always did so himself, but more than that, he introduced the childlike qualities of simplicity and beauty to embrace hope, and be the very necessary foundation for joy.

Francesco Bernardone (1182–1226) lived in a time commonly known as the "High Middle Ages," which began around 1130 and ended around 1250. During his life, Italy was not a unified country but composed of a number of city-states that were either independent dukedoms or controlled by the papacy or the emperor. The emperor at the time was Frederick II, who was born in Assisi's castle. Frederick spoke a number of languages—French and Italian as well as his native German—and, as a result, was able to be more directly involved with his people. Pope Innocent III (another important figure in Francis's life) was elected "guardian" of Frederick II, but later excommunicated him for not providing an army for the Crusades to Jerusalem. During Francis's time, Assisi was an imperial city (under the rule of the emperor) along with its neighboring cities Foligno and Todi, whereas nearby Perugia was under papal control. It was a period of frequent feuds and wars. Lordships and nobility loved war; they even sacrificed their wealth (much of it gained from agriculture) to expend on what they saw as greater enjoyment, glory, and profit. Everybody in Assisi was born armed and grew up armed, always ready to invade, attack, or defend. The city was controlled by the descendents of ancient nobility, whose ranks had been augmented by feudal lords who had moved into the city from the rural areas. Consortiums were introduced and land became commonly controlled in order to defend the area. Many fortified structures were built, and the people prescribed to the common oath "one in blood and war." The classes of people were composed of the "majors"—nobility and successful merchants—and the "minors"—mostly artisans and farmworkers. The Church, too, was not free of the corruptions of power. It resembled a monarchy unto itself, largely due to its religious and political stronghold over the people and to its use of one language—Latin—with its common duties of the clergy. The formalization of the bestowment of the sacraments added to the foundation of its power where rituals such as weddings were snatched away from family and secular life and became only recognized if presided over and witnessed by a priest. With the blessing of swords, priests appropriated other rites of passage, including the dubbing of knights in preparation for battle, so much so that this took on an aspect of sacrament. These ceremonies were controlled by the local bishop; in the case of Assisi, it was Bishop Guido. The other dark side of the papacy and the Church was its abuse of wealth and its renown for pillaging and plundering its enemies, as well as levying heavy taxes. As a result, the movement against Church governance was gaining ground, and there was a growing swell of a free religious sentiment beyond Church dogma, perpetuated by members of radical groups known as Catharists and Waldenses whom the Church labeled "heretics." On the other hand, there was a strong spiritual culture of devotion to saints and relics, and a real belief in the existence of miracles. Due to the growing prosperity of the people, parishes were frequently rebuilt and churches restored or enlarged. The search for adventure was fed by the taking of a pilgrimage, sometimes by foot, sometimes on horseback, to Rome, to Santiago de Compostella, and even to the Holy Land.

Love also seems to have been "invented" in the twelfth century. The promotion of mystical love and courtly love was expressed in the art, songs, and entertainment of the day, and trousseaus had begun to have their influence on the style of marriage.

Francis's parents were well-to-do. His father, Pietro Bernardone, was a fabric maker and trader (he owned workshops for the dyeing of fabrics and a shop to display his wares). With the growing international markets opening up, he frequently went traveling, his favorite destination being France. Francis's mother, Madonna Pica, was French, from Picardy. They had a grand family house at the southern end of Assisi. Francis was the eldest of three sons, and there is a well-known legend surrounding his birth: Pica was alone at the time, as her husband was in France. She was overdue in delivering her first child, and many of her friends were concerned that there was something wrong. One day a stranger came to her house and told Pica that she would not be able to give birth unless she moved into a stable, like Mary, the mother of Jesus. She immediately went to the small barn that was adjacent to the family house and there gave birth to her son. The same stranger who had knocked at her door also appeared at Francis's baptism and asked to hold the baby at the font. Afterward he knelt on the step of the altar and a miraculous imprint of his knee appeared in the stone, after which he disappeared. Pica claimed that he was an angel. She called her young son Giovanni (John) after John the Baptist, a prophetic name for who Francis was to become, but when Pietro returned from his travels, he insisted on naming the boy Francesco (Francis) after the country that was helping him make his fortune.

In his teens, Francis began to display the virtues of leadership; he was confident, sure of himself, even a little "cocky" with enormous charisma and charm. He was always fun to be with, the center of attention, and a leader of revelry. Having an excellent singing voice, he entertained his friends with French songs and lore, and recited poetry. He was rebellious and theatrical, and he savored the delicacies of life. Aspiring to chivalry, he loved women, banquets, and the splendor of springtime. One of the popular songs of the time was

When'er I see the lark take flight
And soar up toward the sun on high
Until at last for sheer delight
It sinks, forgetting how to fly,
Such envy fills me when I see
All those whom love thus glad can make,
I marvel that the heart of me
With love and longing does not break.

Being groomed for merchanthood like his father, Francis would wear the clothes common to the local merchants, who wore silk and carried swords signaling aspirations to knighthood. He had the air of a prince; people loved him and called him "the flower of the young people." There was never any doubt that he was to be called to great things.

When he was sixteen, the people of Assisi laid siege on La Rocca Maggiore (the castle home of the emperor on the hilltop of the town) in an effort to claim independence from imperial rule. Pope Innocent III viewed this attack as an opportunity and directed Bishop Guido to try to regain the old privileges and return Assisi to papal control (like neighboring Perugia). This only caused civil war, as the minors began to mob the majors and started plundering their homes and properties. Francis's home survived, but other families (like Clare's, for instance) moved to Perugia for safety. In their absence their homes were largely destroyed. In the year 1200, a nobleman from Assisi requested Perugian citizenship in order to protect his property from destruction, which began a trend of shifting allegiance. This enabled the Perugians to unilaterally assert taxes over land in Assisi. Along with demands that Assisi rebuild the castle, which the Perugians had destroyed when the emperor left, they also requested payment for damages they had incurred. The Assisi citizens preferred war to this compliance, so they prepared for battle by seizing land owned by Perugia at Collestrada on the plains below. Francis took part in this battle. He was twenty years old and eager for combat, yet unprepared for the slaughter and massacre he witnessed. There were few survivors and those who did survive were placed in dungeons in Perugia. Francis was one of them. Imprisoned in padlocks and chains, he was kept among the nobles in squalid and damp subterranean cells. In prison, while he was still healthy, Francis's warmth and vitality helped his inmates keep positive and joyous, but after a few months, he fell ill, possibly with tuberculosis, and was returned home with the aid of a charitable organization that had taken care of him in an infirmary. His release was probably negotiated by his father, and money would have been paid. Francis returned to Assisi a changed young man at the age of twenty-two.

It took Francis three years and many false starts to give up his desire for chivalrous glory. Obsessed with knighthood and the virtue of bravery, he planned to accompany the Norman knight and conqueror Gautier de Brienne on his travels through Italy. Francis had told others in prison, "You'll see that I'll be adored," which, although accurate, was a desire he later despised. He prepared himself for his journey and left Assisi with the blessings of his family, his church, and his community. But on the road he met a fallen knight, a penniless nobleman. Out of compassion Francis gave him his cloak and some weaponry, and went along his way in more modest attire. He got as far as Spoleto where he fell ill and in a dream was asked, "Who can give you more, the master or the servant?" He answered "the master," and so he was told to return home where he would gain instruction. Although in a weakened physical state, he sold his armor in the main piazza in Foligno (a prominent market town in the foothills of Assisi), and returned home penniless. He probably had to face his father's wrath for such behavior, but after a while he returned to the merry life of carousing and banqueting. He began to talk about being loved by a noble lady, but it lasted only a short while.

DECONSTRUCTION AND RECONSTRUCTION

It wasn't long before Francis stopped attending banquets and sought time alone to pray. He gave alms to every beggar he met, and if he ran out of money, he gave his clothes and the food off his plate. His life was beginning to change. He sought repentance, and confided in a friend (it could have been one of the Benedictine monks in the monastery on Mount Subasio, the mountain that rises behind Assisi) of the enormity of his sins. He spent much time weeping and doing penance in caves on the mountain, causing his parents concern for his well-being and mental stability. In the lives of many great saints, it is common for a period of prolonged penance and weeping, as well as illness, to precede conversion. In medieval times, penitents were people who walked in sackcloth and fasted for their sins and were viewed as heroes of the religious life. This certainly could have held some attraction for Francis as it represented a possible way to fulfill his desire for glory. He was still in the world, seeking a future, and in turning his mind to God and God's ways, he would have found solace in religion. He could, and probably did, have instruction from the monks who would have been his confessors and enlightened him to the meaning of scripture. The monastic life, the alternative offered to a life of trade or knighthood, might have captured Francis's imagination, but his own individualism and creativity, his unique soul, desired much more—which became, as if by a twist of spiritual fate, less!

He began being interested in the experience of the poor; he even went to Rome where he spent time with the beggars outside the sacred sites, exchanging his clothes for their simple rags. He confronted a leper on his return to Assisi—he had abhorred lepers and leprosy in the past—but this time he embraced the leper with a kiss.

The artistic interpretation of the crucified Christ was at the height of popularity in Francis's time. Pictures of the human Christ with the face and clothes of a local man were painted (or sculpted) upon wooden crosses. Jesus was portrayed in a reality that spoke to the people, many of them illiterate and unfamiliar with the written scriptures. One such cross of a Christ very much alive, standing not as a dying man but as if leaning against the cross, and depicted with dark piercing eyes, hung in the small dilapidated Church of San Damiano (St. Damian's), below Assisi. Francis had, during his three years of penance, taken to praying in churches (some abandoned, some not) in the fields and forests outside the walls of Assisi. And it was on one such day that he found himself in front of this crucifix that hung amid the broken stones and rubble of its surroundings. The sober eyes of Christ seemed to pierce Francis's soul, and a voice spoke directly to him: "Francis, go and build up my house which, as you can see, is falling into ruin." According to one account, Francis replied in prayer, "Most High, Glorious God, enlighten the darkness of my heart and give me, Lord, a correct faith, a certain hope, and a perfect charity, sense, and knowledge, so that I may carry out your holy and true command."

Restoring churches would not have been difficult for Francis. Most young men had the skill of stonemasonry (due to the necessary rebuilding of their properties after attack or earthquake), and in Francis's era the building and rebuilding of churches was a competitive activity, one that was composed of outsmarting your neighboring cities or communes by creating even larger, more impressive works of architecture. For Francis, his job was clear, at least at the beginning of his new transformatory path: he was to restore not only Christ's house (represented for him in the little Church of San Damiano), but also create a house for his own future. Little did he know that the effect of his answering the call of Christ would ultimately lead to his restoring the entire universal Church, which was, in Christ's words, "falling into ruin."

Francis decided to get money to accomplish the restoration and naturally turned to his own family for the means. As his father was away, he took bales of precious cloth from the shop and carried them off on the back of his horse, again to the market town of Foligno where he sold everything, including his horse. Returning on foot to San Damiano, he approached the priest residing at the church with the proposal for reconstruction, the money to carry it out in a pouch. The priest, probably knowledgeable of Francis's past and also wary of his father's wrath, refused any assistance, but Francis persisted. The priest finally concurred but refused the money, so Francis tossed the pouch of coins against a window at the entrance. This very act was as symbolic a gesture as he could make. It signified the ending of his relationship with his family and the beginning of his embrace of poverty. Not long afterwards, his father returned from his travels to discover the theft and began searching for his son. Francis hid at San Damiano, and a friend provided him with food and keep, but Francis could not hide there forever. He eventually returned to Assisi, dressed in simple clothes and armed not with fear of his father but with the courage to face him, now that his future direction was clear.

A changed man entered the town, a man not bemoaning his sins or acting in a tearful, penitential way, but a man triumphant, lost in prayer, surrounded by God's love. He was greeted, however, with insults from the people who had once loved him. Children threw stones at him and called him "madman." His father beat him in public and threw him into a domestic dungeon, but his mother gave Francis some new clothes and set him free.

Unable to comprehend or retrieve his son's theft, Pietro registered a complaint with the consuls of Assisi over the stolen money, and Francis was ordered to formally present himself. Francis had renounced his inheritance and his family affiliation; he also refused to abide by any secular rules, claiming that he was free and a servant only of "the most high God." This is when Bishop Guido was consulted, because of Francis's obvious call to the religious life. Francis was ordered to appear alongside his father at the bishop's court. Now, Francis had both the theatrical and spiritual skills to make a point, and he made one that would be remembered forever. And so, in the middle of February 1207, outside the bishop's palace, amid a crowd of onlookers, Francis stripped off all his clothes, renounced the Bernardone name, and, after reciting the Our Father, pronounced, "I shall go naked to meet the Lord." Bishop Guido had him covered in a gardener's shirt and a torn overcoat that had been thrown into the garbage. Francis traced a cross on it with chalk and left the square free as a bird in flight, surrendered to where Christ would take him.

CREATING THE FOUNDATION

St. Bonaventure, the future minister general of the Franciscans, wrote in his biography of Francis, that "the spiritual merchant must begin with contempt of the world, and that the soldier of Christ must begin by victory over himself." Certainly, Francis had been victorious in this respect, moving away from all that he had been in his past, and stepping into a future where Christ would instruct his every move in complete surrender to the poverty of not knowing where or how he would live. After his disinheritance in Assisi, he set off on foot for Gubbio as he had a friend who lived there whom he had met during the battle at Collestrada. On his way, he was attacked by brigands who took his torn overcoat. When asked who he was, he replied, "I am the Herald of the Great King," almost as if he had the same understanding of his role as had John the Baptist.

When Francis arrived in Gubbio, his friend gave him a tunic, along with a simple leather belt and sandals. The tunic's color was gray, like the clothes lepers had to wear, and to prevent people scurrying from him, Francis exchanged it for a brown, coarse tunic, which, to him, resembled the color of swallows. He later said of the coarseness of his robe that Christ praised John the Baptist for wearing such clothes. Francis also said that he endured the cold because "if we burn within with a fervent desire for our heavenly country, it's easy to endure exterior cold."

Francis began caring for lepers in a hospice, but after a few weeks returned to Assisi to begin the restoration of San Damiano. Without money, he turned to begging for the stones he needed. And this is where he started to put the pieces of the Franciscan creation together: He used the language of chivalry in speaking of the virtues of his newfound life, embracing "Lady Poverty" and calling himself the "Poverello" (the poor one). He had once heard a beggar offer *"pace e bene"* as a greeting, meaning "peace and goodness," or "wellness," and he adopted the phrase as his own. He had discovered the joy of freedom and sang all the while he was doing God's work, and because of this joy he attracted many helpers. After finishing San Damiano, he restored another church called San Pietro (St. Peter's), and then went on to his lifelong love, La Porziuncola (The Little Part), a little chapel whose proper name was Santa Maria degli Angeli (St. Mary of the Angels). A primitive country church, it was owned by the Benedictines from the monastery up on Mount Subasio, and was used mostly by foresters and local peasants. One day at Mass, the words of the Gospel of the day had a profound impact on Francis. Christ had sent his laborers out into the fields with the instructions: "As you go, proclaim the good news, 'The kingdom of heaven has come near'....You received without payment; give without payment. Take no gold, or silver, or copper in your belts, no bag for your journey, or two tunics, or sandals, or a staff" (Matt 10:7–10).

On hearing this, Francis threw away his belt, tossed off his sandals, and rearranged his brown tunic in the shape of a cross. Again, Francis took a fresh route even to his adoption of the cross as symbol, because he chose the Tau cross (a cross like a T), which is the last letter of the Hebrew alphabet. In the Old Testament it was an indication of the saving love of God for humans and was imprinted on the forehead of the prophet Ezekiel. Francis began to proclaim the good news of his choice of life, his freedom in poverty, his joy in surrender to Christ. He preached among the poor, the lepers, the outcasts of the rich society, those who would not commonly be seen or heard in the grand churches of Assisi. He preached that God loves sinners and hates only the sin, and he used the language of the people, the vernacular instead of the more-remote Latin, and people marveled at the simple way he could deliver God's message. He was like a breath of fresh air—nobody, it seemed, had spoken of God before in such a refreshing and magnetizing way.

The first man to follow him was Bernardo Da Quintavalle, who had invited Francis to stay at his house one day and witnessed his all-night devotion. Francis's friend Pietro Di Catanio was the second. The three men attended Mass together at Francis's old family Church of San Nicolo, and afterward he asked the priest for biblical guidance for this small band of men by randomly opening the Bible three times. In the three selections, Jesus seemed to speak to them directly:

> "If you wish to be perfect, go, sell your possessions, and give the money to the poor, and you will have treasure in heaven; then come, follow me." (Matt 19:21)
>
> "Take nothing for your journey, no staff, nor bag, nor bread, nor money—not even an extra tunic." (Luke 9:3)
>
> "If any want to become my followers, let them deny themselves and take up their cross daily and follow me." (Luke 9:23)

Inspired by hearing these teachings, Francis proclaimed them as the foundation of their way of life. This was particularly hard for Bernardo and Pietro as they were both rich and had to now sell everything and give it to the poor, but they managed, and took the habit of the Tau cross, the coarse brown tunic. The band of men grew. Soon there were eight of them, and they moved into Rivotorto (Tortuous Stream), an abandoned leprosarium used occasionally as an animal shelter. Francis called it "a jumping off point to paradise." They all squeezed in together with hardly room to stretch their legs as more men began to join them, and they inscribed their names on the beams above them. Francis taught his brothers the basics of their community: "Be patient in tribulation, watchful in prayer, strong in labor, moderate in speech, grave in conversation, thankful for benefits." Work was obligatory. Francis said, "If anyone will not work, let him not eat." In exchange for work, the brothers would receive all necessities except money (which they were not allowed to touch), and if they ran out of food, they would beg for it. Most of their early ministry was with the lepers whom they invited into their hut with them.

THE FRIARS MINOR

Just as Christ had instructed his apostles to travel in twos, the brothers set off in pairs to preach in the nearby towns. It wasn't easy for these friars dressed in rags to be taken seriously, especially in the towns, but in the countryside they became a success. No priest ever visited the poor communities, and most of these people had forgotten what it was like to hear words of the soul. Francis always reminded his listeners of the love that God had for each of them—he would frequently weep as he spoke of the sorrow he felt for their sins, though he never condemned them, and they were moved to repent.

As more men sought out Francis and wanted to join his band of brothers, and as more poor people trusted them to minister to them in word and deed, it became clear to Francis that some order and official acceptance by Rome was required for his poor way of life. Pope Innocent III, aware of the growing popularity of heretical movements sprouting all over Europe (where people took it on themselves to follow Christ's teaching and ignore Church dogma), wanted to infuse the Church with elements of poverty and renunciation. Francis's appearance at the St. John Lateran (the pope's official residence in Rome) brought the compelling issue to a head. It was hard to distinguish Francis and his disheveled group of beggars from any other poor men, and so at first it seemed unlikely that the friars would receive an audience with the pope. Fortunately for them, Bishop Guido was in Rome at the time and, although caught unaware of Francis's intent or his journey to Rome, the bishop intervened on his behalf with the curia, explaining that Francis and his men had not left the Church to pursue their individual calling but were attempting it within the confines of the Church. Bishop Guido had unsuccessfully attempted to steer Francis and his men toward an already-existing religious order—such as the Benedictines—as he was concerned about the harshness of the rules they had set for themselves, feeling they were "beyond human capacity." But Francis defended the teachings of Christ as possible to practice in the way they had chosen, and he finally received his papal audience. There are many stories about how this happened, but the most popular is that Innocent III had a dream of a beggar holding up St. John Lateran as it was about to collapse, and on waking, he recognized the beggar as Francis. The pope gave Francis verbal approval to preach but no official bull was forthcoming, as the pope shared Bishop Guido's concern about the men's capability to endure extreme poverty.

The brothers returned from Rome to their shanty at Rivotorto, only to discover that in their absence, it had been repossessed by a peasant who had pushed his ass into it for shelter, thus pushing them out! Now totaling twelve, the men had already outgrown the animal shelter anyway, so the Benedictines gave them La Porziuncola in return for a basket of fish a year. The friars built grass huts for themselves around the chapel, composing a sort of rustic monastery, and more and more men joined them. Francis, now with papal approval to preach, started to do so more officially, and he went up to Assisi to deliver his sermons in the churches. He taught about God's love and forgiveness, and about repentance. On one occasion he preached to the congregation in the ancient Church of San Rufino, among whom was a young woman called Chiara (Clare) Offreduccio.

THE FIRST WOMAN

Lady Clare was twelve years younger than Francis. She was born in Assisi of noble heritage around 1193–94 and spent most of her childhood in Perugia, as her family was one of the many who had left their Assisi homes during the violent conflicts. According to reports during her canonization process, she was an angelic child who prayed incessantly. As a young woman, she was very beautiful, and had flowing blond locks, but beneath her elegant clothes she wore a hair shirt. She regularly slipped out of her house to feed the poor and give alms. Her mother was a devout woman conscious of her daughter's faith.

Clare was well aware of Francis—she had given food and other gifts to the early brothers while they established themselves at La Porziuncola. She had visited Francis in secret a few times (always chaperoned by a faithful relative), and her cousin Rufino, who had become a friar, acted as an important go-between. What Francis and Clare felt for each other was most certainly love, but it was a mystical love composed of two souls flying toward each other to unite in their love for God. As twin souls, they both recognized in each other the capacity to grow in deeper love with Christ. As Clare's love of Francis was indistinguishable from her love for Christ, it was natural for her to surrender her soul into Francis's care. She had heard his message, seen his way of life, and wanted it for herself. Francis was cautious at first, feeling that such a poor life might not be suitable for her, so he tested her endurance by suggesting she beg in the streets, which she gladly did. On Palm Sunday, March 18, 1212, Clare attended her last family Mass at San Rufino. Bishop Guido, who was presiding and who had been alerted by Francis to what was going to happen, placed a palm in Clare's hands as a sign of the Church's approval. Clare escaped from her home at dawn the following day through a jib door in the side of the house, usually reserved for the removal of the dead in their coffins. Her cousin Pacifica accompanied her as she made her way to La Porziuncola, where the monks were saying Matins in the darkness of the early morning. Francis cut her hair, and she exchanged her noble attire for a brown tunic. With this ritual, Clare became the first female Franciscan, Francis's first sister. She was placed in a Benedictine convent and was soon joined by her younger sister, Catherine, who assumed the name of Sister Agnes. With the defection of two marriageable daughters, the men of the Offreduccio family, furious at the girls' decision, broke into the convent to try to physically force them home. Disturbed by all this commotion, the Benedictine nuns complained to Bishop Guido, who offered Francis's poor ladies their own place at the Church of San Damiano, restored so lovingly by Francis and his early brothers. After Clare and Agnes moved in, they began the task of building a cloistered community for their growing group of nuns, later to become the Order of the Poor Clares.

CONTEMPLATION OR ACTION?

Francis was coming to a point in his life when he had to make a choice about which path to take, that of contemplation or of action. Many of his earlier brothers now lived as poor hermits in caves, but he, as the leader of the order, wondered about his future mission and work. He was receiving hundreds of monks at La Porziuncola (he welcomed each postulant personally), was traveling and visiting his brothers in the surrounding countryside and towns, and continued to preach and heal. He sent word to Sylvester, the first priest to join Francis in the early days at Rivotorto, and to Lady Clare at San Damiano, requesting their prayers and advice on which avenue for him to take. Both sent back messages that action was required and that contemplation would come later. Always a man of obedience and humility, Francis accepted their advice.

One day, while walking toward Foligno, he encountered some birds in a tree beside the path and stopped to preach to them. After he dismissed the birds, they flew off in the shape of a cross, a prophetic sign of the Franciscan work in the four corners of the world.

One of the appeals of action in preaching Christ's Gospel to the world was missionary work and martyrdom, and Francis took this as the next challenge—to lay down his life for Christ, as Christ had done for his followers. Francis introduced missionary work and martyrdom as a call for his brothers at the 1217 General Chapter, in which all Franciscan monks from throughout Italy and parts of Europe converged together in Assisi. This chapter was called the Chapter of the Mats because over one thousand monks built themselves shelters made of wicker and rush matting around La Porziuncola. They were grouped in provinces, and representatives of the Holy See came from Perugia to witness the spectacle. St. Dominic, the founder of the Dominican Order, was also there, being interested in seeing Francis and his brothers in action. Everyone was impressed by their orderliness, their spiritual joy, and their faithful and loving peace. Dominic, like many others present, considered the vow of poverty and the obedience to begging not a particular aid to the growth of the order; in fact, he thought it a deterrence. For example, Francis and his monks had made no provisions for food at the chapter, relying solely on the grace of Divine Providence. Yet at noontime, from the hills of Spello and Assisi, came townspeople with donkeys laden with breads and cheeses and fruits, as well as napkins and tablecloths, and all the necessary condiments for an outside picnic for a thousand. This was the evidence that any doubter needed—the hand of God's gifts among poor men. At this Chapter of the Mats it was decided that missionary work was to form part of the future of the Friars Minor.

But Francis's own travel plans were often foiled: He wanted to go to Spain on pilgrimage but never made it and had to return to Italy, and the same happened with his attempted trips to France. He even set out in a boat for Syria (to follow the Crusaders) but didn't make it there and had to stow away on a returning ship. A group of Franciscans led by Brother Elias did finally make it to the Holy Land and began taking care of sacred Christian sites. In 1219 Francis, after sailing for many weeks, finally arrived in the Holy Land himself, where he was met and welcomed by Brother Elias. From there he journeyed to Egypt on a peace-keeping mission, as one of many battles raged between Christians and Muslims. He met up with the Sultan of Damietta, who like Francis was a lover of religious poetry and mystical things, and Francis and the sultan spent many hours discussing God and religious experience. Even though Francis's intention of converting the Muslims failed, his meetings with the sultan were an unusual event in a time marked by bloodshed between the faiths.

On his return from the East, Francis worked at organizing nearly six thousand friars under his Rule for daily life and prayer, but he still had to defend to Church authorities the difficulty of this life as the way of the Gospel. He wasn't well physically, his eyes had been damaged by the strong sun in Egypt, and he was suspected of having granular conjunctivitis as well as dropsy, which were incurable in those days. Francis turned over the leadership of the order to Brother Pietro Di Catanio in 1220, who died within six months of his appointment. Brother Pietro was succeeded by Brother Elias, who requested assistance from the institutional Church. This signaled a change from Francis's pure and simple life into yet another religious order under the confines and control of the Holy See. Yet Francis formed the Third Order for "all the faithful" because there were so many ordinary folk (families and married people) who wished to follow the way of the Franciscan brothers and sisters in a simple life of repentance and service through the practice of poverty.

With many people trying to tear off parts of his tunic as relics and because of the hazards of his blindness, Francis longed for solitude. The Benedictines and other generous people had given Francis many of their hermitages and out-of-the-way places for contemplation and prayer, and at this point in his life he sought them out.

ATOP THE SACRED MOUNTAIN

Some years earlier, back in 1213, Francis had been traveling with his close assistant and faithful companion, Brother Leo, when he stopped at the Castle of Montefeltro at the time of a knighting celebration. Francis went in "to do some spiritual good" and preached to them. Many were greatly moved and overcome with emotion, and one of them—Count Orlando—approached Francis about the salvation of his soul. They talked together after dinner and to show his gratitude, the count offered Francis a mountain called Mount La Verna. As Francis had been looking for the perfect spot for reflection and contemplative prayer, he sent two brothers to check it out. This they did, taking possession of the mountain by building a hut "in the name of God." But it took Francis himself another eleven years to finally make his way to its summit. He arrived in August 1224 on the back of a donkey. Exhausted from the trip, he stretched out under a bush, and as he lay on the earth, hundreds of birds flew in from every direction, singing and beating their wings, and perched on his arms, legs, and head. Francis recognized this as a sign that the place was a good choice for his fast and retreat in honor of St. Michael, the archangel.

After his companions set up a hermitage for him, Francis was left completely alone except for Brother Leo. They agreed on simple daily rituals. If Francis intoned the second verse of Matins, Leo would join him in the early hours. If there was silence, Leo left him alone. A falcon usually roused Francis for prayer when he meditated on the sufferings and passion of Christ.

On September 14, the feast of the Exaltation of the Holy Cross, Brother Leo—who had witnessed many miraculous occurrences, including hearing Francis conversing with Christ and his mother, Mary, in the woods—saw seraphs with wings of fire, like those mentioned at the beginning of Isaiah 6: "I saw the Lord sitting on a throne, high and lofty; and the hem of his robe filled the temple. Seraphs were in attendance above him; each had six wings: with two they covered their faces, and with two they covered their feet, and with two they flew. And one called to another and said: 'Holy, holy, holy is the Lord of hosts; the whole earth is full of his glory.'" The ancient prophet was then touched by a live coal, by fire, appointed by God, his sins forgiven, his guilt removed, instructed to change the people's ways "and be healed." On top of Mount La Verna these six-winged seraphs, bearing the image of Christ crucified, swooped down from the sky as Francis was outside a cave, lost in contemplation, and they imprinted on his flesh the marks of the nails and the lance wound in his right side. This was the first recorded incident of an individual having received the stigmata, and the physically painful and bleeding wounds were to stay with Francis to the end of his days.

THE FINAL YEARS

In September 1224, Francis left Mount La Verna, asking two brothers, Angelo and Masseo, to stay behind as custodians of this special place. He knew that he was probably not going to live much longer and therefore wanted to return to his beloved Porziuncola. He traveled on an ass with his hands, feet, and side bandaged to protect them from the incessant bleeding caused by his stigmatic wounds. Brother Leo privately cleaned and dressed them, but it was hard to keep this extraordinary anointment a secret, even though that was Francis's wish. After receiving the stigmata, Francis had been elevated to such heights that in his mere presence miracles and healings would occur, and people thronged to see him as he passed through Sansepolcro, Montecasale, and Città di Castello on his way south. The journey took two months, and in November he arrived in the familiar places of his childhood, where he spent many months visiting his local brothers and friends as if to bid them farewell. Brother Elias had ordered an operation for Francis's eyes, and before he went to the doctor, he wanted to say goodbye to his twin soul, Sister Clare. He moved to be near her, staying in the gardens at San Damiano in a darkened hut as he had developed an aversion to light, and there Clare nursed him and took care of him. For almost three months he remained in absolute darkness, with headaches and burning in his eyes, and possibly sinusitis, combined with the sufferings from the stigmata. It was also hard for him to sleep as mice scurried across his body at night. In this state he composed one of the most exalting hymns of joy and praise to the unity of God in all things, a poem that has been hailed as the forerunner to Dante's work. It was written in the Italian vernacular, combining the masculine and feminine energies as symbols of partnership, no doubt affected by his being near his beloved

Clare. "The Canticle of the Creatures" was the first Christian hymn in which the Earth was hailed as Mother. Francis took as his basis for its composition the Canticle of Daniel from the Old Testament; he simplified it, so that his brothers and sisters could recite it with the childlike joy that was the common binding of Franciscan life. They sang it every day—it was reported that Brother Angelo and Brother Leo stopped a war waging in Perugia by singing it there.

In 1225, a year before his death and at the insistence of the bishop, Francis finally agreed to the operation on his eyes, a procedure that cauterized the upper part of the cheeks. This was accomplished by a hot iron that burned both temples from the top of the ear to the arches of his eyebrows. Most of the brothers could not be witness to Francis's painful operation, but Brother Elias stayed by his side and heard Francis addressing the fire beforehand:

> "My Brother Fire,
> The Most High has given you splendor that all creatures envy.
> Show yourself to be kind and courteous to me—
> I pray the magnificent Lord to temper his fiery heat
> So that I may have the strength to bear his burning caress."

The operation was a failure. Advancing dropsy brought swelling to his stomach and legs, and Francis had now also contracted tuberculosis.

He dictated his last testament at the Franciscan hermitage in Cortona and, now completely blind, returned to La Porziuncola for the last time. One of the last letters he dictated was to a longtime friend, a noble Roman woman called Lady Jacopa of Settesoli, whom he called Brother Jacopa. He asked her to come to him if she wanted to see him alive and to bring a haircloth for his shroud and wax for his burial. He also asked her to bring him some of the sweet almond cakes that she used to feed him when he would visit her in Rome. The letter arrived after her intuition had already driven her toward him, and she was present with Francis and his brothers at the end. Clare was sick herself, and feared that she would not be able to see him. He sent her a message through one of the brothers: "You shall say to Lady Clare to banish the pain and the sorrow she feels at the thought that she will never see me again. Let her know that before her death she and all her sisters will see me and will receive great consolation from me."

Francis asked to have passages from the Gospel of St. John read to him as he died; he also wished to die naked on the earth. He asked his accompanying brothers to leave him in this place undisturbed after his last breath for as long as it would take to walk a mile with slow steps. On October 3, 1226, at dusk, he died, aged forty-four, his last words being "I have done my part, may Christ teach you yours." One brother witnessed his soul like a glorious star borne upward on a white cloud, while the others saw an exaltation of larks fly down low singing over the cell in the infirmary.

On the morning of October 4, they carried Francis's body on a stretcher up to the town of Assisi with his brothers and members of the clergy all around singing hymns, saying the psalms, and bearing torches. On their way, they stopped outside San Damiano so that Clare and her sisters could bid their farewell. Francis was buried in the Church of San Giorgio while Brother Elias oversaw the erection of a new basilica to house Francis's tomb. With his love for all men and women, for all creatures and plants, and for all the elements of the natural world, Francis had shown how uniting everything with God, including oneself, is rewarded in ways far beyond the limits of human imagination.

CHRONOLOGY

1182	Born Francesco Bernardone in Assisi.
1202	Battle of Collestrada; becomes a prisoner of war in Perugia.
1207	Called to repair Christ's house at the crucifix of San Damiano. Disinherits from his family by stripping in front of Bishop Guido.
1207	Repairs San Damiano, San Pietro, Santa Maria degli Angeli (La Porziuncola).
1208	Takes words from Matthew's and Luke's Gospels as Rule of Life for brothers.
1209	Begins to build up the Church by his preaching.
1210	Oral approval of Franciscan Order by Pope Innocent III, plus permission to preach. Rule presented as written at Rivotorto.
1212	Foundation of Second Order; St. Clare and her sisters arrive and move to San Damiano. Montecasale given to the Franciscans by the Benedictine Camaldolese.
1213	Count Orlando da Chiusi gives Mount La Verna as retreat for prayer.
1217	General Chapter at Porziuncola; foreign missions begin.
1219	Five thousand confirmed friars. Francis preaches peace among crusaders and Muslims in Egypt.
1220	Returns to Italy and resigns as minister general, succeeded by Pietro di Catanio. St. Anthony joins the order.
1221	Pietro di Catanio dies and is succeeded by Brother Elias. Francis draws up Rule and introduces the Third Order.
1223	Francis builds crib in Greccio. Third Rule written at La Porziuncola.
1224	Receives stigmata at Mount La Verna.
1225	Writes "Canticle of the Creatures" at San Damiano.
1226	Dictates last testament and dies, forty-four years old, on the evening of October 3 at La Porziuncola.
1228	Canonized; first stone laid of the basilica in his name.
1230	His body transferred from San Giorgio to the present basilica.

OFFICIAL FEAST DAY: October 4

Spiritual Essentials

Even after eight hundred years, St. Francis's religious genius and his embracing spirituality continue to influence many aspects of both our spiritual as well as secular lives.

RELIGION

St. Francis and his Friars Minor grew from the roots of Christianity at just the right time. The institutional Catholic Church in the late twelfth–early thirteenth century had become elitist and removed from the needs of the poor, while the dissenting class of critics and reformers was spreading like wildfire throughout Europe. The growing popularity of the life that Francis offered bound the two factions together. The so-called heretics saw that it was possible to live within the Catholic community and still practice their style of poverty and compliance with the teachings of Christ in the Gospels, while the institutional Church, in grave need of reform, was given a gift of huge proportions by the creation of the Friars Minor, the Poor Clares, and the Third Order, who all taught by their example and their preaching and brought what Rome couldn't bring to the masses. Francis also taught the Catholic hierarchy by his exemplary living of the Gospels in simplicity and poverty, thereby exposing the corruptibility of Church wealth and political influence. And he showed that it is possible for one man, with faith, love, and conviction, to change (and restore) an ancient structure from within, as Christ had instructed him to do.

The monastic life, as St. Benedictine had outlined it in the sixth century, was greatly affected by the Friars Minor. Francis brought the medieval monk into the exterior world. Instead of living, praying, and studying behind cloistered walls, the Franciscan Friars introduced an alternative way of living the monastic rule by observing obedience, chastity, humility, and poverty while serving and caring for the sick, the poor, the forgotten brethren of "the minors." The Franciscans were also like the wandering *sadhakas* of the East (especially common in India), but instead of a solitary ministry, they, as instructed by Christ, always traveled in twos.

As men and women joined the Franciscans in droves, the Benedictines lost many novitiates and gave some of their emptying monasteries to St. Francis's burgeoning order.

THE EXPRESSIVE ARTS

St. Francis's love of creation united his spirituality into a poetry of prayer. Not only his writings but his way of life have contributed to the equality of the feminine and the masculine in complete partnership as souls that God created. Even in his male friaries, he referred, in his Rule, to the division of responsibility as "Mothers" and "Daughters" and "Martha" and "Mary." In his "Canticle of the Creatures" where he refers to Mother Earth, he has contributed a Christian hymn that can still be recited by anyone without offending their beliefs.

St. Francis introduced singing for the friars as a means of praise and joy, and composed devotional rituals that would move common people to deeper faith: for example the Stations of the Cross, and the reenactment of the nativity scene—it was St. Francis who created the first Christmas crib, with live animals, in Greccio.

St. Francis's life was an inspirational subject for the artistic masters of the fourteenth century, particularly Giotto, who painted twenty-eight episodes of St. Francis's life in frescoes in the upper Basilica of St. Francis in Assisi. In many paintings both before and after the Renaissance, St. Francis was depicted at the foot of the cross, consoling the Holy Mother, or in surrounding crowds in depictions of gospel scenes, or among animals and birds. As churches were built in his honor in many Italian towns—and elsewhere—depictions of the "poverello," especially with the crucified Christ, also appeared in stained glass.

WAY OF LIFE

St. Francis, by his example and those of his friars and poor ladies, brought the sacred into the everyday by talking about God, by acting with generosity and kindness, by praising the beauty of the natural surroundings, and by making holiness available to everyone. This made many hardships of life sacramental: all hardships had a reason, all were the will of God. Because of Francis's and his followers' empathy with and understanding of the poor, the poor could be seen and heard; they were also shown a way of life that incorporated all of their experiences with hope. As St. Bonaventure wrote, St. Francis, especially sensitive to nonjudgment (and with a sprinkling of humor), would call people "Brother Fly" if they spoiled the good of others, and his own body "Brother Ass" because it was laden with "heavy burdens, beaten with many stripes, and fed with poor and scanty food."

The Friars Minor spread the word of the Gospel by living theology. Innocent as doves and wise as serpents, they had the ability to memorize the scriptures without an academic education. By this example everyone could see that with prayer and belief, God could elevate anyone through grace. St. Bonaventure, referring to Francis as the "Professor of Poverty," claimed that Francis had given poverty the virtues of "stability and mobility," impossible to share with the rich, thus liberating the poor from resentment. Francis too had the ability to see the best of God's gifts in each brother, which he summed up as an ideal portrait of a friar:

> The True Friar Minor should love poverty like Brother Bernardo, should love prayer like Brother Rufino, who prayed even while sleeping; he should be as lost in God as Brother Giles, as courteous as Brother Angelo and as patient as Brother Juniper; he should possess the purity

> and the ingenuity of Brother Leo, the distinction and the good sense of Brother Masseo; and finally, representing detachment be like Brother Lucido, who never stayed more than a month in the same place, under the pretext that on earth we have no lasting dwelling.

St. Francis often referred to himself as just "the little one," and his fellow friars called him "The Brother."

Observing strict poverty, the friars were forced to live in the moment, to be happy and content with "what is." Although a central teaching in the Asian religions and philosophy, particularly in Buddhism, this "being mindful in the present" was refreshingly new in Christian thought and practice. St. Francis, whose sense of unity spilled over toward people of other beliefs, had the extraordinary ability to capture the essence of religions further afield. He was particular over the practice of humility as it related to the teachings of Christ, which he referred to as "the school of the humble Jesus," and emphasized the necessity of practicing simplicity, having a constant and disciplined prayer life, choosing always the path of love, and being in a state of joy. There were many stories of Franciscan friars constantly laughing together—the early English friars who settled in Canterbury were always in such states of joy that they had to impose strict observance to silence during their prayers because of their constant giggling in each other's presence. St. Francis always taught that silence was necessary to avoid "foolish talk."

St. Francis's ecstasies gave rise to an explosion of mystical experiences and teachings, particularly among women (such as St. Catherine of Siena, St. Teresa of Avila, and others), in the centuries after his life. What St. Francis had done was to enliven and to make real the ecstatic interior life of union with Christ in the heart, thus contributing to the acceptance of the vital teaching on individual Christian spirituality.

ANIMALS AND ECOLOGY

The miracles that St. Francis performed involving animals carry a special place in the story of his life. From his bringing peace to the town of Gubbio from the savage "Brother Wolf," to his preaching to the birds near Bevagna, he honored every living being he met and couldn't see any creature without thinking of the spirit of the creator God who lives in all life. He was known to save lambs from slaughter (in memory of the meekest Lamb of God, Jesus Christ), and every time he passed animals they would look at him, or come to him in a knowing way. Turtle doves, too, were special to St. Francis, who saved some as they were being taken to market by a young boy who later became a friar. Inspired by those early days when doves nestled in St. Francis's chest, many Franciscan friaries still breed white doves and keep goats, chickens, and sheep.

St. Francis's praise and reverence for the unity of all life has given him the title of patron saint of ecology. By seeing all life as sacred and a gift of God, St. Francis brought a consciousness to his time that God lives in the fields as well as the churches, in the waterfalls, in the sunlight, in the wildflowers and all wildlife.

CORE SPIRITUALITY

During the last few years of his life, St. Francis had, as he had done before, asked one of his companions to pray and randomly open the Bible for spiritual direction, and it fell open at Christ's passion. St. Bonaventure wrote in his biography, "[He] understood that, as he had imitated Christ in the actions of his life so, before he should depart from this world, he was to be conformed to Him likewise in the sufferings and pains of His Passion." St. Bonaventure isolated the core spiritual path of St. Francis as the path of the cross, from the beginning when he heard his call from the cross of

San Damiano, to the wearing of the Tau cross-shaped tunic, to the creation of the Stations of the Cross. The thirst that Christ had on the cross was what St. Francis also bore for the salvation of souls, and his own physical suffering he saw always as a gift; in fact he called his pains "Sisters." Hence, with the significance of the reception of the stigmata on top of Mount La Verna, St. Francis had not only "reached the summit of evangelical perfection" (St. Bonaventure) but he had become a vessel for healing. By experiencing Christ's sufferings, St. Francis enabled the monks and the people who kissed his stigmata wounds to understand that all tears of sorrow can become tears of joy. An example of St. Francis's pure love of Christ and of love itself is revealed in this segment of his "Love Prayer":

> Love, Love, O Jesus, I am reaching the haven. Love, Love, O Jesus, receive me. Love, Love, O Jesus, come to my help. It is love, love for Jesus which inflames me thus. Love, Love, O Jesus, I am dying of love, let me be near you. O Love, embrace me always; transform me into yourself, O Love, into truth, into supreme charity.
>
> Love, Love, it is the cry of the whole world. Love, Love, it is the cry of everything. Love, Love, such is your depth, that the more one is bound to you the more one desires you. Love, Love, you are the circle that surrounds my heart....

THROUGHOUT THE WORLD

From the beginning when early Friars Minor traveled to faraway lands to preach or to give their lives as martyrs, Franciscans began to make themselves at home and at service in nearly every country. The holy places of Jerusalem were now permanently under their care, due to a decree by the sultan that they could reside there (twenty-two friaries and six monasteries existed in the Holy Land as early as 1263), and fifty years later Franciscans were in India. By the mid-fourteenth century there were over 1,500 friaries, and 40,000 religious worldwide. The first priests to minister in the Americas were Franciscan: the first Mass in America was said by a Franciscan and the first martyr in America was a Franciscan. Franciscans were among the first Europeans in Australia, and took care of the sick and preached in Quebec and parts of Canada in its early formation. The first black canonized saint was a Franciscan (St. Benedict the Moor, son of slaves forced to Sicily in the sixteenth century).

In the nineteenth century Capuchin monks were in Ethiopia, Chili, Brazil, the Amazon, Mexico, Bolivia, Peru, and Somalia. The first women's Franciscan Order outside Europe was established in India. The group of Franciscan missions established in California in the eighteenth century became the foundations of its major cities. San Francisco, an obvious example, was named after St. Francis, and Los Angeles after the first Franciscan monastery, St. Mary of the Angels. Santa Fe in New Mexico is a derivation of its original Spanish name, "The Royal City of the Holy Faith of Blessed Francis."

Individual Franciscans have also made an impact on our world, many of them unsung but the more famous being St. Anthony of Padua, St. Bonaventure, St. Bernardino of Siena, and Blessed Angela of Foligno. Richard le Cordelier was St. Joan of Arc's confessor and followed her into battle. St. Maximilian Kolbe spontaneously sacrificed his life in place of a young father at Auschwitz. More recently, the stigmatic friar and priest from southern Italy, Padre Pio, now St. Pio of Pietrelcina, was also Franciscan.

There now exist many different Franciscan Orders, including the Friars Minor, the Capuchins (known for their strict observance of St. Francis's original Rule, they wear the hooded brown tunic and rope cord, and are bearded), the Conventuals, the Observants, the Poor Clares (and other sisters of St. Francis), and the Third Order of the laity.

The Canticle of the Creatures
by St. Francis

Most High, all powerful, good God,

All praise be yours, all glory, all honor, and all blessing.
To you alone, Most High, do they belong.
No mortal lips are worthy to pronounce your name.

All praise be yours with all your creatures,
Especially Sir Brother Sun, who brings the day and the light
you give us through him.
How beautiful is he, how radiant in his splendor!
Of you, Most High, he is the token.

All praise be yours for Sister Moon and the Stars.
In the heavens you have made them, bright and precious and fair.

All praise be yours for Brother Wind and the Air,
And fair and stormy, all the weather's moods,
By which you cherish all that you have made.

All praise be yours for Sister Water,
so useful, lowly, precious and pure.

All praise be yours for Brother Fire,
Through whom you brighten the night.
How beautiful is he, how gay, robust and strong!

All praise be yours for Sister Earth, our mother,
Who feeds us, rules us and produces various fruits
with colored flowers and herbs.

All praise be yours for those who forgive
For love of you and endure infirmity and tribulation.
Happy are those who endure them in peace,
For you, Most High, they will be crowned.

All praise be yours, for Sister bodily Death,
From whose embrace no mortal can escape.
Woe to those who die in mortal sin!
Happy are those she finds doing your most holy will!
The second death can do no harm to them.

Praise and bless my God, and give thanks,
And serve God with great humility.

The Pilgrimage

Destinations:
Assisi, Foligno, Perugia, Gubbio, Sansepolcro, and La Verna
Suggested length:
Six days

This pilgrimage packs a lot into the six days, so you may want to take a day's break somewhere in the middle of the week, making it seven days in total.

ASSISI

Assisi, a city twinned with Bethlehem and often referred to as "the new Jerusalem," because its name is derived from the word *Asia* meaning "East" (which might have meant east of Perugia), is one of the most holy cities in the world. Because of its many pilgrims each year, it stands as a center of Christian belief, a city that promotes peace and understanding among all faiths, and is host to many international gatherings for such interfaith work. However, it is still quite unchanged in its architecture from Francis's time. With a present population of about 32,000 (6,000 only reside in the city center), it still possesses a feeling of being a small, medieval town that has witnessed numerous miracles and been the home of much light.

DAY ONE: Assisi

"May you be blessed by God, holy city, for through you many souls will be saved and many servants of God will dwell in you and many of yours will be elected to the realm of eternal life." *St. Francis*

The old way in from the north, which St. Francis and his brothers would have taken by foot, can be reached by way of Valfabbrica, following signs to Pieve S. Nicolò onto the Strada Francescani. Enter from the south by SS75, taking any exit.

The following suggested sites are given in the chronological order of St. Francis's life. Begin your visit at the Piazza del Vescovado (Square of the Bishop).

Chiesa di S. Maria Maggiore

The church at the south end of this piazza seems unimposing, but up to the eleventh century it had been Assisi's cathedral. Partly destroyed by fire, it was rebuilt in the early thirteenth century and was the church in which St. Francis was baptized. Usually neglected by tourists, but frequented by locals and spiritual travelers, it would be a suitable place to light a candle and offer your intention and prayers for your pilgrimage.

Exit the church and go to the upper part of the piazza to the right of the well (a well that would have witnessed St. Francis's stripping in front of the bishop). The building at the corner of Via Sant'Agnese is Il Palazzo del Cardinale (The Bishop's Palace), where Bishop Guido lived and where the crowds gathered to see Francis's public initiation into the "poverello."

Walk up through Via Sant'Antonio and weave into Via Arco D. Priori through some steps of any of the alleyways upward toward the Piazza del Comune. At the fountain, turn right down Corso Mazzini, taking the second alleyway to the right (under a bridge/archway) down some steps.

Oratorio di S. Francesco Piccolino

This tiny chapel/oratory here is in the place of the stables of Francis's parents' house where legend claims he was born.

Continue along the alleyway directly in front of the oratory to a small piazza with a bronze statue of St. Francis's parents.

Chiesa Nuova (Parents' House)

The church is worth a visit; part of the original house is at the back, containing the cell in which St. Francis was locked by his father. Inside the church near the altar to the left is an underground chapel and the place where St. Francis's father had his workshops for the making of silks and dyeing of fabrics. There are not many remains of the house except these and the front door, although there are some historic disputes about the exact location of the parents' house. There is another location nearby that many say was actually the house and the shop.

Tempio di Minerva (Temple of Minerva) and S. Nicolò Crypt

The Temple of Minerva that looms over the Piazza del Comune is one of the most well-preserved Roman shrines from the first century AD. It is now a church. The temple is part of the backdrop to Giotto's painting of the prophetic man laying his cloak at St. Francis's feet when he was young (see St. Francis Basilica, p. 40).

There is little left of the original parish Church of **S. Nicolò,** where Francis and his early brothers received the Rule of Life from the priest opening the Bible three times. At the far corner of the northwest side of the piazza, there's situated a small shrine at the entrance of Via Portica (the lower road into the center of Assisi). This shrine is where the church altar used to be and still has a picture of the Madonna. The stone is from La Verna. Via Portica leads to the Roman baths to the right and the crypt of the original church, which now serves as a museum.

Cross the piazza toward the fountain, taking Via San Rufino to Piazza S. Rufino and its church.

Cattedrale di San Rufino and St. Clare's House

The church is where Francis's and Clare's families gathered for special occasions, especially those requiring Bishop

Guido's blessing. For instance, Clare was baptized in this church, as were many of Francis's friends and early brothers—images of them are engraved around the font. The eighth-century church was erected to house the remains of the martyr St. Rufino, who brought Christianity to Assisi in the third century, and whose tomb is still in its crypt; there is little left of its original structures except the foundations and the exterior wall.

On exiting the church, a **shrine to St. Clare** is to the right, which was created at the site of the Offreduccio family's home. Franciscan sisters are in residence in the rest of the building.

Return to the Piazza del Comune toward S. Nicolò and down the Via Portico. Take a left on Via S. Gregorio just past the crypt of S. Nicolò to Via Bernardo da Quintavalle.

Bernardo da Quintavalle's House

There's a plaque on a privately owned house on the opposite side of the street indicating the residence of the first man to follow St. Francis—Bernardo da Quintavalle. He was the one who offered accommodation to St. Francis while he was restoring San Damiano, and on spending the night with him, sold all his possessions, gave the money to the poor, and took the same habit as St. Francis. He later became a renowned preacher.

Return to Via Portica and turn left to a series of steps almost immediately to the right and an alleyway leading to the upper street.

True Bernardone Home?

Some biographers have suggested from historic research and records of the town (and especially as St. Francis's nephew purchased this property to keep it in the family) that this is where **the true Bernardone home** was situated. Presently it houses a candle shop, but before this it was leased by Franciscan sisters who frequented the back stair-

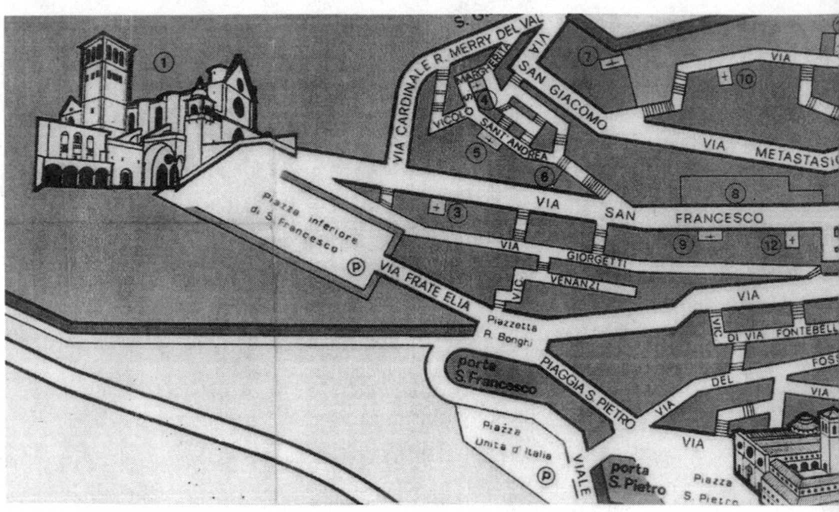

way and had a chapel upstairs and who swore that this was the home of Francis's family.

The alleyway steps that join the upper and lower streets lead to Via San Paolo. Take this upper road away from Piazza del Comune, through Via Metastasio, into the magnificent square that houses the Basilica of St. Francis at the end of the town. Begin by visiting the upper church and then descend into the lower church.

Basilica di San Francesco (St. Francis Basilica)

The present complex has an upper and lower church. The lower church is designed in the shape of a Tau cross and its construction was supervised by Brother Elias and completed in 1230, at which point Francis's tomb was moved to the crypt. When Pope Innocent IV was returning to Rome from Avignon in 1253, he consecrated the upper church, which now houses the famous Giotto frescoes of major events in St. Francis's life. The huge facility attached to the church running the length of the outer wall is the headquarters of the Franciscans.

There are over ninety-two works of art in this basilica depicting St. Francis: sixty-five in frescoes, sixteen in glass,

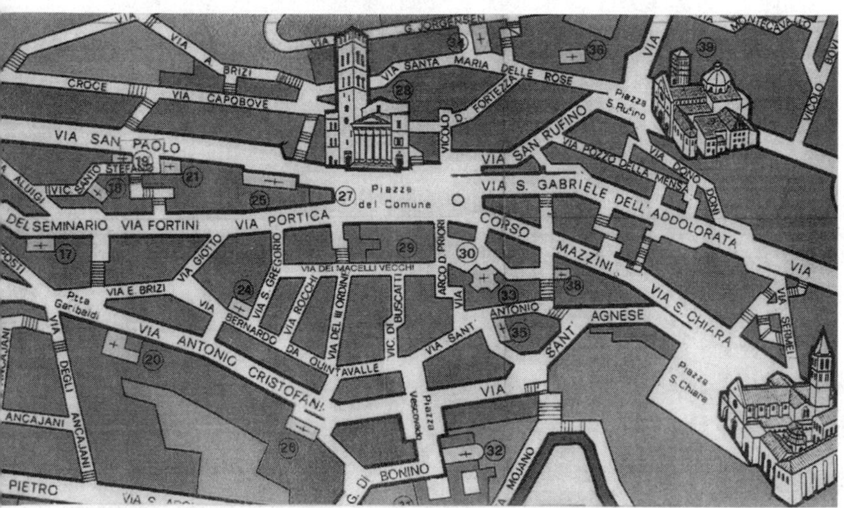

six in wood, two in stone and terra-cotta, two in bronze, and one in mosaic. Some of the more well-known are the stunning Simone Martini portraits of Clare and Francis among other saints, and the Cimabue fresco of St. Francis (and St. Anthony) with the Madonna and Child surrounded by angels.

Il Reliquario (Museum of the Relics)

Near the main altar of the lower church is a small museum exhibiting St. Francis's simple tunics (all patched and sewn) and some of the shoes and undershirts he wore toward the end of his life after receiving the stigmata. In the surrounding display cases are the Papal Bull of the Franciscan Rule and the blessing to Brother Leo that Francis personally gave him, which Brother Leo carried on his body for forty-seven years, leaving it to the Franciscans only on his deathbed. Also displayed are gifts from the sultan, more clothing of St. Francis including a boar's hair shirt, and some altar pieces and chalices from the Benedictine monastery at Mount Subasio (and elsewhere) where Francis attended Mass and studied.

At the crypt and St. Francis's tomb, there's an urn with the remains of Frate Jacopa dei Settesoli ("Brother" Jacqueline, the noblewoman from Rome and a close friend of

Francis who was with him at his death). The stone altar houses the skeleton of St. Francis, exhumed in 1818 and again in 1978, and finally placed for safekeeping in a Plexiglas casket, inside the metal casket of the nineteenth century and in the stone tomb of the thirteenth century. Around St. Francis's tomb are buried his early brothers. The Franciscans offer Masses for private intentions here and also light candles on the altar, which have been donated by pilgrims.

Santa Maria degli Angeli, La Porziuncola (St. Mary of the Angels)

On the plains below the Basilica rises the huge baroque dome of Santa Maria degli Angeli. In St. Francis's time, these plains would have been forests and fields, with occasional buildings like the small churches he restored, leper colonies, animal shelters, and stone huts for the poor. The original church was given to St. Francis by the Benedictines, and he moved in after the overcrowding at Rivotorto. This is the place where he received all the new friars and where St. Clare went for her investiture. It was the original headquarters of the Friars Minor, the place that St. Francis loved and where he died. He said to his brothers, "See to it that you never leave this place," and he offered as advice to visitors, "Whosoever prays with a devout heart will obtain what they ask." He instructed everyone "to honor this worthy place." During one of Francis's visions, Jesus himself granted forgiveness of sins to repentant souls who prayed within La Porziuncola. "The Pardon" was approved by Pope Honorius III, who officially granted the plenary indulgence at the same time he issued the papal bull approving the final Rule of the order. The yearly August festival in Assisi has become known as the Celebration or Day of the Pardon, but the pardon itself is available year-round for pilgrims.

The Chapter of the Mats, and other chapters happened on this site when eventually over 3,500 monks were gathered here in St. Francis's time, and more later on. The huge seventeenth-century structure that adorns the landscape today was ordered by Pope Pius V to enclose and protect the original tiny chapel, as well as to shelter the crowds of pilgrims who came for "the Pardon" each year. The fountain of twenty-six jets outside the church was commissioned by the Medicis to quench the thirst of the pilgrims who came to take advantage of the special blessing of forgiveness and mercy. The large church was later destroyed by an earthquake, and restored into its present state in the mid-1800s. The original chapel survived, and to this day is the church's main spiritual focus.

Chapel of the Transito (Death)

On the right of the chapel, there is a small cell that was probably the infirmary in the original monastery, and is now venerated as the place where St. Francis spent the last hours of his life. The painting on the outside depicts St. Francis on the ground surrounded by friars and Jacopa dei Settesoli. Above the altar there is the girdle used by St. Francis and a statue in terra-cotta by the master Della Robbia.

Il Roseto (The Rose Garden)

The door to the right of the Chapel of the Transito leads to the interior cloister. There you can visit the sacristy and a chapel of the crypt where many of the original structures of the pastoral monastery are still intact. The Rose Garden has a statue of St. Francis, which usually has a dove's nest nearby. According to legend, it was here that St. Francis was undergoing many doubts about the life he had chosen and while praying in his cell (nearby) one winter night, he threw himself into a thornbush as penance for being lured by the devil of doubt. The blood from the thorn pricks seeped into the earth, and roses without thorns grew in their place. Today roses still grow without thorns in this garden. The oratory was built in the thirteenth century by the order of St. Bonaventure over St. Francis's original cell (which can still be seen). The oratory is decorated with frescoes depicting some scenes from people's experiences of "the Pardon."

Il Vecchio Convento (The Old Monastery)

Going through the museum in the outer courtyard, you will find the monastery that was built in stone after St.

Francis's death (around 1230) and was in operation as the center of the Friars Minor up to the fifteenth century. The cell of St. Bernardino of Siena is there; inside it is displayed his Marian sermon that he read at La Porziuncola for "The Pardon" of 1425 where hundreds of thousands of pilgrims were present. Among the other cells is that of St. Charles Borromeo (1538–84) who stayed at La Porziuncola when he was Cardinal Protector of the Franciscans. The room with the common fireplace is where the friars would gather to converse and study.

DAY TWO: Assisi

Begin the day early with a visit to the Sanctuary of Rivotorto. It can be reached by following the signs for "Santuario Rivotorto" clearly marked on the SS75 in the southerly direction toward signs for Foligno. If coming from the center of town, you can hike down if you wish (it would take about one hour) or drive, following the signs to San Damiano and continuing on that road into the valley.

Santuario di Rivotorto

The present church was built in the nineteenth century over the original animal shelter where St. Francis and his first twelve brothers lived. There is a statue inside indicating where St. Francis slept. The dormitory was on the right, on the left was the kitchen/living area, and in the center was the chapel.

Taking the road toward Assisi behind the Church of Rivotorto, turn left at the first junction on Via Francescana. Proceed over a bridge, turning right at a shrine in the middle of a fork. Follow the road up the hill to San Damiano.

Convento di San Damiano

At San Damiano, St. Francis first heard Christ call him from the cross, and it was the first church he restored. The

"San Damiano crucifix" in the chapel today is a reproduction of the original, which hangs in the Basilica of St. Clare. After St. Francis had restored the church and moved to La Porziuncola, he received permission to have the church inhabited by St. Clare and her sister. Here she began her forty-two years of cloistered life with many sisters. They were known as the Franciscan "poor ladies," which later came to be called the Order of the Poor Clares. *(For a detailed tour, with background on St. Clare and her history at San Damiano, see page 121.)*

The garden has a statue of St. Francis because it was here that he spent some time in a hut toward the end of his life and where he composed "The Canticle of the Creatures."

The Poor Clares left San Damiano in 1260 (seven years after St. Clare's death), and the place remained as it was until the sixteenth century when the Friars Minor built the cloister and enlarged the convent. It was bought by an Englishman—Lord Ripon—in 1860, and in 1983 his heirs donated it back to the Catholic Church. Presently it houses a small community of Friars Minor and novices, who spend a year studying to verify their choice of vocation.

Return to the center of Assisi and walk to the Basilica of St. Clare, rising up in front of the dome of San Rufino.

Basilica di S. Chiara (St. Clare's Basilica)

After Clare was canonized, a basilica was built for her tomb, and the Poor Clares moved from San Damiano into a convent attached to the basilica. They live here to this day. This complex was where the original San Giorgio hospital, church, and school stood, the one in which Francis as a boy was educated. Little exists of the original building, but there is an original stained glass of St. George behind the crucifix chapel (which is sometimes obscured and not easy to see). As you enter the church, the chapel on the right is where you can venerate the original San Damiano crucifix.

Abbazia di San Benedetto (The Abbey of St. Benedict)

The total distance from Assisi to the Abbey is approximately 4.5 kilometers, so if you feel like exercising, the road is quiet and convenient for walking. Take the Via San Benedetto (spn. 251) for approximately 3 kilometers. If driving, you can continue on the road down the other side of the mountain, following a map toward the Eremo delle Carceri (Hermitage of the Prisons).

This is the oldest monastery of the area, situated near the top of Mount Subasio. It is probably the place where St. Francis, during his conversion years, spent time with the Benedictine monks, receiving guidance and spiritual solace. It was the abbot here who gave St. Francis and his followers La Porziuncola for a basket of fish a year. The Abbey of St. Benedict was a haven away from the troubles of a war-torn city, and to this day it imbues a spirit of peace. It dates back as far as the seventh century, was rebuilt in the eleventh century, and because of fire damage, restored again in the seventeenth century. It has two ancient crypts, one as early as the eighth or ninth century and the other from the eleventh century. St. Francis would have attended services here and prayed with the monks.

In more recent times, the abbey was run by Benedictine Sisters, who opened its doors to retreatants, but since the Assisi earthquake of 1995, when it suffered damage, it has been undergoing major renovations. At the time of writing, the abbey was still closed to visitors, but it is worth visiting the area, and perhaps picnicking on top of the mountain, or enjoying the breathtaking scenery.

Eremo delle Carceri (Hermitage of the Prisons)

Another small road leads from one of Assisi's town gates, Porta Cappuccini, directly to the Carceri hermitage, and also lends itself to walking.

This was originally the prison of Mount Subasio, and St. Francis and his early companions came here to meditate in the caves in the woods (many of which are identified). Later it was made into a Franciscan hermitage. This is where St. Francis sent a message to Brother Sylvester, who was living as a contemplative in a cave, about advice for his future mission, and it was also a preferred place for meditation by St. Francis's first follower, Bernardo da Quintavalle.

DAY THREE: Foligno and Perugia

From Assisi take the SS75 toward Foligno and exit at Cannara/Castelnuovo. After Castelnuovo, proceed to Cannara. At Cannara follow the "Centro" sign by turning right over the bridge, and then immediately left along the street running parallel to the canal. After driving through fields, turn left at the T junction. Opposite the first gas station is Pian D'Arca.

Pian D'Arca is a monument erected in 1926 to mark the place where St. Francis preached to the birds, and they flew in four directions to mark the beginning of the Franciscan missions around the world.

FOLIGNO

Once a bustling market town in the time of St. Francis, Foligno is still an important commercial and design center. As it is not an obvious place to visit, there are few tourists, but what it represents on a Franciscan pilgrimage is a subtle but powerful witness. In the main square, the **Piazza della Repubblica** (where the cathedral is situated), there is a stone plaque at the far end that states: "This is where it all began" for St. Francis. Here, in this piazza, the young Francis sold his clothes, samples of his father's merchandise, and his horse to raise money for the restoration of San Damiano. This is where his real ministry began, where he gave up his material possessions, in preparation for his later stripping in front of the bishop, his family, and the townsfolk.

Foligno's cathedral, **St. Feliciano,** is magnificent (built in 1133 and expanded in 1201), and its facade exists today much as it would have at the time of St. Francis.

Chiesa di San Francesco (Church of St. Francis)

The Church of St. Francis was built on the site where the first Franciscan hostel stood in Foligno and where Brother Elias lived for a while. The Poor Clare nuns also lived in the convents nearby—St. Lucia and St. Catherine, where many members of the Third Order of St. Francis also worked. One of these was the well-known mystic Bl. Angela of Foligno (1248–1309) who is buried in this church. Her tomb is located in one of the side altars. If the church is locked, ring the bell to the presbytery next door and one of the Franciscan priests will gladly let you in.

BLESSED ANGELA OF FOLIGNO (1248–1309)

Born in Foligno twenty-two years after St. Francis's death, Bl. Angela came from a noble family of wealthy landowners. She had a forceful character and a vain temperament. Married to a rich man and with children, she joined the Third Order of St. Francis after many years of conversion. She sold all her possessions and gave them to the poor, left her family (most had died or moved away), and lived in a shabby hovel as she purified her soul. She was a remarkable woman, attracting followers and becoming a leading teacher of the spiritual life, who, through the grace of the spirit, even became literate and was able to write and understand theology. Her works of teaching appeared miraculously, with nearly thirty manuscripts discovered in the possession of families of the area after her death; these were published in one volume in 1497. Originally published in Italian, this book was translated into Spanish in 1510, into French a hundred years later, followed by German in 1617, and subsequently into Flemish and English. It was the first volume of mystical teachings written by a woman (or even a man), and is so advanced, wise, and explicit that it formed the basis of most mystical works thereafter, particularly those of St. Teresa of Avila, who would have had the chance to study Bl. Angela in Spanish. Bl. Angela's teachings affect our understanding of the course of mystical union and all its attributes, and her work is still an invaluable study.

PERUGIA

Perugia, the ancient rival of Assisi, is where St. Francis spent many months in prison after the Battle of Collestrada. He later returned and preached in the city's main square (today's **Piazza 4 Novembre**) on numerous occasions, and met Pope Honorius III at the pontifical residence attached to the cathedral. St. Bernardino of Siena also preached in Perugia. The **National Gallery of Umbria** exhibits an impressive collection of sacred art, including Piero della Francesca's polyptych of St. Anthony and paintings by Fra Angelico, Boccati, and di Lorenzo.

DAY FOUR: Gubbio

From Perugia take the SS298 north.

Gubbio is famous mostly for its association with the story of the wolf (see below) and St. Francis's intercession in stopping its ravenous attacks, but it is also the place where he headed after he stripped himself at the bishop's house in Assisi because he had a friend from prison in Perugia who lived here. This friend was a member of the Spadalunga family, whose house is now part of the **Chiesa di San Francesco (Church of St. Francis)** in the Piazza 40 Martiri (The Square of the 40 Martyrs). The Spadalungas gave Francis his original garment with the belt, which, with a few changes, became the official Franciscan habit. This is the place, too, where St. Francis decided that helping lepers was to be a part of the novitiate for each Friar Minor.

Inside the church can be seen the door of the original Spadalungas' house, the door that welcomed him after he had closed the door of his old life in Assisi.

Above the houses of Gubbio sits the Duomo, the thirteenth-century cathedral that was built over an older structure (the first bishop's house) dating as far back as the fifth century. Below, on the **Piazza della Signoria,** St. Francis presented the tamed wolf to the people, and had it agree to live peacefully with the citizens of Gubbio.

THE WOLF OF GUBBIO

This wolf was a terrifying predator who attacked many of Gubbio's citizens. Since everyone was living in fear of their lives, St. Francis was invited to help deal with the problem. After his arrival, he went immediately to a deserted stretch of land in the woods (on the plains of the town below) and made a cross on the ground near some bones, recent remains of the wolf's prey. As he was doing so, people called him back in fear because they heard the wolf's howl nearby. When the animal came into view, St. Francis made a sign of the cross over it and said, "Brother Wolf, come here. In the name of Jesus Christ, I command you not to harm anyone anymore. And you will not eat Brother Ass" (referring to himself).

St. Francis then made the wolf promise to rid itself of evil and abide by his request for peace. The wolf wagged its tail, twitched its ears, bowed its head, and much to the amazement of the onlookers, placed its paw in the saint's outstretched hand. He then commanded the wolf to follow him up the hill to the Piazza della Signoria where everyone marveled at the miracle. St. Francis used the opportunity to preach that the sins of the city had brought this scourge upon them and told them each to repent for their wrongdoings. As part of the penance, the people decided to feed food to the wolf so it would not go hungry, and the wolf agreed to live in peace with the Gubbio people by raising its paw.

The wolf became the pet of the town, entering individual houses for scraps of nourishment and making itself at home everywhere. When it died two years later, the whole town mourned.

The bones of the wolf are buried under the altar stone in the **St. Francis of Peace Chapel,** which can be found at the intersection of Via Savelli della Porta (which runs off the Piazza della Signoria) and Via Cairoli. *The chapel is privately owned: to visit, call 075–9275797.*

The **Chiesa di S. Maria della Vittoria (the Church of St. Mary of the Victory)** marks the location where St. Francis tamed the wolf, near the first Franciscan hermitage in Gubbio (around 1213). The inside has images of the miracle with the wolf, as well as a few other paintings, including a unique one of St. Anthony and the child Jesus. In the park outside there's a bronze monument (erected in 1973) depicting St. Francis taming the wolf around the site that it happened. *This church is closed on Mondays.*

DAY FIVE: The Hermitage of Montecasale and Sansepolcro

Take the SS219 toward Umbertide and exit onto northbound E45 following sign for Cesena. Exit at Sansepolcro.

Eremo di Montecasale (Hermitage of Montecasale)

Unless you are a seasoned hiker and wish to spend the bulk of your day walking, the best way to experience a pilgrimage to Montecasale is to drive half-way up the mountain and then walk the rest. To reach the hermitage, follow the signs for Ospedale (hospital), turning off the main road in an easterly direction. After the hospital, at the fork in the road make a right turn and drive up the hill for about one kilome-

ter. Park at the picnic area and walk the second part of the mountain road, which is approximately 2 kilometers and should take thirty minutes.

In the eleventh century, this deserted place, up a mountain, away from the people of Borgo Sansepolcro, was used as a leprosarium. It was later a Benedictine monastery and then was given by the Camaldolese to St. Francis in 1212 (one year after St. Clare joined the order). As it is small in size, only a few monks have lived there at any given time, but it has the original cells where St. Anthony stayed in 1230 while convalescing on his way back from La Verna, and where St. Bonaventure stayed as minister general of the order in 1261 while compiling material for his biography on St. Francis. St. Francis, too, visited many times and his rock bed can still be venerated. His final visit was after receiving the stigmata on the holy mountain of La Verna and on his way to Assisi. Many miracles and healings occurred at Montecasale when he visited.

On arriving at the hermitage, you'll see a monument of St. Francis as Patron of Ecology, a gift by Florentine sculptor A. Berti and inaugurated in August 1980. The inscription over the chapel door inside reads, "Here lived three holy men, Francis, Anthony, and Bonaventure. Here three impious thieves lived as saints. Here numerous venerable men died in the Lord. Hence, blessed are those who dwell here in your house, O Lord."

The Chapel

The thirteen-century wooden statue of the Holy Mother and Child stands on the altar exactly where it was placed by St. Francis, who was given it by the local people on his arrival in 1212. There is a beautiful watercolor of St. Francis on the left wall.

The Choir

Here is where the friars chant, meditate, and pray. The original, ancient plainchant books are on display in front of a moving painting of the friendship of Jesus with Francis, the saint drinking from the wounds of Christ in perfect humility and love.

Saints' Cells

There are few places in the world where a pilgrim can actually experience the presence of a saint's real-life relics. Here their beds and their blankets are preserved in these cells, just as they were eight hundred years ago. The first cell you enter is that of St. Bonaventure, the second of St. Anthony.

St. Francis Oratory

From the chapel take the stone corridor to the right under the archway to an ancient side chapel, which is where St. Francis used to live at Montecasale. This is the oldest part of the monastery. There is an ancient terra-cotta "pieta" and head of Christ that St. Francis would have been able to gaze at from his bed of rock up the stone steps. In the display case are skulls of two of the famous thieves, as well as the habit of Venerable Ramieri, a local shepherd who became a monk. The wooden statue of St. Francis hugging the cross and the Bible was donated to the monastery in 1965.

The Cloister

This simple and beautiful cloister with its well is a perfect place for meditation. On its wall is an eighteenth-century tile-painting of the two rich men undergoing the cabbage-planting exercise with St. Francis. The room beyond the cloister is a gallery of art donated by retreatants. The small door in the far wall in this gallery is where many famous people have retreated, one of the most noted being Blessed John XXIII when he was a priest.

The Fountains

There is a water fountain outside the chapel on the road with an engraving taken from "The Canticle of the Creatures": "All praise be yours for Sister Water, so useful, lowly, precious and pure." Past the gate to the convent, there is a grotto and fountain where St. Francis drank from the mountain stream. This water has been known to heal. To the right of the garage is the original door to Montecasale, with mention of the thieves over its entrance. The terrace garden is where the cabbage-planting exercise took place and is called St. Francis's garden.

Sasso Spicco

Sasso Spicco means "jutting-out rock." The spot is a climb down, following clearly marked signs along a narrow path into the steep valley below, but it's worth it. It takes about thirty minutes to descend to the stream and waterfalls at the bottom where the cool rocks are covered with ivy. Francis prayed here.

TWO TALES OF MONTECASALE

One story tells of two rich men from Sansepolcro who approached St. Francis, asking to be accepted as friars. St. Francis gladly took them in at Montecasale, and the first thing he told them to do was to plant cabbages in the garden with the leaves in the ground and the roots in the air. One man obeyed, but the other remarked that it was the incorrect way to plant the vegetable. St. Francis told the latter that he would have problems as a friar, so it would be better with his knowledge to go back and join the other knowledgeable people of the world. The man who planted the cabbages as instructed, displaying the necessary virtues of obedience and humility, eventually became Friar Angelo and the abbot of Montecasale.

Friar Angelo was put to another test with St. Francis when three famous thieves, who had been terrorizing the area, came to the monastery for food and refuge. After hearing their request, Friar Angelo rebuked them for taking advantage of the innocent monks and sent them into the woods empty-handed. St. Francis, arriving from some travels a few days later and on hearing of the incident, scolded Brother Angelo for acting contrary to charity and the teachings of Christ. He said, "Sinners are brought back to God by kindness, not harsh rebukes." He instructed Angelo to take some food and drink with him, to find the thieves in the surrounding wilderness, and on finding them, to kneel down in front of them, begging forgiveness for his cruelty. He could then invite them to stay at Montecasale, providing they agreed to no longer steal from their neighbors. The thieves were so moved by the friar's behavior that they spent the rest of their lives at Montecasale doing penance for their past misdeeds, fasting three times a week, going barefoot, and depriving themselves of sleep.

SANSEPOLCRO

Sansepolcro is a town rich in cultural and spiritual heritage. Its name in English means "Holy Sepulcher," as its first stones were laid by monks as far back as the ninth century and were from the Holy Sepulcher Church (Christ's tomb) in Jerusalem. St. Francis passed through here many times on his way to and from La Verna and Assisi. There are many interesting churches to visit, but the one not to be missed is its eleventh-century cathedral, the **Cattedrale di S. Giovanni Battista (Cathedral of St. John the Baptist)**. Just east of the cathedral is **Chiesa di S. Francesco (the Church of St. Francis)**. Outside, the white statue of a monk depicts Luca Pacioli, founder of the modern methods of accounting, a gift from the Japanese Accounting Association on the five-hundredth anniversary of Pacioli's *Summa Divina* (which laid out the mathematics for management, including the balance sheet). Pacioli is remembered by most historians as the quintessential "Renaissance Man." As a young man in the fifteenth century, he studied with Piero della Francesca, his hometown compatriot and the genius who helped to work out the geometric principles of perspective. As a Franciscan monk in his adult years, Pacioli studied mathematics at the universities at Bologna and Padua. He met and served popes and princes, taught across Europe, and later in life befriended and collaborated with Leonardo da Vinci.

ART & SOUL: SANSEPOLCRO AND CAPRESE MICHELANGELO

Piero della Francesca: The Father of Perspective

Luca Pacioli's teacher, and a teacher to many artists centuries after him, was Piero della Francesca (c. 1420–92). He was born in Borgo Sansepolcro, and the house of his birth and a monument to him are located on the Via Aggiunti in San Sepolcro just past the Piazza S. Francesco. Della Francesca's father was a shoemaker and desired the same profession for his son. But Piero became a mathematician, geometrician, and painter, this combination of skill enabling him to master the technique of perspective with the genius of introducing a divine order, soul illumination, and almost mystical ambience to his work. As early as 1435 he apprenticed with Domenico Veneziano in Urbino in the Marches. There he met his future patrons from the Montefeltro dukedom and experienced the excitement of the early Florentine Renaissance. The first polyptych attributed to della Francesca was the one commissioned by the Confraternità della Misericordia of Borgo in June 1445 and finished fifteen years later; today it is exhibited in the **Museo Civico, Sansepolcro**. In the Museo Civico, too, can be seen the partly-restored *Portrait of S. Giuliano (St. Julian),* which was discovered only about fifty years ago in the Chiesa di Sant'Agostino (The Church of St. Augustine); the church is just inside the entrance of Porta Fiorentina. The greatest gem in the Museo Civico is *The Resurrection,* a fresco painted on what was originally the far wall of the mayor's council chamber.

Although della Francesca traveled to Rome and Florence, he preferred to live in his hometown of Sansepolcro where he died at the age of eighty-six; some historians believe that he was blind for the last twenty years of his life.

Michelangelo Buonarotti: Renaissance Genius

The childhood home and birthplace of Michelangelo is approximately 30 kilometers from Sansepolcro and is called

Caprese Michelangelo. *(Caprese can be reached on side roads from either Pieve Santo Stefano or on the way up from the valley toward the medieval town of Anghiari.)* The original Buonarotti house amid the sixth-century castle complex above the small town has been turned into a museum. Here in Caprese, the master of sculpture, painting, architecture, and poetry was born March 6, 1475, four hours before dawn. His father was of noble descent and held the position of magistrate for the towns of Chiusi (near La Verna) and Caprese on behalf of the ruling Florentines; his mother, Francesca, died when he was six years old, forcing the family to move south to Settignano. Although seemingly destined for a literary career, Michelangelo always loved drawing and at the age of twelve apprenticed in Florence. There he learned to hone his craft by copying other masters' works, but later specialized in sculpture. He claimed that it was due to him being born in the land of artists in the Tiber valley that he took up painting, and that his wet nurse was the wife of a stonecutter, which gave him the thirst for the familiar sound of chisels being hammered against granite, which as an adult turned him to creating with marble.

There are no original Michelangelo works in Caprese Michelangelo, but there are copies and casts, as well as art by other artists in honor of him. The tiny Church of **S. Giovanni Battista (St. John the Baptist),** where he was baptized on March 8, 1475 (the font at which he was held is still there), can be viewed, although *by appointment only* through the museum desk. The museum is closed on Mondays.

DAY SIX: La Verna

Take the E45 highway from Sansepolcro or the lower road (more scenic) to Pieve Santo Stefano, the next town north. Follow signs for Chiusi La Verna. Try to visit in the mid- to late afternoon on a weekday; weekends can be very crowded and noisy.

Mount La Verna is the sacred mountain where St. Francis received the stigmata two years before he died. The Rule of St. Francis required solitude, silence, and prayer and La Verna inspired him in all three. This place is where

Brother Leo, St. Francis's entrusted helper, witnessed Jesus walking and talking with St. Francis in the woods. St. Francis said of La Verna, "There is no mountain in the world more holy." The sanctuary today is a retreat center built around the original stone buildings.

Cappella S. Maria degli Angeli (Chapel of Holy Mary of the Angels)

Named after the original La Porziuncola, the chapel was built under St. Francis's instruction between 1216–18 when the brothers were erecting little more than simple mud huts and rock caves to live and pray in. The present chapel was restored in 1923 and has a number of fifteenth-century Della Robbia enameled terra-cottas. Count Orlando da Chiusi, who gave St. Francis the mountain in gratitude for spiritual favors, is buried here.

La Basilica

The basilica was begun in 1348, completed in 1509, and consecrated in 1568. The main altar has statues of both St. Francis and St. Anthony adorning each side. In the display case in the Chapel of the Relics is a piece of cloth stained from the blood of St. Francis's stigmata, and a crystal cup, white serving cloth, and wooden bowl from which Francis ate and drank when a guest of Count Orlando.

Corridor of the Stigmata

Erected in 1578, all the frescoes along this alleyway depict stories from St. Francis's life. Halfway along the corridor you'll find St. Francis's bed, where he slept on an iron grille in a damp cave (Francis always chose uncomfortable places to sleep as an act of penance).

La Cappella delle Stimmate (The Chapel of the Stigmata)

This was originally a crude shelter where St. Francis stayed during the last part of his retreat and fast and where he experienced the stigmata. Built over this original shelter, the chapel is highly decorated. The flowers on the floor indicate the exact place (you can see through the glass to the rock below) where St. Francis passed the night of the miraculous appearance of the seraph.

Oratories of St. Anthony and St. Bonaventure

These were the original cells where both these great saints lived while at La Verna for retreat and contemplation. Outside St. Anthony's oratory there is a protruding precipice where the devil allegedly attempted to throw St. Francis over the rock, but he hung on to the hollow and survived.

Sasso Spicco and Cappella S. Maria Maddalena (Chapel of St. Mary Magdalen)

On the way down to the protruding sacred rock that served as St. Francis's pastoral church and where he meditated upon the passion of Jesus Christ, is the tiny chapel of St. Mary Magdalen. This was St. Francis's first cell on La Verna and was built under a beech tree by Count Orlando when St. Francis first arrived. The altar stone is the very stone that served St. Francis as a table, and where some brothers saw Jesus sitting on it conversing with the saint.

La Penna (The Peak)

You can hike to the summit of the mountain on a path cut into the roots of the forest's trees (it takes approximately forty minutes). La Penna is 4,280 feet high and it is here where many of the monks prayed. On the way is the **Chapel of the Beech,** or the **Chapel of Blessed John.** A thirteenth-century friar, John lived in this secluded place, praying in contemplation and ecstasy for thirty years. The chapel at the summit is in honor of Mary, Mother of Jesus.

The Blessing of St. Francis
As Given to Brother Leo

God bless you and keep you.
May God smile on you, and be merciful to you;
May God turn his regard toward you and give you peace.
May God bless you.

PILGRIM TIPS

- You may stay for a private retreat at either Montecasale or La Verna. Get in touch with the Director of Retreatants at either place when you visit.
- If you wish to continue on a short extended pilgrimage within the Franciscan theme, you can follow St. Anthony (northward from La Verna) or St. Bonaventure to the south.

Holy Women of Tuscany and Umbria

The women saints whose lives, teachings, and places are part of this pilgrimage—St. Catherine of Siena, St. Clare of Assisi, St. Veronica Giuliani, and Blessed Margaret—are women who deserve our getting to know individually, as well as followed collectively because of a shared extraordinariness. They exemplified a singular love of God, a firm purpose in their intent to spread God's love in the world, and a unique courage, faith, and ability against tremendous odds. One of these odds was being female in the medieval world with all its restrictions and limitations, yet the world these women inhabited was also conducive to the practice of holiness. Holy women had the power and the authority to be taken seriously, respected, listened to, prayed for, and prayed to—all these women eventually received this acclaim—but it was invariably a lonely journey of mighty faith that got them to the pinnacle of spiritual perfection.

American theologian Rosemary Radford Ruether wrote in her book *Women, Power and the Pursuit of Holiness* that the virtue of obedience was a form of holiness and power for many women saints. "It was an obedience and a listening, self-imposed, which gave an inner sureness of direction and supplied an intellectual and moral clarity." They exhibited a high degree of self-knowledge, a wholeness of human experience, an understanding of suffering, and an embrace of community, prayer, and forgiveness. Above all they had an intimate, ongoing relationship with the Divine within. Therefore all these women were mystics of the advanced order.

It is these women, particularly from this time, who have handed down the prime teachings on mysticism, from their own religious experience and spiritual practices. The time in which most of them lived—the thirteenth and fourteenth centuries—has been hailed as the golden age of mysticism, not only in Christianity but also in the Eastern religions as well. Christian religious women in Italy were particularly supported and encouraged by men, usually members of the clergy, which enabled them to develop in a world dominated by church and state. Because of this support, they received an education and could read, and advanced within and outside the monastic environment. Marriage or the monastery were the usual alternatives offered to middle-class women from artisan families or from nobility, but girls from peasant families and poor backgrounds had no opportunity for such advancement. Therefore, the mystics who have given us written prayers and treatises, teachings from their lives on the mystical path, all hail from advantaged backgrounds or families with prestige and influence. This bred the necessary literacy, without which the teachings could never have survived. In addition, all the women on this pilgrimage were intelligent. They had the capacity to be able to discern and absorb the most esoteric of religious teachings from an advanced interior wisdom deepened by their betrothal to Christ. In order to gain the grace of the mystical marriage, they had to know him, not just through their personal experience and inner reality, but also from study of scripture, in particular the teachings of the Gospel, which they put into action whenever they could.

Catherine Meade wrote in her book *My Nature Is Fire* that holy women "drew townspeople like a magnet once they came to public attention." As their circles widened, these holy women also contributed to the "larger religious and political questions of the day." This is certainly true of St. Catherine of Siena.

ST. CATHERINE OF SIENA
Light of Truth

"In comparison to her, who are the wise men, the conquerors, the great ones of her age?"
Blessed John XXIII

"St. Catherine was not only the most dynamic woman in history but also the best friend to other women that ever lived."
Caryll Houselander

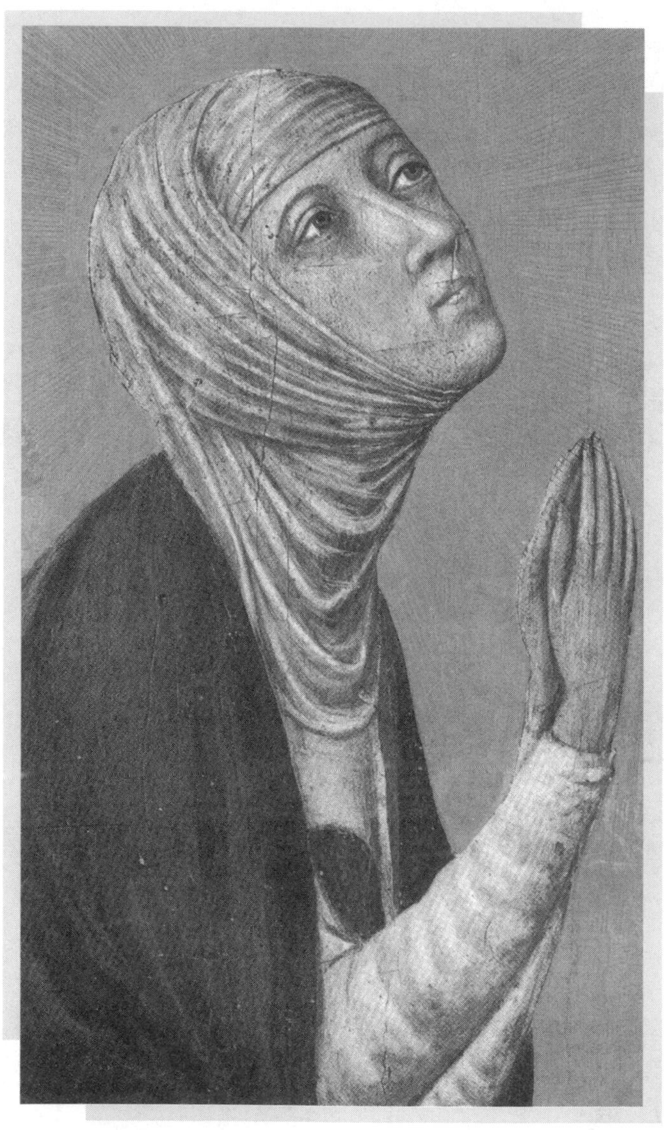

Her Life

The fourteenth century into which Catherine was born and lived was a time of great turmoil, darkness, and doubt. The materialism and corruption of Church leaders, particularly its popes, cardinals, and clerics, bred suspicion and cynicism that undermined faith. The growing scope of secular kings—particularly in France and England—began to shift social power from the Church to the nation state. Trade expanded the consciousness and knowledge of society, even as the victories of the Ottomans and Moors began to threaten the very heart of Christian Europe with subjugation by Islam. In addition to this religious and social upheaval, fourteenth-century Europe was ravaged by at least three waves of Black Plague—each more harsh—that, in the end, wiped out as much as half the population. To a society dominated by the Church, these tumultuous changes were often regarded as punishment by God for sin. The shattering of the social order, the schism within the Church, the encroaching invasions of the Muslims, and the panic from the plague spawned extremes of behavior, unleashing both great violence and destruction, and great piety and reform. Catherine remarkably left her mark on each of the movements that defined her age.

Catherine was born on March 25, 1347, the twenty-fourth of twenty-five children, in the Tuscan town of Siena. Her father was a reputable cloth-dyer called Giacomo Benincasa, and her mother, Mona Lapa di Puccio Piagenti, was a well-organized mother and householder, devout, and a regular almsgiver. Catherine's grandfather on her maternal side had won some fame as a poet so the Benincasa (meaning, in Italian, "well at home") family was endowed with artistry, industry, and faith. Because child mortality was so very high at the time, the Benincasas considered themselves lucky to have half their children live. As the youngest child, Catherine's twin sister, Giovanna, had died in infancy, Catherine became the youngest of the brood, and they all lived in a large house built on the side of a hill in the center of Siena. The house afforded views in all four directions of the activities below; for example, the fountain, Fontebranda, which was steps from Catherine's home, was a common meeting place for women and a source of water for the dyers in the area. Also nearby was the imposing Church of St. Dominic, looming upward as if its roof was reaching for the sky, its bells calling the people to service, a reminder of the vitalness of prayer and faith in daily life. And the courtyard leading to the house, with a well and a garden, was an ample playground for the children among the horses and delivery carts. The house was a hive of activity, and Catherine thrived as a lively, joyous child. Although Siena had been prospering when she was born, things were dramatically changing. Siena and Pisa came into conflict, the schism within the Church was bearing heavy costs, and England and France were in a bitter war (begun ten years before Catherine's birth), which would last for a hundred years.

When Catherine was very young, she began having mystical experiences, which she called "wonder stories." She was fond of visiting churches and shrines, and because education at the time was mostly church-centric, it formed the basis of her learning and fed her already-advancing soul. One incident that happened to her at the age of six changed the course of her life; in fact it ended her childhood as she knew it. She was on her way to visit her married sister, who lived not far from the family home. Accompanied by one of her brothers, Catherine headed up a steep path and, resting at a bend, she saw in the sky above St. Dominic's Church an image of Christ clothed in white, dressed as the pope on a throne, surrounded by several men, some she recognized as St. Peter, St. Paul, and St. John. It was not a vision but a message—in fact it was a prophecy of her future work—and as she turned to answer her brother who was calling her on, the image disappeared and she became distraught. This experience was so powerful for young Catherine that, on returning home, she put childhood games away and distanced herself from her family.

She began spending long periods alone in prayer and even ventured outside the city to sit in a cave, imagining what it might be like to be a hermit. She began regularly fasting and at the age of fifteen decided against the expected course of marriage. Catherine had long blond hair and a lively character and personality, and as the youngest daughter of the family, she was expected to marry well. But Catherine was to prove a masterfully strong character, and took her destiny upon herself, the destiny she had foreseen as a young girl. Tommaso della Fonte, an orphan who had been adopted by Catherine's parents as a boy, had become a Dominican priest, and he frequently visited the Benincasa home. On one such visit, Catherine confided in him about the image in the sky above the church and that she had taken a vow of virginity to God many years ago. Della Fonte casually mentioned the symbolism of cutting hair as a sign of commitment to God. That was all Catherine needed to hear in order to coarsely cut off her flowing locks. To further symbolize this huge bid for spiritual freedom, Catherine requested to live as a hermit in the family home. Her mother was in despair, but after much cajoling, her father recognized his daughter's needs and arranged for a small cell to be available for her. At fifteen years old, Catherine moved into this twelve-by-nine-foot room, in the lower part of the house near the workshops where the smells of dye mingled with the sweat of the workers. It had a high window, no furniture except for a bench, and she spent the next three years there in silence, isolation, penance, fasting, and prayer. She did not sleep much, nor consume any food except for some bread and occasional vegetables and herbs, and passed the time in the interior practice of self-knowledge. She entered into the deepest purification of her mind, soul, and body, to prepare herself, to live peacefully and honestly with her God, and to learn to recognize truth, the truth that would lead her, the truth that would define her, live in her, and guide her for the rest of her life.

Catherine was eighteen when she contracted smallpox, which permanently disfigured her face, and after her mother had nursed her back to health, Catherine requested her help in gaining permission to join the *Mantellatae,* the "cloaked women" of the Third Order of St. Dominic. They were usually composed of widows who lived in their homes but wore the habits of nuns and took similar vows—poverty, chastity, and obedience—as they served the world as religious. Mona Lapa, still unable to perceive of this course for her daughter but wanting to help her after her illness, took some persuading, but eventually she opened the doors for her daughter's acceptance into the Dominican Tertiary Order. The *Mantellatae*'s reception of Catherine, who was not a widow but a young, unmarried woman, was the first of many exceptions in her life. As one of the Dominican *Mantellatae,* Catherine vowed to follow its strict life of penance, prayer, and fasting, and she recited the holy orders of the day as well as went to Mass and received communion. She wore a hair shirt underneath the coarse white fabric of her habit and an iron belt against her flesh. These were common methods of penance at the time, and were perceived to help purify the ego and bring one closer to the suffering Christ, to help surpass one's own physical sufferings to reach a joyous union in pure spirit. And then, like a shroud, there was the black cloak, which identified her religious affiliation.

It was at a time when the whole of Siena was parading in the traditional carnival—the atmosphere full of gaiety and partying—that Catherine was, as usual, isolated in her cell, wondering at the life she was leading. She had learned Latin, which many perceived as miraculous, and was able to read her breviary and study the scriptures. She still kept silent—only speaking to her confessor—but some change was in the air. She wasn't sure what it was, so she carried out her usual activities of penance, fasting, prayer, and study, and experienced frequent torments of darkness combined with extraordinary breakthroughs of mystical light. The family was out of the house at the carnival when Catherine had a unique visitation. She was used to frequent meetings with the saints, the Holy Mother, and her Lord Jesus, but this one was different. Her carnival celebration belonged to the celestial realms: she experienced the mystical marriage, her betrothal period over, a welcome party for all her purgations; she was to be the bride of Christ. Mary put a ring upon her finger—it was a diamond surrounded by four pearls—and Christ said to Catherine, "I betroth you as my bride in perfect faith for all time." He asked her to undertake without protest all the works that he would demand of her, because she was now armed "with the power of faith" and would be triumphant over her opponents. Now, armed with the gift of divine union, the sacred marriage, she was to receive the grace she needed for the next part of her ministry. She said of this initiation, "It is the will of God and my desire."

Soon thereafter Christ appeared at her cell door and refused to enter. Instead, he led her out from her solitude. He requested that she work for the good of other people and the Church. "Go in peace," he said. "In this way you shall serve me and become more perfectly united to me through love of me and your neighbor, and then you will be able to rise even more quickly to heaven, as though on wings." Much to her family's surprise, she emerged from her cell. Her sudden appearance, after avoiding contact for several years, was strange for everyone. For Catherine, there were in-laws and children living in the house whom she had never met. From then on, her life did not consist of a simple embrace of her holiness, but a carrying-out of the domestic duties she had missed during her isolation. She was given most of the load and became a servant of sorts for the rest of the family. She was a fast, fastidious housekeeper, however, and because of her need for little sleep, she would clean the house at night. During these chores, she discovered a way of finding and dwelling in the cell within herself, the cell of the heart, and carrying it around inside her. She also discovered the stocks of the family food, which she readily gave to the poor; she gave so much away that the family had to lock up their provisions in order to feed themselves. Catherine also gave away everything that she possessed (except the objects she needed for her service to the community), like the silver cross from her rosary and even her black cloak. The local *Mantellatae* frowned upon this—the cloak was the proper attire for a tertiary religious—but Catherine responded that she would rather go without a cloak than without charity.

Now that Catherine had returned to the outside world after her years of interior preparation, the first place she practiced the Dominican Rule of visiting the sick and imprisoned was at the local hospital, La Misericordia (Hospital of Mercy, now called La Scala), which was opposite the site of Siena's cathedral. Besides being an ordinary hospital, it also served as a free hospice for pilgrims and a home for foundling children. As was usual for an insomniac like Catherine, she took the night cases, and the hospital allotted her a cell in the bowels of the building, where she could take the occasional nap. The man who ran the hospital introduced Catherine to William Flete, an English hermit Augustinian monk, who lived in the woods of nearby Lecceto. He had great religious fame as both a writer and an ascetic. Later he would become a humble follower of Catherine's counsel. She was known to never disappoint anyone she met. She and Flete developed a loving friendship, although they rarely agreed. She always thought that he was too harsh with others and should be more compassionate, and she would jibe him for his self-centeredness.

To prove that she practiced what she preached, Catherine began to care for two people who had come her way from God. One of them was a prisoner who was to be executed; she wrote in one of her letters to her confessor how moving it was for her to be with him at his death and to witness his soul forgiven and leaving his body into union with the Godhead. The other was a difficult, foul-mouthed, angry, and ungrateful woman who had advanced leprosy. Catherine visited her twice daily to feed, wash, and attend her. These visits were not at all agreeable; it took all her strength to suffer the woman's wrath, but she continued silently to minister to her until she died. Catherine's mother, concerned for her health, despaired when she saw boils appearing on

Catherine's hands, but they disappeared in due course as Catherine continued to give herself in selfless service to the sick, abandoned, and unloved around her.

As Catherine was out of the house and in service in the community, she began to attract some followers, who were moved in her presence, impressed by her strength and faith, and longed for spiritual direction and clarity. Some of these were Dominican clergy, priests, and confessors; others were writers who gladly brought their talents to her service as scribes (she was known only to dictate); and some were *Mantellatae* sisters and friends, including her sister-in-law. Even her mother eventually became one of the *Mantellatae* and a follower of her daughter.

Not everyone was supportive of Catherine, however, because of the strange spectacles of her mystical visions and ecstasies, which she commonly experienced in church, and which made her seem lifeless and unconscious, her body frequently lying as if dead on the floor. She was suspected of being cast into the devil's domain, of being a witch. She certainly was misunderstood by many. But after curing a local priest, Raymond of Capua, of a serious illness, he became her spiritual director, advisor, and closest friend. Her newfound "family" of faith began to call her "Mama," and although in her twenties, she was recognized to be infused with wisdom and other "remarkable gifts." Of her special powers she had said she wanted to "make things and people better."

Wherever she went, it was as if grace flowed from her, and her intent of drawing souls to God permitted her to counsel those who felt the need to be forgiven, to right their lives, and to turn from quarreling and immoral behavior to something purer, somewhere where peace could dwell in them. She began to drop her pearls of wisdom through her teachings and sharing with her disciples. She said that a good person is a prayer, and she advised each one to "pray the prayer of action which is the fragrant flowering of the soul."

Between 1368 and 1375, when Catherine was in her early twenties, many changes took place in her life. One of these was her father's death, upon which her brothers took over the family business. Some of them became involved in the governance of Siena, which not only promoted the family's name but also made its members more vulnerable to attack, especially amid the republic, papal, and imperial discords. But political attack was the least of Catherine's problems; what was worse were the ongoing attacks she received from her own Church, even her order, on charges of suspicions about her behavior, the accuracy of her teachings, and her healing abilities, all of which were novel attributes not commonly experienced in a Dominican tertiary. She was called to Florence to defend herself, which she did admirably. But this brought no end to her struggles. She was continually tested for her theological soundness and the reliability of her faith, and even though she loathed being tested, she knew that it was necessary in the world that she inhabited. Feeling God's love like a burning fire inside her, she could willingly, and patiently, undergo such interrogations, the physical and mental attacks, even the abject failings in her efforts to renew the Church as an acceptance as the will of God for her.

At the age of twenty-five, Catherine's influence widened and she began to move into the political arena. Christ had told her in prayer that she was to "plunge boldly into public activity of every kind with one thought in mind, the salvation of souls, whether they be men or women....I will be at your side....Carry on with courage...." People thronged to meet her, to seek her advice. Her reputation went before her; she was known as a woman of humility yet an intellectual thinker and activist. She was acknowledged as an outstanding peacemaker, and was called to not only mediate among feuding families, but also among city-states.

Meanwhile, the whole of western Europe was in turmoil, due to the devastations of the Black Death, and with the Italian republics and papal states in constant conflict, worsened by the defection of the papacy from its formal Roman residence to a palace in Avignon. The transfer of Church power from Italy to France lent little support to the needs of the Italian people, and as a result fed a growing anarchism. France and England were caught in a bloody war, and the Turks were making inroads into eastern Europe, but were defeated in 1366 at the gates of Constantinople. Catherine saw all the problems of the secular world as religious problems and their solutions, therefore, as religious solutions. She recognized that the sins of the collective Church were also the sins of individuals; she certainly knew how the inner world affected the outer. She did not mince words when she catalogued the sins of the clerical hierarchy: pride, selfishness, avarice, ambition, affluent living, lack of concern for the poor, power-seeking, cowardice, impurity, infidelity, nepotism, simony, and sacrilege! She prayed to the Trinity for divine compassion and mercy on this impoverished and corrupt world.

In the meantime, her world began to widen beyond Siena and she began traveling as a peacemaker, accompanied by her disciples, who called themselves "Pilgrims for Peace." Catherine understood the greatest pilgrimage to be a Crusade, which she called "The Holy Passage" and which for her became the simple and clear solution for every problem of the day. For instance, a third Crusade would certainly unite Italy with England and France into a powerful army. Catherine became almost obsessed with the necessity of this Crusade: everywhere she went she pushed for its recognition and the urgency of its execution. In 1375 on a visit to Lucca and Pisa, she glimpsed the sea for the first time in her life and was inspired to write: "God is the placid sea in which creatures may lose themselves: God is the boundless sea: the sea of light, the fathomless sea."

It was as if the sea was an invitation to chart new territories, and Catherine's international ministry began to take on a structure. She started with letter-writing and wrote to as many influential people as she could. One of them was Elizabeth, Queen of Hungary, whom she warned of the Turkish peril, the threat of Islam at the gates of Europe. The other was the Queen of Naples. She also wrote to the French Pope, Gregory XI, exhorting him to return to his rightful seat in Rome. She preached reform, the way of love, care and compassion for neighbor, a soul devoid of pride, ego, and the common sins of the day. She knew that the power of prayer and her will (in league with God's) could crack any problem. One of her followers said of her, "Angelic and divine she illuminates our hemisphere like the sun."

Her travels to Florence in 1374 to stir up enthusiasm for the Crusade were interrupted by a resurgence of the plague, and she was urgently requested to return and attend the sick at the Misericordia Hospital. This time the hospital was not big enough to house so many, and the streets of Siena became like mass graves. Rotting corpses lay abandoned in alleyways, as survival became the luck of the draw. Catherine and her followers served the sick as best they could, she carrying a scent bottle to combat the stench and a small lantern so she could see in the dark. Six of her beloved nieces and nephews died of the plague, and she buried them herself. She also healed many who were about to die, the most famous case being the rector of the hospital himself, the man whom she admired for his flawless service to the poor and needy. A visit from her was enough to get him out of bed, cured and ready to serve those around him once more.

It was during a trip to Pisa in 1375, when Catherine was praying and attending Mass in the Church of St. Christina, that she entered one of her ecstatic raptures. Her "family" was with her, including Raymond of Capua. He noticed a change in Catherine's body, that she had succumbed to her usual unconsciousness, but at the same time she seemed elevated off the ground in a kneeling position, her arms extended and her face illumined. Afterwards, Catherine revealed to her confessor that she had received the stigmata but that she had begged Christ to keep the marks of his wounds invisible on the exterior of her body. She desired all of him with the deepest of love, which the experience of his holy wounds signified, but only in a humble intimacy and unseen by others. Despite the stigmata being invisible, the news circulated among her followers and further afield. She taught that no one can receive the gifts of the Holy Spirit without "first passing through rigorous purifications in the furnace of suffering, humiliation, and self-denial." Christ had spoken to her in one of her meditations in her masterpiece of spiritual writings, *The Dialogue* (which she produced later), saying, "I am He who is and you are She who is not."

Catherine Benincasa was now one of the most discussed women of her day. All the crowned heads of Europe knew her. Having received papal approval for her promotion of the Crusade, she wrote to the Emperor, Charles V, begging him to join it, and she manipulated many papal army heads to do likewise. Her travels took her far and wide—over the course of her life, she visited and sent delegates from her little army of peace to Avignon, Marseilles, Villeneuve, Genoa, Venice, Milan, Bari, Naples, Rome, and Perugia.

It was at the beginning of the year 1376 that Pope Gregory announced his intention to officially leave France and to return to Rome to "live and die among the Romans." For the papists this was excellent news, something they had been praying for, but the imminent geographical shift in papal power threatened the political dominance of Florence, which actively supported rebellion in the Papal States. This caused subsequent defections in Perugia, Assisi, Spoleto, and many other major Italian towns, including Forlì and Ravenna.

Within two months of the pope's announcement, almost all the states were in rebellion and Florence, the leader of the league for independence, supported movements to promote the ideals of a republic. The pope, furious with the citizens of Florence, sent them an indictment listing the commune's crimes and summoning people by name to appear at the papal court in Avignon. When Catherine heard about this, she wrote the pope a letter in which she tried to placate his wrath and to help him see that the Florentines could not be accused of wrongdoing and injustices when so many representatives of the Church could be accused of the same things. She asked him to offer them mercy, to be compassionate. She offered herself as a mediator and she urged the pope to come to Rome without delay, citing the importance of the heritage of St. Peter and of the renewal of the Church to be "the heart of burning charity." She pleaded for peace and "no more war!" She begged him not to send his army to Tuscany. But her letter arrived too late—the army had already been dispatched. There was no alternative than to go to Avignon to speak to the pope directly.

In Avignon, Catherine was warmly welcomed by the pope, although she raised suspicion among the members of his court, the aristocrats, and particularly the women, who attacked her verbally, emotionally, and physically. The Florentine delegation then arrived and promptly ignored Catherine's role as mediator. She continued to instruct the pope to act from "love and virtue," not "fear and necessity," and refused to return to Italy. The brother of the King of France was in Avignon at the time, and was one of the many who on meeting Catherine was impressed by her abilities and spirit. He asked her whether she would consider settling the war between England and France, but she declined.

The pope finally slipped quietly away from France. He had followed Catherine's advice to engage in what she called "holy deceit" to make sure he got to Rome safely without attack by taking a boat to Genoa. His entourage of cardinals and bishops, his army, and his belongings stayed behind. Catherine also set out at the same time and met the pope in Genoa for counsel when he stopped at port (he came to her dressed as an ordinary priest to protect his anonymity). As the pope returned to Rome, a monumental achievement in the eyes of the Italian Church, Catherine and her followers returned to Siena. Her welcome was slow in coming—her mother complained of her absences, her sisters in the *Mantellatae* questioned the necessity of traveling and interceding in matters far from home.

As if given a consolation gift by God for her efforts (which had no worldly rewards), she was bestowed a castle on the outskirts of Siena near the Lecceto woods where William Flete lived. Flete had introduced her to a rich man called Vanni who needed her help with feuding members of his family, and in gratitude for her peaceful intercession, he gave her the castle Belcaro. She planned to turn this place into a convent for her tertiary sisters; the pope subsequently gave her permission to do so, and the tranquility and peace of the place nourished and protected her. Belcaro had a tiny jewel of a chapel, nestled in a courtyard of roses and lemon trees. Catherine named it Santa Maria degli Angeli (St. Mary of the Angels—after St. Francis's holy place in Assisi), and William Flete said the first Mass at its delicate altar. Belcaro offered Catherine the space and the time to write, and she dictated the conversation between God and her soul that subsequently became the book *The Dialogue*. Today it is considered to be one of the most advanced and comprehensive theological teachings on the mystical life of contemplation and action. For Catherine it was a summary of all her experiences and thoughts of God, all the ideas she had been given, all the teachings she had absorbed from her silent early years. In four days she poured it forth from the depths of her shining soul, using language and symbology of the pastoral, of the body, of blood, water, earth, and wood. She prayed prayers to the spirit, she drew pictures of the universe, she analyzed the state of the pilgrim soul who longs for God. She listed temptations against charity, she plunged into the depths of human misery, and she explained the life of virtue as the solution for a world lost to community. It was as if *The Dialogue* had no other time to be created than the reprise at Belcaro because she would not rest there for long. Rome was in chaos, and she was needed there as soon as possible.

Unfortunately for Catherine, Gregory had died in 1378—only eighteen months after returning to Rome—and had been succeeded by a Roman, Urban VI. He was not a popular man, having an abrupt nature that made him vulnerable to misunderstandings and false judgments. He also lacked political sensitivity, which did not bode well for the future of the Crusade or for peace with Florence, and the atmosphere in Rome was more like a battlefield than the majesty of an eternal city. Urban was a reformist, which Catherine viewed as an advantage, but with his inability to bring about reform in a loving and pastoral way, he upset his own curia. In fact, five months after his election, the cardinals split their loyalties, and the French contingent (which made up the majority) elected to support another pope, a Frenchman, Clement VII.

Two opposing popes and no opportunity for peace created what was referred to as the Great Schism of Europe. Catherine knew that her hopes for resurrecting the Crusade were indeed shattered, since what was more urgently needed was clarity in the papacy and peace in the Church and in Rome. She immediately focused her attention on Florence and began a persuasive pursuit of peace with a series of letters to Pope Urban. She moved to the city and refused to leave until this work was complete. When a courier arrived from Rome containing the long-awaited olive branch (the sign of the pope's peace accord), Catherine left Florence with no thanks from the commune for her help. In fact, she had to slip out undercover due to the volatility of the situation.

Rome was next on her agenda. Urban was in grave need of her counsel and every day without her was proving disastrous. Most of her "family" accompanied her to Rome. She left Belcaro in the hands of others in an act of finality. As she had the gift of prophecy, could she have foreseen that she was never to return to Siena? The pope provided Catherine and her family simple lodgings about one mile from St. Peter's and near the Dominican Church of Santa Maria Sopra Minerva. Her confessor and friend, Raymond of Capua, was pastor of this church, but by some sad twist of fate he was sent on a mission to Genoa as soon as she arrived, so that they had no time together. Most of her friends, and she herself at intervals, begged on the street for alms. But the bulk of her energy and time was spent in writing letters to the pope, meeting him regularly, and praying daily at St. Peter's for the healing of the Church.

Her body was not immune to the collective pain around her. She was physically weak and exhausted by her efforts, and her mental anguish grew daily. She wrote to one of her friends in Siena that the "Divine Goodness" had shown such ineffable love of her miserable soul that God had provided for her "within and without." She viewed this part of her journey as a "thorough trial" made by God and driven by suffering. She said that God had cared for her through this suffering, and she ended the letter: "Let suffering fatten me, suffering heal me, suffering give me light, suffering give me wisdom, suffering clothe my nakedness, suffering divest me of all self-love, spiritual and temporal." She begged for prayer during this time when she said that her Savior had put her on an island where the "winds beat upon me from every side." In faith she had followed where Christ had pointed and had used her gifts to partake of peace, yet her vision and mission for the unity of Europe and of the Church had crumbled in front of her, and she was tormented by her purpose. Her critics viewed her life and work as complete failure. All that she had stood for and aimed for she had not been able to achieve, yet her faithful followers recognized that there was no one else who could teach them the ways of God as she knew them. She had once said "End all pain in pain," which might have alluded to her thoughts on the purpose of her life and her ministry.

Pope Urban's leadership, especially in dealing with the schism and his own place within it, was weakened by circumstance and his ineptness and brusque manner. It was largely due to Catherine's daily wisdom that kept him and his papacy from falling apart. She advised members of the papal armies to enter battle only with "good intention" and after some victories, Urban's position became more secure. Despite increased physical weakness, Catherine continued her letter-writing. She wrote to the churches around Europe pleading for assistance, she wrote to royalty asking for allegiance to Urban's papacy, and she wrote to the government of Siena instructing them to pay their debts to the king of France. She exploited every gift of hers to the utmost. She addressed Urban's lack of diplomacy in letters of advice to him on how to address the Roman government, advising the ways of love over impious acts of anger and irreverence. And in her humility, she always ended her letters asking for his forgiveness for her telling him the things she felt he needed to know, citing love as her guide.

The year 1380 began with little signs of hope. While struggling to quell plots to kill the pope, Catherine was continually tortured by rumors of being evil. Racked by demons and in constant pain, she fell unconscious at the end of January while dictating a letter to the pope (this could have been a stroke). She wrote details of the incident to one of her spiritual family friends in Siena, describing how her soul had left her body and how she tried to talk to those around her with her soul absent. She implored Christ to let her return to the vessel of her body as her memory "was full of the needs of the holy Church and of all Christian people." She wasn't quite ready to die. After ten days of delirium and anguish, she returned to consciousness and continued her activities, dragging her ailing body to St. Peter's for prayer. She had a vision of being crushed by the weight of the Church on her shoulders, and subsequently lost the use of her legs. Paralyzed from the waist down, she lay on a couch, could swallow only water, and developed a high fever.

From February to April her life ebbed away. Her followers were with her, nursing her, her women friends bathing and embracing her. Many of her other followers outside Rome got word of her illness and took to the road to get to her. She blessed all her friends individually, her voice so faint that they had to put their ears to her lips to hear her final words for each of them. She asked for her mother's blessing, and old Mona Lapa, choking with grief, tried to console her. On April 29th, Catherine died. Her last words were "blood, blood, blood." She had taught in her life that Christ's suffering body was the book in which God's love was written, not in ink but blood, in letters so big that no one was unable to read them. The blood of Christ was shed for the life of others. It was as if she knew that her death would lead to life for those who knew her, and it started to become true as Rome's citizens began to mourn her death. Both her devotees and the sick and suffering flocked in a never-ending procession to the bier on which her body lay in the local Dominican church. Her brothers in the order put an iron grille around the bier to preserve it from theft, but still her energy and holiness healed many who revered and mourned her. The pope ordered a magnificent requiem for her, which was carried out with great solemnity. As the presiding priest climbed the pulpit to speak of her, he gave up being heard above the multitude whose voices were raised in prayer. All he said was "She speaks better for herself."

The superior of the Dominicans in Siena eventually made his way to Rome and obtained the pope's permission to have Catherine's coffin opened and her head removed to be brought back home. It was carried through the Sienese streets borne by the bishop in a silver casket while the whole city came out to greet it, with every house decorated in honor of their most celebrated citizen. Finally at rest in St. Dominic's Church, the church where her call for reform began, her head can be seen today in a side chapel dedicated to her and is the church's richest treasure.

In a letter to William Flete, Catherine of Siena had written for prayer that God would have mercy on her and that God would give her the grace to be "always a lover and proclaimer of the truth and to die for that truth." Flete had once said to one of her followers, "You do not know her. You do not realize what she is....Truly the Holy Spirit is in her."

Catherine was thirty-three when she died, the same age as her beloved Jesus when he was crucified.

CHRONOLOGY

1347	Born March 25 in Siena; the Black Death strikes a year later.
1353	Sees vision over cathedral. Is called to a solitary and prayerful life.
1354	Takes a private vow of virginity at age seven.
1362	Makes her first confession; cuts off her hair; retreats to the secret cell within, the cell of self-knowledge, and begins interior spiritual life.
1363	Announces her intent to never marry; begins a life of deeper solitude.
1364–65	Joins the Dominican Tertiaries, the *Mantellatae*.
1365–68	Experiences interior purgations and sufferings. Leaves her solitude to serve the community; attracts disciples. Her father dies.

1369–74	Becomes a peacemaker and healer, but also suffers suspicion from other *Mantellatae* and some friars. Enters into mystical marriage with Christ. Begins her correspondence.
1374	Is called to Florence where her public life is officially approved by Raymond of Capua, her confessor and later biographer. Another epidemic of Black Plague in Siena. She and her followers administer to the sick.
1375	Travels to Pisa to preach and teach; there receives the invisible stigmata in the Church of St. Christina. Advocates for a Crusade.
1376	Travels to Avignon to mediate for Florence and to urge Pope Gregory XI to return to Rome. In September Gregory returns to Rome, and Catherine and her family return to Siena.
1377	Initiates work transforming the castle at Belcaro into the monastery of St. Mary of the Angels. Dictates her *Dialogue*.
1378	Goes to Florence to mediate peace on behalf of the pope, who dies and is succeeded by Urban VI. In September Clement VII is elected pope by rival cardinals and this causes the Great Schism. When peace is restored between Florence and Pope Urban, Catherine returns to Siena. In November, she moves to Rome to support Urban.
1379	Works on behalf of unity and reform in the Church, writing letters, praying, and offering advice to the pope. Becomes physically weaker.
1380	Is paralyzed, possibly from a stroke, and dies two months later on April 29. Her body is laid in the Church of Santa Maria Sopra Minerva.
1461	Canonized by Sienese Pope Pius II.
1866	Pope Pius IX declares her co-patron of Rome.
1939	Pope Pius XII proclaims her Patron of Italy along with St. Francis of Assisi.
1970	Pope Paul VI makes her a Doctor of the Church.

OFFICIAL FEAST DAY: April 29

Spiritual Essentials

St. Catherine of Siena used a unique symbology in her teaching on the life and purification of the soul. These symbols appeared in her *Dialogue* as well as in her many letters to her followers, the pope, members of the curia, heads of state and royalty, army generals, mothers, and families. Catherine's themes and symbols are vital to understanding her teaching and the wisdom she gained from her prayer life (inner purification) and from her own life experience (exterior practice). She also treated many of the same themes over and over.

THEMES

Self-Knowledge

St. Catherine taught that self-knowledge is understanding of self and knowledge of God. She introduced three stages of progression in self-knowledge:

1. Learning the virtue of humility, the soul's need to depend solely on God and to have a burning desire to love God above self.
2. Experiencing the interior transformation that occurs from the infusion of grace for the understanding of the passion and suffering of Jesus Christ, whom she refers to as God-man.
3. Moving outward to practice charity with one's neighbors, the only way that God can be loved in return through compassion toward others.

Love in Action

In her *Dialogue,* St. Catherine heard the divine instruction that she had to be bound closer to God by the bond of love for her neighbor. She was reminded that the two commandments that are the most prominent are the love of God and the love of neighbor. God said that it was impossible to directly return the kind of love that God had for her, so that by expressing her love in compassionate action toward others, she can do for them what she cannot do for God. "Love them without any concern for thanks and without looking for any profit for yourself," God instructed her.

Mercy for Individual and World Suffering

St. Catherine prayed continually for God to show mercy to the people of the world. She also wrote to many people about not falling into the lures and desires of the finite world but to keep their eyes on heaven, their hearts pure, their faith constant in prayer. She outlined the root cause of suffering as being "self-will grounded in self-centeredness." She admonished those who showed too much care for what she perceived to be petty concerns, always reminding them that God's ways were not our ways. Her teaching on suffering (something she experienced all her life, not only in herself but among others) is simple and profound, a way to join with Jesus on the cross.

Divine Providence—God Provides All We Need

To be able to receive Divine Providence and understand its ways, St. Catherine taught that there are many virtues that are required to be perfected in us:

- **Patience.** Patience is the first virtue because patience can never be conquered. Catherine wrote, "Patience is always the victor. Patience is a queen who stands guard upon the rock of courage. She is an invincible victor. She does not stand alone but with perseverance as her companion."
- **Desire.** St. Catherine referred to herself as being "restless with tremendous desire," desire for many things, but most prominently the desire for God and for the salvation of the world. God, who is infinite, desires her; as God's servant, she must serve God with what is infinite, but she has nothing infinite except her own soul's desire.

- **Surrender.** To receive Divine Providence and to understand its ways, one must understand that whatever happens, whatever the Spirit provides and however strange it may seem, it is always done and given to us because of "love."

Intent

St. Catherine was clear that she was to surrender to God's will, without any consolation for herself, only the bestowment of grace to live and teach the truth.

SYMBOLS

The Well

St. Catherine suggests that the quest for self-knowledge is like the digging of a well. Before we can reach the water far below, we have to go through a lot of dark soil, necessary work to achieve the goal. The bottom of the well is the center of one's being. She wrote, "Let us plunge into God's well where we cannot but know ourselves and in this way know also the goodness of God."

The Mirror

Since we are made in the divine image, God in the *Dialogue* speaking to the soul of St. Catherine suggests that she open the eye of her mind and gaze into God. St. Catherine saw that if we look at this mirror of self-discernment with an eye to seeing the blemishes on our own face, we can see more clearly our own defects because of the purity we see in God. She instructed, "The soul cannot live without loving, nor could it love without light. Then if it wants to love, it has to see."

A Fire of Love

St. Catherine wrote that "love is the consequence of knowledge—to seek truth and to be clothed in it." It is love that guides us to better know the goodness of God. In the process of deepening self-knowledge, St. Catherine wrote that as she looked at God she could see her own nature as that of fire, "for you are no other than a fire of love," she said to God, "and you have given this nature to me when you created me in a fire of love." The expression and use of the metaphors "flames of love" and "fire" are common among the mystics' language to describe the love of God burning within.

The Fountain

The fountain of Fontebranda close to St. Catherine's family home must have inspired her prayer life and her teaching. She heard from God in her *Dialogue* that she had to become a vessel to be filled by the fountain of "living water"; she said that if she did not drink continually from it in God, she would become empty. The living water therefore signified the constant grace that is given from God if the soul is pure enough to receive it in quantity.

The Vineyard

God instructed St. Catherine that she should remember that her own vineyard is joined to her neighbor's vineyard without dividing lines, "so you cannot do good or evil for yourself without doing the same for your neighbors."

The Tree

There are several teachings in which St. Catherine uses the tree; there is the tree of the soul made for love that is "delightfully planted" and "bears many-fragranced blossoms of virtue." Uprooted from the soil, it dies without fruit, but rooted in self-knowledge and virtue, it can grow and bear much fruit: discernment; humility; a consistent desire to love; the surrender required to relinquish control and let God choose the best way to serve the world; the purification needed for dynamic growth; courage and steadfastness in conquering self-will, and then in enduring the pruning required, as the soul grows by "means of trials, disgrace, insults, mockery, abuse, and reproach."

The Sea

The sea captured Catherine's spiritual imagination when she saw it for the first time while visiting Pisa. For her, the sea is a symbol of the eternal God, the peace of the water where the soul who conforms to the will of God can be immersed.

The Bridge

The Bridge over the troubled waters of the world, a link between two shores—earth and heaven—is a symbol of Jesus Christ. Catherine taught that the Bridge has three steps upon it. These steps signify the stages that we begin the journey as the servant of Christ, then become his friend, and then become the child who loves him "with no concern for selfish interests."

Tears

She uses the symbol of tears to describe diverse sorrows. There are the tears resulting from the world's evil, the tears of fear of punishment from those who believe, then there are tears of tenderness from those who are more advanced, who weep for their imperfections of heart. The tears for love of neighbor, the sweet tears of mercy of "great tenderness," are a "perfect weeping," and finally the tears of fire are those shed without physical weeping. This final stage of advanced compassionate action is where love is perfected and the soul is united with God.

SAYINGS BY ST. CATHERINE

"Do not wait for time because time does not wait for you."

"Love is had only by loving."

"It would be very displeasing to God if you were to set your heart on something of less value than yourself…for people become what they love."

"Conscience always fights on one side
and sensuality on the other."

"Whoever does not go forward,
by that very fact is turning back."

A Prayer by St. Catherine

"O eternal Trinity, my sweet love! You, light, give us light.
You, wisdom, give us wisdom.
You, supreme strength, strengthen us.
Today, eternal God, let our cloud be dissipated
so that we may perfectly know and follow
your truth, in truth,
with a free and simple heart."

A Pilgrim's Prayer to St. Catherine

O Catherine, irresistible saint,
Your words cannot be resisted by the hearts of doubters,
And neither can heaven resist
Your ardent faith and your insistent prayers.
As then, so now, help us sense the power
of your intercession,
To confirm peace among people,
Liberating the oppressed from injustice
or adversity of any type.
Comfort and cleanse the sick of body and soul.
Pray for world peace,
For unity and faithfulness among the people of God,
the supreme pastor,
And for the well-being of our earth.
Also remember me who has invoked you with faith,
Knowing that you do not abandon in difficulty
Those who consider you mother and teacher.

The Pilgrimage

Destinations:

Central Siena, Belcaro, and Lecceto

Suggested length:

One day

This pilgrimage can be continued in Rome (see pages 315–16).

SIENA

Siena is a winding medieval walled city built on three hills in the shape of a star. It reached its height of illustriousness and power in the Middle Ages during St. Catherine's lifetime. Now famous for being the birthplace of the co-patron of Italy, Siena also attracts tourists for the Palio, a folk festival that takes place in July and August of each year and includes a controversial horse race. Siena has also bred another well-known saint, St. Bernardino, depictions of whom can be recognized around the town and in the churches. He was born the year of St. Catherine's death—1380—and lived until 1444. A brilliant preacher, he joined the Franciscans as a friar and traveled the length of the country by foot preaching and extolling the veneration of the name of Jesus through the use of plaques with IHS imprinted upon them. He became vicar general of the Observant branch of the Franciscans in 1437 and died in Aquila, having refused the three bishoprics of Siena, Ferrara, and Urbino.

Siena can be entered through a variety of gates—called "Porta" in Italian. From the south take the SS223 (either to or from Grosseto), exiting at "Siena Ovest" (Siena West). Follow signs for Centro, Porta S. Marco, and Firenze, taking the road signed for "San Domenico," the Church of St. Domenic north of Porta Fontebranda.

Chiesa San Domenico (The Church of St. Dominic)

This church was St. Catherine's parish church, the place she came to pray and attend Mass and had many ecstatic experiences at the altar; it is also where the Dominican friars and her confessor lived and served the community. It is the church over which she saw her vision in the sky when she was six years old. Its vast Gothic-style simplicity and its hushed reverence are awe-inspiring. Many frescoes from its walls are lost, but the church has the earliest portrait of St. Catherine by Andrea Vanni (who knew her and painted it during her lifetime). It hangs over a small altar at the rear of the church on the west wall. As it is hidden from view in the main church, you need to climb the steps to see it.

St. Catherine's embalmed head is venerated in her own chapel, also on the west side, further up toward the main altar. The frescoes that adorn its surrounding walls are scenes from her life—Catherine in ecstasy witnessed and aided by her *Mantellatae* sisters, and another fresco of her healing the sick. To the right of this chapel in the wall is another relic—part of her finger— as well as a selection of her personal possessions, including her prayer book and breviary. At the front of the church to the right (again on the west side), you can view the glass-and-gold reliquary that had housed her head for centuries prior to the existing enclosure.

You could begin your pilgrimage lighting a candle at St. Catherine's chapel and asking for prayers and intercession for your intentions.

Take the stone steps (going south) to the right of the main doors of St. Dominic's Church.

There's a stone statue of St. Catherine in the lower doorway and also an image of St. Bernardino. Ahead is the skyline of Siena with the magnificent cathedral at its peak. This was the view that St. Catherine would have seen daily from her house.

Santuario Casa di S. Caterina (The House and Sanctuary of St. Catherine)

Take the footpath to the left at the bottom of the steps and walk downward toward an alleyway. Beyond this at the street turn right (going south and downhill) to the main gates of the family house to the right with its deep red stone courtyard stretched at its entrance.

St. Catherine's family home—that of the Benincasas, now cared for by Dominican sisters—is a short walk from St. Dominic's. Busts of the many popes who visited there adorn the walls of the courtyard, and the well was the original source of water for the family. Many of the family rooms have survived in structure but have been turned into oratories and chapels, such as the following:

The Oratory of the Kitchen

Transformed into its present form in the sixteenth century, it has under the altar the remains of the original fireplace with some pots hanging, and the flooring has some of the original tiles of the family kitchen, the place where St. Catherine served her family like a domestic after coming out of her cell of self-knowledge.

Cell of Self-Knowledge

This cell can be reached by the descending stairs.

The first room below has the original cell in which St. Catherine spent most of the years of her girlhood and adolescence, undergoing penance and purgation and preparing herself for the exterior work she was called to in her twenties. On the far wall of the cell are some relics—the lamp she used to serve the sick during the night and the scent bottle she used to combat the stench from the rotting corpses in the street. The frescoes on the wall of the chapel depict some notable scenes in Catherine's young life, including her cutting her hair in the presence of her cousin Tommaso della Fonte, and her experiencing her "miracle stories," witnessed by her mother. If it is open (which it sometimes isn't), the cellar can be visited where her father and brothers' business as dyers took place, as well as where the family wine and food were stored.

The Church of the Crucifix

The church is reached from the entrance portico and was built over the kitchen garden of the original family home. On the main altar is the exact crucifix from which St. Catherine received her "invisible" stigmata in Pisa. Many of the oil paintings that adorn this church are magnificent depictions of incidents in her public life, especially her advising the pope. The Stations of the Cross are particularly interesting and are a recent donation to the chapel.

Fontebranda—The Local Fountain

On leaving St. Catherine's house, take the immediate right street running parallel and walk down toward the fountain.

As old as the eleventh century, the fountain is where St. Catherine's spiritual imagination was fired as a girl to understand the grace of the ever-flowing fountain of water that she referred to in her teaching and prayers. It was also the central meeting place of women in the community for bathing and washing.

The Place of the Vision

Almost opposite the fountain on the other side of the road are steps winding upward toward the cathedral.

On the wall at an angle in the pathway of steps is a painting of young Catherine (accompanied by her brother) as she sees the vision of Christ as pope among some apostles, over St. Dominic's Church. This is the exact spot where it happened.

Take the path upward leading to the street, turn right and then left under an enclosed archway.

At the top is Siena's jewel of a cathedral, its Duomo. Opposite the cathedral is a long building with a clock. This is the old Misericordia hospital, now a museum.

Museo di Santa Maria della Scala (The Museum of Holy Mary of the Steps or Stairs), originally the Misericordia (Mercy) Hospital

The museum has been converted from the original hospice and hospital where St. Catherine offered her services. In the main ground-floor rooms you can view the original tiles and high ceilings. In the hall, with its graphic frescoes of the activities of the commune as well as of the hospital itself, you'll see where the **Infirmary and Pilgrim's Hall** housed the row of beds where St. Catherine served the sick. The images date from the fifteenth century and illustrate the type of hospital work that was carried on within its walls, including scenes of acts of charity—pilgrims being served by the Sienese, the sick receiving sustenance, foundling children being received, their feeding by the wet nurses and their weddings in later life, and those who died being taken up to heaven. There are also scenes of renovations of the hospital that would have happened after St. Catherine's time.

Once through the Pilgrim's Hall, follow the signs to the ***Capella della Notte (Oratory of the Night)*** *in the basement.*

Here is where St. Catherine slept for a few hours in the night when she worked in the hospital. On the left of the altar there's a small devotional chapel with a statue in the hole in the wall where she actually laid (a good place for silent prayer). The devotional art on the surrounding walls and ceilings, and within the adjoining rooms, includes unique icons and a gold triptych. The wooden choir stalls date from the fifteenth century.

On departing the museum, before visiting the cathedral, visit the grand **Church of Santa Maria della Scala** with its altar raised atop a staircase embraced by a vast fresco spreading light and color, almost like rays, upon the pews below.

Il Duomo (The Cathedral)

The present structure was built over the temple of the goddess Minerva. Begun in 1229, it was completed at the end of the fourteenth century, so the erection of the cathedral would have been taking place during St. Catherine's lifetime. As she scurried between her home and the hospital, she would have seen its daily progress—and its months and years of stalling. The problems of finishing it were hampered by the loss of workers during the plagues; in fact it is still unfinished. The original L shape of the exterior (seen at its rear) shows what was planned and never completed.

The cathedral's interior is like the inside of a laden jewel box. The mighty striped marble columns in perfect symmetry soar above the inlaid stone floors. Many of the pavement scenes depict mythical creatures in the Greco-Roman heritage alongside the Christian religious virtues, historic scenes, and the coats of arms of Siena and of the different communes. There are scenes from the Old Testament on the floors of the presbytery, in the transept, and underneath the cupola, and the sculpture of the nativity and other scenes in Christ's life wrap around the impressive pulpit.

A place for private prayer is the Chapel of the Virgin of the Vow (Madonna del Voto), a tiny circular temple with marble statues of St. Bernardino and St. Catherine standing on either side of the Holy Mother.

On departing the cathedral, wind your way to the Piazza del Campo, where the crowds thronged to honor St. Catherine as her head was carried in great solemnity from Rome to its final resting place at St. Dominic's.

The final part of this day's pilgrimage is on the outskirts of Siena.

Eremo Agostiniano (The Augustinian Hermitage) at Lecceto

Leave Siena by the southern route, keeping to the right. At the second traffic circle take the street with yellow signs indicating "Lecceto" and "Belcaro." Go to Lecceto first.

Although Augustinian monks have had a monastery on this land from as early as the fifth century, the present building dates from 1344. The beautiful woods that surround the cloistered community were where many of the hermit monks lived in isolation, one of them being St. Catherine's follower William Flete. Today Augustinian nuns lead a cloistered life there and offer the hermitage as a place for personal retreat. The two cloisters themselves date from the thirteenth and fifteenth centuries, and the church would have been where St. Catherine prayed when she visited William Flete.

Belcaro

Retracing your journey, follow the yellow signs for nearby Belcaro.

Privately owned, the former castle has been open to the public, although at the time of writing it was undergoing major renovation and was closed. If you can see the interior, it is a treat. Most of the buildings were erected after St. Catherine's time—in the sixteenth century—when it fell into ownership of private families. Little is known of what happened to the convent after St. Catherine's death, but the exquisite chapel on its grounds among the lemon trees and the old well in the wall must have been the site of S. Maria degli Angeli and the source of water for the nuns. Within these ancient walls St. Catherine dictated her mammoth theological treatise, *The Dialogue*. Here she spoke with God and God spoke with her soul and revealed the depths of spiritual wisdom she has left us.

A walk atop the walls to the bell tower affords a view of the whole of Siena including St. Dominic's Church.

It will take a leisurely day by car to travel on to Assisi for the pilgrimage with St. Clare. The most scenic and interesting route would be by way of Montepulciano through the northern tip of Lake Trasimeno and through Perugia on to Assisi. There are a variety of secondary roads that will bring you there, so look at the road map and decide what feels best.

Montepulciano is worth the visit if you can stop, especially because St. Catherine spent time there on retreat in a convent (and had friends among the nuns who took care of her as she restored herself after her travels). Also the Jesuit saint John Bellarmine (1542–1621), who among many scholarly books wrote a biography of one of Umbria's holy women, Blessed Margaret (see page 147) that aided her beatification, was born in a house off the main piazza. There is only a wall left now in the interior courtyard of a present apartment complex.

ST. CLARE OF ASSISI
The First Flower

*"The first flower amongst them all, who,
like a sweet spring blossom,
diffused a fragrant odor around her,
and shone like a brilliant star
in the church of God."*

St. Bonaventure in *The Life of St. Francis of Assisi*

*"Her feet stood upon earth while her soul was
already in heaven"*

Pope Alexander IV

Her Life

The life of Clare Offreduccio di Favarone, a noblewoman who left her aristocratic family to live in voluntary poverty, is so closely linked with the life of St. Francis that her story cannot be told without knowing his. They were twin souls who loved God and desired Christ with the same depth of commitment to living what he taught. They were drawn to each other by this desire, recognized it like shining light in each other, and in complement, woman and man, embraced their joint call. There was never any doubt about the love they shared; they knew the beauty of each other's radiant soul and cherished the other like a delicate flower. Clare has frequently been referred to as a flower, the "little plant" of St. Francis, but she was far from a weak and vulnerable woman. Her clarity—in Italian her name is *Chiara* (meaning "to clarify and make clear")—was a virtue she always practiced along with her natural gift of deep faith, which was heralded before her birth.

Her mother, Ortolana Offreduccio, was a devout woman with a broad experience of life. She had, for instance, traveled to the Holy Land (possibly to accompany her husband, Lord Favarone, a great knight) on Crusade. When pregnant with Clare (in 1193 or 1194), she had prayed before a crucifix for safe delivery and was assured that she was going to give birth to "a light which will shine on all the earth." Little Clare was baptized in the Church of San Rufino near her family home and spent most of her childhood in nearby Perugia due to the civil strife in Assisi and the ongoing war between the two cities. During her girlhood in exile, she made many friendships that would last a lifetime; for instance, some of her friends would later join her in her convent.

Clare had three sisters and a brother, all of whom were well-educated. She could read and write and sew and was a talented musician. She also loved flowers and gardens and spent time gardening when she could. Clare had a natural aptitude for religion. She was pious from a young age, regularly prayed alone and with her mother, and gave to the needs of others, especially the poor.

In 1205, when Clare was eleven or twelve years old, her family returned to Assisi and took up residence in their old home. Clare most certainly knew about Francis's imprisonment in Perugia after the battle of Collestrada, and of his subsequent release, illness, and conversion. The affiliation with Francis became much closer when one of her father's kinsmen left his position in the Offreduccio family and joined Francis's early community of friars at Rivotorto.

Clare's inward and outer beauty was renowned. When she reached sixteen, she possessed a peace and strength beyond her years. Although not a slight woman—in fact, she was big-boned and considered stout (which can be attested by the size of her clothes, some preserved at her basilica)—her generosity and kindness toward others was exemplary. Unlike Francis, who had his serious religious calling in his late teens, Clare possessed saintlike qualities early on, advising friends and neighbors to despise the world in favor of the higher realms. She secretly wore a hair shirt underneath her finery, and underwent other personal penance, spending hours in devotional prayer. Unaware of her exact calling, she opposed any plans for marriage, clearly avoiding any commitment, even though she was pressured by her family to make a decision. She was filled with great love, but she waited patiently to see where it was to be expressed, and she was not to be pushed. Many years later, successive popes and cardinals found themselves no match for Lady Clare's tenacity once she was convinced of the rightness of her cause. This tenacity, this clarity, she perfected from an early age.

As Francis was gaining a reputation as an impressive preacher among the poor, it was considered a landmark for him to preach at the Church of San Giorgio (the one affiliated with his old school and the local parish church for the Offreduccio family). Clare would have been present to hear him and soon thereafter requested a cousin, who had also joined the Franciscan brothers, to arrange a private meeting with Francis. This was the first of many subsequent meetings, always in secret, Clare accompanied by a trusted woman friend and Francis by one or more of his brothers. Clare's friend later reported that these meetings provoked Francis to speak about Jesus with great fervor, and this fired Clare, because she wanted Christ more than anyone, and she needed Francis to bring her to him. They also had many other things in common; they both thirsted for the challenge of the spiritual life, and they longed for similar joy and simplicity. Francis's love of animals and the natural world made him speak with reverence about flowers, so special to Clare. He said that gazing upon flowers would remind everyone to remember "the eternal sweetness." The more Clare knew of Francis and spent time in his presence, the more she knew that his was the life she longed for. Her ideal was what he was already living: he made her desires a practical reality. He became what one biographer called "the charioteer of her soul."

For Francis the request of a woman—not any woman, but Clare, his closest soul companion—must have posed a challenge to him. He had not planned to establish an order—even of men—and already he had brothers joining him daily. He certainly had not considered women (they could not live in forest huts and wander the countryside as the brothers did), so advice was needed. As Francis confided in Bishop Guido about Clare's desires, she, quietly and assuredly, prepared for her future.

In the months that followed, there were no outward signs of change while Clare planned to leave her family. The day that was secretly decided upon fell on Palm Sunday, and during Mass at San Rufino, Bishop Guido personally handed Clare a palm during the service, to signify his approval and to give her the sign. That night she fled with her trusted companion. What was extraordinary was that she managed to open a locked and secured side door that was rarely used (it was the exit for dead bodies from the noble household), and she escaped by foot to the rural monastery of La Porziuncola, to the tiny chapel of Santa Maria degli Angeli (St. Mary of the Angels), where Francis received all postulants. All the friars were present, watching and praying, as Lady Clare knelt at Francis's feet for her profession to live in poverty and chastity all her life for God. Francis cut off her long, curly, fair hair; her fine clothes were changed for the rough habit of poverty; and her head was covered with a white veil to signify chastity and a black one over its top to represent penance. Clare was now a beggar for the love of Christ. Francis, who had spoken of the maiden Lady Poverty, now had her alive in Clare. It was a mystical marriage of two souls committed to the same ideal—there was no purer form of love. And with Clare's consecration the second Franciscan Order came into being, that of the Poor Ladies, later to be known as the Poor Clares.

Immediately after the ceremony Francis took Clare to a Benedictine monastery at Bastia where she was to begin her new life, but her days did not go undisturbed. Her family, once they noticed her defection, sent some of its male members (her father was believed to be dead by then) to the monastery to bring her home. At eighteen years old she was still their property, and they threatened her and tried to physically drag her away, as she clung to the altar in the chapel. They finally retreated only when she uncovered her shorn head, as the loss of her long blond locks was a serious obstacle to marriage. The sisters at the convent complained about these disturbances that upset their quiet prayer, so Clare had to move to another Benedictine convent in nearby Panso. Within a few days of her arrival there, her fifteen-year-old sister, Agnes, joined her. This caused further uproars in the family, with visits to the convent and pleas for the two of them to become at least Benedictine sisters and live a more acceptable religious life than follow Francis's life of poverty and begging. As both sisters would not consider this alternative, the men became physically violent, grabbing Agnes to take her back home. She began shouting prayers for protection, which were answered on her way back when she became so physically heavy that no man could carry her over a nearby stream.

Francis had said of Clare's vocation that "the dust of worldliness should not dim the mirror of Clare's immaculate spirit," and it was among the Benedictine sisters that she and Agnes finally lived peacefully, learning and experiencing the rigors—and joys—of religious community.

It wasn't long until they were called to move again, this time into their final dwelling place, at San Damiano, the first church Francis had restored. It now stood empty—the brothers were living at La Porziuncola—so Bishop Guido suggested that the first Franciscan women should take up residence there. Clare and Agnes were soon joined by four other women of noble backgrounds, and a little community began to flourish under Clare's guidance. In her own words, "Thus by the will of God, and our blessed father Francis, we came to dwell in the Church of San Damiano, where soon the Lord, in His mercy and grace multiplied us in order that what had been foretold by His holy one should be fulfilled; for we had sojourned in another place, but only for a short time."

Francis wrote a simple Rule of Life for the sisters and promised to provide for their material and spiritual needs. To protect and preserve the sacredness of their joint vow of chastity, he appointed only friars who didn't want to serve the women to take care of them. Any brother showing an interest in the Poor Ladies of San Damiano was kept at a distance. Clare's community of women grew at a steady rate, with further defections of young and marriageable girls from Assisi households, and they settled into practicing poverty, obedience, and simplicity on a daily basis. The Church granted them the "Privilege of Poverty," which set the ladies apart from the other monastic communities, especially the Benedictines. True poverty is what Francis had embraced as a Rule of Life—"to possess nothing of our own under the sun"—and Clare had embraced this as well. For her this was most vital to community life as a Franciscan sister; the privilege of it was to reject any forms of material and financial support from the institutional Church, relying only on Divine Providence and the gifts of the community, and on what food the brothers brought them by either working in the fields or begging in the streets. In fact, this is what it mostly was—a loaf of bread or two for the community, Clare always preferring just a few crumbs for herself. The Privilege of Poverty was so central to Clare's passion for her chosen way of life and the following of Christ, and so radical for Church authorities (who favored the Benedictine tradition of work and prayer with ownership of land), that she had to fight for it all her life, especially after Francis died.

There was never any doubt of the special bond and relationship that Clare and Francis shared. One of the friars mentioned that Francis rarely had special friendships with women, but Clare was an exception. He was her spiritual director and was in charge of her monastery, and he did not found any other community for women except under her tutelage. Clare in turn advised Francis on his course for God—he often asked her for direction and trusted her wisdom implicitly.

Clare's humility was one of her profound virtues. She practiced it everyday when serving her community. When the lay sisters returned from begging, she would always wash their feet herself. She served at the tables in the refectory, and washed the bed linen, what little they had of it. Clare's commitment to personal poverty went to extremes—she wore one cheap coarse tunic and a cloak, which did not afford much warmth, and she went barefoot on the cold stone floors. She possessed two hair shirts that she wore under her habit, one of boar's hide and the other of knotted horse hair. Her sister Agnes once attempted to wear the boar's-hide hair shirt and found it physically unbearable. Clare also slept on the floor on a bed of vine twigs with a stone as a pillow, which she sometimes changed for a wood log. She ate only on three days of every week and fasted the rest of the time, taking only communion and wine at Sunday Mass. Her health suffered, which wasn't surprising, and due to her extreme practices Francis and Bishop Guido had to intervene and force her, under holy obedience, to eat more regularly—and a more stable diet—and to sleep on a straw-filled mattress and pillow like the other sisters. Clare never insisted that her sisters employ such harsh measures themselves; she always made sure they were comfortable, with as warm a blanket as they could have at night, and took care of them to the best of her ability. Sister Beatrice said of Clare in her testimony for her canonization, "Her sanctity was in her chastity, her humility, her patience, and her kindness. When she issued an order, it was with great humility and fear, and often she hastened to do herself what she commanded others to do; she always made herself the last of all."

By 1215 the Poor Ladies of San Damiano were recognized as an official religious community. As the Franciscans grew, Clare's fame also spread beyond Assisi, and women took up her example of living a simple, prayerful life. Many of these women were already married with children, yet they encouraged their daughters to live a holier life at home, just as Clare had done growing up in the Offreduccio household. In some of the writings of Bishop Jacques de Vitry, who was in Perugia when Pope Innocent III died, he told of other women forming similar orders where they "live in communities in hospices at the gate of the city; they depend for their livelihood on the work of their hands for which they receive no remuneration. They only complain of one thing, that they receive too much honor from the populace." Thus the Third Franciscan Order was born, for non-monastic dwellers who wanted to live Francis's ideals; its formation was largely due to the influence of Clare.

As the Franciscans grew in numbers, the Vatican became more involved in their organization. The man assigned to the task in Rome was a Cardinal Ugolino, who became a close friend of both Francis and Clare. At the Fourth Lateran Council in 1215, it had been decreed and agreed upon that any new religious community within the Catholic faith had to follow one of the existing monastic rules, not write new ones to suit. Ugolino must have discussed with Francis himself his concerns about the Franciscan Rule (which was certainly, in part, not following an existing monastic rule), but Francis's attention was elsewhere as he was preparing to leave for Syria. Francis had, however, appointed Clare as abbess before departing, which Clare did not wish at all, preferring to be a servant to her sisters, which she later defined as the prerequisite of the role of abbess in Poor Clare communities. In Francis's absence, the cardinal himself drafted a new Rule for the Poor Ladies of San Damiano. He insisted that the community have some guarantee of daily food and some land on which they could build a house. Clare was dismayed at the omission of any mention of "sublime poverty," which she considered the cornerstone of the entire enclosure of San Damiano. Things were changing, however, and under holy obedience Clare had no choice than to accept that the other nuns could no longer go out and work or beg in the community, but had to remain enclosed. The sick could be admitted to see Clare and to receive her healing prayers, but it was now impossible for the ladies to be closely linked with the friars who were carrying on with their ideal of "serving and helping all." It was reported that Clare received her new directives with "great sorrow," and she and her sisters lived with this sorrow for nearly thirty years, during which time she never ceased to press for a ratification of the "Privilege of Sublime Poverty" originally granted her and her community by Pope Innocent III.

Although Clare lived in enclosure, away from the world's intrusion, her fame spread far. Members of the nobility and royalty knew of her as an example of pious humility. Other Poor Ladies' communities began to spring up in Assisi's neighboring towns and eventually further afield. Agnes was made abbess of one of them near Florence, and in grief left her sister whom she saw again only when Clare was dying.

Francis, too, was going through his own struggles and doubts. According to one legend, he was traveling from Siena with his faithful helper Brother Leo when he stopped to rest by a well and gazed down into it. After a short while he raised his eyes, smiled, and said, "Brother Leo, what do you think I have seen here?"

"The moon," answered Leo, "which is reflected in the water."

"No, Brother Leo, not our sister Moon, but by the grace of God I have seen the true face of Sister Clare, and it is so pure and shining that all my doubts have vanished."

Francis was becoming physically frailer due to his increasing blindness, especially after receiving the stigmata. He could not walk anymore and was ordered to receive a scalding treatment on his eyes. While preparing for this ordeal, he went to San Damiano in 1225 where Clare had a hut made for him in the garden. It was here that she cared for him over the weeks, making special shoes for his wounded feet. His joy to be in her company overrode his sufferings, so much so that he could write his beautiful "Canticle of the Creatures" during this stay with her. Francis died on October 3, 1226, and his funeral procession stopped at the grating of San Damiano so that Clare and the sisters could mourn his passing. There was much grieving and weeping over his body, but some comfort was afforded them when he was buried in the Church of San Giorgio, whose spire they could see from their enclosure.

On Francis's death, many of his immediate followers turned to Clare for direction and leadership. She became the chief guardian of his ideals and the mother to his brothers. Some were drawn to San Damiano for comfort: it was the first place Francis had restored and lived, its stones had been touched by all the elements of Franciscan life, and the crucifix that hung in its chapel had been the one that had spoken directly to Francis. Around this time, Clare's mother, Ortolana, also joined the community of Poor Ladies, giving up the family home for the life of the cloister and vowing obedience to her daughter. In 1227 Pope Honorious III died and was succeeded by Clare and Francis's old friend Cardinal Ugolino, who became Pope Gregory IX and frequently visited San Damiano. On one such occasion, when it was time to share some bread together in the refectory, Clare requested the Holy Father to bless it, but he replied that he wanted Clare to bless it instead. She argued with him that she was just a "miserable little woman" and would not dare to give such a blessing in the presence of the "Vicar of Christ," to which Gregory had to remind her of her obedience and to do as she was told. As she blessed the loaves with the sign of the cross, it became imprinted on the top of each loaf, a miracle for all to see.

This miracle could have contributed to Gregory's agreeing to insert the old Privilege of Poverty back into their monastic Rule. He confirmed it in a letter, but it needed the stamp of the official papal bull to be enforceable. This did not arrive, but what did arrive were more changes to the sisters' way of life. For instance, the Franciscan brothers were no longer allowed to visit the sisters and provide alms, although some of the early friars, like Leo and Giles, broke this rule continually by secretly visiting Clare to receive her advice and her teaching.

During Clare's later life, there were nearly forty nuns in San Damiano. She taught her sisters by her example and by the study of scripture through the listening of sermons, which she loved. She taught the value of simplicity and silence, reinforcing the motto of the sanctuary, which was "In God and For God."

In her writings Clare likened herself to a mirror: by partaking of the source of Francis with the mirror of Christ's love, she could see her true being. Perhaps the idea occurred to her because of a most sensuous dream she had, which she shared with her sisters soon after Francis's death. One sister reported it with these words:

> "The Lady Clare told me she had seen St. Francis in a vision and she was bringing him a jug of hot water and a towel for wiping his hands and with this she was ascending a long stairway but it felt as if she was walking on level ground. When she reached St. Francis he bared his breast saying 'Come, take and drink.' And as she did so the substance was so sweet and delightful

> that she could not describe it. It was as if it was made of a pure shining gold so bright that she could see her own reflection in it as in a mirror."

Clare was also renowned for her gift of healing. She frequently healed her sisters of ailments, including those of an emotional or spiritual nature, which she had the gift of recognizing before it became serious. One of the sisters in her testimony said that Clare always muttered something when she made the sign of the cross over someone, but when asked what she said, nobody knew, as they said she always whispered. Despite her gift for healing, her own health continued to ail—she had not been healthy for over twenty-eight years though she never complained. Many times she would become bedridden and weak for months at a time. During these long spells of illness, she continued to work, to spin and sew fine materials for the churches of Umbria, and she loved to be carried to her little garden terrace that overlooked the plains below Assisi where she could see the woods around La Porziuncola. There she would indulge her love of flowers, and the terrace became her own personal garden.

Clare shared her love of all creatures with Francis; animals would be drawn to her and obeyed her every word. One incident recorded by the sisters involved the monastery cat. Clare needed some cloth brought to her in bed and, unable to move, with no one around to assist her, she asked the cat to help. As it dragged the cloth toward her, she scolded it for not carrying it properly, whereupon it immediately rolled up the cloth and brought it over to her in its mouth.

The deep spiritual life of San Damiano was enhanced not only by the miracles and loving incidents of everyday life but also by Clare's prayer. When she prayed—sometimes prostrate on the floor for long periods—many of the sisters witnessed a burning light around her. When she came out of her private oratory after prayer, many said that she was filled with a light that shone around her and through her as she spoke about God to them from "the fullness of her heart." One described her as being "as beautiful as the sun as she comforted others with the words of God." It was as if she had come from heaven to be among them.

Her essence of purity in spirituality and strength enabled her to single-handedly defend the community of San Damiano—and the whole of Assisi—against attack by the troops of Emperor Frederick II. The emperor employed Saracens, who had taken up residence in Sicily. Their first stop on their way to the gates of Assisi was the isolated convent of San Damiano. Bent on violating the monastery, they sent their dogs over its walls and followed them into the cloister. The nuns were terrified and began weeping at such an invasion, running to Clare for help. She, displaying no fear, went immediately to the chapel, knelt before the altar, and removed the consecrated host from the tabernacle, placing it reverently in the monstrance (the receptacle used for the purpose of exposition and blessing). Her prayer was for God to deliver her "defenseless children" from the hands of the invaders. "Protect them, good Lord, I beseech you," she prayed, "whom at this hour I am powerless to protect." The sisters all heard a voice like that of a small child assuring Clare as if in answer to her prayer that the sisters would be protected. Then Clare asked her "dear Lord" to deliver the city of Assisi from attack, the city that "nourishes us for love of You," and the same voice answered that the people of Assisi would not be assailed. Then, armed with the body of Christ in the monstrance, Clare turned to her weeping sisters and told them to have no fear and to have "confidence in Jesus." She walked out with the monstrance held high in her hands to meet the dogs and the marauding men. At the sight of her they fled, retreating over the walls of the convent and never venturing closer to the city. They disappeared in a flourish of barking dogs and clattering armor down into the valley of the Tiber.

There was another time that Clare saved Assisi through intercessory prayer. To this day, every year on June 22, she is honored as defender of the city at a special feast during which its citizens visit her tomb and light candles, offering prayers of gratitude to their great saint and to the promise that Christ had made to her that she, her convent, and the town of Assisi would be protected.

Pope Gregory was succeeded by Innocent IV. He had been a prominent disciple of St. Francis and as a cardinal had had five Franciscans in his household. He was also a staunch supporter of the Poor Ladies, among whom was his own niece. His time, however, was taken up with the political challenges of the day, which included the continuing war with Frederick II. Without the pope's attention and with Clare's failing health, she began working in earnest on revising the monastic Rule for her Poor Ladies herself. Clare was the first woman in the history of Christendom to write a monastic Rule especially for women. The original Rule that Cardinal Ugolino had prepared for her was based on Benedictine principles, but she added the "Privilege of Poverty" and some arrangements about silence. The particular Franciscan practices of life in common, working with one's own hands, and the choice of poverty, were reintroduced. For Clare, poverty was not experienced through renunciation and detachment (the Benedictine way of its understanding), but from the basic insecurity of life, of the poverty of not knowing where and from whom God would provide, depending solely on others' generosity.

Clare knew that she couldn't die until she had received the official approval of her Rule from the pope, and, as if her prayers were answered, an opportunity arose in April 1253 when he visited her on his way back from France to take up residence in Perugia. On the pope's arrival at San Damiano, Clare insisted on kissing his foot as well as his hand and requested absolution for her sins. Aware of her holiness, the pope doubted she needed absolution, but he blessed her contrition at her request. When Clare received communion in her bed, many saw the divine child of Jesus appearing over her. After the pope's departure, the ratified Rule was slow in coming and it was not until August 10, 1253, that the pope's official bull finally arrived, delivered by a friar. Clare took it reverently in her hands and kissed it. The following day she died, worn out with patient suffering and with waiting for what she believed was right in the inheritance of what she and Francis had begun forty-two years earlier. She was fifty-nine years old and had outlived her twin soul by twenty-seven years. Surrounded by her sisters and faithful brothers, including Brother Leo, her last few words were "Do you see the King of Glory as I do?" After blessing all those around her, she said, "Blessed be you, Lord, who created me."

All the citizens of Assisi streamed down the path to the San Giorgio Church where her body was placed in a stone coffin. Everyone knew her as a saint in life, and she proved her holiness in death by curing many people, particularly children, at her tomb. She also interceded in saving children from attacks by wolves (a common occurrence at the time). Canonized in 1255, she became one of the three first Franciscan saints, together with Francis and Anthony of Padua. The pope called her "one of those great souls beyond all human praise."

After Clare's death the Poor Ladies did not stay on indefinitely at San Damiano. After seven years, a new church-and-convent complex was built over the San Giorgio Church to house Clare's tomb as well as provide a larger, more secure monastery for the growing number of nuns. The sisters also took the crucifix that spoke to St. Francis from the original little oratory. In an excavation in 1850, Clare's remains were discovered in a stone sarcophagus under the high altar, undamaged by time and emanating a sweet scent. Wild thyme from the hills of Mount Subasio had been scattered all over her.

Near the turn of the last century, about forty-three years after the opening of her tomb, an abbess in Assisi discovered the original Rule of St. Clare, written in her hand, wrapped in a cloak thought to have belonged to her.

During her canonization Pope Alexander IV said, "The life of Blessed Clare shines with wonderful clarity....Her life here on earth shone, after her death it illumined; on earth she radiated, and in heaven she glows. Her brilliant light, hidden in the secret of the cloister, radiated to the outside. From her enclosure she illumined the world."

CHRONOLOGY

1193(4)	Born in Assisi into the noble family of Offreduccio di Favarone.
1210	Hears St. Francis preach.
1212	On March 18, Palm Sunday, is received into the Franciscan Order at La Porziuncola. A few weeks later, moves to San Damiano and is joined by her sister Agnes April 3.
1215	Is appointed abbess.
1216	The Privilege of Poverty is approved by Pope Innocent III.
1218	Instigation of the Rule of Ugolino.
1219	Agnes is sent as abbess to Monticelli near Florence.
1224	The beginning of Clare's long illness.
1226	Clare's mother, Ortolana, joins the Poor Ladies. October 4, St. Francis dies and his body is brought to San Damiano on the way to burial.
1227	Cardinal Ugolino becomes Pope Gregory IX.
1228	Pope Gregory IX renews the Privilege of Poverty.
1229	The entrance of Clare's other sister, Beatrice.
1240	The repelling of the Saracens' attack.
1247	Clare begins work on her Rule.
1253	Clare's last testament is written. Pope Innocent IV approves the Rule of Clare with the bull "Solet Annuere" August 10. Clare dies at San Damiano on August 11.
1255	Is canonized by Pope Alexander IV.
1260	St. Clare's body is transferred to the Basilica of Santa Chiara.
1850	Discovery of Clare's body.
1872	Placement of Clare's body in the newly constructed chapel.
1893	Discovery of Clare's original Rule.

OFFICIAL FEAST DAY: August 11

Spiritual Essentials

St. Clare wrote a few letters (five in all), and these help us to understand her teaching. Four of them were written to Blessed Agnes of Prague. Agnes was the daughter of King

Ottakar of Bohemia and Queen Constance of Hungary and at the age of three was betrothed to a young duke who died prematurely. As a girl she was pursued by Emperor Frederick II, who originally wished her as a wife for his son, later changing his mind and desiring her for himself. When King Ottakar died, Agnes took her life into her own hands. After hearing some Friars Minor preaching in Prague (and receiving permission from the pope), she gave up her royal heritage and moved into a convent attached to the local hospital where she set out to follow the Rule of Clare's hermitage of San Damiano.

The letters, written between 1234 and 1253, were only discovered as late as 1896 by Pope Pius XI when he was bishop and prefect of the Ambrosian Library in Milan. In them, St. Clare's love for Agnes, whom she never met, is expressed with the sentiments of a shared background, a shared faith, and a shared longing for the embrace of poverty and the unity with Christ. St. Clare called Agnes "half my soul, my most beloved daughter." Agnes remained in her monastery in Prague for forty-four years, dying in 1232, and was beatified in 1874.

In his biography of St. Clare, Marco Bartoli wrote that

> St. Clare's originality and theology, over and above that of Francis (which she shared), was her concentration on the themes of mystical marriage, spiritual motherhood and the wider body from the enclosure. There were three characteristic elements of her spirituality—her imitation of Christ in His sufferings, her desire for the eternal wedding feast of her heavenly beloved and her maternal preoccupation with her sisters.

The following is a sampling of Clare's ideas and instructions broken into categories of the prominent symbols she used, the common virtues she extolled, and the unique language and understanding of nuptial mysticism that she possessed.

PROMINENT SYMBOLS

St. Clare wrote about spiritual reflection through mirrors; she also referred to "the narrow door" as it related to the path of Christ's teaching.

Mirrors

In her final testament she taught that God places patterns and mirrors for all believers and especially for the women who are called to the vocation of Franciscan sisterhood. This is "in order that they in turn should be patterns and mirrors for those who live in the world." St. Clare referred to the need to serve as a "pattern and mirror" so that others can see themselves in what you do and in turn be called to become a "pattern and mirror" with others. Through this practice, she emphasized the attributes of a community of grace, how by example we can spread the reflection of truth around the world.

St. Clare also instructed Agnes in her last letter to her, written in the year of her death, to contemplate two aspects of Christ in a two-sided mirror. On the one side is the child Jesus in the manger "in the midst of the utmost poverty and wrapped in miserable clothes," and then on the other side is the Savior on "the wood of the cross there to die an infamous death." She suggested putting down the mirror after this and understanding the message that "falls on each of us" that if we follow the ways of Christ, we recognize that there was no sorrow as great as his. And to this she suggested we must respond to the Master with the words "I will remember You, and my spirit will share in Your sufferings." This, she advised, is the way to marriage to the "celestial Bridegroom."

The Narrow Door

Quoting scripture St. Clare wrote to Agnes that the path is narrow that leads to life, but added that the door "which leads to it is equally narrow." She wrote that there are only a few that "walk in this path and enter by this door!" and then added her wisdom of humanity by noticing that there are only a few who persevere to the end. She also taught that the trial period is relatively short compared to the reward, which is "unending." She advised Agnes not to be discouraged "by the splendor of the world which will pass like a shadow" and told her not to be "deceived by appearances that are false."

THE COMMON VIRTUES

Silence

St. Clare's insistence on silence as part of the Rule of San Damiano in the sisters' daily life was based on her belief that through what she called "unbridled talk," the mind is out of control. She knew that silence "keeps us close to God" and that speech without consciousness and care weakens the heart, and therefore weakens the love one should have for God.

Humility

St. Clare understood the benefits of steady meditation and devotion as a way of living spiritually and warned against the swings of "adversity." She advised all to be "humble in success and unmoved in failure."

Poverty

St. Clare's particular teaching about poverty is that it brings freedom. She explained that poverty brings with it an "ardent desire" for God that cannot be "hampered by temporal things," and from which come a joy and gladness in the soul. No one can rob you of this, she explained, or take it away from you, and therein lie the riches of poverty in her teaching.

Love

"Always be lovers of God and your souls" was St. Clare's advice, to give one's heart over to God "without reserve." Because of God's supreme power to always love us more, we need to strive to love God with more of ourselves all the time. This love needs to be expressed in action—the inward love needs an outward manifestation through what we do. By practicing this, St. Clare advised that the sisters continually grow in the love of God. She also pointed out that we fully understand what love is only by acknowledging suffering as its accompanying virtue. Without suffering we cannot love, she said, pointing to Christ's life, passion, and death.

NUPTIAL MYSTICISM

To express the inner unity with her Beloved, Clare used the language of men and women in courtship and marriage. St. Francis also used the common court language, expressed in his songs and, for example, in his labeling poverty Lady Poverty. St. Clare's language is much more sensual. She mentioned preparing to be kissed by her Bridegroom by being led into "your wine cellar." In her last letter to Agnes, she described her as Queen and Spouse of Christ and even painted a picture of her in beautiful garments, which is the expression of spiritual virtues. Words like "chaste bride" refer to her virginity, her readiness to receive the ultimate delights of mystical union. This she called the "eternal wedding feast" or "sacred banquet," a feasting in the celestial realms of the perfected soul.

St. Clare's call for this unity was ignited by her relationship with Francis. From the early longings of her soul, she found spiritual unity with Francis that contributed to the greater longings for the ideal love, the immortal unity with God.

A Pilgrim's Prayer to St. Clare

Blessed Clare,
Flowering soul of heaven,
Help me to partake
Of the divine fragrance
And love of God.
May I discover the greatness
Of the celestial realms
In the small details
Of everyday life.
Guide me to see the beauty
In serving others,
Of forgetting self, of loving more,
Of finding all that my soul desires
In the prayer of patience, suffering, and joy.
Guide me as my mother and sister
On the course I've been given.
Pray that I will have the courage
To embrace with faith
All that comes my way
From God.

The Pilgrimage

Destination:
Assisi
Suggested length:
One day

Going to Assisi will have some overlap with the places familiar to St. Francis and his friars, so some cross-references to the St. Francis pilgrimage are essential. The St. Clare pilgrimage should start with intention and prayer at S. Maria degli Angeli (La Porziuncola) at the foot of the town.

Take the SS75 from the direction of Perugia and exit at S. Maria degli Angeli at Assisi.

S. Maria degli Angeli, La Porziuncola (St. Mary of the Angels, The Little Part)

This is the church built over the central monastery of the early Franciscan friars, its little chapel its center point. This chapel originally stood in a forest and was where all postulants were received into the order by St. Francis, including St. Clare after she escaped from her family home on Palm Sunday. To visit the other sites nearby, and for more details on the Chapel of the Transito, the Roseto (Rose Garden), and the Old Convent, turn to page 42.

Convento di San Damiano (St. Damian's Convent)

Take the SS75 again in the Foligno direction and exit at "Santuario Rivotorto."

If visiting the Church of Rivotorto (the animal shelter where St. Francis first lived with his brothers is inside), turn to page 44 for background.

To continue to San Damiano, take the side road that winds its way toward the town on the hill behind the church. At the first junction, "Via Francescana," turn left and proceed over a bridge turning right at the large tree and shrine in the middle of a fork. Follow this road up the hill. There is a parking lot in front of the hermitage on the right.

San Damiano was first a priest's house with a ruined chapel, which St. Francis restored after he was called by Christ (from the famous crucifix) to repair his house, which was in ruins. After St. Clare and Agnes spent time in the two Benedictine convents, Bishop Guido assigned San Damiano as the Poor Ladies' place of residence. It was here that St. Clare gathered her sisters around her, expanded the convent by a room or two and a private oratory, and lived out her forty-two years within its walls. After St. Clare's death and the sisters moved, San Damiano remained relatively unchanged until the sixteenth century when the Friars Minor extended the interior cloister and added a new wing of adjoining buildings. In the mid-nineteenth century it was bought by an Englishman called Lord Ripon, and in 1983 his heirs donated it back to the Catholic Church. Now San Damiano's residents are a community of Friars Minor and novices who spend a year studying to verify their choice of vocation.

Outside on the path there's a bronze statue of St. Clare holding the monstrance as she defended her convent—and the whole of Assisi—against the Saracens' attack.

Enter by the door to the right of the building into the **Chapel of St. Jerome.** In earlier times St. Francis would have lived in this space. It subsequently housed the friars assigned to take care of St. Clare and her sisters.

The Crucifix Chapel

This was the chapel that St. Francis restored after being called to do so from the crucifix (an exact replica of which hangs from its ceiling today). The original crucifix has its own devotional chapel in the Basilica of St. Clare and was moved there for safekeeping and prayer when the Poor Ladies left San Damiano after St. Clare's death. Near the wooden tabernacle in the apse is a small window and grille, which separates the church from the choir of the Poor Clares. It was here at this window that St. Clare and her sisters venerated St. Francis's body as it was carried to its final burial place.

The Old Choir

To enter the convent take the right doorway beside the altar into a flagstone vestibule where the original foundations of the sepulcher can be viewed.

This is where the thirteenth-century Poor Clares were buried. The choir is preserved as it was; the present oak stalls and lecterns date from the fifteenth century. This is where St. Clare and her sisters would gather for prayer and hear the Mass being said in the chapel through the grille.

The Garden and Oratory

The stone steps leading to the upper floor reveal a window onto St. Clare's private garden. Here she would sit and tend her flowers, or sew and spin. From here she could see

La Porziuncola, where her blessed Francis lived, below in the plain.

Nearby is her private oratory, which she had especially erected for her own personal prayer and devotion. The frescoes date from the fourteenth century and show scenes in the life of St. Clare and her sisters.

The Dormitory

This is one of the most holy rooms in the Franciscan heritage. In the near corner is where St. Clare slept (and is the place where she died). On the wall is a bronze sculpture of her on her deathbed receiving the papal bull of her Rule. All the Poor Clare sisters slept on straw mats in this one room—there were nearly forty of them when St. Clare died. The view from the stone window seats (carved in such a way as to allow for reading during daylight) looks over the cloister with its ancient well.

Follow the passageway through and down the stairs to the Refectory.

The Cloister and Refectory

It was in this cloister that St. Clare held up the monstrance and saved her convent and Assisi from destruction, and around it is the doorway to the Refectory. Here the Poor Ladies partook of their food (what little there was). A bouquet of flowers or a plant is always placed at the table where St. Clare sat. On the far wall is a fresco depicting the miracle of the blessing of the loaves. This is when St. Clare was asked under holy obedience to bless the bread at table when the pope came to visit the sisters, and a cross appeared on the top of each loaf. Over the Refectory (but inaccessible to the public) are the cells of the old infirmary. Here St. Clare's sister Agnes, the second Franciscan woman, died. Her room has subsequently been turned into a chapel for quiet reflection. There are galleries and an exhibition of more contemporary art inspired by St. Francis's "Canticle of the Creatures," which he wrote while convalescing in the gardens, which can be visited on departure.

The Garden of the Canticle

There is a stone statue of St. Francis in the garden where St. Clare had a hut made for him and cared for him in his sickness for about a month. On the north side of the garden is a contemporary chapel for pilgrims called Chapel of Santa Maria.

Basilica di S. Chiara (St. Clare's Basilica)

Turn right on the hill road toward Assisi proper, heading for the south side of the town. Park and walk to the Piazza di Santa Chiara.

Following St. Clare's canonization, this basilica was built for her tomb, which had attached to it the new convent to house the growing numbers of Poor Clare sisters. On moving from San Damiano, they were officially renamed from the Order of San Damiano to the Order of St. Clare. The headquarters of the Order of St. Clare is now at the basilica. It is still a cloistered convent for contemplative Poor Clares to this day, who take care of the church and say prayers for pilgrims' intentions. Masses and prayers can be requested in the central part of the basilica. The present church stands over the San Giorgio complex (which at the time of St. Francis and St. Clare was composed of a hospital, church, and school, the one that Francis attended as a child). Only a stained glass window of St. George is left of the original complex and can be viewed behind the crucifix chapel. It is sometimes obscured and not easy to see due to recent earthquake renovations.

The Crucifix Chapel

Here hangs the original crucifix that spoke to St. Francis and instructed him on his future work

La Tomba di S. Chiara (St. Clare's Tomb)

In the crypt there's a display of some of St. Clare's possessions. These include her tunics and cloaks and the white dress that she was wearing when she left her home to take up the life of a Franciscan sister. Some locks of her blond hair (cut by St. Francis at La Porziuncola) are also on display.

St. Clare's present tomb contains the remains of her body under a wax model. Sadly, it does not hold as much presence as the stone sarcophagus in which she lay for over six hundred years. It sits an empty vessel in its own marble enclosure in front of the windows that view the more recent tomb.

Cattedrale di S. Rufino (Cathedral of St. Rufino)

From the main fountain in the Piazza del Comune, take Via San Rufino toward the Piazza San Rufino and its church.

This is where St. Clare's (and St. Francis's) families celebrated special occasions, especially those that required Bishop Guido's presence. St. Clare was baptized in this church, as were many of Francis's friends and early brothers. Their engravings adorn the area around the baptismal font. There is only the crypt (where St. Rufino is buried) and the exterior wall of the original eighth-century church existing today.

St. Clare's House

To the east of the piazza on departing the church is a shrine situated on the site of the old Offreduccio family home where St. Clare was born and lived most of her childhood. It is the house she escaped from when she went to join St. Francis. Now it is a private residence for Franciscan sisters.

For details of the other sacred sites in Assisi, please turn to the St. Francis pilgrimage on page 36.

Leave Assisi from the S. Maria Degli Angeli exit and take the autostrada north exiting on the E45 toward Cesena. After about 70 kilometers, exit at San Giustino for the center. Follow the SS73 to Urbino and exit at Mercatello Sul Metauro for continuation of the Holy Women pilgrimage.

If you have the opportunity, a stop in Urbino before continuing on your pilgrimage is worth your time.

ART & SOUL: URBINO

Entering Urbino is always a delight. It rises up on a far hill as you drive through the Marches mountains of Urbania. Its sandy architecture, dominated by the splendid **Ducal Palace,** immortalizes one of the greatest cultural and socially-just cities of the Renaissance. This was due to the leadership of a single superior human being, the famous Duke Federico Montefeltro (or Federico da Montefeltro) who put this small duchy on the international map.

Federico da Montefeltro: Enlightened Ruler

Federico ruled Urbino between l444–82, and came to his heritage by a circuitous route. Born illegitimate, he assumed power only after his half-brother, the legitimate Duke of Urbino, was brutally murdered and the citizens of Urbino voted for Federico to succeed him, providing he not accuse the killers. The new duke was a trained man of war and an unbeatable warrior, renowned not only for his endurance and courage, but also for the virtues of mercy, justice, and generosity, which he practiced on and off the field. He also had a keen nose for business and the needs of his duchy.

As a ruler, he was a generous and honest man, open-hearted and open-minded. He reduced taxes, provided back-up grain in case of famine or flood, introduced public education and medical services for all, and almost as a precursor of democracy, permitted the common people to vote in the election of magistrates. Devoutly religious he attended Mass daily, was well read in the scriptures in Hebrew, Latin, and Greek, and had an extensive theological library.

Federico Montefeltro is frequently compared to the other great Renaissance man, Lorenzo di Medici, because of his patronage of the arts and love of culture. He wanted to—and did—create one of the greatest libraries in the western world, composed of ancient and modern literature, at one time superior to the library at Britain's Oxford University. A patron of contemporary writers of his time, Federico also supported the painters, especially Piero della Francesca who captured

Montefeltro's essence in the famous twin portrait of him and his wife, Battista, from side views.

A man whose reputation went before him, in and outside Italy, Federico Montefeltro received many honors, among them the Honor of the Garter from the English king. Its emblem can be seen today in the Ducal Palace.

He died, presumably from malaria, while fighting in the swampland of Ferrara. Urbino was eventually swallowed up by the papacy. Frederico's famous library is now housed in the Vatican library in Rome, and the more famous paintings in internationally renowned galleries. However, his palace, an architectural jewel, still stands as the evidence of a time when human excellence, creativity, and the practice of virtue and democracy lived for a while in perfect harmony.

Palazzo Ducale (The Ducal Palace)

The palace was Federico's great love—it is a monument to his passion for architecture and form. It was built slowly between 1450 and 1468 and was large enough to house his family, visiting guests, and a staff of four hundred: of these, two hundred were servants and teachers, including a resident astrologer; five were readers who read at mealtimes; four were scribes for the library, and there were two organists and a bloodhound keeper. The duke also collected musical instruments—as music was also a passion—and regularly had concerts in the palace.

Ground Floor

This is the oldest part of the palace and includes the main entrance, the courtyard, the rooms where the library was kept and the archeological museum. The emblem for the Montefeltros was the eagle, which is in evidence throughout the palace with the exception of the Porta della Guerra (Door of War) off the courtyard, which bears the symbol of the Order of the Garter.

First Floor

The Jole apartments include the room of "men of arms and heroes," Duke Federico's alcove with its splendid example of a fifteenth-century bed and other artifacts from the time, and the guest apartments, including the king of England's room. Then there is the duke's apartment, the audience chamber, his son

Guidobaldo's chapel, and the duke's study—the extraordinary *studiolo* with inlaid wooden engravings in perspective. Next to this is the duke's dressing room, the spiral staircase leading to the Chapel of Forgiveness and the Temple of the Muses, the duke's bed chamber, and the "room of angels."

Following on is the magnificent throne room and the hall for musical gatherings. The duchess's apartment, vestibule, salon, and bed chamber, including her dressing room and prayer room, are in a section of their own.

The Art and Paintings

Among the many paintings exhibited in the palace, the most famous are Piero della Francesca's *The Flagellation* (of Christ) and *The Madonna di Senigallia;* also here are *The Ideal City,* which is not attributed to anyone in particular (although della Francesca has been mentioned as the possible painter due to the perspective being explored), and Raphael's *Portrait of a Gentlewoman.* The collection of ancient crucifixes is also worth viewing.

The Underground Levels

Access can be gained from the main courtyard on the ground floor down a brick staircase. Here, near the large saddle room and stables for the horses, are the intricate plumbing and sewage systems that served the palace; they are important to see as evidence of the time, including the Roman baths used by the servants.

Raffaello Sanzio (Raphael): "Too Happy" to Be a Genius

Raffaello Sanzio was born in Urbino, one year after Federico Montefeltro's death, and lived between 1483–1520. His father was a painter called Giovanni Santi and his mother Magia di Battista Ciarla. Santi recognized the talent in his son at an early age and introduced Raphael to works of other artists before sending him to apprentice with Pietro Perugino. Raphael proved to be a child prodigy who found it easy to study and assimilate quickly. He became a man Montefeltro would have been proud to call a prime citizen of Urbino; his reputation of having "good character" was enhanced by the virtues of grace and humility, along with his love of beauty in expression and way of life.

At seventeen he was contracted for his first assignment as an assistant painter of an altar piece—the *Coronation of St. Nicholas of Tolentino*—in the Church of Sant'Agostino in Città di Castello. The painting was later severely damaged in an earthquake in 1789 and segments of it are preserved today in the Museo di Capodimonte in Naples and the Louvre in Paris. Aided by one of his father's assistants, Raphael lived and worked in Città di Castello for four years. His father died in 1494 before Raphael became famous.

In 1508, while other contemporary better-known and more-senior artists were commissioned by Pope Julius II to decorate the papal apartments in the Vatican, Raphael visited Rome and so pleased the pope that he turned the entire commission over to Raphael. Spending much of his time in Rome from then on, Raphael adjusted his style and work to the needs of his most steady employer, the pope. He was—and still is—considered one of the greatest painters of his time, though through his skill and artistry more than his creative genius. Some considered him to be "too happy" to be a genius, citing Michelangelo's temperament as an example. But Urbino was different from Florence, and those born under the protection of the great Montefeltro inherited something special, the secret of contentedness in the beauty of life.

Raphael's House

Rafael's home, which is a typical Renaissance house, is a short walk from the Ducal Palace.

Take the Via Veneto to the left on exiting the palace to the Piazza della Repubblica and continue over the other side along the Via Raffaello, following the signs. Just after Via S. Margherita the house on the left is Raphael's.

The ground-floor rooms include his father's studio, where Raphael was born; the Madonna-and-child fresco in the room is attributed to him. (Most of the other Raphael paintings in the house are copies of the originals, although his father's *Annunciation* is original.) The courtyard and kitchen are original, and mementoes and records belonging to Raphael are upstairs.

Please note: *The remaining part of the Holy Women pilgrimage has some overlapping in places. St. Veronica and Bl. Margaret, although they lived hundreds of years apart, were born in the same area, baptized in the same church, and ended their lives in the same Umbrian town of Città di Castello. For this reason their two biographies are introduced together and the pilgrimage details are combined afterwards.*

ST. VERONICA GIULIANI
Love's Mediator

"For the very thing that tortures her and gives her
the greatest suffering makes her whole
and what wounds her most deeply
is the source of her greatest relief."

Beatrice of Nazareth in *Seven Degrees of Love*

Her Life

Veronica Giuliani is often called "a true daughter of St. Clare" as she was a Capuchin Poor Clare, and became abbess of her adopted monastery in the Umbrian town of Città di Castello. She lived during the latter part of the seventeenth and early eighteen centuries and was an extraordinary example of an advanced mystic. Her vocation was particularly unique in that it was lived in her interior, which required her to suffer ceaseless pain and sorrow and to be able to love at the deepest level in that pain and sorrow. As a result, she was able to humanly exemplify the mysterious teachings of the alchemy of Christ's cross. Throughout her sixty-seven years, she recorded the process of her lifelong devotion to the suffering and loving heart of Jesus in thirty-six volumes of personal diaries, providing us with the fine details of a mystic's journey, culminating for Veronica in complete surrender to feminine sanctity. She began her journey with the embrace of religious life in the heritage of St. Clare, and ended it in holy sisterhood with Mary, the mother of Jesus.

Veronica's life began on December 27, 1660, in Mercatello, a peaceful village in the Marches region, which formed part of the diocese of Urbania. Her father, Francesco Giuliani, was a standard-bearer at the local garrison; her mother, Benedetta, was very devout and caring. Veronica was the youngest of five children and was baptized Ursula. As a child she displayed a strong character accompanied by much religious fervor. Surrounded by sacred pictures on the walls of the family home, she would cry and beg her parents to be lifted up to them, particularly to those of the child Jesus so she could kiss him. When she grew older, she would go herself to stand in front of these pictures and carry on conversations with the divine child. She wrote that these conversations were simple exclamations of love and devotion, such as "I am yours and you are all mine, dear Jesus," to which she heard in reply "I am yours and you are all mine!"

Little Ursula was nicknamed "Fire" by her mother. She had said that it felt as if she had flames in her womb while she was carrying Ursula. Ursula's mischievousness was another reason she had this name. She was burning to know everything about everyone in the house, and in her busyness broke many objects, but her parents always forgave her.

When Ursula was seven, her mother became terminally ill and was administered the last rites. As the priest was giving her mother communion, Ursula saw the child Jesus in the host and ran toward it, wanting to partake. But she was denied the Eucharist because of her young age, and this, along with the distress of her mother's impending death, was something she would always remember. What she also vividly remembered was the gift her mother bestowed upon her: the dying woman offered her five children to Jesus. She entrusted one each to the five wounds of the body of the crucified Lord. Ursula she entrusted to Jesus' pierced side, so she would reside near the heart of God "where not only will you find protection but you will also learn to desire to speak love," her mother said. This incident marked the beginning of Ursula's lifelong union with the heart of Jesus.

After her mother's death, her father moved the family from Mercatello to Piacenza in the northern part of Italy where he took a job as a customs officer. They were to remain there for three years. Ursula remembers the joy of her first communion at the age of eleven and wrote in her diary that she stayed awake the whole previous night with excitement. She pondered what she would offer her Lord and decided that she would offer her whole self, requesting only his love so she could carry out his holy will. When she received the host, she described a "great heat" that overwhelmed her interior. "I felt my heart was burning," she wrote, "and I could not get back into myself." A transformation had clearly taken place as she began to spend her days in prayer. She always prayed to Jesus and Mary while she carried food, grain, and candles to the poor, and even when she was just eating and taking walks.

Around this time, Ursula began having visions of the wounded body of Christ. Christ instructed her that she was to devote herself to his passion, and on another occasion he imprinted his sufferings on her heart. Ursula could think of nothing else but these experiences that were happening to her, and she isolated herself in the family home, beginning a series of voluntary penances. Still a young girl, she did not have access to instruments of mortification commonly used by religious, so she beat herself with stinging nettles from the fields and made knots from the ribbons of her pinafore and hurt herself with them. She also discovered some wood in the cellar of the house and made a crucifix out of it and carried it around so she could feel the weight of Christ's sufferings on her young shoulders.

One day, while looking out of the window of her home, she saw a beggar, dressed like a pilgrim, who asked for her help. She had nothing to offer him except the new shoes that she had just been given and liked very much. She threw one of them out of the window, and the pilgrim on catching it said that one shoe wasn't going to help him. On tossing the other out, it missed the street and landed on the archway over the front door. Ursula remembers how the pilgrim jumped up to reach it. She recorded in her diary that she was touched by the beauty of the man, and many years later she experienced a vision of Christ dressed as a pilgrim beggar carrying the same pair of shoes.

During her early teenage years, Ursula's lively personality, her intelligence, and her generosity, combined with her natural feminine beauty, made her a source of admiration. She was proficient at playing cards, dice, and draughts —she even handled a sword with alacrity—and she had a natural inclination for sociability, entertaining friends and strangers with warmth and a sense of fun. She frequented masked balls and dances, always chaperoned by her father, and there was no doubt that she would marry well and be a special gift to a lucky man. In fact, she had one suitor who called frequently at her home, bringing her flowers and pestering her for attention. Although she gave the appearance of an extroverted young woman who loved the world, it was not truly who she was. Her interior call was to leave it all behind. She felt that the world wasn't made for her, and she began talking about becoming a nun. This was not what her father wanted to hear from his youngest, especially when all his other daughters had already entered convents. Giving permission for Ursula to take the veil would shatter his last hope for grandchildren. Ursula was thirteen when she returned home to Mercatello to live under the care of her Uncle Rasi. While there, her health declined rapidly, mainly due to her father's lack of support for her vocation. However, Ursula's tenacity and strength (which would serve her well all her life) at last won her father's favor. At the age of sixteen, writing became part of her prayer, and even though she had acquired only an elementary education—possibly from a priest—she managed to write a letter to her father laying down the sincerity and true desire she had for the religious life, and he gave in.

There were three monasteries in the area—in the town itself, in nearby Sant'Angelo in Vado, and further away in Città di Castello in the Tiber valley of Umbria with the Capuchin Poor Clares. Ursula was attracted to the latter because she had heard of the nuns' austerity and spiritual discipline, and was accepted as a postulant by the abbess. Three months later she set out with her Uncle Rasi on the treacherous road to Città di Castello, with its hairpin bends through the mountains and the danger of bandits and thieves. Their journey became a pilgrimage of sorts—this was Ursula's last view of the world outside, as she journeyed toward the cloister for the rest of her life. She stopped to visit the shrine of the Madonna of Belvedere on the outskirts of town, with its breathtaking view of the valley stretched below it, the walls of the church adorned with stone statues of local saints, one of them being Bl. Margaret.

Ursula entered the streets of Città di Castello dressed in the white clothes of a Franciscan postulant, resembling a beautiful bride. The people on the street begged her to change her mind, that it wasn't too late to keep her beauty and character among them, to marry, to find fulfillment as a woman of the world, but none of these temptations swayed Ursula's resolve. All she replied was that she was sorry that she hadn't been given permission to do this sooner. She was still underage for a postulant, but exceptions had been made for an exceptional girl. The bishop of Città di Castello, Giuseppe Sebastiani, was asked by the abbess to examine Ursula as a suitable candidate for the convent. Ursula managed, much to his amazement, to recite Latin prayers from the breviary, reading them as easily as if she had always known them.

On October 28, 1677, Ursula's bridal dress was replaced with the heavy brown habit of the Capuchin Franciscans—the habit that symbolized complete surrender to God, top to bottom—and she stepped from the exterior world through the narrow doorway into the interior world of the convent. She had written of this time that she knew of the significance of its finality, that she was only to be in contact with people from outside the convent in the church itself, and that she would never again set foot outside the enclosure. The bishop gave her the name *Veronica*, which partly means "wedding ring"—*vera* in Italian and *unica*, which means being "God's alone, united with the One."

Settling into convent life was very hard for the novice Sister Veronica. She called these first few months a time of torment between the "big temptations" of the world and the "divine consolations" of her newfound life; it was as if her human nature was full of discontent while her soul was at peace. It was not as easy a transition as she had imagined, and she began to suffer swings between her soul's desire and her body and mind's limitations. In the middle of this, she received visions of being welcomed in the heavens, of the "delights of paradise," and she saw a "multitude of men and women saints," as well as Holy Mother Mary. In this celestial vision, her Lord Jesus welcomed her by saying to everyone, "This one is ours now," and turning toward Veronica, he asked her what she wanted. She replied that she wanted the grace to love him and to be able to live up to the state of life he had chosen for her, to never depart from his will for her, and to keep her on the cross with him. She heard his promise to grant her what she had asked for, and thus began her vocation to "suffer for love's sake." With the theme of her religious life now given to her, she was tested in the fire of everyday suffering, which included being unfairly gossiped about by fellow novice sisters to her novice mistress. This provided Veronica with her deeper struggle—between the human need for revenge and the spiritual way of loving those who are against you in surrender to God's will.

Veronica's interior struggle was about learning obedience, giving away any personal sense of power and opinion through daily experiences in humiliation. In addition, she was undergoing what she called "interior evil," which she felt physically in her stomach. In her sleep she had dreams of darkness, of temptations of evil, and many times she felt utterly forsaken. In her waking hours her mind was foggy, her life seemed in turmoil, and strong feelings of a nonexistent God and of saints made only by imagination pervaded her being. She wrote that her soul—her "poor soul"—was "in the hands of the enemy and, being full of fear, has nowhere to turn." But she did turn, slowly and surely, to the place where she would find consolation—the cross of Jesus. She began at the foot of the cross, the place where the original women disciples had gathered in sorrow and prayer, and she progressed into the embrace of the whole of the crucified Christ, an inevitable progression in the traditional mystic's experience and teaching.

The first level of transformation was Veronica's desire to be forgiven, what she termed "washed in the blood of Christ," and she did this with her usual fervor and discipline. She confessed to a priest sometimes up to five times a day. It was on Good Friday 1697 that her process of reconciliation and contrition culminated in "the whole court of heaven" where she made one general confession in the presence of Christ, Mary, and all the saints. This took the form of her asking forgiveness from Christ for her offenses; that was all she had to say as the blessed Mother Mary moved to stand at the feet of Christ facing Veronica and began praying for her. "As she was praying for me," she wrote in her diary, "I received illumination and knowledge of my nothingness, and this light gave me the insight to know that all of this was the work of God." She was given understanding of the divine love for souls who come to God, "and in particular, ungrateful ones like mine." Asking for pardon with all her heart, Veronica offered her own blood, sufferings, and pains in retribution, which included the deepest pain of "everything I had ever done in my lifetime. The Lord said to me, 'I forgive you, but I want faithfulness in future.'" Veronica emerged from this confession renewed. She described the result of this renewal as feeling lighter, as if "a mountain of lead" had been lifted off her back, and of a heavenly embrace that enabled her to "exude the love of God."

Veronica's vocation of suffering for love's sake matured over the years to transform itself into something extraordinarily unique in mystical experiences. Over the course of her twenty years in the convent, she came to see herself as being chosen by God as a "victim for sinners," as a mediator, a "go-between" who stands at the gateway between God and her brothers and sisters whose souls were about to be lost forever in the chasm of hell. Her work of salvation, of praying for those who needed mediating atonement, enabled her to assume their sufferings so she could relieve them and bring them back to God.

On April 5, 1697, Veronica received the stigmata, and her experience, recorded in her diary, is similar to that of St. Catherine of Siena three hundred years earlier. Praying at the crucifix, she saw "five shining rays issuing from His wounds and coming toward me," turning into little flames. Four of these contained nails, which pierced her hands and feet, and one of them was a lance, "golden and all aflame," which pierced her heart.

But it was not enough for Veronica to suffer only the exterior physical suffering of the wounds of the stigmata. She always wanted to suffer more because, in that suffering, she had experienced the utmost joy of the soul beyond the physical, an advanced understanding of the way of suffering both interiorly as well as exteriorly. She was proving what all mystics have experienced, that the way of expressing their commitment and maturing marriage with Christ was to understand and partake in whatever way they could with his sufferings. By doing so they learned the paradox of how unity is achieved in opposition, that from exterior suffering, the interior joy is heightened, and that the severer the practice, the greater the breakthrough. Now a senior sister, Veronica returned to one of her early devotions as a child, carrying a wooden cross on her shoulders feeling its weight, and this she did during the night around the cloister while the other nuns slept. She sometimes carried pieces of heavy oak as well. These processions she ritualized by wearing an embroidered robe lined with tough thorns against her bare flesh, to symbolize the beauty of interior suffering to the outside world. She also branded herself with red-hot pincers—burning Jesus' name on her breast and Mary's on her forehead. This also signified her commitment to Christ's suffering in her heart and to Mary as the instructor of her mind, the woman who became her prime teacher as Veronica's years advanced, and in whose heart she felt she had transformed herself.

In 1704 at the age of forty-four, Veronica wrote about entering what she termed the "Purgatory of Love." This purgatory (meaning an in-between place of torment and confinement) provided opportunities for greater pains of purgation and transformation for her soul. She wrote again of the symbolism of "Fire"—her nickname as a girl—now matured to burn in the cells of her body, and deep within her bones. This pain, this fire, is what she called the "Fire of Divine Love," which she experienced as a confining bonfire of flames where she could not escape and even if she cried out, no one heard her.

The second stage of her purgatory of love was the burning up of her bowels and marrowbone, which became "eaten by the fire." Veronica shared that her humanity seemed "about to die," which made her spirit feel even stronger, "taken up in God." There she felt the divine: "God is in it and itself in God." A true unity took place in the soul, while the body lay forgotten, languid, lost in the lower world. Of this experience Veronica wrote that she could not find the words to describe it; it was not in the religious teachings as she had studied them because it was impossible to write of this love. Through this process, Veronica taught that even though the experience itself may be short in finite time, the purification that comes from it has a long-lasting effect.

The third "fire" in the Divine Love experience is when Veronica felt "set alight by Divine Love" in a quick and simultaneous flash. During this experience, she was given clarity about what she was to do to attain perfection. She said, "The things we do will never be of any value, despite every possible effort on our part, unless we unite our works with the works of Jesus: our suffering with the suffering and the merit of Jesus." She instructed that Jesus alone can make our imperfections perfect.

During the years when Veronica underwent more internal suffering, she was still prone to humiliation from her superiors. They suspected her—as did the Holy See—of all sorts of sorcery and madness, and denied her any responsibilities, even though they were her due. She was segregated for prolonged periods in the infirmary, prevented from eating with her sisters in the parlor, and subjected to regular medical examinations. However, by 1716 much of this suspicion subsided and she was elected abbess of the convent, and a month later the superior of the local Capuchin Franciscan community. She proved a valuable leader, not only in spiritual matters where vocations flourished under her guidance (one of her novices was later beatified—Blessed Florida), but also in temporal matters, modernizing her convent with the installation of lead pipes so that the sisters could have ready access to water.

Throughout her life she had documented her spiritual growth in her diaries, sharing the process of her wounded heart becoming the loving heart of God. It was through her devotion to the crucified Jesus that she had found union in the heart of the divine. This union, this merging, had three components to it, made up of the trinity of herself, Jesus, and Jesus' mother (and her mother guide and teacher), Mary. In an alchemy of purification and graces, in suffering and joy, she had won the seal of what she termed the "Fount of Grace," also composed of a trinity of virtues in its total oneness—the will of God, fidelity, and obedience. These were what defined her life, the divine life in her soul, the gift of what she called the "grace of the three graces." And it was through their reception that her life was divinized into God's.

But Veronica didn't stop there. She ended her teaching with an even more advanced stage of unity than other mystical teachings recorded by women religious. She became absorbed into the unique feminine spiritual teachings that Mary represented. Just as her Lord Jesus had given his mother to his disciple John before he died on the cross, after Veronica's mystical marriage with Christ, he gave her over to his mother, to a merging into the heart of Mary. Mary told her that Veronica was "heart of my heart," and soon after she was appointed abbess, Veronica turned herself over to Mary completely, who, in turn, dictated her diary to her and supervised her work in the convent and the community as the abbess and superior, instructing Veronica to be only her "slave." Mary told her not to be concerned about anything at all, just surrender all to her.

On the feast of the Annunciation, March 25, 1727, Mary instructed Veronica to stop writing her diary. There were no more words, only silence. Three months later, on June 6, Veronica suffered a stroke while receiving communion and endured severe agony for thirty-three days thereafter. These were combined with moral sufferings and "diabolical temptations," which she had predicted would accompany her death. Her last words on July 9 were "Love has let Itself be found."

Veronica's whole life and vocation had been centered in her heart; it was there that her spiritual efforts and experiences dwelt. With the wisdom of an advanced mystic, Veronica had drawn an image of the interior make-up of her heart in her diary. There were outlines of the instruments of Christ's passion—the cross, the lance, pliers, hammers and nails, the scourging rod, and the pillar. Among them were also the seven swords of Mary, and a number of letters representing the virtues. After her death, a tissue examination revealed mysterious incisions in her heart shaped like the instruments she had drawn, as well as other unexplainable markings.

Pope Leo XIII said of Veronica Giuliani, "No other being, save the Mother of Jesus, was more endowed than her with preternatural gifts."

CHRONOLOGY

1660	Born Ursula Giuliani on December 27 in Mercatello, Urbania.
1667	Mother dies; family moves to Piacenza.
1670	Receives her first Communion.
1672	Returns to live with her uncle in Mercatello.
1677	Enters the Poor Clares Capuchin convent in Città di Castello in Umbria.
1697	On April 5 receives the stigmata.
1698	On December 25 the diary descriptions of exterior sufferings and penance cease.
1704	Writes of the Purgatory of Love.
1716	Elected abbess and superior of the community.
1720	Diary dictated solely by Mary.
1727	Dies on July 9.
1804	Beatified.
1839	Canonized a saint.

OFFICIAL FEAST DAY: July 10

Spiritual Essentials

St. Veronica's vocation was to love God so as to atone for others' lack of love. There are three aspects to her mystical life and its teaching: mystical marriage, transformation, and divinization.

MYSTICAL MARRIAGE

St. Veronica wrote in one of her prayers that she wanted to be holy, to love and serve Christ in everything: "I want to be your spouse but with the pact that I also want to be crucified."

The more advanced Christian life that Veronica exemplified in her understanding of interior prayer and purgation leads to a perfection of the soul that experiences divine love and that, beyond ego and all other human frailties, is united into the One and the All from which it came. Her biographer, John Leonardi, wrote that by understanding love in its fullest sense, Veronica made her life an enactment of the process of unity of the body and soul with the Beloved.

TRANSFORMATION

St. Veronica's whole being was transformed into the suffering Christ. He adapted her constitution into his. He provided her with the experiences of the love and woundedness of his heart. He perfected her through the instruments of the passion. Veronica cried to him in prayer that she wished to be washed in his pure blood. And then, when at last prepared, she took on the suffering of others by mediating for their own transformation. "My God, I ask nothing else of you but the salvation of sinners. Send me more pains, more torments, more crosses!" she exclaimed.

DIVINIZATION

Throughout her spiritual journey, St. Veronica is led toward Holy Mother Mary as her ultimate teacher and guide. It is Mary who takes over from her surrender; it is Mary who brings St. Veronica to the pinnacle of spiritual perfection in the experience of the Trinity of God. Veronica wrote of the Holy Mother, "She it was who did and said everything." Mary taught Veronica that when the soul is pure and simple, it has "God's gaze constantly upon it, and is favored with God's graces and gifts." St. Veronica explained in her diary that she had been favored with so many gifts—nearly five hundred of them in her lifetime—and she wrote that these graces of "union and transformation" are the same on earth as are enjoyed by the "blessed souls in heaven. They enjoy God in God: it is a continuous banquet of love with love."

Thus St. Veronica taught that it is possible to reach the state of enlightened love with God on this earth, the pinnacle of holiness enjoyed by the saints and guided by feminine wisdom.

A Pilgrim's Prayer to St. Veronica

St. Veronica, fire of love,
Pray that God's love will burn through me.
Teach me purity of thought,
Clarity of mind,
Wisdom of hidden realities,
Of the richness of interior life.
Help me contemplate the truth of my existence.
Pray for the healing and opening of my heart
That I may be compassionate toward suffering and sickness
In myself and others,
Open to change,
Humble in experience,
Persistent in faith,
Never forgetting the teaching of Christ's crucifixion—
That we are to die to the sufferings of life
And be reborn into the joys of the love of God
In this life and the next.
Unite me in your prayers
So that I may receive
The gift of ceaseless grace.

The Pilgrimage

For the combined St. Veronica–Bl. Margaret pilgrimage, turn to page 160.

BLESSED MARGARET OF CASTELLO
Unheralded Survivor

"If my father and mother forsake me,
the L*ORD* *will take me up."*
Psalm 27:10

Her Life

In 1287 a blind, lame, hunchbacked dwarf was born. The unnamed baby was to become Blessed Margaret of Castello, patroness of the unwanted and of the disabled. This is her story, a story not revealed through diaries or letters, or by any sublime poetry or famous paintings. All we have are some facts of her life recorded by an anonymous man who knew her and who talked to others who knew her. A canon of the cathedral of Città di Castello branded this text "a tissue of lies," but the locals protested against his proclamation. He later retracted his accusations after discovering documents in the archives revealing truths of Margaret's life. Other books appeared in the fourteenth century: one by a Franciscan monk, Hubert of Casale, and a few biographies, including one by the Jesuit saint Robert Bellarmine. Most recently there's been a revival of interest in her, especially in the United States, which has ignited a new movement to press for her canonization. She was a remarkable woman, an extraordinary soul who loved and served joyfully against odds that were unremittingly stacked against her.

Margaret's father and mother lived in a castle at Metola, quite near Mercatello (where St. Veronica came from), and where the family also had another home. Margaret's father was a military man, a strong warrior who was famous for his ruthlessness but not much else. He had inherited a large amount of land and had many serfs and peasants working for him, and his wealth was renowned. His wife was a weak and compliant woman, but there was much rejoicing when she became pregnant. In preparation for the birth, the locals had planned a fanfare of festivities to herald the anticipated son, who was to inherit his father's wealth and military prowess, but all fell silent on the day Margaret entered the world. An ugly, deformed, and blind baby girl was not what anyone expected. Instead of a multitude of flags fluttering on the high tower and gaily dressed horses clattering across the castle bridge to proclaim the news of the birth and start the banquets and singing and dancing, there was only darkness and the early stirrings of deceit.

When her parents had recovered from their initial shock, they dismissed the child and put her in the care of a maid in the castle with strict instructions to keep the baby's existence a secret from everyone outside their immediate staff. The local priest, however, demanded that the baby be baptized. To ensure secrecy, it was the maid who took the infant to the church in Mercatello, where she chose her name *Marguerita,* which means "pearl."

By the time Margaret was six, she knew the name of everybody in the castle. She could make her way unassisted, hobbling on a crutch, through the various passageways of the fortress and the outbuildings. She was warm, friendly, and sociable with everyone, yet she was always warned to stay away from her parents.

One day Margaret was making her way down a corridor when she met a woman visitor to the castle, a guest of her parents, who was openly moved with pity and began asking her questions. Margaret's maid, who had forgotten to warn the girl to stay in her room when guests visited, quickly squirreled her away. On learning of the incident, her parents decided to ensure it didn't happen again. Her mother suggested putting the child into the care of a peasant family, but her father thought that this was too risky. He had heard of some holy saint in Florence who had spent years holed up in a prison cell to become closer to God, and recognizing his own daughter's devotion to prayer, decided instead to imprison her in the local parish church in the mountains, not far from the castle. He ordered a mason to build a cell at the side of the church, a low-ceilinged affair with a doorway; after putting his six-year-old daughter inside the cell, he walled it up. There she could feel the altar nearby through a hole in the wall, and this hole would also serve as a means of passing food and drink to her. Her parents intended to leave her there until her death.

Luckily for Margaret, the chaplain of the parish visited her regularly and educated her in the ways of the soul. He found her mind to be "luminous" and her patient understanding of life and its problems truly remarkable. He taught her how to accept not only her physical afflictions but also her imprisonment as a special gift from God. Margaret began to fast at the age of seven and was known to do so for four days a week. She also secretly obtained a hair shirt, though conditions in the cell were uncomfortable enough; she suffered intensely from the cold in winter and the heat in summer. She spent twelve years walled up in this cell.

In 1305 a French cardinal was elected Pope Clement V. Because of the threat against papal security in Rome, he moved his residence to France. This made many of the Italian Papal States and republics vulnerable to attack with no guarantee of military defense. Trabaria, the republic of which Metola was a part (sandwiched between rich republics in the mountains of the Marches), was particularly exposed and was attacked. Wary of Margaret being discovered and identified by intruding soldiers, her father arranged to move her from her cell on the mountain to the safety of the family palace in Mercatello. Disguised by a veil, she traveled by carriage to the palace with her mother. Any hope that Margaret had of reconciliation with her parents was dashed, as she was placed in an even more miserable prison, the underground vault of the palace, furnished only with a simple bench and table. She was instructed to remain absolutely quiet, to never call out, and to speak only with the servant who brought her daily meals. Here Margaret's suffering was intensified by her isolation—there was no visit from the priest, and she could not partake of Mass and the sacraments. She had nothing but darkness and total solitude.

In the meantime, when the invading army advanced on Trabaria, neighboring states came to its defense. This forced the invaders to retreat, and a peace treaty was signed with Margaret's father.

A couple of years passed before an incident in the main piazza in Mercatello resulted in another move for Margaret. Some German pilgrims traveling through the country stopped in Mercatello and spoke of sacred places where miracles occurred. One of these places attracted Margaret's mother's attention. It was the tomb of a Franciscan brother called Fra Giacomo in nearby Città di Castello. Evidently there had been many cures of the disabled and sick there. After two years in solitary confinement in the vault of her family's home, Margaret, who was now about twenty, was led out in a party, including both her parents. They left town early on a foggy morning with full military enforcement due to the bandits on the road, arriving in Città di Castello to stay in an inn for the night. The family attended early morning Mass next day at the Church of St. Francis, and then prayed at Fra Giacomo's tomb for a miracle cure.

Margaret's happiness at her parents' attention was to be short-lived, however. With no visible signs of a cure, they left her at the church, promising to return for her in the late afternoon, but they never did. When evening arrived, and her parents had still not returned, the warden asked this lone diminutive figure to leave the premises, as the church had to be locked. Margaret found herself cold, hungry, and lost on the steps of a church in a town she didn't know. The following morning, she was discovered by a couple of beggars, a man and a woman, who had come to sit in their usual place on the steps of St. Francis's Church. They saw a woman of twenty years old resembling a small girl, who told them that she was waiting for her parents to come for her. Moved by compassion, the beggars made inquiries on her behalf among the townsfolk, only to discover that Margaret's parents had left town the previous day. With this news, Margaret resigned herself to begging for survival. Her two new friends taught her the streets of Città di Castello so she could locate the fountains for drinking and washing, and the sheltered doorways where she could spend the nights.

One time, close to Christmas, her friends discovered Margaret covered in snow in a doorway, so they invited her to sleep inside with them in a stable they had found. This had profound spiritual relevance for Margaret as she took it as a sign that she was no longer the daughter of nobility in Metola, no longer orphaned from her background, but a daughter of God. God was now her only parent; Jesus, Mary, and Joseph in Bethlehem, her family.

Margaret's joyful and loving disposition in the face of such hardships seemed incongruous to the townsfolk who knew her. People became suspicious of her because there was so much she shouldn't be joyful about, but over time she won their admiration and respect and was invited into their homes. For Margaret, a warm welcome was an invitation to sleep on a dirt floor, sometimes with eight to ten others, surrounded by the usual dogs and animals of a household. It happened that every small act of kindness and hospitality extended to Margaret was miraculously given back hundredfold: families experienced extraordinary healings, feuds were brought to peaceful solutions, those with persistent misfortunes were given abundant peace, and the sick were cured.

Within a year of Margaret's arrival in Città di Castello, her faith, zeal, and devotion to God had impressed so many that she was recommended for convent life, and the local abbess invited her to join their community of nuns. The qualifications required for entrance to the convent were an irreproachable character, legitimate birth, and freedom from serious physical disabilities, so some exceptions had to be made. After investigation by the bishop, who had received from the rector of Mercatello confirmation of Margaret's baptism, the truth of her background was also exposed—that she was of noble birth and her father was a heralded military hero. Concerned about the future of his position should this information ever be revealed, the bishop decided to keep it secret and informed the abbess only that confirmation of Margaret's legitimacy and her baptism had been received. Margaret, happy to join a religious community, began to make waves almost as soon as she stepped into the enclosure. She lived a heightened discipline due to years of isolated prayer and suffering, and she committed herself wholeheartedly to the Rule of the convent (it probably was Benedictine), spending her days in obedient observance. This fervency made her stand out among the other sisters, who had become slack toward the Rule. None of them, for instance, honored the designated times of silence in the day; there was much idle chatter, and the vow of poverty had little effect, as the sisters regularly received personal gifts from visitors. Margaret began to point out these idle defects to her novice mistress, who tried to dissuade her from her tenacity, but Margaret had committed to the Rule of the community and she was going to keep it. Unfortunately her persistence backfired. Her attitude and strict behavior disrupted the nuns so much that they had no alternative than to ask her to leave.

Life on the streets was not the same as before. Cast out of the convent, Margaret was now perceived as a victim of shame, and gossip about her spread. She was called all sorts of insulting names, and children ridiculed her, calling her "the saint," but Margaret never spoke unkindly about the nuns or her time in the convent, only remorse that she had disappointed them. She never answered or defended the accusations against her. In humility and love she carried on, spending much of her time praying in the local Dominican church, which became her favorite, the Chiesa della Caritá (the Church of the Charity).

After she had spent a retreat with local Dominican friars, it was suggested that Margaret join the Third Order of Penance, the *Mantellatae*. Single women were not usually permitted—only widows or senior women who wished religious life outside a convent—but Margaret's faith, character, and reputation forced a committee of women to review her suitability to be one of the *Mantellatae* and she was admitted. This decision was historic, because as far as records show, it was the first instance of a young, unmarried woman being permitted to join the Order of Penance of St. Dominic, and undoubtedly paved the way for St. Catherine's special acceptance fifty years later.

Margaret felt sincerely blessed by her newfound Dominican family and entered a life of ceaseless prayer, contemplative action, and loving service to others. She was a light sleeper and passed many of her nights in meditation. Serious in her vocation and supported by the habit of the Dominican *mantella* (meaning cloak), she began to visit the sick and dying and spoke with wisdom and love of the ways of God. Her presence always brought healing, and her holiness became renowned. She also gave religious instruction to many children of wealthy families, and as they became friends, she was offered a bed in their homes.

After four years of this ministry, Margaret moved permanently into the palatial residence of the Venturino family on the outskirts of town. Lady Gregoria Venturino had also joined the *Mantellatae* and invited Margaret to teach her children religion. But Margaret, although happy with the family, decided that the luxurious surroundings in which she now lived were inappropriate for her state and her vows, so she requested a room in the garret on the property. She said she wanted something plain and simple—a cell out of everybody's way—and for her a room with a low ceiling that was cold in winter and hot in the summer reminded her of her childhood home. This time, however, she had deliberately chosen her cell-like home, and this time she was not abandoned by those around her, but loved and respected. At Margaret's suggestion, she and Lady Gregoria and some other *Mantellatae* began to visit the local prison, especially ministering to the sick there as nobody considered caring for them. It was viewed as an unsafe environment for women, but that did not stop Margaret. At times during her visits, she fell into ecstatic prayer, and prisoners reported that when she was in this state, her physical ugliness disappeared, and she became beautiful and beatific.

In 1320 Margaret announced to her close friends that she was probably not going to live much longer. She quickly fell into a fever, suffering greatly at the end, but she never complained about the pain. On receiving the last rites by a Dominican priest, her face became radiant with love. She died with that serenity, a smile upon her lips, surrounded by tearful friends and sisters. The day was April 13, 1320, and she was thirty-three years old.

The burial tradition for the Dominican *Mantellatae* was to wash the body and then enshroud it in the famous black cloak. Because of the warm climate, it was customary in Italy to bury a person on the same day, so in the late afternoon of the day of Margaret's death, a few pallbearers carrying her diminutive remains on a wooden frame made their way to her favorite Dominican church, where she had requested burial. The local priest greeted the mourners at the side entrance in order to bury her in the inner cloister, but there was so much commotion from the townspeople that they had to put her body down in the street while they argued about her final resting place. The locals called for her burial in the church itself. "She's a saint!" they shouted. "That's where she belongs." The pastor tried to subdue them with reason—that the Church would, of course, go through the official process of beatification and canonization, but that until then it was appropriate for Margaret to be buried in the cloister. The people were going to have none of it, and insisted on a church burial. In the crowd was a young couple whose child could not walk due to an extreme curvature of the spine. Amid all the commotion, they managed to push their child through the crowd and up to Margaret's body, and prayed that she would cure their daughter. Much to everyone's astonishment, Margaret's left arm loosened itself from her shroud, moved upward, and reached over to touch the girl lying beside her. A moment later the child stood up for the first time and walked unaided. This miracle, witnessed by all, decided Margaret's final resting place. Without further ado, she was carried into the church, where she was specially embalmed (a procedure given to holy people) and buried in a side chapel. Throngs of people—some from neighboring republics—visited Città di Castello and Margaret's tomb for healing and prayers (and continue to do so). There are over two hundred affidavits in the Vatican records testifying to permanent cures of blindness, deafness, and other afflictions.

CHRONOLOGY

1287	Born in the Castle of Metola to noble parents.
1293	"Imprisoned" in the local parish church of Metola.
1305	Moved to the family's palace in Mercatello and kept in the vault.
1307	Trip to the tomb of Fra Giacomo in Città di Castello. Abandoned by her parents in the Church of St. Francis.
ca. 1308	Enters the local convent.
ca. 1310	Asked to leave the convent.
1311	Joins the Third Order of the Dominicans as one of the *Mantellatae*. Lives with the Offrenducci family.
ca. 1315	Takes up residence in the garret of the Venturino family's palace on the outskirts of town and begins her ministry in prisons.
1320	Dies on April 13.
1609	Beatified on November 18.

UNOFFICIAL FEAST DAY: April 13

Spiritual Essentials

To create a composite of Bl. Margaret's spirituality, we have only the elements of her attitude and actions in her story as we have been told it. The most prominent teaching from her life is the paramount virtue of surrender. In this surrender she accepted her physical condition, her abandonment and isolation, the continual shame and rejection of her early life with a constant attitude of joy and humility. This was evidence of her inner spiritual freedom, the permanent peace wherein her soul dwelt. Unlike St. Catherine's, St. Clare's, and St. Veronica's choice of enclosure as the training ground of perfection, Bl. Margaret had no opportunity to choose anything. The choice was made by others. Placed in isolation in a cell because of who she was as a child, she still managed to reach the same heights of mystical union as her sister saints. It could be argued, then, that due to her life as an involuntary hermit—and her surrender to it—she advanced to an even higher degree than those who voluntarily chose the mystical life, but this cannot be proved. Despite this, she gave the world invaluable lessons regarding perceptions of normality, physical beauty, and social acceptability.

RESIGNATION

Even if we are not happy with our families, our physical appearance, or our status and feel that our lives are lacking in excitement, or laden with duty, we can find grace in the surrendered resignation to carry on anyway, to live in the moment, to care for those around us, and to learn that we are cared for in turn.

COURAGE

Margaret is an inspiration that, whatever happens to us, whatever God wills for us, we can find the courage to accept all as God's plan and not be defeated by others' attitudes, slander, discouragement, and resentments. We can also pray for the wisdom to know we are loved in the exact and unique way God has created us.

SERENITY

Margaret is a model of someone at peace in all of life's challenges, with the constant serenity of a prayerful life, a knowing of the infinite, and the realization of the temporariness of our worldly life.

HUMILITY

She shows us the humility to accept that we may know nothing of why and how God acts and yet to trust in God's ways as given through others. This humility is realized through deep prayer and a relationship of trust with the Divine.

TO LOVE ANYWAY

Margaret is a model of love; even when devoid of love, even when alone, she still loved others with passion, generosity, and care.

TO BE AWARE

Margaret is an obvious example that all is not what it seems when we judge a person by his or her outward appearance or disabilities, obvious or hidden. Sometimes the greatest gifts come from the most unlikely people, the biggest healings from those who suffer most. Even without sight, Bl. Margaret was not blind to those around her, to God's will for her, or to the needs of others.

THE CROSS

Unlike St. Veronica who voluntarily carried a heavy cross to become closer to her suffering Lord, Bl. Margaret was born with her cross and carried it with dignity and faith throughout her life. It could be said that she came into the world for a short while just to exemplify what good can come from rejection, what magnificence from horror, what love from hate. She truly embodied her suffering Lord from the beginning to the end.

A Pilgrim's Prayer to Bl. Margaret

With your inner eye,
Teach me to see the purity of spirit.
With your inner beauty,
Teach me to love my soul

And the souls of others.
With your heightened surrender,
Teach me acceptance and resignation
To all that God sends me.
With your courage,
Guide me to be heroic for God.
With your serenity,
Teach me constancy in peace.
With your great heart,
Be an example to me of how to love
Always in any situation.
With your suffering,
Prod me into the joy
Which comes from surrendering
To God in all things.

The Pilgrimage

for St. Veronica Giuliani and Bl. Margaret

Destinations:
Mercatello sul Metauro, Metola, and Città di Castello
Suggested length:
Two days

DAY ONE: Mercatello sul Metauro and Metola

Mercatello sul Metauro is a special town because it was home for both St. Veronica and Bl. Margaret. St. Veronica's first family house still exists and is now a Franciscan convent, but there is no evidence of the location of Bl. Margaret's family home where she spent two years in the vaults.

The best way to see Mercatello sul Metauro is by foot as the streets are narrow and it is a small enough town to walk around. Park outside the walls and take any entrance to the main piazza.

The main piazza was the grand meeting place of all the townsfolk, and in it stands the church where both St. Veronica and Bl. Margaret were baptized (the latter in secret with her maid). It was the rector of this church who sent the documents confirming Bl. Margaret's baptism to the bishop in Città di Castello, and this was the main square where Bl. Margaret's mother heard about the healing tomb in Città di Castello.

Chiesa Collegiata

The church's two stained-glass windows, each side of its interior doorway, are of St. Veronica (portrayed in brown, the color of the Franciscan Capuchin sisters) and Bl. Margaret (in white with the black cape of the Dominican *Mantellatae*). One chapel is dedicated to St. Veronica and the other has an interesting altar image of the Madonna. This church would be an ideal place to offer your pilgrimage intention and prayer.

Monastero S. Cuore (The Monastery of the Sacred Heart)

Take any street west off the piazza to the convent where a statue of St. Veronica marks the place. The convent used to be St. Veronica's family home. It includes the original inner courtyard garden (seen only through the sisters' windows); also, one of the original main rooms has been turned into an oratory. The oratory can be reached by taking the stairs to the upper floor, where framed pictures of events in St. Veronica Giuliani's life line the walls. In the intimate chapel, the ceiling, walls, floors, and fireplace are the originals from the family home. Many of the artifacts and images were also part of St. Veronica's early life—for example, the picture in the enclosure is the actual picture of the child Jesus that she prayed to when young and where she heard him speak to her. The tomb is a replica of the original, which is in Città di

Castello. The door to the right of the tomb is the original one leading to St. Veronica's childhood bedroom.

The relics on display include a pair of her sandals, a walking stick, her habit and cloak, some instruments of penance, as well as samples of her handwriting. On the wall is a framed image of the Giuliani family tree and the symbols that St. Veronica knew were imprinted on her heart. There's also an image of the miraculous child Jesus, lying on a cushion and decorated in gold and white, made by St. Veronica herself. The hearts and other objects are in thanksgiving for prayers answered.

The **chapel** of the convent on the main floor has a special fresco of Mary dictating to St. Veronica, who is writing her words in her journal. The farthest door in the corridor leads to the anteroom of the cloistered convent. At the window grille the sisters can be met by ringing the bell (provided they are not in their prayer times, which are listed).

On departing the town of Mercatello, drive toward Urbino and Sant'Angelo in Vado on the SS73 (the only main road out of town). There is a stone statue of Bl. Margaret in a parking lot/play area off the main road just outside the walls.

Torre Metola (The Metola Tower)

Visiting the mountain where Bl. Margaret was born and where lie the ruins of her parents' fortress castle requires hiking and climbing. It is worth every step!

From Sant'Angelo in Vado (about 4 kilometers from Mercatello), turn off at the Stadio sign. Make a left at the T junction, veering right after the Sant'Angelo in Vado signs and following the road with the brown "Agriturismo" signs to the country beyond. After 2.8 kilometers, turn right at the two "Agriturismo" signs and a sign for "Metola." Follow this dirt road at the fork to "Caselle." Park at the hamlet of houses and follow the "Torre" sign by foot. Go past the farm and at the fork in the slate part of the path, keep to the left. It takes thirty-five minutes to reach the tower.

The tower of the castle at Metola has been single-handedly preserved by the young man who presently owns it. Some ancient castle walls and cisterns can also be seen as well as a staggering, almost 360-degree view of the Urbania region.

La Cappella Beata Margherita (The Chapel of Blessed Margaret)

On your way back from the tower, watch for two signs to the left at the second bend in the path. One points to a pathway to Sant'Angelo in Vado, the other to Capella Beata Margherita in the opposite direction. The pathway ends in a steep decline of slate, which needs to be crossed to reach the chapel.

The chapel is the presumed place where Margaret was imprisoned for most of her childhood and teens (although some believe it was the church at the foot of the hill). The chapel is cared for by the local women, who tend its altar and light its candles. A terra-cotta statue of Bl. Margaret stands below a plaque noting that the chapel is her birthplace. This, as explained in her life, is only half the story.

N.B.: The chapel is also accessible by car off the road from Mercatello. Follow the sign for it that appears several kilometers before arriving at Sant'Angelo in Vado.

End the day by driving to Città di Castello. There are two alternatives— Sant'Angelo in Vado and San Giustino or by way of Apecchio on the SS257.

CITTÀ DI CASTELLO

Originally the site of a Roman camp erected over an Etruscan town, Città di Castello (meaning the "City of the Castle") was built in the lowlands of the Tiber valley. Unlike other towns perched on hilltops to facilitate defense, Città di Castello protected itself by two high stone walls, which can still be seen today. A town with much history and heritage, it has been the home for many saints, among them St. Veronica and Bl. Margaret.

Raphael also lived in Città di Castello for four years after leaving Urbino and produced his early paintings here. *The Standard of the Holy Trinity,* painted in thanksgiving for deliverance from the plague, is hanging in poor condition in the Pinacoteca Comunale in the center of town. His *Crucifixion,* an altarpiece commissioned in 1503 for St. Dominic's Church (where Bl. Margaret's body is preserved), now hangs in London's National Gallery. Raphael was also commissioned to paint *The Marriage of the Virgin* in the Church of St. Francis (where Bl. Margaret was abandoned), and a reproduction of that painting is situated on the original side altar. The original painting is in the Pinacoteca di Brera, Milan.

In a nondescript side square of Città di Castello called Piazza Incontro (the square of the meeting), behind the Cathedral of S. Florido (another local saint), is where it is believed St. Anthony of Padua personally met St. Francis of Assisi for the first time.

Now host of many cultural, spiritual, and design events, Città di Castello has much going on in its streets. It is loved by Umbrians and upheld as an example of civilized living. It was also one of the first members of the "slow movement," a now-international philosophy that avoids the mindless speed of modern life and instead emphasizes awareness and appreciation of the moment. Città di Castello prides itself in being a "slow town," where all aspects of life are respected.

DAY TWO: Città di Castello

Park outside the walls as most of the interior streets are pedestrian.

Convento di S. Veronica (St. Veronica's Convent)

The convent is at 21 Via Mario Angeloni. As a working cloistered community of Franciscan sisters, it has not changed much since the time when St. Veronica joined it as a young postulant and where, within its walls, she experienced the fullest mystical life. She lived here all of her religious life, and here was where she died. The chapel of the tomb of St.

Veronica is accessible from the vestibule. There is also a museum within the cloister.. The museum has some original paintings of Veronica, items used in the kitchen and the apothecary, the crucifix she prayed to, and some vestments she wore while carrying the cross in prayer. There are samples of her mystical writing, some of her clothes, and the drawing of her heart. Her room in the convent cannot be visited but a sign on the cloister walls indicates its location.

To view the museum, an appointment needs to be made with the sisters. It is possible to speak to someone in English and be shown around by an English-speaking volunteer. The telephone number for the convent is 075–8550956.

La Chiesa di S. Francesco (The Church of St. Francis)

The church's interior has been restored many times, due to fires and earthquakes, but most of its original exterior remains. There are two sets of steps to its entrance; one of these would have been where Bl. Margaret spent her first night as a beggar and met her future friends after being abandoned by her parents. The miraculous tomb of Fra Giacomo is situated under the main altar.

La Chiesa di S. Domenico (St. Dominic's Church)

This vast, imposing church can be reached from the main piazza (Piazza Matteoti), via Corso Vittorio Emanuele, turning right at the second street, Via Signorelli, leading to the landmark of the old hospital. St. Dominic's is on the opposite side.

Although it hasn't been proven, this church may have been built over Bl. Margaret's favorite Dominican church where she prayed and was finally accepted into a religious community. Today its treasure is Bl. Margaret herself. She lies below the main altar, a diminutive figure preserved for nearly eight hundred years: her teeth, skin, and fingernails are still intact, and she's dressed in the clothes of the

Mantellatae. The marvel of her life is expressed in the marvel of her body's preservation, which astounds scientists who cannot explain its incorruptibility. There are images of Bl. Margaret's life in the modern stained-glass window behind.

La Cattedrale di S. Florido (The Cathedral)

Although destroyed by earthquakes and rebuilt many times, the ancient cathedral is still home to silent prayer and much devotion. Its art and architecture are particularly unique. The fresco behind the high altar depicts local saints, including Bl. Margaret, and its side altar with a statue of the Sacred Heart is unofficially recognized as a place of holy presence.

Santuario Madonna di Belvedere (Sanctuary of the Madonna of Belvedere)

End this pilgrimage at the sanctuary on the outskirts of town. In the past, most pilgrims stopped here as they traveled through the mountains. As a young girl, St. Veronica visited the shrine on her way from the Marches to cloistered convent life. It is now a Franciscan oratory.

To reach the sanctuary, take the ring road (SS257) to Fano. Follow signs for Hotel Termi di Fontecchio on the Viale Raffaelle de Cesare. The circular church can be seen perched high on the hill.

The spectacular dome of the church is unique to its time, designed in the seventeenth century by Antonio Gabrielli. Inside the building, the style is overly ornate, but the statues of local saints encircling the church (Bl. Margaret being one of them) have made this a special place of worship to the locals. Outside is a small bronze statue of St. Veronica with her arms raised as if blessing the valley below; built more recently, a life-size statue of St. Pio of Pietrelcina (Padre Pio) stands in its own garden.

The ceramic Stations of the Cross by local sculptor and artist Enrica Conte are worth walking.

ST. BONAVENTURE
Prince of Wisdom

"The labor of wisdom is plainly better than corporal toil."
St. Bonaventure

His Life

Bagnoregio is a medieval town perched atop a mountainous mass of volcanic rock. What makes it exceptional is that its surrounding terrain seems to belong to another world, a celestial landscape of orange and red formations uncommon to the natural undulation of southern Tuscany. Yet it is a fitting birthplace and hometown of the man who has been called the second founder of the Franciscans.

Giovanni (John) di Fidanza was born in 1217, the year that the General Chapter of the Franciscans had gathered in Assisi, during which St. Francis and his followers decided to extend their ministry outside Italy. His father, Giovanni, was a physician, and his mother's name was Maria di Ritello. It could well be that growing up in a house built on the edge of a cliff with breathtaking 360-degree views contributed considerably to young Giovanni's spiritual formation. Bonaventure described God as "an intelligible sphere whose center is everywhere, and whose circumference is nowhere."

Giovanni was given the name *Bonaventura,* which means "good fortune," after he was cured of a serious illness when he was nine years old through prayers to St. Francis. He was educated by local Franciscan friars who recognized his keen intellect. At the age of eighteen, he went to study preparatory theology at the University of Paris—at the time the epicenter of academia—eventually gaining a master's degree in arts, which included logic, math, physics, metaphysics, and ethics. Nine years after his arrival in Paris, he entered the Franciscan Order under the provincial of Rome, and furthered his studies in canon law, medicine, and theology with many scholars, including the renowned professor Alexander of Hales. One of his fellow students, who would become a lifelong friend, was Thomas Aquinas, who joined the Dominican Order. Both Bonaventure and Aquinas received their degrees of bachelor of sacred scripture at the same time in the year 1248. During the subsequent two years, Bonaventure pursued advanced studies and received his master's of theology, which entitled him to teach. He began to write what would eventually become an extensive collection of scholastic theses, spiritual works, and sermons, including the *Commentary on the Sentences, On the Knowledge of Christ, On the Mystery of the Trinity,* and *On Evangelical Perfection.* He was also appointed regent master of the Franciscans in Paris and master of theology at the Parisian School of the Friars Minor.

The Franciscans were struggling with numerous challenges that had emerged over the thirty years since their founder's death, and the minister general, a man called John of Parma, was forced to resign on suspicion of heresy. This suspicion was largely caused by his belief in, and promotion of, Joachite philosophy, which held that the coming age (supposedly begun with St. Francis) was that of the Holy Spirit. The Church feared that this increasingly popular view would ultimately usurp Christ's central role in Christianity. With discontent rife among the Franciscans over its administration, combined with the added threat to the dogmatic power of the institutional Church, John of Parma had no choice than to bend to the control of Rome and resign. He recommended Brother Bonaventura in Paris as his successor, and Bonaventure was elected minister general of the Franciscan Order on February 2, 1257.

The first delicate task Bonaventure had to undertake was handling the charge of "heresy" against his predecessor. Bonaventure had no recourse than to have him tried before a group of learned friars. Parma spoke little in his defense, so the tribunal reached a verdict of "life imprisonment," but this was later changed to a lighter sentence because of the pleas of one of his old friends, Cardinal Ottobono. John of Parma spent the rest of his thirty years in obscurity at Greccio near Rieti.

Next Bonaventure turned his hand to the immense administrative and theological challenges that lay before him and began introducing a systematic way of renewal for the order. Still headquartered in Paris, he took to the road to meet his friars, sometimes spending months going to and from Assisi. Undaunted by distance and time, he traveled to England, Spain, Germany, and around Italy and France, mediating the differences among about thirty thousand friars. As he threw himself into pastoral duties, he also wrote and preached to Isabella, the sister of King Louis of France, who had founded a Poor Clare community. Bonaventure's intelligence, his love for the Franciscan way of life, his understanding of the theology of St. Francis (never before recognized as such), and his efforts to renew theology (e.g., introducing more systematic interpretation) were all a departure from the ways in which Franciscan spirituality had been previously understood and followed. Bonaventure was firmly established within the academic milieu and brought a unique marriage of mind and heart to the work of guiding the Franciscans into some semblance of security, clarity, and direction. Only a man who loved St. Francis's original Rule (and who was able to link the original Primitive Rule, the subsequent Rule Bullata, and then the papal bull together for posterity) could write in a "Letter to an Unknown Master" that it would be wise not to be

> disturbed that the friars were simple and illiterate men in the beginning: this should confirm your faith in the Order even more. I confess before God that it is this that made me love the life of blessed Francis above all, because it is similar in its beginning and perfection to that of the Church, which began with simple fishermen and grew to include the most illustrious and learned doctors. And so you will see in the Order of blessed Francis, as God displays, that it was not invented by human discretion but by Christ.

Yet Bonaventure himself was not widely popular among the Franciscans. He had not only sentenced John of Parma, but he also subsequently weeded out the practitioners of what he saw as abuses, taking dramatic steps to expel any

Franciscan who publicly tarnished the order by either word or deed. One of the extra tasks he gave himself was to write a biography of St. Francis, something he considered vital to help the preservation of the order because it would enable its members to fully understand its formation. Bonaventure especially wanted to express St. Francis's theology as "the way of the cross," beginning with San Damiano and the call of Christ from the cross, and culminating at the end of the saint's life with the sacred stigmata at La Verna. He said of St. Francis's spiritual genius that it enabled him to penetrate "the hidden depths of the mysteries, and where the knowledge of the masters stands outside, the affection of the lover entered within."

During his travels, Bonaventure interviewed many who knew St. Francis personally or had stories about him to share, and in 1259, two years after his election, he stayed for many months at La Verna, combined with lengthy visits to the hermitage of Montecasale near Sansepolcro. He not only worked on his biography of Francis but also began to have mystical experiences about the suffering Christ, which resulted in his writing his spiritual classic, *The Journey of the Soul into God*.

Around this time, Thomas Aquinas arrived from France to begin ten years of teaching not far from Bonaventure's hometown, in Orvieto, Viterbo, and Rome. Both he and Bonaventure most likely met and compared notes on their theological writings and experiences.

In 1260 Bonaventure presided over his first Franciscan International Chapter, held in Narbonne, France. Here previous statutes were reviewed, many of them precariously agreed upon—and sometimes practiced. There was still much confusion among the friars, and Bonaventure's job was to get it sorted out. For instance, one question was the appropriate age to enter the order as an oblate, which was changed from fourteen to eighteen. The habits of the friars had to be approved and had to be uniform, fasts properly observed, novices properly trained; the order had become clerical and monastic but needed to now become more academic. The teaching and study of theology were promoted, and the use of books and attendance at university for selected friars were recommended. The authority of the superiors in the order was more clearly defined, and by the end of the chapter, the Constitutions consisted of a Prologue written by Bonaventure, and two hundred and fifty-five decrees arranged under twelve sections. It was later considered a masterpiece of legislative flexibility because it condensed the realities of the previous forty years of Franciscan experience without comprising new initiatives and the natural evolution in the spirit of future directives. In later chapters that Bonaventure presided over—Pisa in 1263, Paris in 1266, and Assisi in 1269—there were variables appended to the Constitutions that included more liturgical additions, as well as changed boundaries for provinces. Bonaventure did all this work to promote what he called "the perfect way of life" that the Franciscans strived for. Bonaventure's "way of life" was not understood or accepted by some of the friars who preferred the original ideal of perfection through poverty and simplicity, but it offered, under his guidance, a stability and peace not experienced before, and created greater prestige for the Franciscans among the intellectuals of the Church.

The typical friar would no longer be "a wandering evangelist who worked in the fields, tended the sick, slept in barns and churches, a simple, devout, homely soul content to take the lowest places but a member of a religious house, well educated and well trained, a preacher and director of souls, a man whom the community could respect and whose services would be valued." The future Franciscan friary would be equipped with a library, a place to study, pray, contemplate, and serve the community. The Franciscan friar was still a preacher, but educated in theology, always in service to souls. And to this day, this form of Franciscan life is the one most embraced and practiced.

In 1265 the pope offered Bonaventure the prestigious post of archbishop of York in England, but he graciously declined, citing his need to concentrate on his work for his order.

A year later Bonaventure and Aquinas were invited by Pope Pius V to prepare and present a definitive theological summary. This was to be vital for the Church at the time when Christendom was at the apex of its influence. Bonaventure had begun his summa of systematic theology when he was completing his university degree and had been working on it through the subsequent years. He was to present his summa after Aquinas at the papal court in Rome, but in a sign of profound humility, he tore up his own treatise upon hearing Aquinas's *Summa Theologica.* A masterpiece of theology, Aquinas's *Summa* became the standard text for many schools and universities, although Aquinas never fully completed it due to his being recalled to teach in Paris.

Another incident illustrates the depth of Bonaventure's humility. In 1273, he was made cardinal bishop of Albano by Pope Gregory X. The pope's messengers, who officially announced Bonaventure's appointment by delivering his cardinal's hat, had to wait in the anteroom of the Franciscan friary near Florence where Bonaventure was residing at the time, because he was busy washing the dishes and wanted to finish the job at hand before receiving his guests and his hat!

Pope Gregory X also summoned Bonaventure to assist him in preparing for the Ecumenical Council at Lyons in May 1274. The thrust of this particular council was to find ways of reconciliation between the Roman and Greek Churches after centuries of disagreement. Bonaventure had already played a crucial role in integrating insights from the Greek East and the Latin West in his writings and teachings, thus contributing new insights into the shaping of the spirituality of his time. The spirit, the intellect, and the physical substance of Aquinas and Bonaventure were meant to intersect at the council, but Aquinas died on the way to Lyons. Then, as if Bonaventure's life was intertwined with Aquinas's, he died on July 15, 1274, and did not live to witness the council's outcome. He was buried in the Friars Minor chapel in Lyons with the pope presiding at his funeral.

Canonized in 1482, Bonaventure was called by a papal chronicler "a man of knowledge and distinguished eloquence, illustrious in holiness, life, conduct and customs. Loved by God and people, he was good, affable, pious, merciful and full of virtue." Bonaventure, the man of "good fortune," healed as a boy by the intercession of St. Francis, was savior of the Franciscans, bishop, cardinal, scholar, and theologian. He left an extensive body of written work that was translated into English only in the nineteenth century and is being avidly studied today. He was a prince of wisdom far ahead of his time, understanding the mystical, theological, and philosophical ways of the Divine, and embracing the cosmos with a heart of gold. He was awarded the title *Seraphic Doctor* by the Holy See in 1588, a seeming reward for his embrace of the pure love of Christ as the way of prayer. A true son of St. Francis, who foresaw the exigency of theological understanding and wisdom as the way forward for many of his followers, Bonaventure must have surely surpassed even St. Francis's expectations as the friar of the future.

CHRONOLOGY

1217	Born Giovanni di Fidanza in Bagnoregio, Orvieto.
1226	Is miraculously healed through his mother's prayers to St. Francis.
1235–43	Studies at the University of Paris, gaining master of arts degree.
1243	Enters the Franciscan Order.
1243–48	Studies theology in Paris under Franciscan professors.
1250–52	Writes expositions on the *Sentences* of Peter Lombard, later is included in the 4-volume *Commentary on the Sentences.*
1252–54	Partakes in theological disputations at the University of Paris. Obtains master of theology degree; is licensed to teach theology.
1254–57	Holds position of master of theology at the University of Paris.
1257	Is elected minister general of the Order of Friars Minor.
1257–73	Travels throughout Europe as minister general.

1259	Stays at La Verna and Montecasale compiling biography of St. Francis and the *Journey of the Soul to God.*
1260	Presides over the first international Franciscan Chapter at Narbonne. Introduces reforms.
1265	Turns down papal invitation to archbishopric in York, England.
1266	International Chapter at Pisa. Tears up his "summa" on hearing Aquinas present his to the pope.
1269	International Chapter at Assisi.
1273	Made cardinal bishop of Albano.
1274	Attends Council of Lyons and dies on July 15. Buried in the Church of Friars Minor in Lyons, France.
1482	Canonized by Pope Sixtus IV.
1588	Made Seraphic Doctor of the Church by Pope Sixtus V.

OFFICIAL FEAST DAY: July 15

Spiritual Essentials

ON PRAYER

St. Bonaventure advised the friars that those who wished to walk in the footsteps of Christ needed to place the Word in the center of their contemplative prayer life, especially as they entered the order from the outside world. He advised in the novitiate that the contemplative path was essential, including the ancient practice of recitation of the psalms and learning words of scripture by heart, known as *Lectio divina*. He called Christ "the lamp, the door, and also the foundation of the whole of Scripture."

ON STUDY

St. Bonaventure said that study of sacred scripture must be "approached in an orderly way." He suggested reading the original writings of the saints as well as more secular teachings (like philosophy), but, in the end, he summarized that scripture stands alone as the foundation for all other readings and interpretations. He said that all writings of saints were born from knowledge of scripture. He teaches that in scripture there are three truths—

1. The eternal generation and incarnation of Christ
2. The pattern of human life
3. The union of the soul with God

From this he merges theological understanding (science of divine knowledge) with mystical and religious experience. St. Bonaventure therefore exemplifies his gift for synthesis between the intellectual study of theology and the living experience of mystical life. He said that "knowledge without love is not perfect," that knowledge alone can distort our perspective. Knowledge and love together are the prescription for the practice of wisdom, and to enable us to practice this wisdom we need to unlearn ignorance: whatever knowledge we have gained that keeps us away from authenticity, truth, and unity needs to be disassembled to make room for holy wisdom. He wrote in his prologue of *The Journey of the Soul to God* that one cannot believe that "reading is sufficient without unction, speculation without devotion, investigation without wonder, observation without joy, work without piety, knowledge without love, understanding without humility, study without divine grace, the mirror without divinely inspired wisdom." He later taught that "unless you are able to consider things in terms of how they originate, how they are brought back to their goal, and how God shines forth in them, you will have no understanding."

THE SOUL

St. Bonaventure teaches that all the arts and sciences are vital for the understanding of the journey of the soul. He teaches that the nourishment of the soul is in deep and constant prayer. Prayer makes you receptive to the "free grace of God," without which the mystical journey cannot be traveled successfully.

The soul cannot recognize the divine light unless it is given by divine grace, "and only those who strive for it will receive such grace," he explains.

A SELECTION OF HIS WRITINGS ON WISDOM

"The door to wisdom is a yearning for it and a powerful desire. Therefore the Psalm says 'open wide your mouth and I will fill it.' That is the road by which wisdom comes to me; by which I enter into wisdom, and wisdom enters into me. The same is true of charity. Hence, 'God is love, and those who abide in love abide in God and God in them.' Such wisdom cannot be obtained without supreme mutual pleasure, but where one looks for supreme mutual pleasure, supreme desire must be there first."

"We need to know that there are three things in us the use of which will enable us to proceed in this triple way: the sting of conscience, the ray of intelligence, and the little flame of wisdom. If you wish to be cleansed, turn to the sting of conscience; if you wish to be enlightened, turn to the ray of intelligence; if you wish to reach perfection, turn to the little flame of wisdom."

All creatures are nothing other "than a certain likeness of the divine wisdom; a kind of statue."

"The highest form of wisdom is not won by our efforts but is the gift of the Holy Spirit, infused with contemplation."

The human knowledge of Christ can only be understood by someone who has experienced it, therefore no one will experience this unless they are "rooted and grounded in love....And this is what true, experiential wisdom consists of. It begins on earth and is brought to consummation in heaven."

ST. BONAVENTURE'S LEGACY

During Vatican II in 1962–63, St. Bonaventure's work was referred to as the way of assistance through the study of sacred scripture. Unlike the literalists, he taught that to study holy scripture it is important to do so in different ways: first by reading it literally, then by understanding what it offers in way of redemption for humanity, and finally by discovering what this redemption means in terms of faith and morals. This he explained was why the mystery of salvation is sometimes plainly written and sometimes obscurely recounted. Scripture is not just a historical record but a living testament that resonates and provides guidance for contemporary situations. He defines humanity as a community, groups of people made up of the opposing forces of good and evil.

Among his extensive written works are *The Journey of the Soul into God, Defense of the Mendicants, Soliloquy on the Four Spiritual Exercises, The Threefold Way, The Tree of Life, The Mystical Vine, On the Five Feasts of the Child Jesus, On the Perfection of Life,* and *The Life of St. Francis.* His many sermons and lectures, called collations, include *On the Ten Commandments, On the Seven Gifts of the Holy Spirit,* and *On the Six Days of Creation;* the last was his final work, unfinished at his death.

A Pilgrim's Prayer by St. Bonaventure

Lord Jesus Christ,
Pierce my soul with your love
So that I may always long for you alone
Who are the bread of angels
And the fulfillment of the soul's deepest desires.
May my heart always hunger and feed upon you,
So that my soul may be filled with
the sweetness of your presence.
May my soul thirst for you, who are the source of life,
wisdom, knowledge, light,
and all the riches of God.
May I always seek you and find you

And do all things for the honor and glory
of your holy name.
Be always my only hope, my peace, my refuge and my help
In whom my heart is rooted so that I may never be
separated from you.

The Pilgrimage

Destinations: Bagnoregio and Orvieto
Suggested length:
One day (or two days with a trip to Arezzo)

This pilgrimage can follow on the back of the St. Francis of Assisi pilgrimage, which ends at La Verna, traveling directly to Bagnoregio and Orvieto with a stop in Arezzo on the way.

Take the E45 in the direction of Rome. About 30 kilometers south of the Perugia exit, follow Todi/Orvieto and the SS448 to Castiglone di Tev. After 3 kilometers follow the Bagnoregio sign for about 11 kilometers. Go to Centro Storico and Cività (little town) as there are two Bagnoregios, the larger and the smaller. Drive to the end of the road in the large town to Piazza S. Agostino where there's a monument in its center to St. Bonaventure the Seraphic Doctor, erected by Pope Leo XIII. Proceed to Piazza Alberto Ricci and the Café Belvedere.

Grotta di S. Bonaventura

At the end of the garden is the grotto where the saint used to pray and contemplate. Unfortunately on the last visit, it had been abandoned and not cared for, but it is worth visiting even just to see the spectacular view of the Cività of Bagnoregio.

On leaving the piazza take Via Bonaventura Tecchi (by car or foot) to the bridge.

Cività (Little Town)

Walking the bridge over the vast, volcanic rock to the ancient town requires a test of courage for any pilgrim who has a fear of heights! However, be assured that this bridge, built with the aid of the University of Virginia, is far more secure than the old one of wood and rope, which used to swing at every movement (including when donkeys passed carrying provisions).

At the entrance of the old town through an archway into the first courtyard, turn right and follow the road to the left for about thirty paces to **La Casa Natale di S. Bonaventura (The house where St. Bonaventure was born).** *On the wall is a granite etching portrait of him. Follow the cobbled pathway to the church in the square, which would have been St. Bonaventure's childhood parish.*

Orvieto

The whole town of Orvieto is built around their grandest treasure, the **cathedral** itself, which is one of the biggest and most beautiful in the whole of Italy. The cathedral is built in a pinkish marble and took about four hundred years to complete from its beginnings in the late thirteenth century. It was erected by order of Pope Urban IV as testament to a miracle. At the time of the pope's visit to Orvieto, the Holy See was experiencing resistance to the teaching of the doctrine of transubstantiation. A Bohemian priest called Peter had also stopped on his way to Rome and was invited to celebrate Mass in the town of Bolsena (just south of Orvieto). This priest had been among the skeptics to the said doctrine, but when he held the host at the Consecration he noticed that it dripped blood onto the altar linen cloth. Believing he had witnessed something miraculous, he took the cloth to show the pope, who instantly declared the incident a miracle and appointed the date as the feast of Corpus Christi (Body of Christ) in honor of it. This is still an important feast in the Church calendar. St. Thomas Aquinas was also visiting

Orvieto at the time and on invitation composed an office for this special feast day.

The cathedral is still the temple for the bloodstained relic and is a testament to faith in architecture. The essence of its front facade depicts scripture, from Creation to the Last Judgment. Inside, the twelve pillars in gray and sand stripes complement the twelve upper windows, which represent the apostles. The main altar is resplendent with frescoes, and to its left is the Chapel of the Body of Christ (the relic of the stained cloth is over the altar). The organ in the Corpus Chapel is one of the largest in Italy.

To the right of the main altar is a gem of a chapel called Capella della Madonna di San Brizio, which is decorated with frescoes of the Last Judgment. The painting was begun in 1447 by Fra Angelico, while others—Gozzoli and Signorelli—also contributed. These extraordinary works of art can be clearly viewed because of the immense quantity of natural light that pours in the chapel's windows as if bathing it in divine illumination.

Chiesa di S. Domenico (Church of St. Dominic)

On the outskirts of the northern part of town on the Via della Pace is the first Dominican church built after St. Dominic's canonization in 1233. Beside it is the former Dominican monastery where St. Thomas Aquinas taught for a while.

ART & SOUL: AREZZO

Arezzo is the ancient capital of the province, and was one of the richest cities in the Tiber valley as far back as the Etruscan times. Guido Monaco, the creator of the musical stave, lived here; the fourteenth-century poet and writer Petrarch was born here; and many great artists painted here.

Guido Monaco (also Guido of Arezzo)

In the center of Piazza Guido Monaco (near the railway station) is a statue of Guido Monaco. Born around AD 990 (and died in 1050), Monaco was a Benedictine monk who became famous for his invention of the five-line stave on which to record music (almost unchanged to this day). A musical theorist, Guido wrote the work *Micrologus, which* is one of the earliest documents on musical practice, polyphony, and plainchant.

Take the Via Guido Monaco from this piazza to the Piazza S. Francesco.

Chiesa di S. Francesco (Church of St. Francis)

In this church, in the corner of the square, is one of Arezzo's greatest artistic treasures, Piero della Francesca's grand floor-to-ceiling frescoes of the legendary story of the True Cross, popular in the thirteenth century. Its writer, Varagine, told of a branch received by Adam that was eventually grafted onto the tree from which was made the holy cross on which Jesus died. The cross was returned to Jerusalem with the help of Emperor Constantine's mother, St. Helena. Piero painted events of his day into the elements of the legend—for example, the victories of the Christian army against the Turks in Belgrade. There are scenes from the Crusades, as well as a meeting between Solomon and the Queen of Sheba (representing a reconciliation between the Churches of East and West). For full details on the recently restored paintings, it would be wise to pick up a book, or follow the information in the church itself.

Guido Monaco's House

Climb uphill on the Via A. Cesalpino to number 47 where on its wall is engraved the musical scale of "Ut re me fa so la...."

This is the house where Guido Monaco was born and where he spent his youth. To this day, the eight-note musical scale is almost unchanged from when Guido invented it here a thousand years ago.

Il Duomo

Continue up the hill to the Piazza Duomo and its imposing cathedral.

The Duomo has many treasures including a life-size fresco of Mary Magdalen by Piero della Francesca; the image is painted as if it forms part of a door to the left of the main altar.

Chiesa di S. Domenico (St. Dominic's Church and the Cimabue Crucifix)

Leaving the cathedral take the Via Ricasoli at the opposite side of the Piazza and walk through it to Piazza Landucci. Turn right along the Via Sassoverde into the small piazza where St. Dominic's Church is situated.

Here one of the world's most famous crucifixes hangs over the altar. It was painted by the great Florentine artist Giovanni Cimabue (1240–1302), who found fame not so much for his own work but more for having influenced the post-Byzantine style of Giotto's work. Also recently restored, this masterpiece is indicative of the tradition of wooden medieval crucifixes, but what makes it remarkable is that, while Christ's face expresses torment and suffering, his outstretched arms embrace the feminine and the masculine—his mother on his right, and John the apostle on his left (whom he had assigned to the care of each other).

Francesco Petrarca

Born in Arezzo in 1304, Petrarch was a poet and scholar, and is considered one of the founders of the Renaissance. Though he wrote extensively in Latin and was interested in Latin literature, it is his work in Italian for which he's most popularly known, specifically his love poetry written in the vernacular, which had a dramatic impact on his contemporary Boccaccio and later on Elizabethan and Jacobean literature. This love poetry was the result of pure chance: In 1327, Petrarch caught sight of a beautiful woman in church, Laura, and the experience moved him to write hundreds of love poems to her over the space of two decades, even though they would never meet, and there are some who say she never existed and was only always an ideal.

His many works include *Canziones,* the collection of love poems; *Africa,* an epic poem on Scipio; *Trionfi,* an allegory in verse, in which Divinity triumphs over Love, Death, and Fame; and *Secretum,* a book he wrote for his private meditation consisting of imagined dialogues between himself and St. Augustine.

Petrarch's Monument and S. Maria delle Pieve

Proceed along the Via dei Pileati to the park behind the cathedral that has a monument of Petrarch, whose house (before it was bombed) was at the corner of the Piazza Duomo and Via dei Pileati; this was the house in which he was born.

Continue on the Corso Italia to Via Dei Pileati where the ancient twelfth-century Romanesque church, S. Maria delle Pieve, is situated.

Recognized for its stunning architecture, this church boasts one hundred full arches, which wrap around the rear into the Piazza Grande or Piazza Vasari where the circular apse can be viewed. Inside, the church is an example of the way of worship in the early Middle Ages: the priests and clergy elevated above the people—the crypt open to view.

II

Pilgrimages in Northern Italy

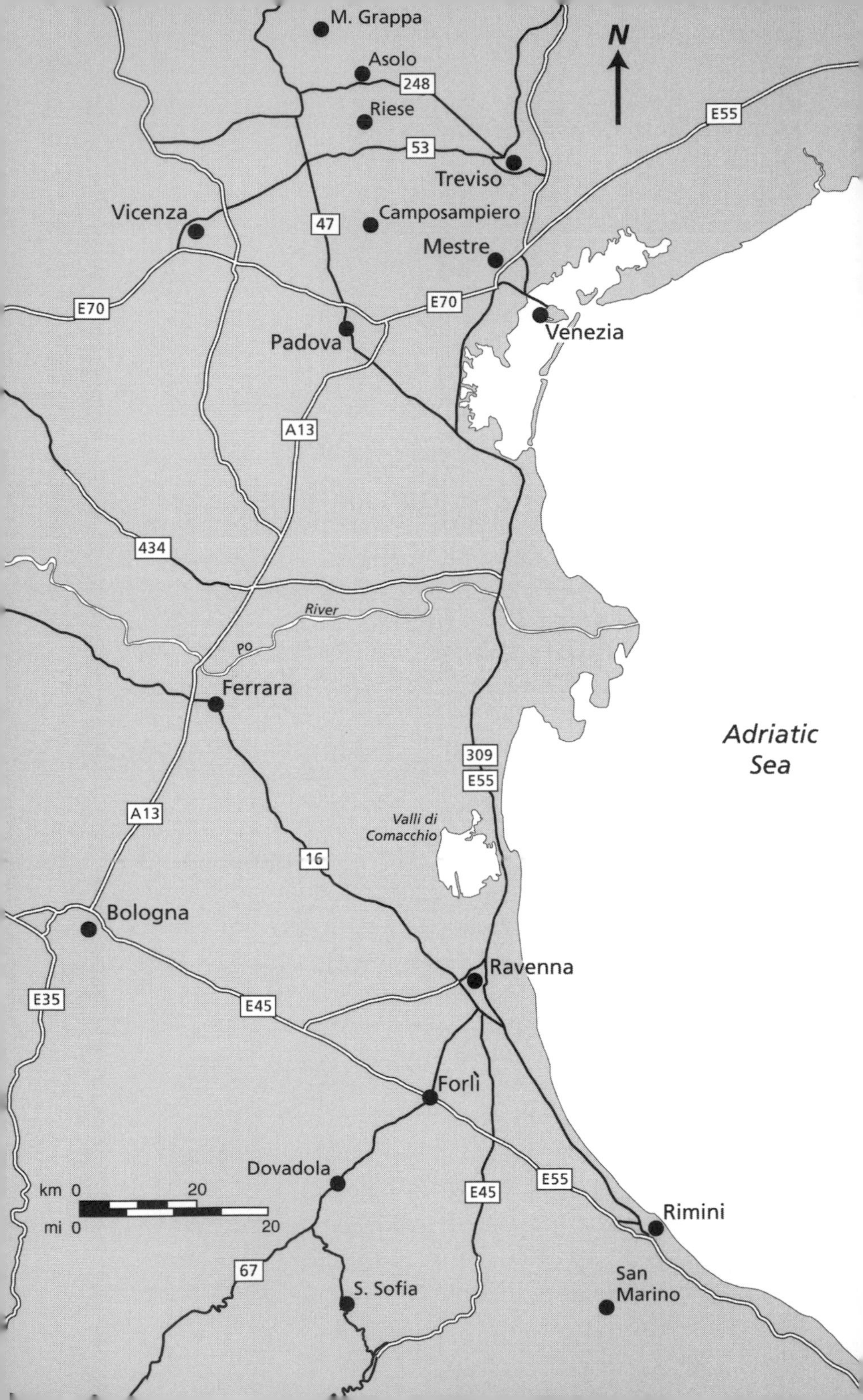

M. Grappa
Asolo
248
Riese
53
Treviso
N
E55
Vicenza
47
Camposampiero
Mestre
E70
E70
Venezia
Padova
A13
434
River
Po
Ferrara
Adriatic
Sea
309
E55
A13
Valli di
Comacchio
16
Bologna
Ravenna
E35
E45
Forlì
Dovadola
km 0
20
mi 0
20
E45
E55
Rimini
67
S. Sofia
San
Marino

ST. ANTHONY
The Miracle Worker

"If then you ask for miracles,
Death, error, all calamities,
Leprosy, and demons fly,
And health succeeds infirmities.
The sea obeys and fetters break,
And lifeless limbs you do restore;
Whilst treasures lost are found again,
When young and old your aid implore."
Traditional Prayer to St. Anthony

· S ANTO
NIUS ·

His Life

Fernando de Bouillon was born in 1195 in Lisbon to a well-to-do Portuguese family with aristocratic roots on both his parents' sides. His mother was a pious woman named Teresa Tavera; his father, Martin, was a knight of King Alfonso and a direct descendant from Godfrey de Bouillon, who was infamous for leading the first Crusade and becoming the initial Frankish King of Jerusalem. Fernando (meaning "bold fighter for peace") was baptized in Lisbon's cathedral near his family home. How many siblings he had is unknown except for a sister Mary, who became superior of a convent.

There were early miraculous occurrences in Fernando's life but most of them are legendary. What we do have as fact is that he was a special student who was educated at the nearby cathedral school in the subjects that were customary for the time—grammar, dialectic, rhetoric, math, astronomy, geometry, music, and religion. Fernando was especially influenced by a wise uncle who taught at this school, and who could have certainly guided him in the direction of religious life. One of his biographers wrote about the boy that he "was a natural enemy of idleness; was instinctively studious and of a sweet solemnity, which did not oppress but rather edified his associates, and endeared him to them."

At the age of fifteen Fernando chose to follow the life of a religious and entered the monastery of Sao Vicente de Fora of the Canons Regular of St. Augustine in Lisbon, probably through family connections with King Alfonso, who was a generous patron. About two years after Fernando's arrival, conflicts began between the king and the Church—a common occurrence when royalty or nobility tried to gain greater influence over the Church—so Fernando made a decision to look elsewhere to pursue his studies in sacred scripture in preparation for the priesthood. He was granted permission to move to the mother cloister of Santa Cruz, about 120 miles outside Lisbon in a place called Coimbra. This abbey was aptly equipped for study and contemplation, with its well-stocked library and its reputation as being a center of high learning. Two men who lived in its confines were Doctors of the University of Paris, and Fernando flourished as he proved himself an outstanding student. He learned quickly and well, and had an impressive memory (he evidently knew the Bible by heart). Yet the monastery was not immune to the cares of the world. Fernando witnessed many squanderings of its possessions by the abbot and there were other conflicts with the monastery's Rule and way of life. Nevertheless Fernando spent eight years in the community, absorbed in his studies and contributing as best he could. Even though we have no evidence that he was ordained earlier than normally accepted, it is probably safe to assume that he did enter the priesthood there, especially after he exemplified his outstanding gifts of religious understanding.

Fernando's first encounter with Franciscans (three priests and two lay brothers who had traveled to Portugal around 1219) proved fateful. Francis of Assisi had sent the friars to Portugal to undertake missionary work among the Saracens. At the time they had been given by Queen Urraca a small and simple house called St. Anthony of the Olives, not far from Santa Cruz. (St. Anthony was one of the founding desert fathers who established a Christian way of contemplative life that became a precursor for the monastic life of solitude, simplicity, poverty, and chastity). The Franciscans had been causing quite a stir in Portugal, especially as their fame was spreading throughout Europe. Fernando probably met these men when they had come begging at Santa Cruz, and he took them in. He discoursed with these brothers (which is probably where he learned Italian), and they recounted their experiences, telling stories about Francis, the friars, Assisi, and all that they stood for and practiced in their lives. The twenty-four-year-old Fernando was deeply moved by the Franciscans. They seemed to have what he had been searching for, but hadn't found in Coimbra. What also impressed Fernando was that these Franciscan brothers possessed no formal training in theology, yet they showed great knowledge and love of God and a clear understanding of their mission as it related to the Gospels. This, perhaps, was the missing link for Fernando—that his intellectual capacity and his comprehension of scripture, nourished by ten years of religious community life, had not brought him opportunities to practice what he knew.

In their fervor for missionary work among the Saracens, for which they were outspoken and had been imprisoned in Seville, the Franciscan friars went on to carry out missionary work in Morocco, where they were eventually killed. Their bodies were brought back for burial at Santa Cruz, and at their tombs Fernando became convinced that his calling was not only to the Franciscan life but also to martyrdom: this was the call to walk in the footsteps of Christ in a more heroic way. He decided to join the Franciscan Order and head for Morocco, so he requested permission from his superiors to leave the Augustinian Order and move in with the handful of remaining monks at St. Anthony of the Olives. His superior reluctantly granted his request, but as he blessed him, he exclaimed in prophecy, "Go on your way, you will surely become a saint," to which Fernando replied, "When they tell you I am a saint, then bless the Lord."

Fernando exchanged his Augustinian habit for the rough brown tunic of the Franciscans and chose as his new name Anthony—Antonio—(probably in honor of his new hermitage home). He began his Franciscan life of the same chastity and obedience that formed his previous life, but with the added vow of "poverty" as the essential Franciscan ingredient. In one of his later sermons Anthony wrote, "The Lord will comfort all the ruins of Sion. Only when the proud house of earthly comfort is reduced to a ruin can the Lord prepare a dwelling place for his inward comforting. Her wilderness shall become a garden of the Lord, for out of the desert of outward poverty the Lord makes a garden full of inward delights."

In 1220 Anthony's provincial minister gave him permission to leave with another brother for Morocco, their sights set on martyrdom. As soon as they arrived there, Anthony fell seriously ill with a fever (which could have been malaria), and was bedridden for four months, cared for by the other brother yet still not well after that time. In the spring of 1221, when the weather made it easier to sail, they were both summoned back to Portugal. God had other plans, however, because their vessel was struck by a huge squall and was blown in a different direction, ending up on the shores of Sicily. Here they made their way to the nearest Franciscan hermitage at Messina, where Anthony recovered and his strength was restored.

During his two-month Sicilian sojourn, he learned about the upcoming General Chapter gathering for all the Franciscans at Assisi. Anthony made his way with his brothers to the "cradle of the order" at La Porziuncola (S. Maria degli Angeli), on the plains outside Assisi. Here was his opportunity to be in Francis's presence; although with the company of two thousand friars' it was unlikely that they personally met each other at that time.

This 1221 Chapter was to be the last that Francis attended anyway. Already weakened by sickness, he spoke in a voice so faint that he could barely be understood. Francis had appointed Peter of Catanio as head of the order, but Peter had died within the year so Brother Elias was then made minister general and became Francis's "mouthpiece" during the Chapter. At this Chapter many aspects of the Franciscan Rule were discussed, one of them being the ways of keeping order amid what was becoming a rapidly growing community. It was decided that every monk needed to be associated with a provincial. Anthony, an unknown Portuguese newcomer recovering from illness, was not a ready candidate for any provincial to consider—especially since most accounts say that he kept his training and past religious life to himself, being humble about his theological achievements. But he took it on himself to approach Brother Gratian of the upper Italian province of Romagna, appealing also to Brother Elias to grant his request to be sent there, and he was accepted.

Anthony was twenty-six years old when he was sent to Montepaolo near Forlì (between Rimini and Bologna) to a poor farmhouse that was probably not unlike St. Anthony of the Olives in Portugal, composed of a few men undergoing the year's novitiate to become Franciscan friars. The Montepaolo community was in need of a priest, so Anthony provided his services.

Life in a Franciscan hermitage in those days was arranged so that one half of the residents took care of the material needs of the house, while the other half gave themselves to contemplation and prayer. Each week these arrangements were reversed, and those who had been active became contemplative, and those contemplative, active. Francis likened these complementary responsibilities to those of Martha and Mary in the Gospel. Anthony first assumed the ordinary household duties of washing dishes, cleaning floors, and saying Mass, and took up his contemplative time in an old stone cell in the woods below the farmhouse, where one of the brothers kept his tools. Eventually he moved into it full-time and spent a year in the cell in silent prayer, penance, fasting, and contemplation; he also worked on commentaries on the psalms. He wrote, "The contemplative man goes his way alone, keeps himself far from the restless throng, and lives in the sorrow of penance. He seeks solitude for body and soul." This solitude Anthony was happy to have found at Montepaolo.

In the summer of 1222, a year after Anthony had come to Montepaolo, a number of Franciscan and Dominican men of the area were called to ordination at the Church of San Mercuriale in nearby Forlì. Bishop Riccardellus Belmonti was to preside and Brother Gratian invited Anthony to accompany him and the men. At the dinner celebration after the ceremony, Brother Gratian suggested that instead of the usual tradition of scripture reading, it might be more edifying to hear a sermon from one of the newly ordained. Those first asked refused, but Brother Gratian was adamant, so he turned to Anthony and asked him. Anthony also resisted, citing his inexperience, but on Gratian's insistence and out of obedience, Anthony spoke. This was his "coming out"—his very first public sermon, one that astounded the friars because he spoke with eloquence and wisdom on the mysteries of faith and revealed a wealth of theological knowledge that no one knew he had. From then on, Anthony's time in solitude and housekeeping at Montepaolo ended. The preacher had preached, and there was no turning back. Later in life, he wrote, "The saints are like the stars. Through His providence Christ keeps them hidden so that they do not shine openly even though they would like to. Yet they are always ready to exchange the quiet of contemplation for the works of mercy as soon as they sense the call of Christ in their hearts."

At this time in Anthony's life the call was clear, and it came with the approval of his superior—as well as Francis: he was to preach and to study theology in order that he might speak with authority. Anthony's humility prevented him from revealing that he had already undergone ten years of theological training in one of Portugal's leading seminaries. Instead, he began his course in theology at St. Andrew's in Vercelli, which was supervised by one of Italy's leading doctors of theology, Abbot Thomas. Anthony took up residence in a nearby Franciscan convent and was joined by other erudite young men, one an Englishman called Adam de Marisco, who was later appointed bishop of Ely. Some of Anthony's teachers recorded their experience of him during this time. One remembered that when he was teaching the "celestial hierarchy," Anthony explained the different orders of celestial spirits "with great precision and wonderful intelligence; and it seemed to all who heard him as if he were in the very presence of that hierarchy."

Anthony, now a confirmed Franciscan, was concerned that he not fall back into the trap of learning and forget the real call of Francis for a life of poverty and service. He also knew that the Franciscan Rule clearly allowed for preaching but in a special way. The Rule said, "All the brothers should preach by their deeds." In an effort for clarification, he wrote to Francis for advice. Francis's reply read,

> To dear Brother Anthony, my bishop, Brother Francis sends greeting in the Lord: It is my wish that you teach the brethren sacred theology; yet in such a manner as not to extinguish in yourself and others the spirit of prayer and devotion, according to the prescribed Rule. The Lord spare you! Brother Francis.

Speaking in a language that was not his native tongue, Anthony began his extraordinary ministry as a renowned preacher and teacher. He preached throughout northern Italy—Padua (Padova, in Italian), Verona, Bergamo, Milan, and Rimini—and he preached with authority and love. This combination of abilities and virtues was what attracted people to him. As his reputation grew, so did his congregations, and because the churches couldn't hold the crowds who swarmed to hear him, he took to preaching outside in the piazzas and surrounding fields.

One of his major challenges in his ministry of preaching, and one he was more than suited for, was to speak on behalf of the Church with the breakaway religious factions that were growing in popularity throughout Europe, and particularly in France and northern Italy. These movements were numerous, but the most prominent were the Partorini, Cathari, Waldenses, and Albigenses. They were united in their attempts to revive Manichaeism—the beliefs of St. Augustine before his conversion to Christianity in Milan. They all believed that humans were so evil that it was impossible for them to be saved without God's singular intervention and that there was no redemption to be had beyond fate. This stance denied the freedom of human will and the humanity of Jesus, as well as the saving power of the resurrection. Manichaeans were naturally against papal and Church dogma, and this increased the threat to the Church's theological authority.

This opposing force found favor among the emerging middle class of the time, especially its artisans and trades people. One of them, Peter Waldo (the Waldenses were his official followers), was a wealthy merchant from Lyons, France, who followed gospel teachings exactly as instructed. He sold all his possessions and gave his money to the poor.

This shift of power from the Church to the ordinary people in following Christ allowed them to preach about their own experiences of the Gospel without yielding to what many believed was the corrupt authority of the clergy. This caused the Waldenses and other groups to verbally attack the Church, and the Church, in turn, responded with accusations of heresy.

Anthony was the perfect mediator. He had the courage and the ability to stand among the various factions as well as to build upon what Francis had begun—living according to the Gospel but within the institutional Church. Anthony's deeds were always as pure as his words. He could hardly be accused of hypocrisy, and, more importantly, his behavior reflected a loving understanding of others' beliefs. It was written of him that he always adapted himself to the circumstances and needs of his listeners. He himself wrote as part of his instructions to other Franciscan preachers, "The preacher must by word and example be a sun to those to whom he preaches. You are, says the Lord, the light of the world. The sun is the source of light and of warmth: a symbol of our life and our teaching—for like two streams these must overflow from us to others: our life must warm the hearts of people, while our teaching enlightens them."

There is a particularly moving story from *The Little Flowers of St. Francis* about Anthony's preaching trip to the Adriatic coast town of Rimini. At the time Rimini was home to many of the alternative Christian movements, and Anthony's preaching fell on deaf ears. So he went to the mouth of the river at the place where it ran into the sea and began to preach to the fishes instead.

> No sooner had he uttered these words than a great shoal of fish approached the shore, large, small, and medium in size, so that such vast numbers had never been seen in the sea or river before. And they all raised their heads from the water and remained attentive, completely still, tame, and orderly; for the smaller fish remained in front close to the shore, the medium-sized fish lay beyond them, and the larger fish lay further out where the water was deeper. And when all the fish were thus disposed in their species and order, St. Anthony solemnly began to preach to them.

His sermon continued with a blessing of the fish and an acknowledgement of them as one of the few species to have survived God's great flood upon the earth. He spoke of their composition, how the fins that God had given them enabled them to swim wherever they willed; the fact that one of them had housed Jonah for three days; and also that they had been food for "the Eternal King, Jesus Christ, both before and after His Resurrection....Because of these things," *The Little Flowers* quoted him as saying, "you are under a deep obligation to praise and bless God, who has given you blessings above other creatures." Evidently at these words the fish opened their mouths and bowed their heads and offered other signs of reverence to give thanks to their creator. Anthony then blessed the fish again, this time in gratitude for their attention and continued to preach to them as they all stayed in their positions in the water. Some of the townsfolk came to the shore to witness this miracle and were so touched by what they saw, as well as what they heard, that many converted to Catholicism.

While he was traveling (always on foot accompanied by a brother or two) to preach in nearby towns, Anthony also began, at Francis's insistence, to teach elements of theology to the Franciscan brothers. This he primarily did at Bologna, which was already a famous school, one of the original universities in Europe. Anthony became the first professor, then called lector, of the Franciscan Order. It was vital for the friars who were on the road preaching to know enough sacred scripture to be able to stand up to the scrutiny of the alternative movement's religious; many of them were erudite and well versed in the Bible.

After two years of Anthony's preaching and teaching and bringing people back to the Church, his superiors requested him to go to France where the Cathari and Albigensians had gained more power and influence. His three years in France (1224–27) were spent mostly in the areas of Montepellier, Toulouse, and Limoges. He traveled everywhere on foot, taking no possessions and accepting hospitality as he went. He also founded a friary at Brive.

In 1227 Anthony, now in his early thirties, returned to northern Italy, having been appointed the Franciscan provincial for Romagna, and took up residence in Padua. Many feuding families and political groups there, such as the Guelfs and Ghibellines, were caught in interminable disputes and bloodshed and presented him with an enormous challenge. As was usual with him, he met it with a compassionate heart and a vital intellect. He performed most of his major miracles during his time in Padua, bringing peace to many feuds, his zeal for bringing lost souls back to God his primary purpose. His preaching was as popular as ever—merchants were known to close their shops and leave their market stands to hear him. As a confessor, he imposed penances on those requesting it, and they felt the impact of his intercession. He had many willing helpers among the Franciscans, but the burden of this large territory fell mostly on his own shoulders. It is said that he assumed this responsibility with patience, endurance, calm judgment, and wise and deliberate action. His time was selflessly devoted to his duties all day and night, whether it was preparing for and giving a sermon, sitting all day in the confessional bestowing the mercy of God, or administering to the sick and dying. Anthony also taught theology at the university, second only to Bologna in fame and reputation in Italy at the time. He loved the people, and they loved him.

With all this outward activity, Anthony needed time for contemplation, and toward the end of his life this became, as in earlier years, a necessity. During his travels (especially to and from Assisi), he was given cells and grottos by the Franciscan brothers to dwell in, to pray, and to be silent, and many of these are preserved today, especially at Francis's holy mountain, La Verna, and at the lesser known hermitage near Sansepolcro, Montecasale. Anthony wrote, "The taste of God in contemplation is more precious than everything else; for no matter what a man might wish for, it is nothing when compared to this."

In the meantime in Padua, his influence continued to cause waves of conversions to the Church, which Anthony said had no effect unless each person sought reconciliation with God and practiced it with one's neighbor. The Paduans began to experience the effect of Anthony's three years with them, and the city carried a hue of peace and genuine goodness. His presence was like a channel of God's grace, as he healed the brokenness of people's lives. One key area in which he brought mercy and relief was to those in debt, accusing the usurers of the day for their harsh and hardened hearts, and persuading the town's courts to abolish imprisonment for debtors. The statute of this law, dated March 15, 1231, is housed in the Biblioteca at the basilica in Padua, where there are files of documents and papers written and published since then, on Anthony's influence on the cause of human rights and his contribution to the foundational laws of bankruptcy and freedom of will.

In 1230, due to poor health (he might have suffered from diabetes), Anthony resigned as provincial of Romagna at the General Chapter in Assisi. Since Francis's death four years earlier, there were rival opinions on the future direction of the order, some wanting to maintain the spiritual influence of Francis, and others, led by Brother Elias, proposing a more traditional institutional approach. Anthony suggested a middle ground between the two so that the Franciscans could grow in an orderly fashion and yet still be faithful to the life and legacy of its founder. Anthony was assigned the role of leading a delegation to consult the pope (Gregory IX at the time) in Rome. As a result of his intervention, the papal bull of September 28, 1230, was published, which maintained poverty as central to Franciscan life.

In 1231 Anthony became more frail and felt the need for solitude. He went to the country (about twelve miles north of Padua), to a place called Camposampiero, which had been given to him by Count Tiso. There he had a hut built in a nut tree on the property and moved into it. Legend tells us that Count Tiso was walking one evening by the tree and saw a light shining from the hut. Curious, he peeped in and saw the child Jesus playing in Anthony's arms. Anthony made the count swear not to tell anyone about this, but Count Tiso revealed all after Anthony's death, and this is why he is often depicted with the Christ Child in his arms. Anthony's sojourn in the nut tree lasted only a few weeks because when he knew that he was going to die, he asked his brothers to take him back to his beloved Padua. The brothers borrowed a cart to transport him, but he was so weak that he didn't make it to the city and died outside its walls in a convent of Poor Clares in Arcella, which he had founded during his time in Padua. His last words were "I see my Lord," and his eyes lit up.

The children of Padua announced his parting. The Franciscans wanted to keep Anthony's death quiet while they decided who was to have his body for burial. The sisters sorely wanted to keep him within the confines of the convent, while the brothers wanted to bring him back to the center of the city. The latter were granted their wishes. But it was the children who miraculously ran through the streets of Padua shouting, "The saint is dead, the saint is dead!"

Armed guards were brought in to protect Anthony's body, which lay in a marble sarcophagus supported by four columns in the Church of Santa Maria Maggiore while all the people of Padua came to pay their respects. The miracles began occurring almost immediately at his tomb: the blind saw, the lame walked, the deaf heard, and the sick were healed. The crowd of mourners was so huge that even those who could not enter the church were healed outside as if they had been touching his tomb.

Anthony was canonized a year after his death (his mother and his sister were present at the ceremony in Spoleto), and thirty years later, St. Bonaventure, then minister general of the Franciscan Order, gave permission for a new church to be built in St. Anthony's honor. When they moved the remains of his body to this new church, they discovered a naturally corrupted skeleton, but with the tissue of his tongue still intact, a sign they took of his saintly preaching.

It seemed as if St. Anthony of Padua had hardly left the people since he interceded for them in a such remarkable capacity after death. To this day, devotion to St. Anthony is as alive as ever, and he has gained a reputation for being a "wonder worker" to those who call on his intercession. He is the patron of finding lost objects and for saving those in peril, especially at sea. He is acknowledged by the Catholic Church as the "Saint of the World." Because of his miracles, big or small, no one who has experienced his answer to their prayers for help would dispute his very real presence in their lives.

Many of St. Anthony's miracles were actions of "life-giving" love. The following are a few of the more famous miracles that occurred during his lifetime. Those after his life are so numerous that it would be impossible to chronicle them.

In 1228 St. Anthony was asked to Rome to preach to the papal curia and the throngs of pilgrims. People from various ethnic backgrounds were in attendance—Greeks, French, Germans, Slavs, and English—and they each heard Anthony's sermon in their own language.

Another reported miracle was of bi-location, that is, St. Anthony being in two places at the same time. One instance was when he was preaching in France at the Cathedral of Montpellier on Easter Sunday and had forgotten that he had promised to sing High Mass the same day in a convent chapel nearby. While in the pulpit in the cathedral, St. Anthony covered his head with the hood of his habit and sank back in a seat. The congregation waited patiently for a long while before St. Anthony delivered his eloquent sermon. While visible to the cathedral congregation at Montpellier,

St. Anthony had in fact sung his office and performed his duties simultaneously at the neighboring convent.

Another occasion of bi-location had much more dramatic circumstances. In Lisbon, St. Anthony's father had been wrongly accused of murder after a dead man was found in his garden. St. Anthony received permission to travel to Portugal to defend his innocent father, so he set off on foot on what was to be an arduous journey of a few weeks. In defending his father at his trial, he requested the judge to open the dead man's coffin in order to confirm his father's innocence. The dead man momentarily came back to life to tell the truth of the real murderer, and after begging St. Anthony for absolution for his own sins, which he received, he sank back dead into his coffin. When Anthony reappeared in Padua, he had been absent for only two nights.

CHRONOLOGY

1195	Born August 15th in Lisbon, Portugal, as Fernando de Bouillon
1201–10	Attends the Cathedral School.
1210	Joins the Augustinian Order at the cloister of Sao Vicente de Fora in Lisbon.
1212	Changes residence to the Priory of Santa Cruz, Coimbra.
1220	Enters the Franciscan Order. Goes to Morocco.
1221	Arrives in Sicily. Attends the General Chapter in Assisi. Takes up residence in the hermitage of Montepaolo.
1222	Attends ordination of Franciscan and Dominican brothers in Forlì. First public sermon. Begins preaching. Receives appointment in northern Italy.
1223–24	Studies at Vercelli, becomes Professor of Theology in Bologna.
1224–27	Spends time in France in Montpellier, Toulouse, and Limoges.
1227	Elected Provincial of Romagna Province.
1228	Stays in Milan and Vercelli.
1229–31	Preaches in Romagna, teaches in Padua.

1230	Resigns as provincial. Participates in the Franciscan delegation to Pope Gregory IX to define the Rule. Writes Feast Day sermons.
1231	Dies on June 13 in Arcella.
1232	Canonized in Spoleto on May 30.
1263	Transfer of relics to new basilica in Padua.
1949	Made a Doctor of the Church with the title "Doctor of the Gospel."

OFFICIAL FEAST DAY: June 13

Spiritual Essentials

St. Anthony's spiritual teachings are very much based on Franciscan ideals. St. Francis took these directly from the Gospels, through the examples and teachings of Jesus Christ. What was vital was that humility, patience, willingness, and perfect surrender to the will of God be part of everyday life.

THE MIDDLE WAY

St. Anthony wrote that we cannot escape the world, that we cannot live "remote from the tumult of cities to keep oneself unspotted from their vices." The only way was the middle way between contemplation and action, between mystical prayer and deed, always dwelling on the rock that is Christ:

> Establish yourself in Him. Let Him be the constant theme of your thoughts, the object of your affections. Jacob reposed upon a stone in the wilderness; and while he slept he saw the heavens opened, and conversed with angels, receiving a blessing from the Lord. Thus will it be with those who place their entire trust in Jesus Christ. They will be favored with heavenly visions; they will live in the company of angels; they will be blessed as Jacob was.

THE COMPANY OF ANGELS

St. Anthony himself enjoyed the company of angels, which made his soul of an advanced order. He was often referred to as being "not of this world." By living on the rock, in the love of Christ, he was able to perform miracles that Christ had foretold any of his apostles could do with the grace of his spirit—speak in tongues, heal the sick, raise the dead. Miracles are understood as marvels that cannot be explained by our known laws of nature. For St. Anthony, they were not precipitated out of any will of his; but dwelling in Christ, he let Christ do through his own actions what came from his heart.

THE SECRET OF THE HEART

St. Anthony wrote that the secret of the heart is as a veil that hangs between ourselves and our neighbors, a veil that only God looks behind. "For Jesus alone is our High-priest. All hearts are open to Him and He sees everything despite that veil, for he searches the heart and its deepest thoughts." St. Anthony's further teaching is that when we have grasped in our hearts what is good, "we must show outwardly also in our good deeds; and what we have tasted of God in meditation must be reflected in our love for neighbor. So must our countenance shine as the sun."

He also advised that no matter how burdensome life becomes, nothing is impossible, and everything becomes sweet and easy and can be put into practice if we are motivated by love.

PEACE AND RECONCILIATION

"You ought to have external peace with your neighbor, internal peace within yourself, and eternal peace with God in heaven."

"Let us ask Jesus Christ to fill us with His mercy, so that we may practice compassion with ourselves and others, not judging nor condemning, but forgiving those who hurt us and helping those in need."

TO KNOW AND TO LOVE

St. Anthony taught that we need to know ourselves, we need to know God, and we need to know as much as we can about God's ways. Then we will find that love is where God is, love is where we give out of our faith. Anthony asks us to know, to study, to believe, to learn, but also to act, to move into action out of these beliefs, and to live them fully.

A Prayer by St. Anthony of Padua

O light of the world, infinite God of eternity,
Giver of wisdom and knowledge,
And ineffable dispenser of every spiritual grace,
Who knows all things before they are made,
Who makes the darkness and the light,
Put forth Your hand and touch my mouth,
And make it as a clear bell to utter eloquently Your words.
Make my tongue, O Lord, as a chosen arrow,
To faithfully declare Your wonders.
Put Your spirit in my heart
That I may perceive:
In my soul
That I may retain:
And in my conscience
That I may meditate.
Do this lovingly, holily, mercifully.
Gently inspire me with Your grace.
Teach, guide, and strengthen
The comings in and goings out of my senses
and my thoughts.
Let your discipline instruct me even to the end,
And the counsel of the Most High help me
Through Your infinite wisdom and mercy. Amen.

The Pilgrimage

Destinations:

Montepaolo, Forlì, Camposampiero, Arcella, and Padua

Suggested length:

Two days

This pilgrimage is recommended as a short northbound extension to the pilgrimage of St. Francis, which ends at La Verna in Pieve Santo Stefano, Tuscany. The drive from Pieve Santo Stefano to Montepaolo takes about two hours.

DAY ONE: Montepaolo and Forlì

From the south:

From Pieve S. Stefano, take the E45 exit at "S. Piero in Bagno." Follow signs for S. Sofia or S. Sofia/Forlì on the SS310. From S. Sofia, follow signs to Forlì and when in Galeata, turn left in the middle of the town onto a cobbled narrow street. IGNORE the sign for Forlì here, but follow signs for Firenze, Predappio, Rocca, and S. Zeno. Turn left outside the town and follow S. Zeno sign on the SP 24. In S. Zeno, again IGNORE signs for Forlì at the junction but follow signs for Rocca S. Casciano and any other signs to Rocca on SP 23. When in Rocca, NOW FOLLOW signs to Forlì, taking the SS67 to Dovadola. On exiting Dovadola, watch for the sign to Montepaolo almost immediately to the left on a steep incline. Take the road up the hill to a small church and hermitage sanctuary of S. Antonio, Montepaolo, at the top.

From other directions:

Head for Forlì and take the SS310 marked to S. Sofia and Galeata and look for signs as instructed above on the SS67 outside Dovadola.

Montepaolo

Montepaolo is the name of both the mountain and its hermitage where St. Anthony spent two years in a community when he settled in Italy. No trace of the original building exists. Although some stones were used in the erection of later structures, these buildings were damaged and rebuilt over the years.

Franciscan friars still live and work here, together with the Sisters Minor of Mary Immaculate, and it is possible to stay on retreat. *For reservations, telephone 0543–934723, or e-mail montepaolo@office.it.*

The Oratory

The old oratory was built in 1629 by a man called Paganelli in gratitude for a miraculous recovery from illness through praying to St. Anthony. An earthquake in 1905 destroyed much of it and the present oratory was rebuilt in the last century by the friars.

Recently renovated inside, there's a new mosaic altar to St. Anthony with a sacred relic (probably a piece of bone). On the opposite wall is a painted scene of St. Anthony preaching to his fellow brothers in France when St. Francis miraculously appeared to them. The main altar has the Madonna and Child leaning toward St. Anthony with St. Francis kneeling to their right. Over the altar and also in the front of the church is a stained-glass window that depicts the lilies St. Anthony is usually portrayed holding, which are a sign of spiritual purity. This could be the place to offer your intention and prayer.

Grotta (Grotto)

The path to the grotto is left of the oratory. The grotto is where St. Anthony spent a year in solitary prayer in a cell here. On the path are shrines of scenes from his life.

The Walkway

The mosaics on the way to the cell depict the friars' life at Montepaolo.

Forlì

Take the SS67 to Forlì and follow signs for "Centro." Metered parking is easy to find on the side streets. Walk to Piazza Aurelio Saffi.

Basilica Romanica di S. Mercuriale (Basilica of St. Mercuriale)

This ancient church with its tall steeple was built in the late twelfth century. Much of it is still intact—for example, the original wood ceiling is unchanged. This was where St. Anthony was present at the ordination of the Franciscan and Dominican friars and where, at dinner in the rectory, he was first asked to preach. At the back of the church is a statue of St. Anthony sharing bread with a young child.

Other Forlì Sites

Il Duomo di S. Croce (The Cathedral of the Holy Cross) is on the Via delle Torri, which is opposite the San Mercuriale on the other side of the Piazza Aurelio Saffi. This street runs into Piazza Ordelaffi. Like many Italian cathedrals, this one was rebuilt on the site of a previous edifice, which was destroyed by fire.

Being in Forlì would not be complete without a visit to the **Basilica S. Pellegrino (Basilica of St. Peregrine).** *From the Chiesa del Soffracio on the Piazza Aurelio Saffi take the Corso della Repubblica. Turn right on Via Biondo Flavio to a piazza with a statue of Morgagni. Behind this is the Church of St. Peregrine.*

ST. PEREGRINE, PATRON OF FORLÌ AND SAINT FOR CANCER SUFFERERS AND THE SERIOUSLY SICK

Born in Forlì in 1265 (thirty years after the death of St. Anthony), Pellegrino Laziosi was a proud and confident teenager when a priest called Father Philip Benizi came to visit the town. Because of their antipapal sentiments, all of Forlì's citizens had been collectively excommunicated by the pope. Father Philip was the prior general of the Servite Order of friars in Florence who, on visiting the local Servite monastery in Forlì, offered to mediate in the ongoing dispute. Young Peregrine was one of the belligerent hecklers and became violent, punching the priest in the face. It wasn't long thereafter that Peregrine felt remorse for such an action and sought forgiveness from Father Philip. Peregrine developed an interest in the Servite Order and joined it as a lay brother when he was about thirty years old. He served his novitiate in Siena, then returned to his native Forlì where he lived the rest of his long life in the monastery attached to the church (the plaque on its wall verifies the fact). As a monk, Peregrine's main ministry was to serve the poor and the sick of the town. Even with no medical expertise, he became the man the sick wanted by their bedsides, the compassionate peaceful messenger who brought the dying closer to God.

Brother Peregrine, however, was not without his own afflictions, one of them being varicose veins in his legs. Later in life his condition worsened, and he suffered ulcers and gangrene (which could have been cancer) in one of his legs. The solution at the time was amputation, so after consulting with the friars, Peregrine decided to undergo this radical operation. As the only anesthesia at the time was opium, it was common to die during surgery. Worried and in pain, Peregrine found it hard to sleep the night before his operation. He dragged himself out of bed and into the monastery chapter room and lay on the floor in front of its crucifix. He fell into an altered state and had a vision of Christ coming down from the cross and being with him. The following morning, the surgeon arrived with his bag of instruments, and was astonished to discover Peregrine's leg completely healed with no sign of tumors or gangrene.

Peregrine died in 1345 at the grand age of eighty, and people were miraculously healed when visiting his coffin. He was canonized in 1726 at the same time as the great Spanish mystic St. John of the Cross, and his feast day is May 4. Veneration of St. Peregrine and prayers for his intercession for those with cancer or leg problems can be said (and a candle can be lit) in the chapel to the inside right of the church. There his uncorrupted body, dressed in the Servite habit, rests in a glass sarcophagus and can easily be viewed. The Chapter Room (left of the main altar through a corridor and what must have been the original cloister of the monastery) is where Peregrine received his healing.

A Prayer to St. Peregrine

O Lord Jesus,
who liberated us by sacrificing your life for love,
enduring in your heart and your body
all of the suffering of humanity,
fortify our faith so that we can be united with you in God.
By the intercession of St. Peregrine
that you most miraculously cured,
free [add the name of person]
from sickness and suffering
so that [we/they] can love you and serve you forever.
Amen

For the remainder of this pilgrimage, drive north toward Padova (Padua) either up the coast road via Chioggia or via Ferrara. Avoid the coast road in the summer months due to heavy beach traffic.

DAY TWO: Camposampiero, Arcella, and Basilica of St. Anthony

The suggested itinerary for this final day follows the chronological sequence of the last weeks of St. Anthony's life.

Drive north of Padua on the SS307, following the signs for Castelfranco and Camposampiero. Camposampiero is about 10 kilometers from the turn-off. Follow signs to Santuario Sant'Antonio.

Santuario Sant'Antonio

This Franciscan monastery is built over the original small hermitage that St. Anthony established. It is here that he spent the last month of his life, living in a hut created for him in a nut tree. The stone rendition of his being carried in a cart to Padua (accompanied by his brothers) is in the parking lot. The narrow avenue leads to the Chapel of the Nut Tree (erected at the place of St. Anthony's tree home where Count Tiso saw him with the Child Jesus). This special place is cared for by Franciscan cloistered sisters. If the gates are closed, ring the bell of their convent to gain entry.

Santuario Antoniano dell'Arcella

Take the SS307 south to the outskirts of Padua where it becomes Via T. Aspetti. Before the Piazzale della Stazione, turn left at the sign for "Il Santuario Antoniano dell'Arcella" to the modern church, designed and built in the early part of the twentieth century.

The church site was originally a Franciscan monastery founded by St. Anthony to house the Poor Clares (Franciscan nuns), with a few Friars Minor to take care of them. This is where St. Anthony died, unable to reach his own hermitage in the center of Padua, and where there was a major dispute between the nuns and monks of the order to claim his body's final resting place. The old monastery was destroyed in a siege, and a church was built in the seventeenth century at the request of the Paduan citizens. In the mid-nineteenth century it was reconstructed into a neoclassical design before the present church was built. During World War II, 90 percent of the Arcella area was destroyed by bombs but, as is usual with the miracles of St. Anthony, the present church remained standing and intact.

What has also survived is the original cell in which St. Anthony died. It now forms the center altar and is called the cell of transition, **La Cella del Transito**. This simple cell is a devotional masterpiece. It depicts St. Anthony at his death (the sculpture was by one of Canova's pupils), and the ironwork surrounding the cell is designed of the famous lilies, with tongues of fire forming the decoratives. There is a side altar depicting the most famous Franciscans—St. Francis, St. Anthony, and St. Bonaventure—and some later Franciscan saints—the Holocaust martyr St. Maximilian Kolbe and, more recently, St. Pio of Pietrelcina (commonly known as Padre Pio). St. Pius X can also be seen here, surrounded by first communicants. In the Chapel of St. Francis lies the uncorrupted body of Blessed Elena, a Poor Clare sister who lived in the Arcella monastery for a few months after St. Anthony's death. It is claimed that he was her teacher and she led a holy life. The road outside is named after her.

Basilica Sant'Antonio (St. Anthony's Basilica), Padua

Return to Padua and to the Piazza del Santo in the center of the walled town. Here the magnificent basilica to St. Anthony stands on the site of his original friary and the first basilica consecrated by St. Bonaventure. The present basilica (built in 1745) is one of the most famous churches in the history of Christendom and has been a vital place for pilgrimage for centuries. The peace, artistry, love, and respect for one of the world's most famous saints can be clearly seen in this multidomed temple in memory of a man from eight hundred years ago, who is buried within its walls and whose spirit is as alive today as ever.

There's a tradition of writing prayers, and prepared pamphlets are available at the door, for offering at St. Anthony's tomb. Another tradition is to place your hand against the wall of his tomb and lay your head against it in prayer.

The chapel beyond St. Anthony's tomb on the left of the church is dedicated to his close colleague and friend **Luke Belludi,** who is buried beneath its altar. Brother Luke guarded St. Anthony throughout his life and was also recognized as a holy man and excellent preacher in his own right.

The **chapel of the reliquaries** is worth a visit at the curve of the nave. In the first glass exhibit are the cover and seals of the original box where the relics were housed, and the box itself. Pieces of St. Anthony's rope cord from his habit and other sacred objects (e.g., cloths, chalices, and missals) used at the friary during his time are also exhibited. The medallions around his tomb are gifts for miracles granted. In the lower display case are the remains of his last Franciscan tunic. His lower teeth, tongue, and vocal chords (which are uncorrupted by time) can be viewed in the center display case, and beyond it are the drapes that were used over his coffin.

In the sacristy is a unique painting of St. Francis over the doorway, and to the left of it is a fresco of St. Anthony preaching to the fishes at Rimini.

In the cloister there's the **Musei Antoniani** with art and precious statues of St. Anthony, but the most intriguing display is the **Mostra Antoniano della devozione popolare (The Display of Popular Devotion).** From as far back as 1855 and as far away as China, the heartfelt objects on display are all gifts to St. Anthony for "PGR" (in gratitude for prayers received and granted). The exhibit is organized by individual themes—for example, transportation (being saved from accidents involving machinery, cars, trucks, trains, etc.); relationships (married couples and family); other accidents (being saved from falls, near drownings, fire). When sick children are being prayed for, it is traditional to dress them in mini-Franciscan habits while praying for the saint's intercession.

When prayers are granted, the little brown habits are given to the church. Young girls give their hair.

On exiting the church there is a large picture of St. Anthony in his nut tree over the door, a reminder that he is never far away from a pilgrim's heart and desire.

ART & SOUL: PADUA

Scuola del Santo (School of the Saint)

In the piazza in front of St. Anthony's Basilica is the school where St. Anthony taught. Today it houses paintings of him by such well-known masters as Titian.

Cappella degli Scrovegni

This chapel is packed full of frescoes by Giotto. Enrico Scrovegni was a rich banker from Padua who erected this private chapel dedicated to the Virgin of the Annunciation to expiate the sins of his father who had been found guilty of usury. Giotto decorated the walls and ceiling of the chapel between 1303 and 1305. Advance reservations are required to view it. The telephone number for the chapel is 049–200020.

STS. APOLLINARE & VITALE
Early Martyrs of Ravenna

The blood of the martyrs is the seed of the Church.
Tertullian, *Apologeticus*

Their Lives

ST. APOLLINARE

Apollinare was a contemporary of St. Peter and accompanied him from Antioch to Rome. He was consecrated bishop by St. Peter and sent to found a Christian community in Ravenna during the reign of Emperor Claudius (AD 41–54).

Apollinare's entry into the port of Ravenna (called Classe) was not received enthusiastically by its mostly pagan citizens. This did not sway Apollinare in carrying out his mission and establishing a church as he was instructed to do. During the time he lived in Ravenna, he performed many miracles, but he was continually harassed and was continually under suspicion. Arrested and sentenced, he was exiled to Corinth and Thrace, but was released after three years. He returned with renewed passion for his fledgling church community. He was arrested again, put on trial, and eventually killed. He was buried within his community, which had become one of the first episcopal sites in Italy. His tomb is now in the basilica bearing his name, as his remains were moved there in AD 549.

Apollinare's official feast day is July 23, the day of his death in the year 74. He has been honored and written about by subsequent bishops, one of whom was Peter Crisologo. In the fifth century Crisologo wrote, "The Confessor spilled his blood many times and with his wounds, and the faith of his soul, bore witness to his Lord. He sustained and nourished the Church throughout its fragile infancy and, as he wished, was kept alive. He lives, and just as the good shepherd stays with his flock, the spirit of he who came before us in body and in time will never leave us."

Devotion to St. Apollinare grew over the centuries. He is not only the patron saint of Ravenna but also of the Byzantine Age in the West. In the Ravenna mosaics, St. Apollinare is usually depicted as a Greek bishop, dressed in the vestments of a pallium and dalmatic. His image appears in cathedrals around Europe; for instance, there are a few scenes from his life in the Cathedral at Chartres in France. The best place to find him, however, is in his hometown and in his own basilica. Here he lives through glorious mosaics, a gray-bearded man in the company of the Church's early martyrs.

ST. VITALE

Vitale is usually portrayed in the mosaics as a young soldier (because of his intercession in defending Ravenna after his death), although what we know of him in life is that he was a servant of a rich man. Born in the fourth century, he worked for a prominent citizen from Bologna called Agricola. A confirmed Christian, Vitale was advised by many of his friends to denounce Christ, but he was firmly resolved in his faith, so much so that he was tortured and crucified in the presence of his employer. Agricola was so overcome by the faith and courage of Vitale that he, too, converted to Christianity and went to his death in the same way. Both men were buried in a Jewish cemetery, which has led historians to believe that they were Jewish because the capital punishment for a Roman citizen was decapitation, not crucifixion.

Vitale's feast day is April 28, and though considered a Roman martyr, he became particularly connected with Ravenna in the fifth century due to a noblewoman called Galla Placidia. Daughter of Theodosio the Great, Galla represented her imperial family and moved to Ravenna from Constantinople in AD 409. She lived there for twenty-five years, bringing with her peace and religious devotion. She gained permission from Ambrose, bishop of Milan, to have relics of St. Vitale's remains brought to Ravenna from their original burial place in Bologna. As a result, popular devotion to St. Vitale grew among the Ravenna townsfolk, who built the famous basilica that bears his name.

The Pilgrimage

Destination:
Ravenna
Suggested length:
One day

This visit to Ravenna is suggested not only to honor the early Christians, but also to celebrate the rich spiritual and artistic achievement of the human race. There are many places to visit in Ravenna, but the following should not be missed.

RAVENNA

Ravenna made an impact as a city as far back as the first century. Its perfect location was invaluable to the Romans—it had a seaport and was easily accessible from Rome. The Emperor Tiberius established naval bases here in AD 23, to be able to launch military campaigns and control the Adriatic. Later, under Emperor Claudius, the grand Porta Aurea was constructed in his honor. Also during Claudius's reign, Christianity came to Ravenna through the ministry of St. Apollinare. People arrived from the East and stayed in Ravenna, and many passed through on traditional trade routes.

From the beginning of the fifth century, Ravenna became the capital of the Western Roman Empire, establishing itself as a place of wisdom, law, dogma, art, and cultural interchange. Ravenna survived many wars and invasions and remained the intersection point between Byzantium and the West up to the seventh century.

Much more recently, in June 2002, this meeting of East and West was further enforced by the visit of Bartholomew I (ecumenical patriarch of Constantinople) who officiated at a divine liturgy in St. Apollinare in Classe. This signified closer ties between the Eastern Orthodox Church and the Holy See of Rome.

Basilica di S. Vitale (Basilica of St. Vitale)

Enter by the cloister to the main church.

This eight-sided, sixth-century church is designed in a geometric marriage of circle and square to represent the perfection of heaven. In the mosaics at the altar, St. Vitale stands in the center of the dome with Christ in the archway, accompanied by "fourteen apostles"; the two additions to the original twelve are probably St. Paul and St. Apollinare.

On the left side of the altar are details from the life of Abraham, and below them Emperor Justinian stands, his halo the symbol of imperial power as a divine bestowment. Around him are deacons and bishops. Opposite him on the other side is Empress Theodora with some of her women, wives of generals, and members of her court. She, as well as Justinian, brings gifts to the Church like the Magi did to the Christ Child in Bethlehem. The design patterns are from early Christian symbology; the dove represents the Holy Spirit, the peacock the resurrection.

The central dome in the church would have been painted much later than the mosaics, probably in the time of the Renaissance. All the hanging flower garlands look sculpted when, in fact, they are painted on the plaster.

Mausoleo di Galla Placidia (Galla Placidia's Mausoleum)

In the gardens behind the basilica there's another stunning example of devotional mosaics at the burial place of Galla Placidia and members of her family. St. Peter and St. Paul stand side by side in the archway. From the hill of heaven flow four rivers: one of them is the Mystic Lamb on the hill with the monogram of Constantine, the other with Galla Placidia's monogram; two doves at the fountain represent Christ as the living water, and the Holy Spirit in the doves.

Battistero (The Cathedral Baptistery)

In previous times, the as-yet unbaptized, who were called catechumens, would not be permitted to enter a church until after their baptism. Naked catechumens were submerged in baths of holy water, in memory of Christ's full-body baptism in the River Jordan. The baptistery is designed for this glorious entry into the Christian faith and the Church community, with four chapels in a circle around the baptismal font representing the four Gospels. The throne is the symbol of sovereignty. There is a prominent mosaic illustrating St. John the Baptist baptizing Christ, and the sculptures are of Old Testament prophets.

Battistero degli Ariani (The Arian Baptistery)

Situated beside the **Chiesa dello Spirito Santo (Church of the Holy Spirit)**, the Arian Baptistery was built by the Arian Gothic King Theodoric between the end of the fifth century and the beginning of the sixth. It later became Catholic.

Basilica di S. Apollinare Nuovo (New Basilica of St. Apollinare)

Erected by King Theodoric in the first half of the sixth century, this church was reconsecrated by Bishop Agnello in AD 561. The mosaics portray the different structures of religious hierarchy. On the left are women martyrs (including St. Cecilia and St. Agnes—see Rome, pages 302, 303). Holding their crowns of martyrdom and looking toward the altar, they bear gifts to the Christ Child along with the Magi. The exquisite Holy Mother is flanked by four angels. Around them are scenes from the Gospels, mostly healings and miracles: the woman at the well speaking with Christ, the hemorrhaging woman touching Christ's hem, the apostles casting their nets and catching fish, Lazarus being raised from the dead. All images are linked with the fire of the Holy Spirit. On the right are male martyrs (including St. Apollinare), with St. Martin nearest to Jesus who is represented as Messiah and Savior and flanked by four angels. The images depicted are of the passion of Jesus Christ. The image at the end of the right wall is of Emperor Theodoric's palace, again giving the impression that the secular kings have divine connections.

In St. Anthony's chapel to the left of the main altar, there is also a statue of St. Bonaventure with a book in his hand. St. Francis, St. Anthony, and other Franciscans are also represented in mosaics around the church.

ART & SOUL: RAVENNA

Dante Alighieri

Dante Alighieri (1265–1321) was the first poet to write in the Italian vernacular—independent of Latin used in prose and other formalities. Florentine by birth, he was exiled from that city for political reasons, under pain of death if he ever returned. He spent the rest of his life wandering Italy. During that time, he devoted himself to discovering, and composing in, the ideal Italian language, although he also wrote extensively in Latin. His best-known work is the *Divine Comedy,* an allegorical poem in which Dante is given a vision of hell, purgatory, and heaven. His writing has been ranked with that of Homer, Sophocles, and Shakespeare for both the virtue of his art and his influence.

In 1316, Dante found some peace in Ravenna, living here for a while, and he died here in 1321. The people of Ravenna claimed his body as theirs, even though the Florentines tried to have his remains returned to Florence. It wasn't until the fifteenth century that Dante received a special monument in Ravenna.

Sepolcro di Dante (Dante's Tomb)

Dante's present tomb, designed in a neoclassical style, was built in 1780. This small shrine was decorated with onyx only in the 1920s. The lamp hanging from the dome inside is filled with oil donated by the Dante Society in Florence, a tradition begun in the early twentieth century and continued to this day. To ensure against plunder and possible theft during World War II, Dante's actual remains were moved to an ivy-covered mound in the adjacent cemetery. Still intact today, the mound represents a more natural monument to Italy's founding poet.

Further Afield

The largest and earliest Christian basilica is that of **S. Apollinare in Classe (St. Apollinare in Classe).**

Take the SS12 for about 5 kilometers south toward Rimini along the coast.

ST. PIUS X
The Man in Between

"I was born poor, I have lived poor, and I wish to die poor."
Giuseppe Sarto, Canonized Pope

His Life

Giuseppe Sarto (Joseph Tailor, in English) was born, not into nobility or privilege, but into a peasant family on June 2, 1835, in Riese, Treviso, at the foothills of the Dolomites. He was the second son (the eldest, also called Giuseppe, died at birth) of Margherita Sanson and Giovanni Battista Sarto, who married when she was in her early twenties and he in his mid-forties. Giuseppe was closely followed by eight siblings, six girls and two boys, the last also dying in infancy. Like many poor farming families of the area, the Sartos did not own much, but rented a house, which brought with it two hectares of land and a cow. Margherita helped with the family income by working as a dressmaker, and as a woman of faith and example, she greatly influenced her eldest son. Giuseppe (or Bepi, for short) was also influenced by the local pastor, Don Tito Fusarini, whose sermons he loved. He received his elementary education from him, which involved some grammar and reading, at the local church school about two hundred yards from his home.

Father Tito noticed that Giuseppe was an intelligent and devout child, possibly a candidate for the priesthood, which required him to continue his education. This put Giuseppe in a quandary. He certainly wanted to further his education but he was also needed at home and in the fields to help his family, especially with his father being so much older. The local priest still continued to teach Giuseppe on the side, introducng him to Latin. Because young Giuseppe exemplified a love of learning, he was accepted in a college in Castelfranco, six kilometers from Riese. He made the journey to this college every day for three years by foot—literally without shoes! During his last year of attendance between 1849 and 1850, he went by a horse-drawn carriage that his father had managed to acquire.

Giuseppe was fifteen years old when he passed his examinations in his final year. He did so well that his results gained him automatic entry to the seminary. Whether to attend the seminary was another tough decision for Giuseppe, as it would cost his family money, which, naturally, they didn't have. However, through the intercession and recommendation of Don Tito, he was granted a place for free, an exception the Church sometimes made for outstanding students from poor families. He entered the seminary on November 13, 1850, and immediately made an impression on his teachers. They noticed his disciplined way of learning, his excellent memory, and his devotional faith. He was ordained a priest by Monsignor Farina, the bishop of Treviso, in Castelfranco in 1858.

All of Don Giuseppe Sarto's family and friends turned out for his first Mass at his local church, San Matteo (St. Matthew's) in Riese, the one he had attended as a young boy. The only missing member was his father, who died in 1852, the same year as Giuseppe's six-month-old baby brother. Bepi's priesthood brought not only joy to his family but also much prestige. A priest in a family always elevated it within the community.

Don Giuseppe's first pastoral duty was in the parish of Tombolo in the Treviso province, assisting the local priest who suffered from tuberculosis. Giuseppe liked this work and remained in the parish for nine years. He gained a reputation as a generous and dedicated leader within the community, and during his spare time he furthered his education through private study. Perhaps to give back what he had received as a child, he founded a school for the illiterate people in his area, and he also served the poor by providing financial assistance and food as the needs arose.

In the mid-nineteenth century, there were many disruptions to the tranquil, pastoral life in which Don Giuseppe had been brought up. Much of the turmoil was due to the changing political environment and to new technology, such as the electric telegraphic wire and the increasing use of the railway. The people of Italy were still reeling from the effects of the revolutionary war, which had been led by Garibaldi to establish an Italian state independent of the old ruling establishment of the papacy, emperors, and influential families. Giuseppe found himself living amid the struggle for peace and victory as troops continued to move up and down the country. The Veneto area, where the parish of Tombolo was located, had not been liberated, and the poor, still largely ignored in their needs, were pressed to give much of their meager earnings to the ruling parties.

One of Don Giuseppe's parishioners wrote of his popularity, "We have not missed our old priest at all—quite the contrary—this young chaplain amongst us is full of good sense, zeal, and other precious gifts that I learn a lot from him." Many of the unschooled from nearby towns and parishes would come to hear Don Giuseppe preach and teach.

In 1866, toward the end of Don Giuseppe's time at Tombolo, another war was waging for the liberation of the Veneto, and this time the people won. After the battle, Vittorio Emanuele II entered Padua victoriously and placed the tricolored Italian flag in the center of the town. The local clergy were largely supportive of this independent movement, and Don Giuseppe was asked to help establish a local civic administration by compiling lists of candidates.

In July 1867, the thirty-two-year-old priest was posted by the local bishop to a larger parish, Salzano, near Venice. He received a cold reception at first, but in his nine years of service there he gained a reputation for generosity and accessibility (never closing his parish house door), and for openly sharing the resources of the parish with everyone. During this period, the themes that would shape the early twentieth century were already revealing themselves: a cholera epidemic was taking its toll on families, while little education and few jobs for the poor resulted in a wave of emigration by farming families to America. There was growing fear of contamination by cholera, hostility at not being provided enough medicine, and protests about the economic conditions. In short, the atmosphere of the parish was anything but peaceful. Instead, it offered a challenge to local clergy who could not remain aloof to the needs of the people they served. This was the time when Giuseppe Sarto began to realize how to be a man "in between"—in between changing times, in between the responsibilities of the Church and the needs of the people, in between representing the poor in pastoral ministry without inciting civil demonstrations against the authorities for the prejudice they felt. This was Don Giuseppe's challenge while witnessing the struggles of a nation being born, as the passions of patriotism that create community on the one hand were also creating division and destruction on the other. And in between all this stood a Church forced to change as well.

In the summer of 1875, Bishop Zinelli, who had recognized Giuseppe Sarto as having special abilities far ahead of most of his contemporaries, asked him to teach at the seminary in Treviso. Four years later, Don Giuseppe was elected the canon of Treviso and after a further six years was appointed bishop in Mantova. During Bishop Sarto's first year in this new post, he began a period of reevangelization to strengthen the sacramental life the Church offered its congregation. There was increasing slackness toward devotion and discipline, mainly because of clerical haughtiness, the result being that many had turned against the Church. Strong feelings of anticlericalism took hold, especially outside the cities, where an aggressive socialism was taking root. A backlash of anarchy and violence struck society, including the old pillar of religion. The backlash even reached the villages, where the apathy among the rural priests prompted them to either abandon their communities completely or to simply turn a blind eye. Bishop Sarto recognized that, to break the clergy's apathy and to reinvigorate the people's sentiments, it was necessary to make faith relevant again, bringing it to the people without foregoing the very traditions the faith was built upon. He wrote in a letter, "Few people understand, other than superficially, the science of religion and fewer still practice it. Its laws have become so rigid and its teachers so distant that it is impossible to maintain the high integrity of Church law without accusing the Church of being too severe in its morality."

He set about his process of reevangelization with reform in mind, although many of his critics felt he was not going forward but backward. He first introduced basic instruction of the catechism (the core teachings of Catholic doctrine and faith), making it accessible in schools. He was given permission to design the curriculum, he invited preachers from his diocese, and he provided books. He advanced the necessity of devotional singing and resurrected the ancient Gregorian chant to imbue more traditional sacredness into the rituals of sacramental life.

Seven years later, Bishop Sarto was promoted to one of the highest positions in the Church, that of patriarch of Venice as well as to the college of cardinals. Pope Leo XIII said that Sarto's appointment to cardinal was because of the quality of the man himself. But things did not then become easy for Cardinal Sarto. On returning to Mantova, he was celebrated by some and parodied by others due to his traditional views. With his persistence—one of the qualities he had learned from his childhood—he eventually won over most of his critics.

In 1894 he returned home to Riese to bless his sick and dying mother, who had, during her lifetime, seen her Bepi become not only a priest, but bishop, and then cardinal.

It took some time for Cardinal Sarto to move from Mantova to Venice, due to political upheavals that were plaguing the city, including assassination attempts on counteranarchists, who stood for equal power between royalty and the papacy (their motto was "Long live the Cross, long live the King!"). During this particularly volatile time, Cardinal Sarto couldn't enter Venice to take up his position as patriarch unless the government gave him permission. The government first wanted a promise by the Church to create a mission that would set up Italian dioceses in colonies abroad. It was the government's way of using Church power outside

Italy to gain land strongholds for the Italian populace—an ambition that cast its shadow in future world wars.

There were many conflicts facing Cardinal Sarto in Venice, which were only heightened by the Church's weakening position with the monarchy and its colonial interests. The municipal authorities greeted his arrival with little enthusiasm, as he ended up immersing himself in much more than he wanted. Like it or not, the Church was inextricably entangled in the political arena. All the cardinal said at the time was that the objective of his mission was to reunite all things in Christ, referring to chapter one of Paul's Letter to the Ephesians; that through God's grace, God would act "when the times had run their course; that God would bring everything together under Christ, as head, everything in the heavens and everything on earth."

All of Giuseppe's familiar passions became part of his Venetian ministry. He revitalized the seminary, established a faculty of canon law, promoted catechism teaching in schools, and encouraged the regular use of Gregorian chant. He hired a young maestro to develop the musical agenda in the famous St. Mark's Church by the Grand Canal. And, as if it were a metaphor for all that he stood for, he began the reconstruction of the collapsed bell tower in the Piazza San Marco.

Even though he was now at the top of his ecclesiastical profession, Giuseppe Sarto did not lose touch with the places and devotions that lived in his heart and memory. One of these was the mountain of Monte Grappa, not far from Riese, which towered above the Veneto valley between Bassano and Treviso. There was already an established tradition of climbing the many pastoral paths to its summit—1,775 meters (5,823 feet) high—from as far back as the locals could remember. Monte Grappa was a challenge, especially in winter when it was wise to leave it alone, its icy peaks disappearing into the clouds. In 1899 Cardinal Sarto proposed for its summit a sacred monument to Mary, the Holy Mother, thus sanctifying the mountain. The statue of Mary was originally commissioned to be made by local artist Augusto

Zardo out of the red rock of the Grappa itself, but it became impossible to find the means of transporting its heavy weight. Instead, it was created in three parts in bronze and taken to Monte Grappa's summit by treacherous and narrow paths on the back of a mule. One month later in August, in the company of nearly six thousand people, the cardinal processed up the mountain to consecrate the monument. He, too, was transported by a mule (a photograph exists of him in the saddle wearing his cardinal's hat!). As the trip took two days, he stayed overnight in a primitive church house halfway up. Among the pilgrims was an eighteen-year-old young man called Angelo Roncalli. He was to follow Cardinal Sarto in more ways than either man could have imagined. Sixty years after their climb on Monte Grappa together, Angelo Roncalli became Pope John XXIII.

Looking through the eyes of history, one wonders whether Cardinal Sarto had a premonition of what was to happen on Monte Grappa. During half of the First World War, it became a battleground, the Italians defending their country against the invasion of the Austrians. Tens of thousands were killed on this mountain—men (young and old) digging trenches; blasting holes in the stones to make roads for armament transport; being chilled to the bone; sometimes having no food; sleeping in damp, overcrowded tunnels; becoming sick and dying of disease or being splintered into pieces by random bombshells. The summit of Monte Grappa is now a memorial and a burial site for these thousands of men, many of them unidentified.

After a papacy of twenty-five years, Pope Leo XIII died in Rome at the age of ninety-three on July 31, 1903. Sixty-two out of sixty-four of the Church's cardinals arrived for the conclave at the Vatican to begin voting for his successor. This was something that the Church usually had sole jurisdiction over, although it was common in the past for popes from the nobility to be elected through political maneuvers or pressure from emperors. This conclave became a turning point between the old ways and the unexpected new. At the end of the second day of voting, a Polish cardinal announced that the emperor was exercising his power to veto his choice of a popular Sicilian cardinal. This caused disruption among the rest of the cardinals, who resented the intrusion from an outsider, and the Sicilian cardinal himself declared his disdain at the threat to the Vatican's liberty. In the end, he lost his preferential place to a disbelieving Giuseppe Sarto, who burst into tears and asked to be forgiven for his nonacceptance, preferring, he said, to renounce his cardinalate and become a Capuchin friar. The archbishop of Milan, who was one of many who pressured him to accept the papacy, said to Giuseppe, "Return to Venice if you want, but you'll be full of remorse to the end of your days." Giuseppe took the name of Pius (Pio). He explained that all the previous nine pontiffs with this name had suffered much. He behaved like a robot during his investiture in his effort not to break down and cry.

Giuseppe's election was so much more significant than it seemed on the surface. Since St. Peter himself, and certainly since the Middle Ages, Pius X was the only pope who came from peasant stock. As the white skull cap was substituted for his red one in the ceremony that had not changed for centuries, Giuseppe broke tradition by putting his cardinal's cap in his pocket, instead of rendering it to the master-of-ceremonies. He also didn't nominate a seasoned cardinal as his secretary of state—or the Sicilian who had lost to him—but gave the honor to an unknown thirty-eight-year-old Italian of British origin called Merry del Val, whom Giuseppe had never met.

Giuseppe wished for a complete break with the old traditions; he wanted to be a pope of his time. He was certainly not interested in maintaining the Vatican's "ivory tower" mentality (which had isolated the papacy from the world), but wanted it to have a more global presence. While he first blessed the crowd in St. Peter's square, he was blessing the young Angelo Roncalli, then a seminarian in Rome, also from a northern Italian farming family, who would be so influenced by Pius X's reforms that he was to take the papacy even further into the modern world between 1958 and 1963.

For a man who did not want the position, Pius X began his papacy with a surprising surety of attitude. He desired to become international; he wished to develop missionaries and to bring Catholic ideas and ideals to social action. Even though the Church had established some social teachings, they had been politically blighted. Pius X wanted to transform the role of the pope from the regal model to a reconciler of differences. And he knew that the Church could not stand silent on secular issues.

Pius X reformed as best he could with a combination of intelligence and love. He immediately changed the way of papal living; instead of moving into the palatial state apartment, he took a few simple rooms on the third floor of the Vatican, which have since remained the pope's official residence. Pius X also refused to be vested, instead waking himself and washing and dressing himself. In the past, popes would always eat alone, but Pius X invited the company of secretaries and cardinals to his table.

Although criticized and dismissed for his harsh stand on modernity, Pius X still managed to stand "in between" the forces of change at a very dangerous intersection. It was certainly vital to relinquish the political stronghold of the Church, but at the same time it was also vital to prevent science or the political powers of nations from imposing their authority upon it. Pius X remained in touch with the poor and the needs of the people, which eventually opened the doors to the Church's greater involvement in the work of social justice.

Pius X's theological wisdom was composed of all that had been important to him as a young priest, a bishop, and a cardinal, and he continued to put it into practice during his papacy but on a much larger scale. He brought the sacraments out of the shroud of mystery and made them gifts of grace to the common person. He introduced the Eucharist as a daily sacrament available to all, and instituted first communion to children at the earlier age of seven years. On being complimented for being as good a navigator in Rome as he had been in Venice, he said, "Yes, but there's a difference between navigating a gondola and a battleship!"

Many people underestimated him, but he had a real strength of character and persisted with his work, "resolved and urgent" in everything he did. Where his associates would drag their feet, he plowed ahead and got on with the job at hand. One of his early international challenges was in France. With its growing anticlerical sympathies and its political extremes, with parties forming on the far left and far right, Pius X again claimed the middle way between the two as the best. He sacrificed ecclesiastical property for the sake of Church independence from state control, requesting the clergy and the people to materially sacrifice much in their lives for this purpose. He knew the French language well, but denied being able to speak it sufficiently, and referred to his "gross French" by saying, "Since I don't easily tolerate those who abuse language, I'm very careful not to follow their example." One French journalist called him "The Ardent Fire."

Even though much of what he did was not popular, he changed the world by changing the way the Church was in the world. He sent—and received—apostolic delegates from as far away as South and Central America, and closer to home throughout Europe and into Turkey. He established twenty-eight new dioceses in his eleven years as pope, most of them in the United States, Brazil, and the Philippines. The scope of this foundation contributed to the growth of the Church in territories that had been previously ignored. His idea of strength for the Church didn't come from the old way of exercising its power, but through its traditional capacity of bringing grace to the world. In retrospect, his papacy could be viewed as a turning point of realization in the modern world; the Church was already more diminished in its temporal power than it had ever been in history, but it gained instead a liberty, the freedom to grow and change and form into a more profound spiritual resource.

In his efforts to promote piety and purity of faith among the religious, Pius X formalized the use of Gregorian chant and classical polyphony in liturgy. He evidently had a good voice himself and often sang a cappella prayers with his secretary. He instituted many reforms to canon law, including suggesting the removal of priests involved in "grave circumstances." Violence, brutality, and vulgarity always weighed heavily on him, so he introduced censorship of some books and magazines in an effort to ensure purity of thought and opinion. Closer to home, he created an institute for biblical study in Rome, which he placed under the direction of the Jesuits, and he restored the picture gallery in the Vatican. With the advent of radio communication, he broadcasted a weekly Sunday discourse to the churches in Rome. Explaining the Gospel of the day, he'd then give examples on how to bring the catechism into the Gospels. And he did all this on his feet, standing in the studio as if he were in a pulpit, giving all his efforts to make religion more relevant to the time. He always spoke with clarity and simplicity in an animated, energetic way. He said, "We shouldn't infer from simplicity that this style of teaching is without life. We can't teach fruitfully without reflection."

His sisters would often visit him, and some moved to Rome to be nearer him. He kept a tradition of having caffe latte with them after Mass. As he grew older, he suffered leg problems and spent time slowly walking in the gardens of the Vatican, where he would also sit for long periods of reflection under its shady trees. He was known to be meticulous with money. He kept detailed accounts of expenditures, especially when calling on worldwide assistance for the victims of the earthquakes in Calabria and later for those around the erupted Vesuvius. All that was given to the Church through charity he dispersed with clear directions on where it was to be spent. He did likewise with assistance for other natural disasters in the world.

Toward the end of his life, the burden of world brutality weighed heavily on his heart. Europe in 1912 was like a tinderbox ready to burst into flames. He realized that his efforts for peace in Europe would not come to fruition. All he could do was counterbalance the fear that everyone felt with the hope that comes from faith. He was preoccupied with how these problems of the world were to be handled by his successors, believing the outbreak of war was looming on the horizon. In one of his sermons in 1914, three months before World War I began, he said, "The people as never before seek peace but nations are hostile towards them. With this intense hatred, we can see now more than before that war will consume us all." On another occasion he said, "There are solutions offered for peace but these will bear little fruit unless they also procure justice, and unless Christian charity profoundly takes root in the soul."

His last message, delivered on August 2, 1914, was a call to all Catholics to pray for Europe as it was being pulled into a vortex, the consequences of which were the waging of a megawar.

Mid-August of that year he became unwell. He developed bronchitis and a fever as well as heart problems and did not communicate much. When he did, he maintained his sense of humor. He remarked that with the war in Europe it wouldn't be easy for the cardinals to get to the conclave in Rome after his death.

On the morning of August 19, the pope's secretary noticed that Pius hadn't risen, so he entered the bedroom to find the pope's fever high and his breathing and heartbeat irregular. While still conscious, Pope Pius X received the last rites, all the while holding the hand of his secretary of state and clasping a crucifix. He died—some say of a broken heart over the coming war—in the early morning of August 20. He left no testament but a few requests for prayers for the Holy See, some suggested financial provision for his sisters and his chamber man, and a few thousand lire for his nephews. He had said, "I was born poor, I have lived poor, and I wish to die poor."

Due to the many miracles that occurred after his death, as well as the reforms he introduced during his lifetime, he was canonized by Pope Pius XII in 1954, significantly in the "in between" time of the Cold War. Pope John XXIII erected a tomb for St. Pius X in the Basilica of St. Peter and brought his remains up from the crypt. John's reason was that, as the first pope to come from poverty, Pius deserved a special place of honor among the noble classes on the upper floor. Before St. Pius X was finally laid to rest there, Pope John sent his body to Venice for veneration. This was to fulfill St. Pius X's promise to the people of that city when he left as a cardinal for the conclave in Rome, hardly aware of his future, that he would be back, "alive or dead."

CHRONOLOGY

1835	Born June 2 in Riese, Treviso.
1850	Enters the seminary.
1858	Ordained in Castelfranco.
1858–67	Priest in Tombolo.
1867–76	Priest at Salzano.
1875	Teaches in the seminary at Treviso.
1879	Appointed canon of Treviso.
1885	Made bishop in Mantova; begins reforms in ritual, singing, and school catechism.
1893	Nominated patriarch of Venice and made a cardinal by Pope Leo XIII.
1899	Makes a pilgrimage up Monte Grappa.
1903	Becomes Pope Pius X.
1914	Dies on August 20.
1954	Canonized a saint by Pope Pius XII.

OFFICIAL FEAST DAY: August 21

Spiritual Essentials

IN BETWEEN

St. Pius X felt that the old traditions should not be tossed aside or forgotten for the sake of contemporary sentiments, nor should the issues of the day be tossed aside for the sake of tradition. Instead, being "in between" the two is where the challenge for growth lies and where we must look for signs of the future. Thus, the middle path is the only path to walk during change.

PIOUSNESS

St. Pius X was a model of inner personal sanctity and outward leadership. He showed by his example how to be humble, clear, simple, and courageous. He felt that generosity and kindness to others were vital. One must always do one's best and act with perseverance, but to remember that rewards came in God's time.

EVERYDAY SACREDNESS

St. Pius X believed and taught that we need to be conscious of the sacredness of everyday faith, ritual, belonging, and community. Sacramental life has a scientific source that cannot be proved unless experienced with discipline and devotion.

A Pilgrim Prayer to St. Pius X

St. Pius, please listen to my intent,
And help me with your prayers
To more fully understand
The ways of God.
In our daily lives
We are tossed between old and new.
There is much that is constantly changing,
And I am lost to myself, and in myself, in my busyness.
Help me to stand back and reflect on what matters.
Speak to me with your wisdom and clarity.
You always did your best for God;
Guide me to my best with calmness and simplicity
On this pilgrimage in your memory,
And stay with me afterwards as helper and friend.
Amen.

The Pilgrimage

Destinations:
Riese, Monte Grappa, Asolo, and Treviso
Suggested length:
Two days

Take SS667 north from Castelfranco and turn left at Valla. Or from Bassano del Grappa or Montebelluna, drive south after the turn-off for Asolo.

DAY ONE: Riese, Monte Grappa, and Asolo

Begin the day in St. Pius X's hometown of Riese. At the crossroads of central Riese is a statue of St. Pius X in front of his childhood home, now a museum.

St. Pius X's Family Home

Days for visiting are Wednesday–Sundays only.

The house is very much the way it was in his time—the furniture is all original and the kitchen is particularly special. The ground-floor backroom has a picture of Giovanni Sarto in which his gaze follows every movement. Upstairs is the double bedroom where he was born, with mementos of miracles on the walls, along with photos of subsequent popes who made their own pilgrimage to the house. The pink bedroom was St. Pius's, and the bed is the one he slept in when he visited as a cardinal in 1894, his last time in the house. The crib in the room was made by him as a boy, probably for his brothers and sisters.

At the back of the house, in the field that was worked by his father, is a museum of artifacts from St. Pius's life, including a selection of his clothes and vestments, objects he used, as well as the saddle in which he rode on his way up

Monte Grappa. Also included are some of his shoes and his last stole. There is a chapel attached to the house.

Chiesa di S. Matteo (Church of St. Matthew)

Walk along the road in an easterly direction to the Church of San Matteo.

This was St. Pius's church, the place where he said his first Mass with all his family and friends. About one hundred yards further on is the elementary school he attended; it is still an elementary school, now named after his mother, and at its gates stands a monument to him. Inside the church, there is a picture of St. Pius over the altar offering blessings; a side altar is also dedicated to him. This would be the most appropriate place to offer the intention for your pilgrimage.

Monte Grappa

If you desire to make this part of the pilgrimage, be prepared for some walking and simple climbing. So wear suitable clothes and take provisions (although there's a restaurant at the summit).

Head north on the road toward Asolo. At the final junction take SS248 west toward Bassano del Grappa. At Piazza Onè, turn right toward Crespano del Grappa and follow the signs. At Crespano follow signs for Borso Bassano and then Borso to the right. Take the Via S. Pio X through Borso (the route he originally took). Turn right on the main road, and then almost immediately turn toward Semonzo. Follow signs for Campocroce, and keep on this road to the top of Monte Grappa. It takes about one hour by car, more if you walk. I suggest walking only the last part.

Fifteen minutes up the road there's a shrine in honor of Pope John XXIII, who, as a youth, accompanied St. Pius on his Monte Grappa pilgrimage. There's still a tradition among the locals of processing to the Madonna every year on the first Sunday of August to mark the anniversary of the erection and dedication of the chapel on the mountain's summit.

At Campocroce, there's a shrine (erected in 1959) at the small house where St. Pius X stayed the night while ascending Monte Grappa. In the chapel there's a mosaic of him on the altar, and on the side wall is a photograph of him on the mule with the crowd of pilgrims following him.

Just beyond this shrine there's a spot where you may park your car. Signed footpaths indicate where you can climb the rest of the way. Follow the red-and-white markings up through the meadows of the mountain. The walk is 2.3 kilometers in length. If you decide to drive, continue upward as the road curves in switchbacks through rock-strewn meadows.

At the summit *(la cima)* are the military memorials for the thousands of Italian and Austrian men who lost their lives on this mountain. After the 1918 Italian victory of the Battle of the Solstice, a military commander remarked, "Each soldier defending Monte Grappa felt every inch of the mountain was sacred to the country." The solitary monument erected by St. Pius X to the Madonna has been rebuilt since its damage in the war, and the original bronze statue now stands inside its circular structure. As a reminder of the polarities of light and darkness (life and death), there are the Stations of the Cross around the chapel walls. There is also a bust of St. Pius X.

Outside, on a clear day, you can see the vast plains of the Veneto stretched out for what seems like infinity, confirming why the Italian people have so much respect, love, and gratitude for their Monte Grappa.

Descend the mountain either by the way you came or by the northwest alternative route via Possagno del Grappa.

ART & SOUL: POSSAGNO AND ASOLO

The Temple of Canova

Possagno is the birthplace of the sculptor Antonio Canova (1757–1822), renowned for his neoclassical works. The temple, an imposing white circular building, was designed by Canova himself; it's where he had his studio and is now home for his tomb. Most of the works displayed are plaster copies of the originals except for his last sculpture, *Descent from the Cross.*

Asolo: A Poetic Interlude

This jewel of a town in the foothills of the Dolomites has no direct connection with St. Pius X except that he visited it as his neighboring hill town, wrapped around its pre-Roman *rocca* (the rock castle). Many poets have left their mark on Asolo. Robert Browning lived here for a time—the main street is named after him—and the Italian actress friend of Gabriele D'Annunzio, Eleanora Duse, also made Asolo her home and is buried in the cemetery of Sant'Anna. There are picturesque Palladio villas dotted around the landscape.

Take the SS248 east through Montebelluna, and then the SS348 to Treviso.

DAY TWO: Treviso

Treviso is an elegant city, full of walled villas, winding streets, and canals.

Chiesa San Nicolò (Church of St. Nicholas)

This church is on the outskirts of the main town (but within its walls) on Via San Nicolò between Porta Calvi and Piazza Vittoria. Attached to it is the seminary where St. Pius X taught. It is a seminary still to this day. The church belongs to the Dominicans and is one of the most architecturally breathtaking churches in Italy. It certainly would rank as having the highest ceiling. Built in 1303 by Pope Benedict XI to honor Nicolò Bocassino, a local Dominican (later canonized), the church features a roof shaped like the bottom of an overturned ship. Many churches are designed to be like ships on their way to heaven. Huge and simple, this one is packed full of art that is unique and different. There are frescoes the height of the church—for instance, the one of St. Christopher—and preserved frescoes still exist on its pillars. All the side altars are individual and special unto themselves, and there's a very old *pietà* on the upper side altar. A beautiful cloister (which was previously part of the monastery attached to the seminary) can be visited through an entrance in the side wall of the church.

Il Duomo (The Cathedral)

The final spot of the pilgrimage is at the cathedral, where St. Pius X would have spent many hours, especially as the canon of Treviso. On the right of the main altar, where a gilt crown hangs over the crucified Christ, is a simple altar dedicated to St. Pius X. Under the gold statue of him is the inscription "San Pio prega per noi": St. Pius, pray for us.

Venice and Rome

If visiting either of these cities, there are special places of significance to St. Pius X. In Venice, the Patriarchal Palace *(Il palazzo patriarcale)* is where St. Pius X resided when patriarch of Venice, and there is a bronze statue of him in St. Mark's Church (Chiesa San Marco) in the main piazza. The bell tower in St. Mark's square was restored through his instruction. There is also another statue of him in the Church of San Salvador.

In Rome, the tomb of Pius X is on the main floor of St. Peter's Basilica in the Vatican, and if you write ahead, you can receive permission to view the Vatican gardens where he used to walk, pray, and contemplate.

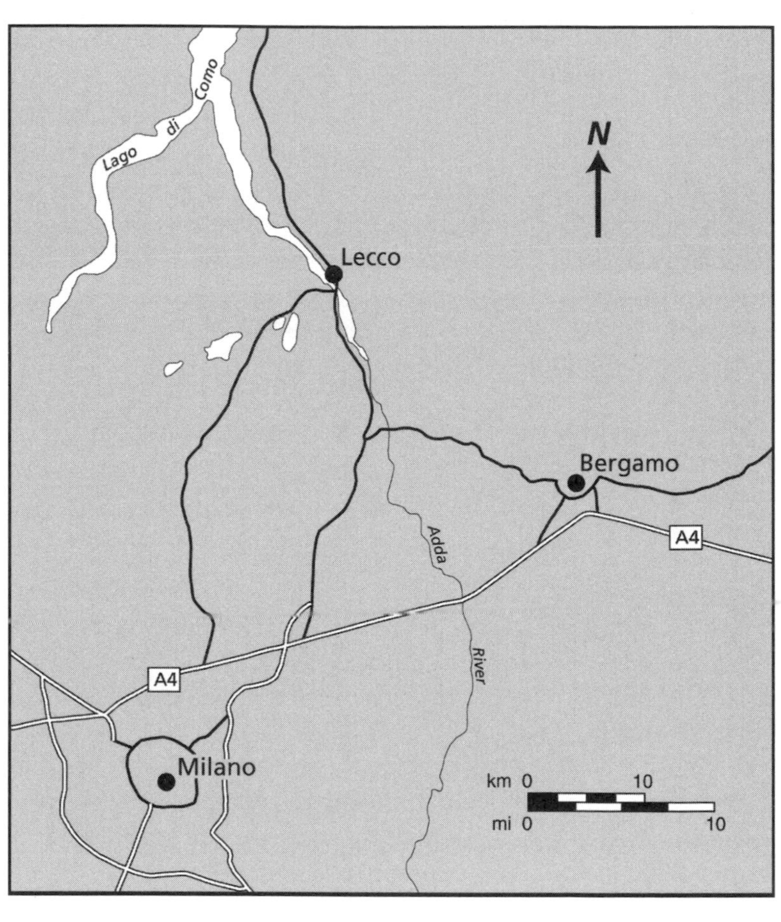
Lago di Como
N
Lecco
Bergamo
Adda River
A4
A4
Milano
km 0 10
mi 0 10

BLESSED JOHN XXIII
Hero of the Sacred Mountain

"We are not on earth as museum-keepers,
but to cultivate a flourishing garden of life and
to prepare a glorious future."
Angelo Roncalli, *Journal of a Soul*

His Life

This is a story of a man from a humble background who, through the force of his faith and reliance on God's will, became first a priest, then bishop, Vatican envoy and nuncio, cardinal, and finally pope. It is also a heroic story of a soul who was born into a farming family in a village outside Bergamo in northern Italy. Having learned to read and write, he kept a diary for sixty-seven years, which charted the intimate details of the joys, challenges, and struggles of his soul's growth. Because of this diary, and his generosity at willing it for publication after his death (to enable it to help people, he had said), he has opened up the course of his interior mystical life, spiritual purification, enlightenment, and final unity with God. One of his biographers, Peter Hebblethwaite, wrote that the end of the diary (now a book called *Journal of a Soul)* "crowns and explains the beginning."

This is also a story about a traditional priest who longed for simple service and chastised himself for his personal imperfections, who journeyed to faraway and exotic places to minister to those of diverse faiths, learning language upon language to be able to understand and serve the people, never knowing the reason until the end of his life. It is a miraculous story of how a soul thirsting for perfection, who began life "under the mountain" (the name of his village being *Sotto Il Monte*), pulled himself and all Christians up a spiritual mountain to view their lives of faith from a higher and different perspective. After three years of preparation for the Second Vatican Council, Pope John XXIII wrote that "we are now on the slopes of the sacred mountain." He reached the pinnacle by embracing the world like a great-grandfather, making everyone feel part of one family. But there is far more to "Good Pope John."

Angelo Giuseppe Roncalli was born on November 25, 1881, in his parents' bed in a peasant hamlet in Sotto Il Monte, a village of about twelve hundred inhabitants. His birth was cause for much rejoicing in the Roncalli household. His father, Giovanni, and his mother, Maria, were delighted to have a son, a brother for his three sisters, and a future helper on the land. As was the custom, he was baptized the same day at the local church. Called Santa Maria di Brusicco, it was about a hundred yards from the Roncalli home. His godfather was the patriarch of the Roncalli clan, Zio Zaverio—although he was only his great-uncle, being his deceased grandfather's brother. Zaverio was pious and well-read, and, without children of his own, took it on himself to become a second father to Angelo. In his diary, Angelo wrote, "Hardly had that good old man, my uncle Zaverio, presented me, a newborn babe, at the baptismal font, than he consecrated me there in the little church of my own village to the Sacred Heart, so that I should grow up under its protection, a good Christian."

The significance of his given names—and later the name he chose as pope—was always foremost in his mind. Angelo, meaning angel, was a compelling challenge; he once remarked that he felt under an obligation to always behave like one, when he knew, on the contrary, that he was "no angel at all." His second name, Giuseppe, meaning Joseph, was in honor of "the dear Patriarch" of the family of Jesus, and St. Joseph became his spiritual protector.

Angelo's earliest memory was when he was four years old. It was on the feast of Mary's Presentation in the Temple, November 1885. His pregnant mother had dragged all her young children on a short pilgrimage to the shrine of Madonna delle Caneve on the edge of the surrounding woods. When they arrived, the chapel was already full so they had to stand outside. Angelo remembered being lifted up by his mother so that he could see through the small window, and she said to him, "Look, Angelino, look how beautiful the Madonna is. I have consecrated you wholly to her."

Life for the Roncallis was not easy. Like most peasant families, they were professional sharecroppers, which meant that half the land's produce was shared with their landlords and the rest kept for feeding a family of up to twenty people at a time. Angelo remembered that his parents would also invite hungry strangers home, so there would sometimes be less food for the children. There was never bread on the table, only *polenta* (cornmeal), and he had only one pair of shoes to last all his childhood.

Angelo spent more time in church as an altar boy than he did in the village school, although he was the brightest pupil. Nurturing his young nephew's devotion and vocation, Uncle Zaverio arranged for Angelo to take Latin lessons with a priest from the next village. Although Angelo recalled it as a harrowing experience with beatings for grammatical errors, he came to passionately love Latin.

The local parish priest, who resided in Angelo's baptismal church, was Don Francesco Rebuzzini, a model of holiness exemplifying the perfect priest to young Angelo. What he noticed in Rebuzzini's ministry, which would become a teaching he would later cherish, was that he practiced holiness in virtual obscurity. Angelo called his parish priest "the saintly guardian of my childhood and vocation" because, after Angelo declared his intentions for the priesthood, Don Francesco prepared him for the entrance exams to the seminary in nearby Bergamo. Later, when Angelo came home for the holidays, he was about to serve at Mass when Don Francesco dropped dead in the sacristy. Angelo recalled it as the first great tragedy of his life; he wrote how heartbroken he was, and how looking at the seventy-three-year-old priest's body on the floor reminded him of a statue of the dead Jesus. Don Francesco had bequeathed his personal copy of the *Imitation of Christ* to Angelo, which he treasured all his life.

Bergamo was a bustling city that had been under Venetian rule for over three hundred years. At the time Angelo entered the junior seminary at the age of ten, it was undergoing modernization with railway links to nearby

Milan and Brescia, and with a growing industry in textile manufacturing. Angelo loved the city and embraced its historic and spiritual culture with vigor, but even more important for him was its link with St. Charles Borromeo, the sixteenth-century archbishop of Milan and founder of his seminary. Recognized by the Council of Trent as a "model bishop," Borromeo became an example for the young seminarian to follow. Angelo wrote in his diary that he would "try to make this great saint more and more familiar to my heart and mind, to pray to him frequently for his help and to imitate him." In fact, Angelo always felt called to imitate not only Borromeo but also other saints especially close to him. Among these were Francis de Sales, patron of writers and journalists; John Berchmans; Gregory Babarigo, who reformed the seminary after Borromeo and whom Angelo, when pope, canonized; Philip Neri; Ignatius of Loyola, founder of the Jesuits; and Catherine of Siena. Angelo often chided himself for not being more like them when they were his age. Yet, the lives and examples of the many saints he loved became, in fact, the link to holiness that he had witnessed from his parish priest. He was beginning to put together a composite of what holiness was, what he himself was perhaps striving for. Two of the most vital teachings that emerged from his diary were that holiness is not dependent on the sensational but on "little things which seem but trifles in the eyes of the world," and that saints, especially in their youth, looked as if they were taking a quite different route than the one in which their "natural gifts and brilliant qualities had seemed to indicate." He noticed that their practice of "holy detachment" allowed them to be able to hear God's voice, the way that he could hear God speaking to him. He also indirectly admonished himself by claiming that there was no cause for pride in anything the saints succeeded in doing while they worked at reforming and founding orders, healing and transforming the world. All they did, he wrote, was to "cast themselves blindly into all that God wanted them to do...."

THE WAY OF PERFECTION

In the senior seminary in Bergamo, Angelo began to set out on a series of disciplines for the deepening of his interior life. His spiritual aim was "at perfection," and his course became one of daily obstacles and struggles with his humanity. He wrote that although he aimed at perfection in practice, he was far from succeeding; in learning surrender, he knew that it was not to be mapped out by him but by God. However, he also knew that he needed a spiritual discipline to tame him and keep him on his course, and he advised himself to be careful not to get sidetracked by thoughts and activities that would take him away from his "pursuit of the interior life. Every stray thought that enters my mind breaks off a bit of my inner self," he wrote. He faced the challenge of duality that battled inside him for dominance—which he viewed as a battle of interior good and evil—and he would catch himself on the vice of pride, writing that if he continued with his captive pride prominent in all that he said and did, then "in the end, what shall I be?—a windbag!" He had to convince himself of what he called "the great truth," which was that "Jesus wants me, the seminarist Angelo Roncalli, not just a mediocre but a supreme virtue; he will not be satisfied with me until I have made myself, or at least have done my utmost to make myself holy. The graces he has given me to this end are so many, and so great." He listed the gifts and graces he had received so far—that he, "a country lad…with the affection of a loving mother," was taken from his home and given all that he needed. He was hungry and Christ fed him, had nothing to wear and Christ clothed him, had no books to carry to his studies and Christ provided those also. He recalled that many times he forgot Christ but that Christ never forgot him, and "gently recalled me. If my affection for him cooled, he warmed me in his breast, at the flame with which his heart is always burning." These early expressions of the motherhood of Christ contributed to his model of behavior as a future pastor.

Part of the challenge of growing up, growing away, and practicing "holy detachment" was his changing relationship with his mother. He had been very close to her as a child, but on one vacation visit home from the seminary, he felt ostracized by the family. This was largely due to their misunderstanding of his call to the priesthood. Some family members viewed his departing for Bergamo as an irresponsible desire to avoid farm work. Sitting in the parlor studying during the summer didn't make sense to them. In addition, his mother, feeling his emotional distance, accused him of not liking her, which upset him tremendously. In order to cheer him up, the local priest (the successor to Don Francesco) gave Angelo a trip to Rome to celebrate Pope Leo XIII's ninetieth year, along with a short pilgrimage to Assisi and Loreto. On his return to Bergamo, Angelo reached out to his mother in a letter of prophetic consolation: "Even if I was pope, you would always remain for me the greatest lady in the world."

"GIVE ME A SOLDIER'S HEART, A KNIGHT'S VALOR"

In 1900, at the age of nineteen, Angelo took the overnight train from Bergamo to Rome to take an exam for a theology scholarship. He wrote of his love of the pomp and pageantry of the Vatican. Receiving a blessing from the pope at St. Peter's, he also received an award for Hebrew and he excelled in his exams. His studies were interrupted, however, in November 1901 when he was called to compulsory military service in the Lombardy Brigade in Bergamo, which he called his "year of Babylonian captivity." His time in the military also tested his way of perfection. It was far from a perfect environment for a seminarian twenty years old. He wrote of the locker-room ambience, of rough language and blatant sexuality, and he prided himself more for remaining "unpolluted" than for being promoted from corporal to sergeant. Fearful that he might lose his vocation, he found that it was strengthened even more by his year in the military, and he felt restless to continue his studies and to familiarize himself "with the scientific moment in all its manifestations."

He saw his move to Rome as a gift from the motherly care of God, that God through "countless acts of kindness" had brought him to the headquarters of his Church. He mused that it must be for a purpose that he was there, and that even if he were made pope in the future (with all its fame and prestige), he would still have to stand for divine judgment at the end of his life, and be asked the question, "What should I be worth then?" His personal and spiritual scrutiny continued in earnest as, at the age of twenty-one, he became a subdeacon, which was prior to final vows, at a solemn ceremony at St. John Lateran. He felt a newness in himself, a sense of moving forward, as he took the sacramental steps toward the priesthood.

His doctorate in theology then in preparation (and supervised by Eugenio Pacelli, who was the future Pope Pius XII), Don Roncalli was ordained in 1904 at the Church of Santa Maria in the Piazza del Popolo in Rome. Almost as a reminder of his mother's early consecration of her son to the Madonna, he said that at the altar, when he was swearing his eternal fidelity to his superior bishop, he looked up above the tabernacle at the "blessed image of Our Lady" who he had not noticed before, and she seemed to be smiling down at him. He felt a "sweet peace" in his soul and "a generous and confident spirit," and he heard her tell him she would watch over him and was pleased with his ordination. His first Mass was said, aptly, in the crypt at St. Peter's Basilica, and one of his professors had arranged for him to have an audience and blessing with Pope Pius X. He knelt at the feet of a man whom he had followed as a cardinal, who had been patriarch of Venice, and the first pope from peasant stock.

Don Roncalli's first assignment as priest was secretary to the newly appointed bishop of Bergamo, Msgr. Radini Tedeschi. He also became professor in the seminary at which he had been a student.

"LOOK AND MAKE IT AFTER THE PATTERN"

As a newly ordained priest, Don Roncalli took his duties seriously and his soul growth continued under meticulous scrutiny. He experienced "indescribable joys" and gratitude for the many graces he was receiving and feeling, although he made sure to add that he was a most unworthy recipient. He continued to monitor his pride, his unnecessary conversations; even his natural ability for leadership and teaching was not something to celebrate. He confronted himself on various incidences where he was not following his way of perfection, and wrote prayers pleading for heavenly intercession for his errors. He expected himself to be an example of a good "priestly character" in his gestures, speech, and dress (as it was defined by the Council of Trent). He noted that Jesus Christ during the first thirty years of his life "offered me a whole series of shining examples," to which he added the scriptural quote from Exodus 25:40: "Look and make it after the pattern."

His bishop was a man he admired and respected, who took the place of his first parish priest, Don Francesco, as mentor, advisor, and example, and Don Roncalli served him loyally and efficiently until the end of Tedeschi's life. They traveled together to the Holy Land in 1905, as well as to the original Benedictine monastery at Subiaco, south of Rome. Tedeschi guided his secretary through many of the challenges prompted by secular life in Italy at the time, particularly what was referred to as "the social question," which caused the Church to respond to the emerging changes between civic and ecclesiastical life. This also provided the seedbed for Roncalli's future ministry of opening the Church to the world. In the meantime, the keen professor loved his seminarian students, wanting to be able to teach them in humility and prayer.

"*WAR* IS AND REMAINS THE GREATEST EVIL"

During the outbreak of World War I in August 1914, after Pope Pius X had died, perhaps of a broken heart, Don Roncalli's Bishop Tedeschi also passed away, his last words being "for peace, for peace."

Don Roncalli began his war ministry as a medical orderly and later an army chaplain at the Bergamo hospital. He remembered this time as one of long vigils among the bunks of brave soldiers, receiving their confessions, preparing them for death. He remembered the hymns to Mary that "rose up around simple, improvised altars," Masses in the fields, sacrifices of families, losses, and grief. Demobilized in December 1918, the young priest promptly destroyed his uniform. But this time in the army had been different from his military service as a seminarian. This time he had been able to bring the principles he had been working so hard to achieve in himself into action for service to others.

The new pope in Rome was Benedict XV, who was a political "neutralist" like Don Roncalli, and, as soon as he was out of his military uniform, Roncalli was appointed spiritual director of the seminary. He founded the student's hostel, which he called "the darling of my heart," installing a huge mirror in its hall with the words "Know Thyself" over it. He began lecturing there on topics that showed his own intellectual interests: "The Church, Science, and the School," "Christianity and Greco-Roman Science," "Astrology, Alchemy, and the Intellectual Aberrations of the Middle Ages," "The University and Scholasticism," "The Church and the Renaissance," and "Modern Struggles for Freedom in Education." He also lectured on St. Catherine of Siena to the National Union of Catholic Women, to which he was serving as chaplain.

"I DON'T WANT TO LIVE HERE"

Don Roncalli had written in his journal after a visit to Rome that he didn't like the Roman atmosphere, that he felt only like a pilgrim in Rome, and that, even though there was always good to be done everywhere, he wouldn't want to live there. He had been working through his interior journey dealing with his imaginings of what lay ahead for him, and then scolding himself for not living accordng to Divine Providence and doing God's will in the moment. Just as if he was ready for the next stage in his inner life, which was to practice obedience without question, he was appointed to work with the Roman curia in the Vatican in the distinguished department of the Propagation of Faith. In 1921, despite his desire to never live in Rome, he arrived there with his belongings, turning down a seven-room apartment for something cheaper and inviting his sisters Ancilla and Maria to become his housekeepers. He stayed for four years.

A "PROLONGED MISSION" IN BULGARIA

Don Angelo Roncalli must have proved himself during his time working at the Vatican, although he frequently wondered where God would put him next. His appointment by the new pope, Pius XI, to become apostolic visitor in Sofia, Bulgaria, was certainly a surprise. It was 1925, and Don Angelo was in his mid-forties. A promotion came with the job, and before leaving he was consecrated bishop on March 19, the feast of one of his namesakes, St. Joseph; what's more, it took place in San Carlo al Corso, a church in Rome dedicated to another one of his patrons, St. Charles Borromeo, who was also the subject of Roncalli's labors on what was to become a five-volume edition of Borromeo's writings and teachings. Members of the Roncalli family from Sotto Il Monte came to Rome for this special occasion. A photograph taken at the time shows a stout man who seems naturally suited to the vestige of bishopric. He had written in his diary that bishop's robes are a reminder of the "splendor of souls," which they signified, and that this was the bishop's "real glory." He now had to assume new aspects in himself—*"digne, attente, devote"* (with dignity, attentiveness, and devotion), which he needed to express in his work and solely "for the edification of souls." He advised himself to do "ordinary things day after day, without over-anxiety, without ostentation" and to carry these out with "fervor and perfection." His way of perfection was still unfolding, but another thing that needed his attention was his physical weight. He disliked exercise so he had to find a way to curb his appetite and his "greedy palate." He set out diets for himself, cutting down his food portions, watering down his wine, but his attempts at losing weight seemed hopeless. Perhaps he was promising too much to God and himself about dieting. He hadn't the discipline because he liked to dine, and he relished building community by eating together at table like one large family. He accepted his destiny as being "fat and heavy," and later, when elected pope, the Vatican tailor had to hold together the largest cassock in the papal wardrobe with safety pins so that the new Pope John XXIII could appear in the appropriate garb on the balcony at St. Peter's. He was by then old and disinterested enough to make jokes about his physical appearance, which he did frequently. Once he said that, when he felt too fat, he would go and stand next to Cardinal Cicognani (the stoutest man in the curia), which then made him feel as "thin as a rail!"

The post as bishop in Bulgaria was to prove invaluable in his later ministry, although he admitted that the "prolonged mission" of his ten monotonous years there caused him "acute and intimate suffering," which he tried not to show. His lonely isolation from friends and family combined with the many trials he endured representing the papacy in a country where the Orthodox Church was the prominent religion. He was, of course, sowing seeds in a ground that had hardened to the concepts of reconciliation and dialogue. He befriended Orthodox Church leaders, among them the

Armenian patriarch, who later asked to die with a papal medal that Bishop Roncalli had given him, placed upon his heart. There were small signs of hope between the various religions, as Roncalli set about to be "good and kind," to persevere with patience to represent the pope and the Roman Catholic Church, and to "exercise pastoral and fatherly kindness, such as befits a shepherd and father," which he defined as his "whole purpose of my life as Bishop." Ultimately he came to love the Bulgarians and learned of the importance of understanding a people and the history of a place. He became able to adequately explain to others the philosophy of the historic, not only of the past but also of the present, "even the history that is now before our eyes."

What Angelo Roncalli was creating was a widening path through the world. Still checking in on his interior motives—of the need to be moderate in speech, tranquil in thoughts, loving and caring, open and embracing—he was learning the elements of spiritual and secular precepts in his own particular style and way, which would benefit him greatly in what lay ahead.

"IF IN ROME CHRIST IS A ROMAN, IN TURKEY HE MUST BECOME A TURK"

In 1935 Bishop Roncalli was posted as Vatican envoy to Turkey and Greece. He arrived in historic Istanbul (previously Constantinople) to face the challenges of unity among the Christian Churches in a prominent Islamic country, which disallowed the wearing of clerical vestments. As a man who favored robes of dignity, he accepted civilian wear as an opportunity to practice priestly attributes and virtues without the external trappings, although he didn't find it easy. The experience, however, might have enabled him to more fully understand and sympathize with the role of the laity, those followers of God who attempt to practice Christ's teachings in ordinary life. But this was not ordinary life, because ill winds were blowing through Europe that would eventually lead to the outbreak of another world war. In Rome, Pius XI passed away, and one of Bishop Roncalli's former theology professors, Eugenio Pacelli, was elected Pope Pius XII. It is reported that Roncalli said, "Being pope today is enough to turn your hair as white as your soutane" (the papal cassock).

Matters back in Rome made things difficult for Roncalli; he alluded to the toughness of dealing with the curia on affairs of diplomacy as well as ecumenism. He began to learn Turkish and would introduce Turkish words into the liturgy (an early sign of what was to come in liturgical and vernacular reform at Vatican II). While in Turkey he never wanted to visit Greece, but once he got there, he always felt "like a fish in water." During the late thirties, he was viewed with suspicion in Greece, especially when Italian troops were posted at its borders prior to their North African defeat, but he stepped in to help trace prisoners of war with the Red Cross, as the Vatican became central to gaining information on the whereabouts of prisoners of war from all sides of the fighting. While the Holy See remained silent about the persecution of Jews, Bishop Roncalli offered as much practical help as he could. With the aid of King Boris of Bulgaria, whom he had befriended when he lived in Sofia, he gained transit visas to Palestine for many Jewish people who were vulnerable to being sent to concentration camps. The chief rabbi of Jerusalem, Isaac Hertzog, wrote to Roncalli expressing his gratitude "for the energetic steps that you have taken and will undertake to save our unfortunate people, innocent victims of unheard of horrors, [and I acknowledge the] noble feelings of your own heart."

At a peace service he led in Istanbul's cathedral, Bishop Roncalli offered a concluding prayer for unity citing that whatever race we are, whatever religion we belong to, or whatever tradition or social position we have, we are in the end all members of the same human family. It was the crowning statement of his appointment, one that was to be his primary link to the desires he knew of Christ for the unity of the world. He said of war that it is instigated by the "prince of this world," who has nothing to do with Christ, who is "the Prince of Peace." And then, as if forecasting hope and healing, he announced in 1944 that the Holy Spirit may seem lost to the world, but was still at work—"mysteriously and powerfully"—within it.

THE ONLY MAN IN PARIS...

Much to his—and everyone else's surprise—Bishop Roncalli was made papal nuncio to France, an appointment announced soon after Pius XII's meeting with General De Gaulle and the liberation of Paris to the allied armies in August 1944. In December Roncalli arrived in a divided Catholic France, due to the aftermath of the Resistance movement. However, there were other divisions, the most prominent created by members of the clerical hierarchy who didn't know him at all. He was perceived to have been shunted off to the Balkans for twenty years, which were a "backwater" to France and not part of the central diplomatic scene, and at sixty-three he was considered, according to one prelate, "an old fogy." Yet this prestigious diplomatic post, probably one of the highest accorded by the Vatican, did not intimidate the new nuncio. He was more than well prepared: for most of his adult life, he had been working on his way of perfection; it was clear, simple, and directive. And, with his caution for not being inwardly distracted by the ways of the world, he could offer the world something different, something intimate.

From the start, everything Roncalli did was considered right. He wrote to all the bishops of the Church of France in a friendly and open manner, respecting everyone's opinion, and treating them with openness and kindness. He took to decorating his diplomatic apartments—something he said was important for the work he had to do. He became a familiar figure in the streets, walking around his quarter of Paris, even though Pope Pius XII suggested that it was undignified for a nuncio to do so. He began learning French, meeting and speaking with as many people as wanted to see him, and he said, “A good table and a good cellar are great assets.” He also gained a reputation for being a brilliant conversationalist, a master of diplomacy who weighed his words carefully. One Venetian commented that his “graceful conversation was like lacework or subtle embroidery.” After Roncalli hired a chef who later became the proprietor of the reputable restaurant La Grenoville, his dinners were considered the best on the circuit. But more than that, he gained a reputation as a man who was imbued with the grace of God. Author Robert Schuman said of him that he was the only man in Paris in “whose company one feels a physical sensation of peace.”

France provided the ground for further education for Roncalli. Although he was careful to walk what seemed to be a conservative and conventional line in his work as nuncio, his eyes didn’t miss the “signs of the times,” a term he adopted as pope from the then-banned French theologian Chenu. Social changes were in the air as the priest-worker movement was expanding and challenging the Church to look seriously at social action, equality, and justice as central to the work of Christ. Roncalli took up reading Simone Weil, the Jewish/Christian French writer and activist, and he began introducing ground rules of dialogue to the Catholic members of UNESCO; he also continued his work on the writings and teachings of St. Charles Borromeo.

It was ten years before he was called back home to his beloved Italy, closer to his blood family, who had visited him frequently, his brothers astonished at having been whisked around the great European city in a black Cadillac.

As he prepared to leave Paris, Roncalli was visited by many dignitaries to say good-bye and wish him well. The Canadian ambassador, Georges Vanier, told him that he had three of the characteristic products of Bergamo—wine, silk, and steel—wine representing his warmth of heart and vivacity of spirit, silk for his “sense of nuances,” and steel for the firmness of his character, which “makes no compromise where truth is concerned.”

"I COULD NEVER HAVE IMAGINED OR DESIRED SUCH GREATNESS"

Throughout Roncalli's career he had heard rumors about the greater things that were in store for his future, although he attempted to make a joke of them, seeing them as an opportunity to further his interior detachment from expectations of honors and promotions. He also wished to perfect the same virtue in cases of humiliation or opposition, and had begun to feel the fruit of his interior labor when he wrote in his diary, "Nothing of all this causes me any anxiety or preoccupation." As if to gauge how he was doing with his practice of detachment, his next appointment was, naturally, to the college of cardinals in 1953, along with the added prestigious position of patriarch of Venice three months later. He was at last to return to his native soil, and to the Veneto region of the north so near his Bergamese home. "It is he [the Lord] who has really done all, and done it without my help, for I could never have imagined or desired such greatness," he wrote in his diary. He saw this appointment like an arc beginning in his native village and curving over "the domes and pinnacles of St. Mark's" (the great church in the main piazza of Venice). At the same time he received sad news from home. His beloved sister Ancilla, whom he called "the most precious treasure of my household," died of stomach cancer. In his absence abroad, he had rented part of a house called Casa Martino in his hometown to spend a month a year there during his vacation. His unmarried sisters lived—and died—in that apartment, which he wanted them to have as a home especially after their parents had passed away.

Roncalli viewed his purpose as cardinal as a sacred mission: "To save souls and guide them to heaven." He was happy—and possibly relieved—to be out of official diplomacy and back to where he began as a young priest, a pastor and shepherd to his Venetian flock.

As someone who favored ceremony, he kept the tradition of entering Venice in a procession of gondolas and cut a fine figure as the people lined the canals and streets to greet him. Following in the footsteps of Pius X, he moved into the Episcopal Palace near St. Mark's overlooking the Piazzetta Dei Leoncini, choosing the second rather than the first floor as his residence. He provided an open door policy to all and put a sign over his study that read "Shepherd and Father." He also referred to himself as mother "of a poor family who is entrusted with so many children," as his time was stretched with endless requests for meetings, help, care, sacraments, and other calls for ministry. One of his first appointments, which he had to defend for breaking tradition, was of Don Loris Capovilla as his secretary. Capovilla, like Roncalli himself, was from a poor background instead of the traditional nobility and came from the Padua diocese with experience as a journalist. Peter Hebblethwaite in his biography of Pope John XXIII wrote, "In Capovilla, Roncalli got much more than a secretary: he got a spiritual son, a literary executor, a confidante, and a Boswell."

During his five years in Venice, Cardinal Roncalli witnessed and celebrated the canonization of Pius X (whom he honored by giving communion to Pius X's grand-nephews and nieces), and he continued his ecumenical work by regularly meeting with leaders of other churches, including the Melkite patriarch Maximos IV Saigh, whom he later invited to the Vatican Council. Roncalli noted, maybe for the first time by the official Church, that Catholics cannot blame—and accuse— solely the Protestant and Orthodox Christian Churches for the split with Rome, but need to take some responsibility themselves for possibly prompting the split by the actions, or inactions, of the Holy See. So as to prove his point, he opposed the official papal consecration of the feast of the Queenship of Mary, which he saw as an obstacle to ecumenical dialogue. All the while, he continued to reach out to those he considered opponents, "if not enemies," and provided a basis for cooperation between the Church and the political parties of the left. The themes of his lectures also illustrated his ministry and reflected his pastoral experience: "The Church in the Slav World," "The Church and Separated Oriental Christians," "The Church and Protestant Confessions." Now that he was in Italy, he didn't forget the people he had served in other parts of the world. He wrote that he remembered France, Turkey, Greece, and Bulgaria in his daily prayers.

The fact that, at his age, he was probably nearing the end of his life was a truth he wanted to ignore. "My mind resents this and almost rebels," he wrote, because on good days he still felt young, "agile and alert." But he admitted that he was feeling "on the threshold of eternity" as he prepared his last will.

"I'M READY"

Cardinal Roncalli had always been interested in the papacy. His love of history and the Church motivated his study, and he knew much more about the popes of the past than most of his contemporaries. Summoned to Rome in October 1958 after the death of Pope Pius XII, he and the other cardinals arrived for the conclave. Kneeling in the crypt of St. Peter's (a place so close to his heart from the first Mass he had said there as a young priest), Roncalli prayed to St. Peter to protect and guide the conclave. Almost immediately, he was among the favored—one cardinal exclaimed that he could imagine kneeling at his feet. During the conclave, Cardinal Roncalli wrote to the then-bishop of Bergamo, exclaiming that his soul had found comfort and confidence "that a new Pentecost can blow through the Church, renewing its head, leading to a new ordering of the ecclesiastical body, and bringing fresh vigor in progress toward the victory of truth, goodness, and peace." He was hopeful that the new pope would be a part of this divine plan, and became delighted when his popularity seemed to be diminishing during the early rounds of voting. But the cardinals had agreed that they needed a man with spiritual strength and charity, one who belonged to all peoples—especially the poor and those under totalitarian persecution—someone who could exemplify the subtle art of diplomacy, who could comfort the doubters, who could listen, encourage, and bring hope. No one fit the bill more perfectly than Cardinal Roncalli.

When he was elected by thirty-eight votes, with heavy support from the French delegates, he wrote in his diary at the end of the day, "I'm ready." He prayed to the saints, particularly St. Pius X, for "calmness and courage." He chose the name John—not Pius or Leo or Benedict, as expected. There was a spirit of change in the air, and his choice of name was another sign. He explained that he chose John because of St. John Lateran (the official church of the bishop of Rome, a promotion he had just assumed), and it was also the name of the fourth evangelist, one who had so beautifully recorded Christ's teachings of unity and oneness and of the final message, "Love one another as I have loved you." It was because of John the Baptist as well, not only the great biblical prophet but also the name of Roncalli's own father, Giovanni Battista. And it was the name of a tower on top of the mountain behind Sotto Il Monte, which he loved and recalled as part of the joys of his childhood. Last, but not least, with his knowledge of the troubled succession of all the Pope Johns (particularly the last, an antipope in 1410 by the name of Baldassar Cossa, who took the name Pope John XXIII), Roncalli wiped him out in the apostolic succession by assuming the same name. He announced that he was to be John XXIII.

There was much excitement as he stood waving to what he called "an invisible crowd" from the balcony of St. Peter's. The dazzling television lights prevented him from seeing anyone as the world cheered and applauded him. He reported that he blessed the people as if he were a blind man and, turning from the crowd, became acutely aware of the responsibility he had now been given. He reminded himself that if he didn't remain a disciple of "the gentle and humble

Master," he would understand nothing of "temporal realities. Then you'll be really blind," he told himself.

His first speech on Vatican radio announced the major themes of his papacy: unity in the life of the Church, including the embrace of the Orthodox Churches and peace in the secular order, particularly as the nuclear arms race, which he deplored, was accelerating at an alarming rate. He said the money spent on defense and destruction was better spent on "the least favored" in the world.

Almost from the beginning, everyone was aware that this pope was different. Now that he was pope, Roncalli was free from his vow of obedience to his superiors and didn't have to heed warnings of the decorum expected of his ecclesiastical rank. He made members of the Roman curia very uncomfortable—they were being taken places they had never trod, and almost with an added twist of John's inevitable pastoral love, the reverse was experienced by the laity. The Roman people and his staff, which included the Vatican gardeners and the Swiss guards, were made more comfortable and felt like members of his family. He stopped to talk to the common people—he even embraced them—he didn't want to be removed and kept apart. It was a freedom that came naturally to him. He made everyone feel real and was present to them as one human being to another human being. He had been perfecting and practicing this way all his life; now he could show the world exactly what it meant to be "catholic" in the true sense of the meaning—to unify and be inclusive. There was going to be much more reform ahead, but these early signs of papal collegiality and informality set the scene. It was as if Pope John had, because of his previous study of the papacy, begun to exemplify what a pope in the modern world should be. He had frequently said that the Church had only one diplomacy, the priesthood, and that the responsibility of his priesthood was to see and speak the truth, and to do so with "the utmost simplicity and tranquility," with a "radiant and serene kindness," always joyful and generous, "patient, equable, and forgetful of self," and to be loyal to God "for life and death."

THE CHAIR OF TRUTH

As a young priest working for the curia in Rome, Pope John in his journal had hailed St. Peter's as "this beautiful place of meditation and rest," praising its majestic dome rising to the heavens. He honored it as the Chair of Truth and paid fervent homage to it with his mind and heart. Now he was being crowned to sit upon it. On November 4, 1958, the feast day of his beloved St. Charles Borromeo, he was carried into St. Peter's on a portable throne by twelve footmen. It reminded him of when he would ride upon his father's shoulders as a young boy, but this time, he said it was quite windy "up there." He automatically abandoned the regular wearing of the heavy, bejeweled papal tiara, and restored some of the early, medieval costume of red velvet cape and cap with white fur border. He also dismissed the terms "the most Supreme Pontiff," "Your Holiness," and "Holy Father," which he admitted embarrassed him greatly, and instead asked to be referred to as Pope John, or just plain John. It didn't take long for plain Pope John to become "Good Pope John" to almost everyone who met him.

Pope John gave Rome further signs of what was to come during his coronation. He was not going to be a pope who sat back, remained in seclusion, and led by appearance only; he had much to share and he had little time to do it. Never before had a pope preached at his coronation Mass. Pope John stood up and delivered his homily with verve, passion, and signs of a keen intelligence, worrying many in the conservative curia who had thought they had voted in a transitional, tow-the-line pope, someone who would guide them safely through a changing period without too much trouble. Political positioning began to take hold, with its "squalid maneuvering," which tried to undermine many reforms that were to come, but Pope John was ready; he knew what he was dealing with. He once said to an American bishop that when he faced Jesus in eternity, Christ was not going to question him about how well he got along with the Roman curia, but how many souls he saved.

Two days after his coronation he met with the Italian press in a friendly, informal way. Many commented that it was like talking with a "grandfather," he made them feel so at ease. Toward the end of November he took possession of his cathedral as bishop of Rome, the St. John Lateran (where he had been blessed with his diaconate fifty-five years before), which he said was one of the most wonderful days of his life. In his private apartment, he took to eating with his staff—Capovilla was still with him as his secretary, and eating alone with him was not something John enjoyed as he commented that Capovilla picked at his food like a canary. In a visit with John Diefenbaker, then prime minister of Canada, John commented that the realization of his solitary arrival at "the top of the heap" was on waking in bed at night with a question he wished to discuss with the pope. On remembering that he now was the pope, he turned to discussing it with Christ.

"WE ARE EMBARKED ON THE WILL OF THE LORD"

At Christmas, Pope John ventured out of the Vatican walls again to visit local hospitals and the prisoners at the Regina Coeli prison. Without a prepared speech, he spoke personally about his feelings, he embraced, he touched. The smiles and laughter captured on the faces of the men in prison, filmed for television, were enough to show the effect he had on those he met. He began getting the Vatican systems in some order and started discussing his thoughts of a Vatican Council with his closest confidantes. Capovilla was opposed to the idea of a council as he felt Pope John couldn't handle it at his advanced age, but the pope answered him that being caught in one's ego disables you from being "fully and truly free." "It's not a matter of personal feelings," he once said about Vatican II. "We are embarked on the will of the Lord."

John prepared to announce the Vatican Council to the bishops and cardinals at the Basilica of St. Paul's Outside the Walls. The renewal and reforms needed in the Church had already been drawn up with Pope Pius XII's authority early in 1949, but its obsession with "modernism" and its need for retrenchment was not what Pope John had in mind. He saw the Holy Spirit working in the signs of the times and felt himself called to lead something more expansive, an *"aggiornamento,"* a renewal that was a radical departure from what had gone before. His announcement, followed by his request for prayers for "a good start," was received with what one cardinal described as a "devout and impressive silence." Pope John generously responded that the clergy were probably all stunned. But he was being made aware of the load he had to personally carry up "the slopes of the sacred mountain."

Even in his previous positions, Pope John had always taught that change requires patience, that all change is slow to come about, and that the course of change requires an awareness of three elements at play. He outlined these three elements when referring to the Vatican Council as (1) when the devil tries to mix up the papers, (2) when human beings help with the confusion, and (3) when the Holy Spirit clears everything up. He continued to refer to the priority of trusting the working of the Spirit within himself and throughout the community of the Church. He taught that nothing was perfect in the world and that it was necessary to "ride the storms to find the truth." He single-handedly did that during Vatican II's first stages when clearly the devil was mixing up the papers.

The changes were indeed slow in coming, even from himself. The Roman Synod in 1960 was anticipated as a practice run for the Vatican Council, but at the synod John delivered no reforms that were perceived as new. The curia responded with accusations and negative comments, which he continually referred to as "a suffering." However, he looked only for the good in all and kept his eyes fixed on the tasks at hand. He continued to publish encyclicals, including *Mater et Magistra,* an important document with a new tone in Catholic social teaching, and was kept busy with the open-door policy that he had introduced in Venice. He received anyone who wished to see him—heads of state, political leaders, royalty, religious leaders from other faiths. He welcomed the archbishop of Canterbury for the first time since the Reformation, which resulted in having Anglican representation at the Council. On one occasion, he gave his own personal breviary to a visiting Anglican priest, because he thought his looked a bit tattered. He continued to make people feel at home in his company; he guided a bishop from the traditional ritual of kissing his feet up from the floor and into a comfortable armchair to chat, and after being briefed about the right protocol toward Jacqueline Kennedy, he shocked his staff by spontaneously stretching out his arms and greeting her by her first name.

The political pressures that were gaining ground in the world during the early sixties were not something that could escape Pope John's attention. He read the reports on the ever-increasing tensions of the Cold War and the mounting missile crisis between the Soviet Union and the United States over Cuba. He dispatched a message of peace to the Conference of Non-Aligned Nations in Belgrade, and was honored by Nikita Khrushchev in the Russian newspaper *Pravda*, who said that lay Catholics should heed the pope's advice about peace negotiation over war. Pope John and Khrushchev began a correspondence, while the pope also reached out to newly elected U.S. president John F. Kennedy, who was attempting to downplay his Catholicism in the American political arena. But the pope didn't back down and drew the parties together to ensure peace. It was Khrushchev who told Norman Cousins in an interview that "what the pope has done for peace will go down in history." Pope John had said that in a nuclear age there was only one choice—dialogue or catastrophe.

The pope's seeming friendliness with Khrushchev only added fuel to his critics. Due to his "communist sympathies," he was perceived to be responsible for Italy's communist political party gaining prestige and popularity. Even as he was dying in later years, the same accusations were made of him in the press, which only added to his physical sufferings. But in preparation for the upcoming Council, he needed representatives of the whole Church present. He started dialoguing with China as well, although with little luck. Friends in Hong Kong sent him a gift of gratitude for his efforts, a small altar that he cherished and erected in his private tower in the Vatican gardens. This ninth-century tower he had renovated for prayer and solitary retreats. He called it the Torre San Giovanni (The St. John Tower), named after the original above Sotto Il Monte, of which he was so fond.

Meanwhile, he continued to appoint cardinals from all corners of the world, men from the Philippines, Japan, Mexico, and Africa, and he finally invited his first black cardinal into the Holy See, Laurean Rugambwa, archbishop of Dar-es-Salaam, Tanzania. The Church's official face was no longer made up of white Italian nobility, which worried the white Italian nobility: it was becoming obvious that there would be no turning back.

On his eightieth birthday in 1961, Pope John began feeling unwell. Many of his siblings had died of stomach cancer, and he was concerned that he would follow the same fate. He continued on his mission, however, fueled by grace, prayer, and his total surrender to the will of God. He reminded himself and others that "everything comes from God."

"HISTORY IS THE GREAT TEACHER OF LIFE"

With just under a year to go until the opening of the Council, themes, programs, and agendas began to flood not only the Vatican but the public press. The more radical and liberal theologians, prominent in Germany and North America, who had been researching, writing, and teaching the elements of ecumenism already, contributed the subjects and the needs for a fresh look at theology, dogma, papal infallibility, liturgy, education, social justice, and other areas of required reform. Many, like the Swiss theologian Hans Küng, were considered to have more Protestant than Catholic leanings, but they could not be dismissed or diminished by the more conservative curia. What they were contributing was a vocabulary, a succinct interpretation of the elements that made up the reform required to facilitate change. Many were later invited to the Vatican and contributed in the sessions largely due to Pope John's appointment of the seasoned Jesuit Augustin Bea, who was called in to oversee the planning in the preparatory commissions.

In the beginning of October 1962, when the Vatican Council was to begin, Pope John made a pilgrimage to Assisi and Loreto, two places that had touched him when he had traveled there as a young priest with Bishop Tedeschi. It seemed apt for him to pray to St. Francis for his intercession and guidance, the man who had centuries before been called by Christ to restore and renew a Church corrupted by power and greed, and lost to the needs of the poor. The first-draft documents prepared by white First-World Italians did not have much, if at all, on the needs of the poor. This was to come later when the missionaries arrived with their experience of ministering to those with nothing. Addressing the needs for social action gave way to the emergence of liberation theology.

Pope John requested prayers from the whole Christian world for the Council. He spoke openly of the need for renewal, dialogue, and conversion. He said that the Council needed to reflect both St. Peter and St. Paul—Peter representing order and stability and Paul for his zeal in the missionary spread of the Gospel. Bishops began pouring into Rome as never before—217 came from the United States alone and eight hundred from missionaries. There were 296 Africans, 84 from India, and 93 from the Philippines, Japan, and Indonesia.

Among the 2,500 bishops who ultimately came were those from Eastern Europe, including the young Pole Karol Wojtyla from Krakow (the future Pope John Paul II), and members of the Russian Orthodox Church. In addition, there were ecumenical observers, translators, journalists, support staff, and secretaries—all of whom needed to be accommodated within the confines of the Vatican, which posed a physical challenge. All the hotels and houses in Rome were packed to the limit and, for the first time, St. Peter's Basilica reached capacity, filled with rows and rows of clergy, and sections erected for secretaries and staff.

Pope John's inaugural speech was a tour de force. It was the moment that summed up his entire life, all his interior preparation, all his pastoral experience, all his faith and love, and more than anything, his hope in the ways of God. He appeared youthful and manifested a sense of adventure. His main themes were the celebration of faith both old and new, the optimism of Spirit to combat the despair and gloom that was evident in the world, the intent of the Council, and the approach to dealing with errors.

He reminded everyone that history was the great teacher of life and that it was necessary not to turn a blind eye to what has happened in the past but to see how it can inform the present. He spoke of the *moment*, of becoming conscious of how the Holy Spirit was working *in the moment,* what the present age demands of the Catholic Church, and the vitalness of the education of conscience.

That evening he stood on the balcony of St. Peter's and told the crowd that he hoped to contribute to world peace, asking for their prayers, referring to the beautiful moon that shone down on them in the night sky. Then, in his usual grandfatherly style, he told everyone to go back home and give their children a kiss from Pope John.

"WHEN THE BODY GETS WORN OUT, THE SOUL GETS IN SHAPE"

The first sessions of Vatican II ended in December, and subsequent sessions took place regularly over the next three years, guided by Pope Paul VI. As if Pope John knew he had completed his part, he worked over the final months of his life in 1963 on his last encyclical, *Pacem in terris,* or "Peace on Earth." He was in continuous pain, and an inoperable tumor was found in his stomach that Spring. Though frail, he still appeared at his papal window and spoke and blew kisses to the crowd, who wept and prayed and stayed in vigil for him in the piazza below. All the world was struck by sadness. Here, at last, was a holy, accessible, open man as pope, and in the shortest years of any papacy (five in total) he was to be taken away. It was a slow fade. On the eve of the Feast of the Ascension on May 22, he said to the night nurse attending him (a friar from Sotto Il Monte) that he wished he could say Mass, to which the friar replied, "Your bed is your altar." His secretary, Capovilla, wept by this same bed when he heard there was no hope. Pope John turned to him and asked him to help him die "as a bishop or a pope should." In a Christ-like way, he entrusted the surviving members of the Roncalli family to Capovilla's care and told him, "When this is all over, get some rest and go see your mother." His brothers and one of his sisters arrived from Sotto Il Monte, and they kept prayerful vigil by his bed.

The family and the crucifix were the last themes of his life. He told those around his bed that his entire ministry was guided by the crucifix opposite his bed, which he had seen on his waking and sleeping every day of his life since 1925. "Look at it, see it as I see it," he said. "Those open arms have been the program of my pontificate: they say that Christ died for all, for all. No one is excluded from his love, from his forgiveness."

On June 3, 1963, Pope John, the man who had embraced the world with the open arms of Christ, died into the arms of his beloved. Many called his death the most untimely of the twentieth century yet he had completed what he had worked toward; he had come to the top of the Sacred Mountain, what Peter Hebblethwaite called "an accurate and farsighted prophet." John had written in his journal many years before: "Certainly on the day of judgment we shall not be asked what we have read but what we have done; not how well we have spoken but how virtuously we have lived...."

Angelo Roncalli's diaries were published under the title *Journal of a Soul*. Don Loris Capovilla, who was to take care of all the pope's writings and personal possessions, wrote in its Introduction,

> People called him the good Pope, everyone's Pope, the parish priest of the world: he persuaded people to pray, to ponder the Gospels, to reform the morals of the world by reforming themselves. And at the end he drew everyone to be present not at a spectacle of splendid liturgical pomp but at a death bed as solemn as a Papal Mass. He ennobled death. He made people say it was a beautiful thing to die like that. The crowds who gathered in St. Peter's Square, many of them for the first time and feeling astonished at such an unexpected occurrence, looked each other in the eyes and suddenly, mysteriously, felt they were all of one family. They wondered how this had come about.

THE SECOND VATICAN COUNCIL

The Second Vatican Council threw open the doors of the Church with the twofold intention of letting the modern world, with its issues and problems and ideas, *into* the Church, and bringing the Church, with its wisdom and healing and good news, *into* the modern world.

The Church had stood apart for centuries, even resisting the changes that were affecting the world, until it was shocked by the reality of the Second World War, the Holocaust, and the development of nuclear weapons with its added possibility of mass destruction. These events led the Church to recognize the need to reengage itself and move into the center of the questions of our age, rather than stay on the periphery where it would have little effect. Pope John XXIII had the courage to gamble: he encouraged liturgical reform and made Church teachings more accessible, even knowing he was making the Church more vulnerable to scrutiny. But he believed, in the end, that the changes were part of God's plan in contributing to the unity of humanity. John recognized that the precarious position of the divided world called for a truly ecumenical council with representatives from East and West. He also had the wisdom and vision to invite Lutheran and other Protestant representatives so that the Christian Churches could find a united voice.

The numerous commissions that tackled the topics for debate, discussion, and agreement originally returned with nothing new, a set of orthodox teachings, which the pope and his bishops sent back again and again until some quite progressive ideas began to emerge. The first was that the hierarchy of the Church is at the service of the people and that the people make up the Church, which led to the reform in the liturgy with celebrants facing the congregation instead of being custodians to the mystery of sacrament. This also included the reform in language, from the historic Latin to local vernacular, and the change from medieval-inspired clerical habits to clothes of the everyday. A second progressive idea to emerge from the Council was to view the Church as a player in history, not a witness to it, removed and apart. This meant that the Church had to be involved in issues such as justice, peace, social action, and economics. Third, Church authority as it had been accepted for centuries was forced to break down and change. For instance, the structure of the Church around the primacy of the pope—the leader at the top of the pyramid with the minions of the curia all around—became more balanced between the head and the college of cardinals, enabling an important and progressive step to be taken toward reunification with other Christian Churches.

But despite these essential changes, the Second Vatican Council was called "the unfinished symphony" because it had created large movements and initiated some radical changes, but then realized that there was much more work to do in theology and lay involvement. There was more to understand, for instance, in recognizing the movement of the Holy Spirit in religious experience (and theological teaching), which was the intent of the Council itself. This spirit of renewal, of change, of embrace, would, perhaps, take generations, maybe centuries, to see it played out to its fulfillment. Steps were taken forward—and then taken back—but some permanent new movements have come from these steps. Liberation theology is one of them, the ecumenical dialogue and exchange another. The recognition of women, the laity, and the oppressed (which did not go far enough) have also become vital contributions to the understanding of the living Church. Most Catholics recognized that there would be no turning back: some lamented the loss of traditional ceremony, while others welcomed the rush of fresh air.

Pope John XXIII always emphasized dialogue as the way to peace, a way to bring people of faith into a united whole. The dialogue that began in the first years of the Council was, in a number of cases, not acted upon, especially under the leadership of the succeeding popes. John began a challenge that pulled the rug from under the safety and security of Catholic dogmatic teaching. To this day many Catholics are either trying to replace the old rug, or are intent on weaving a much more contemporary covering, full of the vibrancy of multicolored threads.

The Church in the twenty-first century is still changing, the Holy Spirit still working at breaking up the old to make way for the new. The Catholic Church has taken a lead among furthering the cause of interfaith dialogue and embracing people of other faiths, yet forgiveness and reconciliation were necessary before any radical changes could be put in place. Due to the work of Vatican II, Pope John Paul II could apologize to the Jewish people. Because of Vatican II, he could offer prayers at the Jewish Holocaust museum in Jerusalem.

The Second Vatican Council published sixteen documents of reform covering all life of the Church, including priestly sacraments, decision-making, the role of the laity, the role of the Church in the modern world, and reformation of canon law. The work continues to unfold.

CHRONOLOGY

1881	Born November 25 in Sotto Il Monte, Bergamo, as Angelo Giuseppe Roncalli.
1892–1900	Seminarian in Bergamo.
1900–4	Seminarian in Rome.
1901–2	Compulsory military service.

1904	Ordained priest at the Church of Santa Maria in Monte Santo, Rome.
1905–14	Became private secretary to bishop of Bergamo, Msgr. Radini Tedeschi, and also professor at the Bergamo seminary.
1915–18	War ministry as medical orderly and later as army chaplain.
1918–20	Spiritual director of the Bergamo seminary. Founds student's hostel.
1921	Works at the Propagation of Faith at the Vatican.
1925	Consecrated bishop; appointed apostolic visitor to Bulgaria.
1935	Appointed Vatican envoy to Turkey and Greece.
1944	Becomes papal nuncio to France, stationed in Paris.
1953	Appointed cardinal and patriarch of Venice.
1958	Elected pope on October 28.
1962	Commencement of Vatican II.
1963	Dies June 3 in Rome.
2000	Beatified September 3.

Spiritual Essentials

"I will never recommend anything unless I can serve as an example to others...."

Blessed John XXIII lived this teaching and because of his example and his writings, we can glean the essence of the virtues required for soul purification and spiritual leadership according to the way of Christ.

DISCIPLINE

The spiritual discipline and practice of self-knowledge is the training of the self and the mind to surrender, to be humble, to love, to shepherd, to obey, and to be free and in peace. Following the teachings of Thomas à Kempis, Bl. John XXIII said that all these virtues can be practiced by

- Seeking to do another's will, not yours
- Choosing to have less rather than more
- Taking the inferior position, the lowest place to others
- Desiring and praying that the will of God be fulfilled in you

SPIRITUAL JOY

Through devotion to the Blessed Sacrament, Blessed John discovered the experience of spiritual joy, which he said was the most important element of the spiritual life. Spiritual joy was achieved by

- Practicing courage
- Being intuitive
- Experiencing the genius of God
- Giving free rein to natural expressions of love
- Controlling the wandering mind and desirous flesh to enable the spiritual joy to flourish

LITTLE BUT WELL

During his studies, Blessed John took up the mantra of "reading little, but well," and he eventually lived this "little, but well" philosophy through all aspects of his life.

DETACHMENT

This virtue Blessed John referred to as the "supernatural virtue." He stated that we achieve it by

- Serenity and calmness
- Nobility of soul
- Concentrating on the higher ideals of spiritual growth and worth
- Becoming holy

HOLINESS

Holiness, he taught, was an "interior calm," an ability to smile amid the trials and crosses of life. This calm is found in the words and promises of Christ, the interior calm that is always with one. Its expression is in a "conquering charity," a feeling of renewed physical and spiritual energy, a sweetness in the soul and body.

UNITY

Blessed John's passion for unity is, he said, central to the teachings of Christ, the practice of which he recommends as the basis of Christian life, "the wholehearted practice and constant practice" of unity. He asks us to consider why today's prayer and desires cannot be tomorrow's reality.

The practice of a constant interior union with God "in thought, word, and deed" is essential for understanding that part of the Lord's prayer that says, "Thy kingdom come, thy will be done." He recommends we see everything in relation to these two ideals.

In the world the two evils that poison this thirst for and practice of unity are secularism and nationalism. Blessed John prods us to aim for what unites instead of concentrating on what separates. Moved by the first pictures of our planet sent back by space, he points to the "one planet" as our home, our spiritual aim for preservation of the oneness of life. He called the world "my family."

ON LEADERSHIP AND DIPLOMACY

Blessed John exemplified how the spiritual leadership and diplomacy of even one person can affect the world. The following are the vital elements he taught and practiced in portraying leadership.

- Have no expectations of being anybody except God's.
- Take on the tasks you are given, however humiliating, and do them without agitation "for goodness sake."
- Leaders must remember the problems not only of the developed world but also of the undeveloped world, including the poor, those who lament, and those with nothing.
- In all things be humble, with spiritual fervor, courteous to all, cheerful with a serenity of mind and heart.
- Show yourself by your actions, not your words.
- Avoid distractions, keep firm.
- Take the middle path in all conflict.
- Be loyal to God "for life and death."
- Be wary of honors and distinctions; they can be the "vanity of vanities." Fear flattery.
- Delegate—allow others to work and not keep everything in your own hands.
- Learn from not only the wise, but those whom you perceive as foolish.
- Free yourself from longings for change and promotions.
- Preserve "a fine simplicity" in conversation and behavior without affectation. Be afraid of saying too much on occasions, and always practice charity.
- Speak the truth and "be reprehensible in nothing."
- Remember that Christ is the solution to every problem.

SAYINGS

"The heart is the will and the spirit is the understanding. So we need a purified will and a renewed understanding."

"Simplicity contains nothing contrary to prudence, and the converse also is true. Simplicity is love: prudence is thought."

A Pilgrim Prayer to Blessed John XXIII

Blessed John, Papa John, our good pope,
Guide us as we step in your footsteps
To become closer to God, to touch the truth
Of what it is we need to learn in our lives.

To become courageous, surrendered, humble,
holy, and open
To all that will come our way
According to the will of God.
Pray for our intention, and guide us with your wisdom,
Your experience and acceptance of everything
coming from God
In the moment, in the heart of Christ, in exactly
where we are meant to be.
Help us with our responsibilities, with the healing
of our families,
With the necessary spiritual virtues in leadership.
In service, in ministry, in shepherding, in parenting,
In seeing all as one in divine unity,
Our planet, one family of love.
Pray for our protection, for the reign of good and
righteousness,
For justice to overcome evil,
For the light of God's grace,
For the teachings of Christ to live and be practiced,
Starting with me.

The Pilgrimage

Destinations:
Sotto Il Monte and Bergamo.
Suggested length:
One day

[If you want to complete this pilgrimage in Rome, see pages 309, 312, 317, 321–23.]

Sotto Il Monte is reached from Milan, from the Dolomites, from Venice, or south from Bologna and Padua via the exit at Bergamo near the great and famous Lake Como off the A4 or on side roads via Lecco. Take the northwest outskirts of Bergamo, follow signs to Lecco and then Ponte San Pietro (a plaque from President John F. Kennedy is on the right of the road). Follow the yellow signs for Sotto

Il Monte or "Casa Natale Papa Giovanni XXIII." Turn left off the Lecco road before Lecco and drive for 8 kilometers to the village.

Park at La Chiesa di S. Maria. The Roncalli family home is just west of the church.

Via Brusicco 42 (Roncalli family home)

This is where Angelo Roncalli was born and spent his childhood; it is typical of a farmer's dwelling of the area in the late nineteenth century. A modern sculpture of Roncalli as pope stands in the courtyard. The family rooms downstairs have photographs of his brothers and sisters, his parents, Zio Zaverio (his great-uncle who fathered him as his own), of the pope as a young seminarian, the card from his first Mass at St. Peter's tomb in Rome, and a picture of him with Bishop Tedeschi in Bergamo, when he was his secretary. Other photos show him during the First World War, when he was consecrated bishop, and during his diplomatic appointments. Upstairs off the terrace is the matrimonial bed of his parents where he was born, with the family's original simple furniture, and over the bed is a painting of the Madonna with a sword through her heart. In the next room are many of Roncalli's vestments from the time he was priest, cardinal, and pope.

Through the courtyard at the back of the building there is a new church built on the property, and in the hall leading to its entrance are many photographs of Blessed John XXIII's ministry. There is also a room packed full of thanksgiving mementos for answered prayers and the many miracles that have occurred through his intercession.

Return to the small Church of S. Maria on Via Brusicco.

Chiesa di S. Maria (Holy Mary Church)

The local parish church for the Roncalli family, this is where Angelo Roncalli was baptized on the day of his birth. His parents were married here. Young Angelo served as altar boy in this church, and was supported and taught by his beloved parish priest, Don Francesco Rebuzzini, who died suddenly here on his way to say Mass, a trauma that Angelo as a young seminarian never forgot. Built in 1450, the church is simple and not particularly attractive. John had acknowledged that it was "not much to look at, but inside what richness!" Much of the richness came from the many important events that happened here in Blessed John XXIII's life—his baptism, his first communion, and his early aspirations for the priesthood. He offered his first solemn sung Mass here after his ordination. Many pilgrims leave messages, gifts, and prayers in the baptismal font. This church would be the best place to offer your pilgrimage intention and prayer.

Chiesa di Madonna delle Caneve (or delle Cantine)

Behind the Church of S. Maria follow the signs on the paved road to the woods.

This stop commemorates Bl. John's earliest childhood memory, of when his mother took her young children up to the little shrine for the November feast day of Mary's Presentation in the Temple, and lifted him up to its window to consecrate him to her loving care. It still is a restful, holy place unspoiled by time. It was a place of pilgrimage, particularly at the turn of the century, when the locals would come to pray for their work and families. They would also come here for blessings before emigrating to North America or entering the military. It was in this chapel that John celebrated his last Mass in his hometown, two months before he was elected pope.

Drive into town to the parish church.

La Chiesa Parrochiale di S. Giovanni Battista (The Parish Church of St. John the Baptist)

Constructed between 1902–27, this church was consecrated by Bl. John when he was Bishop Roncalli and stationed in Bulgaria. He would always return to Sotto Il Monte for his summer vacations and taught adult catechism on Sunday afternoons at this church. Now there is an additional chapel of peace erected in his honor, where his miter and some other objects and relics are displayed, as well as a side altar dedicated to him.

In the crypt of the chapel is a moving painting of John F. Kennedy and Pope John sowing seeds of peace together. In this crypt are also the remains of Angelo Roncalli's parents, and evidence and gifts of all favors and miracles granted through his intercessionary prayers.

Ca'Maitino/Casa del Beato Giovanni XXIII

In the center of town, by Piazza della Pace (the Square of Peace), you will easily find a large and imposing yellow house with a garden in front, in which there's a bronze statue of Bl. John with two children. The steps to the right of the house lead to the entrance to what had been his summer apartment.

Ca'Maitino's history dates back to the fifteenth century, when Martino Roncalli originally built the house. Because of the family connection, Bl. John rented an apartment in it from the then-current owner, a Baron Gianmaria Scotti, and used it as a summer retreat for his annual vacations for over thirty years. It was here that his sisters Ancilla and Maria, who helped him with housekeeping, lived after their parents died. Msgr. Capovilla, Bl. John's secretary, now resides in this house along with the Poor Sisters of Bergamo. Capovilla is responsible for the magnificent restoration of articles from Bl. John's life; he has given us a gift of familiarity, a feeling that we are a part of Roncalli's intimate life by stepping through the door. It is as if Bl. John were shuffling toward each pilgrim in his papal slippers, with his arms open wide. Capovilla himself said of Ca'Maitino that it is "the most eloquent witness to [John]'s service for God and for souls."

The sisters will offer a tour of the house, but their language ability may be restricted. For this reason many of the important items of information are outlined below.

Ingresso (Entrance Parlor)

Exhibited throughout the house are artifacts, gifts, personal possessions, and photos that Bl. John had not only at Ca'Maitino but also in the Vatican, in Bergamo, and during his ministry outside Italy. Here there is evidence of his rich life, beginning with the entrance parlor that has a mixture of photos of his family, pictures of favorite saints (e.g., St. Bernardino of Siena), and St. Francis's crucifix from San Damiano over the door. Also, the crib in glass was his own. Additional busts and figurines of him were made by artists and others who wished to offer something to him during, and after, his life.

Soggiorno (Second Floor Yellow Room)

Much of the furniture and books in this room come from his time in Bergamo—the things that were in his student hostel, as well as the reference books for his lectures when he taught at the seminary. His parents' pictures are over the fireplace. There are also exhibits of his prayer books and objects of his personal devotion.

Studio (The Study) and Stanza Radini (The Radini Room)

Most of the objects in these rooms were left to Don Angelo Roncalli by the bishop of Bergamo, Radini Tedeschi. They include the pictures, the desk, and the chairs. The clock was a gift from an American Jewish couple. Other gifts are a statue of Mary from Milan Cathedral (due to his devotion to Milan's patron, St. Charles Borromeo), framed photos of his favorite popes, Pius X and Pius XII, and a portrait of his bishop. Walking between rooms you will see his old radio on a table by the wall. Bl. John liked the radio, although he would accuse it of distracting him. He had said, "The wireless takes up too much time and puts everything else out of joint." Even so, he managed to listen to his favorite programs between prayers. He found it necessary to follow the news, which he did daily and loved "some good program of music."

Camere (the Dining Room, Devotional, and Adjoining Rooms)

Again, many of the pieces of furniture here were gifts from Bishop Tedeschi. There are souvenirs of him and pictures, and also the leather chair, which Bl. John loved (and had by his bed in the Vatican). All the heart-shaped objects are of gratitude for prayers answered through the intercession of Bl. John.

Exhibited in the devotional are mostly sacred objects of Bl. John's clerical life. There are gifts and mementos from his trips with his bishop (to the Holy Land and elsewhere), as well as artistic gifts from others.

Galleria del Mappamondo (The Gallery of the Globe)

The huge globe of the world was special to Bl. John, and he had it in his study at the Vatican. It was a reminder of his family—the whole world—and his duty to shepherd its people to unity in peace. Also exhibited here are photos of King Boris III of Bulgaria and his wife, who became influential friends when John was bishop in Sofia. There is also a photo of Pope John Paul II praying to Bl. John. The typewriter has the indentation in its ribbon of the words of his last will and testament.

Stanza da letto (His Bedroom)

The bed here (including the mattress, covers, and pillows) is the bed on which Bl. John died in the Vatican. It was in this bed that he spent his final days and hours preparing for his death. This was the bed referred to as his altar by his nurse from Sotto Il Monte. On the wall opposite is the crucifix John mentioned when he was dying. There is a mold of his right hand after he had signed his encyclical "Peace on Earth," and many of his personal objects and furniture are those that were in his bedroom at the Vatican, including his last rosary.

Capella della pace (Chapel of Peace)

This room is as near as anyone could get to a pope's private chapel. All the items—the altar, kneeler, Stations of the Cross paintings on the wall, pictures, and liturgical objects—

were in Bl. John's private chapel in the Vatican, his personal place of prayer.

Scala (the Stairwell)

The stairs leading down to the first floor have portraits of all the Pope Johns, from the first to the twenty-third, along their walls. Also there are portraits of St. Philip Neri and St. Charles Borromeo.

Sale delle vetrine (Rooms of Vestments and Relics)

In the downstairs rooms there are many of Bl. John's clothes, shoes, hats, special items, and gifts that he used or was given throughout all his life, from priest, to bishop, cardinal, and pope. There are also the many medals of honor he received, his walking cane, his death mask, and another sculpture of his hand at death. The historic papers of Vatican II with his signatures are laid out and the last official photograph of him, a side view, is also exhibited. The briefcase he took to the conclave before he was voted pope is there, and many statues of Mary, who had told him she was his protector along with St. Joseph (his special saint whose name he shared). The photographic portrait of American president Eisenhower was sent by him directly to Bl. John as pope.

La Macchina (The Car)

In the garage is John's special car with the license plate SCV 20, the car of his cardinalship in which he was driven to the conclave in Rome on October 25, 1958.

Sacrarium S. Sepolcro e B. Giovanni XXIII (Holy Sepulcher Chapel to Blessed John XXIII)

This was originally the domestic chapel of the house, now named in the honor of the beatification of Pope John XXIII.

Torre di S. Giovanni (St. John's Tower)

From Ca'Maitino continue up the steps to the hilltop behind.

Here is a small chapel erected in honor of Bl. John because of his love of the tower from his childhood. The original tower here was the prototype for Bl. John's Tower in the Vatican gardens.

Bergamo

Bergamo is one of the central towns of Lombardy, a grand commercial center with a vibrant arts community. It is divided between the upper and lower towns, both distinct from each other, the upper being the older part.

No cars are allowed in the upper city of Bergamo, so it is necessary to park in the lower town and take the Funicolare *(cable car).*

La Città Alta (the Upper City)

Begin your walk around the old city of Bergamo by visiting Bl. John's seminary, now named after him. It is on the Via Arena and is written in Latin as Seminarium Papa Giovanni XXIII.

Rising over the door of the seminary is a huge bronze statue of John with his coat of arms. This is still a working seminary today. The upper city has evidence of students, and the feeling is of a university town, with not only the seminary but also a music school and a school of languages. This is the town where Bl. John, as a young priest, put a sign over the mirror in the hallway of the student hostel he created: "Know Thyself." Here he delved deeply into the knowledge of self and offered his early priesthood to the service of Christ in the world.

Follow the signs back to the Duomo in the main piazza.

La Basilica di S. Maria Maggiore

Although originally a twelfth-century church, the basilica has been remodeled in the Baroque style of the late sixteenth and early seventeenth centuries. There are extraordinary tapestries on the wall, and the engraved wood around the altars and on the doors is a special feature. Many of the painted frescoes depict the life of St. Francis.

Before visiting the basilica, view the **baptistery,** which is a unique building directly opposite it. Also the **Colleoni monument** next to it is a perfect example of Bergamese devotional artistry.

Duomo di S. Alessandro (The Cathedral of St. Alexander)

This is the official church of the bishop of Bergamo and his diocese and would have had personal significance to young Don Angelo Roncalli during his service to his bishop as secretary over the ten years he spent here. There's a chapel within dedicated to Bl. John and a statue of him with the doves of the Holy Spirit and of peace. There are also some relics as gifts from the Vatican: three of the crosses he wore, a piece of his bone, his episcopal ring when bishop, the papal tiara from 1958–63, and a chalice he personally gave to the cathedral in 1959. The box and the robe he was originally buried in at St. Peter's are shown here. In 2000 when he was beatified, he was removed from this coffin wearing these exact robes. His remains were brought up from the crypt at St. Peter's into the church where he can now be viewed in a glass sarcophagus.

La Capella di San Giovanni Battista (The Chapel of St. John the Baptist)

Located inside the *Duomo,* this chapel would have been a favorite place for Don Roncalli to have prayed, and he would have spent much time here in devotion to the Blessed Sacrament, part of his regular spiritual practice. A modern statue of St. Charles Borromeo greets you at its entrance. End your pilgrimage with your petition, your offering, and your intention by lighting a candle for the intercession of Blessed John XXIII.

III

A Pilgrimage in Rome

"From there we have received the pledge of our faith, in that we sigh for her beauty while on our pilgrimage."

St. Augustine in *City of God*

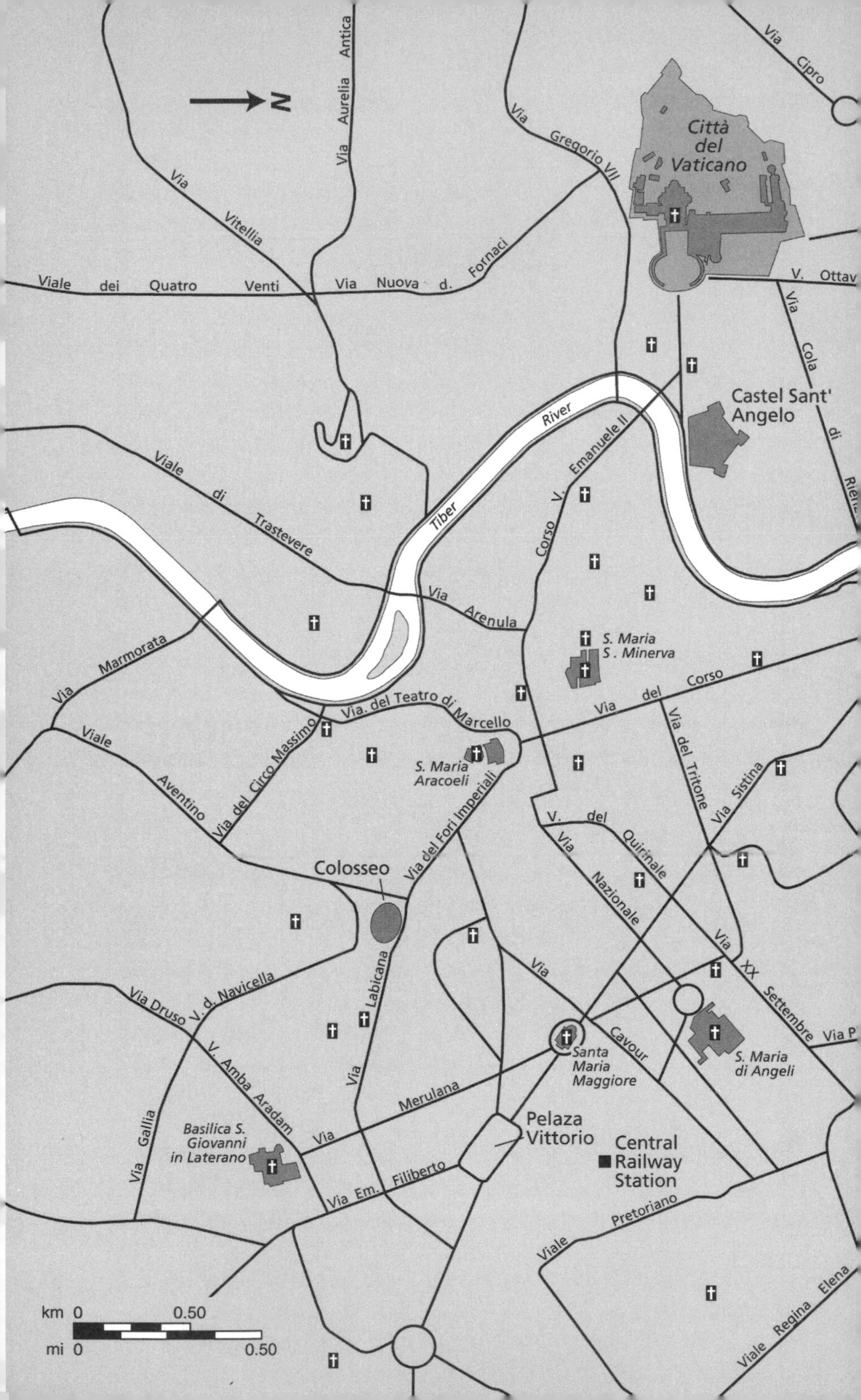

N
Via Aurelia Antica
Via Vitellia
Viale dei Quatro Venti
Via Nuova d. Fornaci
Via Gregorio VII
Via Cipro
Città del Vaticano
V. Ottav
Via Cola di Rienzo
Castel Sant' Angelo
Tiber River
Corso V. Emanuele II
Viale di Trastevere
Via Arenula
S. Maria S. Minerva
Via Marmorata
Via del Corso
Via. del Teatro di Marcello
Viale Aventino
Via del Circo Massimo
S. Maria Aracoeli
Via del Fori Imperiali
Via del Tritone
Via Sistina
V. del Quirinale
Via Nazionale
Colosseo
Via XX Settembre
Via Labicana
Via Cavour
Via Druso
V. d. Navicella
V. Amba Aradam
S. Maria di Angeli
Via P
Santa Maria Maggiore
Via Merulana
Via Gallia
Basilica S. Giovanni in Laterano
Pelaza Vittorio
Central Railway Station
Via Em. Filiberto
Viale Pretoriano
Viale Regina Elena
km 0 0.50
mi 0 0.50

A Brief Overview

Like a magnet Rome has drawn pilgrims to its center from the very beginning. As early as twenty years after Jesus' death, it was the place where his apostle Peter was to live, minister, and die, and where Paul also preached and died. It was where the early Christian Church flourished in secret, where martyrdom was common for believers who denied the traditional Roman ways of worship, and where faith was tested in the fire of cruelty and suspicion.

It was the center of authority and power for the Roman emperors and the capital of the empire for many centuries. Its architecture, language, arts, religion, culture, philosophies, and politics have influenced most of the civilized world.

During the reign of Emperor Constantine in the fourth century, the pagan empire converted to a Christian empire. This conversion laid the foundations for Rome to be the headquarters, not only for the "Roman" Catholic religion, but also for the Catholic Church worldwide, its influence overseen and guided by the pope and the Holy See. The Christianized city was hailed as the New Jerusalem and the Eternal City. Its shrines and churches were sanctified by the many relics transported from the Holy Land, and the heritage of the saints began in earnest with devotion at their tombs. A pilgrimage to Rome was central to any crusader, who came to be blessed by the pope. Ordinary citizens, too, made their way on foot to honor the joint feast day of St. Peter and St. Paul (now June 29). Rome was the official residence of the pope, and site of the rituals over which he presided (including the sacrament of forgiveness in the Jubilee years); it was also the place of the beatification and canonization of saints. All this made pilgrimage to Rome a priority for Christian devotion.

Not everything that Rome has to offer can be seen in one trip, but the following four days are an introduction to the overall elements of experiencing Rome on pilgrimage within a framework composed of four themes:

1. The early Christian Church
2. Legends and traditions
3. Saints mentioned elsewhere in this book
4. Rome's magnificent sacred art

The following selection of places to visit are composed of "the best" or "must sees" in relation to an initial visit to the city and can, with further reference and research, be expanded in future visits.

ALL ROADS LEAD TO ROME

Any of the pilgrimages in this book probably already includes arriving or departing from Italy's capital. And because of Rome's pilgrimage tradition, a few days here can be complementary to any other pilgrimage in this book. For instance, if you plan a St. Benedict or St. Pio pilgrimage southward, or a St. Francis and Holy Women trip northward, both could begin in Rome. And it is also a perfect finale.

In any case, in Italy all roads certainly do lead to Rome and out of Rome, but it is easier to find your way *in,* if you are driving in a car, than to discover the right exit *out,* which is a challenge to any visitor. As this four-day Roman pilgrimage can be taken by foot or bus or taxi, it is best to leave any car outside the main center.

All major highways link with the ring road around central Rome, and once you're on this, it is easier to find your way in or out. The exits and entrances are clearly marked by name and number.

An Introduction to the Early Christian Church

The city of Rome was founded by Romulus and Remus in 753 BC on the banks of the River Tiber. Known in Latin as Tiberinus, the river was originally revered as a god. Curling through the city, Tiberinus was invoked in periods of drought and celebrated at the temple built on an island between its shores, especially on its feast day, December 8. Fisherman would honor Tiberinus each June in the area near Trastevere, and at its estuary in Ostia, the port of Rome, where another temple existed.

For the early Christians, the Tiber River also wound its way around *their* places of significance. The tradition of baptism in a river, established by St. John in the River Jordan, was continued by St. Peter who offered similar-style baptism to Roman converts in the Tiber. And on the road into Rome from the great port of Ostia, called the Ostian Way, St. Paul was executed.

The Romans did not start out as persecutors of Christians: the first martyr, St. Stephen, was stoned in Jerusalem. Ancient Rome, by comparison, was at first tolerant toward the practice of traditional religion by its conquered peoples (like Judaism, for example), as it was believed to be a necessary part of binding the community and the race of people. Christians got into trouble because they were accused—first by the Jewish community, which later influenced the Romans—for breaking ties to custom and being irreverent toward what was considered sacred. They were assumed to be atheists for believing in a more informal and freer way of life and worship with a personal God. Suspicion was later compounded and spread due to the secrecy in which persecuted Christians gathered and practiced their beliefs. This practice united all believers together, whatever their class; for instance, slaves and nobles would equally share the same eucharistic table. This contributed to the common assumption that Christianity was not a religion as understood (based on community and race of people), but a cult or sect, which in the Roman Empire was considered a heretical threat. During the first thirty-five years after Jesus' death, the Roman magistrates afforded Christians a fair trial. St. Paul asked to be tried as a Roman citizen for that reason, after being imprisoned in Caesarea in AD 57. But Emperor Nero's enthusiasm for liberal and judicial fairness dampened after the pettiness of politics wore down his optimism. He turned his attention instead to his greater love—the arts and the Greek theater—remaining for the most part away from Rome in his pursuit of fame as an actor and performer; he preferred partying and the pursuit of entertainment to battle, supremacy, and leadership of the senate. Though he despised taking life, he murdered his mother, Agrippina, who was responsible for his election and whom he considered a threat to his reign. He also killed his first wife, whom he had divorced. Then fear and suspicion crept more dramatically into his character. In AD 64, Rome suffered the Great Fire, which destroyed much of the city's holy temples and monuments. Needing a scapegoat, Nero focused his rage on the Christian community in Rome, blaming them for destroying the sacred places. He condemned them as criminals and had them put to abominable deaths, the most common being crucifixion, sewn up live in the skins of wild beasts, or devoured by lions and dogs. Others were smeared with combustible liquids and torched to death. Nero committed suicide in 68 after having killed many of his own supporters in the senate and after being abandoned by his praetorian guards. It was during the final year of Nero's reign that both St. Peter and St. Paul suffered the common fate of martyrdom.

ST. PETER AND ST. PAUL (DIED AD 67)

Simon Peter, a Jewish fisherman from Capernaum, was an apostle of Jesus Christ who, on recognizing him as the Messiah, was appointed by him in AD 30 to lead the community of followers. Simon was a married man with children. In some accounts it is noted that his wife also suffered martyrdom, but we do not know where. Christ gave Simon the name *Petrus* (which means "rock" in Latin), and after Christ's death, resurrection, and ascension, St. Peter began missionary work and traveled to the surrounding towns. Spending the early years of his ministry in Jerusalem, he left after Herod Agrippa I (AD 42–44) had imprisoned him (and he had miraculously escaped) during the ongoing persecution of Christianized Jews. Peter led the communities in Antioch and later in Asia Minor and Corinth, and ended his missionary work in Rome (where it's possible he lived for another twenty-five years). He finally suffered imprisonment and execution under the Neronian persecution.

Originally St. Paul was a persecutor of Christians. He became a disciple of Jesus Christ after his conversion on the road to Damascus. After visiting St. Peter and the apostles in Jerusalem, Paul evangelized in Tarsus and Antioch, bringing Gentiles into the early communities. Returning to Jerusalem a number of times, he was captured on his fifth visit and spent two years in a prison in Caesarea, departing for Rome in AD 59 at his request for trial as a Roman citizen. Imprisoned in Rome for a further two years, he then spent four years in ministry there before being arrested again in AD 66 and executed in 67 at the age of sixty-eight. It is commonly believed that both St. Peter and St. Paul died on the same day, or within the same week.

SOME LATER ROMAN MARTYRS

After Nero, for about 250 years, Christians in Rome were still exposed to constant suspicion and persecution, interspersed by the occasional years of peace caused by lenient (or absent) emperors. All Christian gatherings and rituals were carried out in secret, mostly in private homes, their cemeteries being the only public places of reverence. It is believed that the first house church in Rome was established in the home of Mary, the mother of Mark the evangelist (who might have written his Gospel in Rome), and even with the threat of death, the new religion quickly spread among Roman citizens.

Through the hundreds of years of persecution there, two women emerged whose deaths lived on in the hearts of the church communities and whose tombs and places of worship became the earliest pilgrimage sites: the martyrs Cecilia and Agnes.

ST. CECILIA (DIED AD 230)

A young Roman woman, Cecilia was a Christian betrothed to a pagan man called Valerian. She vowed herself to virginal purity as an oblation to God, and never physically consummated her marriage. At her wedding it was believed that she sang to God in her heart as part of her religious commitment and because of this became the patron saint of music. After their marriage, Valerian and his brother, Tiburtius, both converted to Christianity and were executed. Shortly afterwards, Cecilia was brought before the tribunal for refusing to offer sacrifices to the Roman gods, and she was also sentenced to death by scalding and suffocation in her own steam bath. As she did not immediately succumb to this torture and was found to be miraculously alive, a soldier decapitated her. Even the blows to her head and neck failed to kill her outright, and she bled to death over the next three days. Originally buried in the St. Callisto catacombs, she is now in the crypt of the church erected in her name over her original house, which she had hoped would become a place of worship. Her life—and death—have been the inspiration for many artists and composers, especially in the early mosaics of Ravenna and in the fifteenth century by Raphael (the original painting is in Bologna). St. Cecilia is usually portrayed holding a lute or other instruments. Musical pieces, odes, and Masses were written and dedicated to her memory by many of the great composers from the sixteenth century onward.

ST. AGNES (DIED AD 304)

At the age of thirteen—after refusing marriage to the son of Symphorian, the prefect of Rome, who later tried to rape her—Agnes openly declared her dedication to Jesus Christ by refusing to sacrifice to the gods. After being stripped, she was exposed naked as a public spectacle outside a brothel in the Piazza Navona and then was physically tortured and killed by a sword through her throat. Praised by early Christian writers as an example of faithful courage, St. Agnes is mentioned in the Roman Canon and her feast is celebrated in both the Eastern and Western Churches. In art—including the early mosaics—she was often portrayed with a lamb in her arms or at her feet, as her name in Latin (Agnus) means "lamb."

There are two churches consecrated in her name, one built over the place where she was tortured and killed, and the other, a basilica with her tomb, built over the family cemetery in which her parents were believed to have buried her.

THE SIGN OF THE CROSS

Around the turn of the fourth century, it slowly became safer for Christians to practice their ceremonies outside their homes and begin to erect churches for worship. This was partly due to Emperor Constantine's father, Constantius Chlorus, who admired the virtues of his many Christian servants . His wife, the Empress Helena (who was to become St. Helen), also shared his tolerance toward the Christian religion, although Constantius divorced her after becoming emperor in AD 292. But it was their son Constantine who made Christianity the official religion of Rome through a personal experience in battle. Finding no solace or aid from the Roman gods and suffering from continuous defeat, he was informed in a dream to entrust the future of his empire to Jesus Christ. While summoning his troops against his adversary, Maxentius, he saw a cross in the sky above him inscribed with the words *In hoc signo vinces* ("By this sign, you shall conquer"). The standard was then created, the heraldic symbol that included the Sign of the Cross, and from then on, the Christian religion of selfless generosity and forgiveness, portrayed by the symbol of a fish, emerged instead as a force of might and power. Constantine's subsequent victories led him to impose Christianity as the official religion of Rome—and the empire—and with the marriage of the two came the influence and security that led to the appropriation of Rome as the center of the Church. Having the artistic influence and economic means to do so, Constantine started erecting shrines to the Christian God—the first two being San Giovanni in Laterano (St. John Lateran) and the Santa Croce in Gerusalemme, The Holy Cross of Jerusalem, with a donation from his mother. Converting to Christianity herself at the age of sixty, Helena embraced the religion with zeal—even traveling to the Holy Land (where she died) to arrange for the transport of irreplaceable Christian relics, including what was believed to be the remains of the true cross, as well as the holy steps Jesus Christ walked on during his trial. The cross became not just the symbol of salvation (through the understanding of Christ's death and resurrection) but the sign of Rome's redemption. Over the next sixty-seven years, Roman paganism as it was known, revered, and practiced was dismantled and destroyed, replaced by a Roman-influenced Christianity that then existed for centuries until the break with the Eastern Orthodox Church and the Protestant Reformation. From then, it continued as Roman Catholicism, the religion that owes a large part of its cultural and ritualistic heritage to Roman paganism, and its forms of governance, leadership, and Latin language to Roman imperialism.

The Pilgrimage

Suggested length:
Four days

DAY ONE

Morning: Colosseum, Mamertine Prison, S. Pietro in Vincoli, and S. Pudenziana
Afternoon: S. Stefano Rotondo, Catacombs of S. Callisto and S. Sebastiano, and San Paolo Fuori le Mura

The Colosseum

Start the morning early at the Colosseum, the massive amphitheater commissioned by Emperor Vespasian in AD 72 and built on the grounds of Nero's palace. It probably got its name from the Colossus of Nero (a huge bronze statue that stood near it). The Colosseum was used for free public spectacles and entertainment that included gladiator combats and wild-animal fights. It was also used as a circus, as exotic animals were brought in from North Africa and the Middle East and kept in cages around its circumference. Its eighty arched entrances led fifty thousand spectators to their seats. Later a common site for Christian martyrdom, the Colosseum was dedicated in 1749 to the passion of Jesus.

Mamertine Prison

Walk toward the Forum from the Colosseum to the sixteenth-century Church of San Giuseppe dei Felegnami (St. Joseph the Carpenter) at its edge. This is Mamertino, S. Pietro Incarcare, Civio Argentario 1.

Mamertine Prison is below the church. It is where, according to legend, Sts. Peter and Paul were imprisoned before their execution, as the prison was commonly used for Christian incarceration. The column to which St. Peter was reputedly chained still exists today; the chains themselves can be viewed in the Church of S. Pietro in Vincoli. The upper part of the two levels of the prison is where the condemned would be held, and the lower, called the Tullianum, was where their bodies were thrown into the sewer. There is an altar over the place (with a relief of St. Peter in chains) where a spring miraculously rose up in the ground of Peter's cell so that he could baptize two of his guards. The water still flows today.

The Basilica of S. Pietro in Vincoli (St. Peter in Chains)

From the Mamertine Prison it's an easy walk to this church not far from the Colosseum, in Piazza di San Pietro in Vincoli, 4A (off Via Cavour).

Vincoli means "chains" in Italian, and in the fifth century Pope St. Leo I ordered a church to be built over the site where St. Peter was sentenced to death by the Roman tribunal. The bishop of Jerusalem had bequeathed to Empress Eudoxia the chains by which St. Peter had been imprisoned there (and which had broken during his miraculous escape under the Roman consul, Herodotus). Eudoxia brought the chains back to Rome and gave them to the pope. After Pope Leo discovered that the Jerusalem chains were almost identical to the Mamertine Prison chains in Rome, he had them placed together in this church where they are still displayed today in a bronze reliquary under the high altar. Centuries later Pope Julius II, a great patron of the arts, commissioned Michelangelo to design his epitaph. The imposing sculpture of *Moses and the Dying Slaves* can be seen over Pope Julius II's tomb to the right of the altar. The twelve columns on each side of the church represent the apostles.

The Church of S. Pudenziana

A short walk to Via Urbana, 160, leads to this church with its mixed history.

A first-century Roman senator called Pudens lived on the site and had hosted St. Peter as one of his guests who, in turn, converted his whole family and baptized them in their house or garden. Believed to have been the site of an early Christian church, one hundred years later it was turned into a public bathhouse and then, in the fourth century, the Church of Pudens was erected. A legend was later established about a St. Pudentiana, a woman in the Pudens family who sheltered persecuted Christians. Although declared invalid as official saints, members of the family are portrayed in the church in fourth-century mosaics. The apostles are also represented as Roman senators in togas, and along with the Pudens sisters they accompany the enthroned Christ. The Pudens family members are also portrayed on the outside facade of the church.

Church of S. Stefano Rotondo Sul Celio

At *Via di Santo Stefano 7* is one of the oldest churches in Rome, built over an early Roman military camp; the circular dome of the church's roof could have been part of a temple to petition one of the gods in battle. Originally constructed to be architecturally similar to the Holy Sepulcher Church in Jerusalem, it was built in the late fifth century in honor of Christianity's first martyr, St. Stephen. It is believed that St. Stephen's remains were brought from Jerusalem back to Europe around the time of Constantine and distributed to parishes that built churches in his honor. This church was certainly one of the earliest, if not the first. Those who prayed to St. Stephen found that he miraculously interceded in healing physical infirmities. In this church there are many Byzantine mosaics from the seventh to the ninth century, as well as frescoes, depicting stories of St. Stephen's life, the horrifying deaths of other martyrs, and portraits of early Roman martyrs whose remains had been moved here from the catacombs.

Catacombs of S. Callisto and San Sebastiano

Go to Via Appia Antica 110 and 136.

As it was the law of Rome that people could not be buried within the walls of the city, all the cemeteries of the early times were on the outskirts of town. Christians adopted the Jewish tradition of burying their dead in catacombs—underground corridors where bodies could be safely stored. Because Roman law also prevented desecration of burial places, Christians felt safe to use them for other means including gathering for eucharistic celebrations and the administration of the sacraments. On the walls of the catacombs are still preserved early paintings of Christians seated around a table. Miles of these underground catacombs exist to this day and can be visited as part of a pilgrimage, as they were honored as shrines to the saints. Some of the catacombs (like those at Via Latina) were individual cemeteries for richer families who owned the lots and buried their relatives together. The most common are the S. Callisto and S. Sebastiano catacombs, so these are the ones to visit first.

Many of the saints (and most of the fourteen popes prior to Constantine's reign) were buried in S. Callisto and were later transferred to churches in the fourth century. St. Cecilia's body was found here in 820 and taken to the church in Trastevere built over the site of her home. The sculpture of her in the catacombs is a copy of the original in her church.

The catacomb named after St. Sebastian was an important place of pilgrimage from antiquity. Many converted to Christianity after receiving healings and revelations visiting this catacomb. Many of the miracles were attributed not to St. Sebastian himself but to Sts. Peter and Paul, who were believed to have been originally buried here.

St. Sebastian is himself one of the more famous Christian martyrs. A third-century Roman soldier who converted to Christianity, he was condemned to die by the arrow (which is why he is depicted standing with arrows in his body). Left for dead, he was discovered to be still alive, and when he recovered, he faced his accuser, the Emperor

Diocletian, admonishing him for his persecution of Christians. Due to his belligerence, Sebastian was bludgeoned to death and his body thrown into the sewers. A pious Roman woman took his body and buried him in the catacombs, now under the church in his name created by Constantine, and his remains rest in the chapel dedicated to him. **The Chapel of the Relics** contains the arrows that were hurled at St. Sebastian, the column that he was tied to for his final beating, and some alleged footprints of Christ (who met St. Peter on the Appian Way). The present church was rebuilt over the original basilica. The drawings of St. Peter and St. Paul on the original walls point to the possibility that both men were actually buried here in the years before or between being transferred to their own basilicas. This might have taken place during the Valerian persecution in 258 to ensure that their remains were not desecrated.

S. Paolo Fuori le Mura (St. Paul Outside the Walls)

From the catacombs, take a taxi to Via Ostiense 186, which is not too far away from the catacombs.

Built in the fourth century, St. Paul's still retains some of its original structure. There's an impressive statue of St. Paul outside, holding a sword. To the left of it is the "Holy Door" with scenes from the Old and New Testament in bronze (which was returned to Rome from Constantinople in the eleventh century). The church was mostly rebuilt in 1832 after a fire destroyed it, although the medieval cloisters that survived the flames are considered the most impressive in Rome. St. Paul's tomb is believed to be under the main altar and the outstanding mosaics of every pope run like a frieze around the nave. All two hundred and sixty-three of them are portrayed with space for only eight more after John Paul II. Roman tradition believes the world will come to an end when there is no more room on the St. Paul's wall for another pope. Other art depicts St. Paul's life in chronological order including some scenes taken from the Acts of the Apostles.

It was here in this basilica that Pope John XXIII officially announced his intention for the Second Vatican Council to the bishops and cardinals of the Catholic Church, asking them for prayers for "a good start."

DAY TWO

Morning: Basilica of S. Cecilia and S. Francesco a Ripa, both in Trastevere; and Sant'Agnese in Agone

Afternoon: Sant'Agnese Fuori Le Mura (St. Agnes Outside the Walls), San Giovanni Laterano (St. John Lateran), Scala Santa (Holy Steps) and Sancta Sanctorum (Holy of Holies Sanctuary), and S. Croce in Gerusalemme (Holy Cross of Jerusalem)

Basilica of S. Cecilia

Depending on where you are staying in Rome, you can walk or take a cab to the Trastevere region of the city. In its quiet village atmosphere, it is easy to walk around. Go to the Piazza di Santa Cecilia, and visit the church in the name of the early martyr who is the patron saint of music.

St. Cecilia was executed in AD 230 in her own home, which stood at this site. Parts of the house can still be seen under the church where there are also remains of a Roman tannery. This is the house she wished to become a place of worship before she died. Her remains, when exhumed from the S. Callisto catacombs, were found to be still intact, and they were brought back to be reburied here in the ninth century when Pope Paschal I rebuilt the church. The apse mosaic comes from this period. In 1599 the tomb was opened for viewing and, on seeing the incorrupt body, Clement VIII had the sculptor Maderno create the famed statue that is now in front of the altar. There are also scenes in paintings of her life throughout the church. In a side chapel are the remains of the steam bath where she was left to die. Her tomb is now shared with her husband, a brother-in-law, and two popes in the crypt.

S. Francesco a Ripa

Still in Trastevere, go to Piazza San Francesco d'Assisi 88.

S. Francesco a Ripa is the Benedictine monastery where St. Francis of Assisi usually stayed when he came to Rome. The monastery later became a hospice for pilgrims. Rebuilt by Franciscan followers and restored in the seventeenth century, the monastery has the stone pillow and crucifix Francis used in his cell, as well as other relics, displayed in the **Chapel of San Francesco**. The panel painting of him (attributed to Margaritone d'Arezzo) is meant to be as true a likeness as any, although this is only a reproduction (the original is in the Vatican picture gallery). The church contains many sculptural treasures including Bernini's *Ecstasy of Beata Ludovica Albertoni.*

Sant'Agnese in Agone

Take a cab to Piazza Navona to the Church of St. Agnes in Agone.

It is believed that the church was built over the site of a brothel where in AD 304 young Agnes was exposed naked in the piazza to force her to deny her Christian faith. Martyred at this site, she was buried in the catacombs, over which was built a church that houses her tomb. This is the Sant'Agnese Fuori le Mura that can be visited next.

Sant'Agnese Fuori le Mura

Take a taxi to Via Nomentana, 349.

This church was described in a book by author Margaret Visser as "...a place where you could almost reach out and touch the early Christians of Rome....This church was uncommonly close to what they would have known and liked." It is one of a cluster of early Christian churches built over the tombs of martyrs in the extensive catacombs below. Here is where St. Agnes was originally buried in her family's own private cemetery. The church in her name was erected over it at the request of Emperor Constantine's daughter, Constantia, whose petitions to the saint were answered. St. Agnes's tomb is now in the crypt of the church with the original stone monument; the shrine is from the seventh century, as are the mosaics. St. Agnes is portrayed in gold holding a lamb, a symbol for her name and youth. In 1901 excavations in the church revealed a reliquary that measured the length of a young girl, and soon thereafter a skull was discovered in the St. John Lateran Palace, the teeth of which confirmed it as that of a girl of about thirteen years of age.

The Basilica of San Giovanni in Laterano (St. John Lateran)

Go to Piazza di San Giovanni in Laterano.

Originally built as a church by Emperor Constantine on the property of the palace of the Lateran family, who were Christians, it was later rebuilt in 1646. For centuries it was the official residence of the pope (prior to the move to Avignon in the fifteenth century). After the papacy returned to Rome, the church lost its central importance, being usurped by the restoration of St. Peter's, which was only a cemetery before. Like St. Peter's Basilica today, St. John Lateran was the place of prime importance to any pilgrim in Rome. This was the palace of the popes, the headquarters of the Church, where all coronations took place up to as late as 1870. All decisions and dialogue happened here, as did the definitions and refinement of official Church teachings. Audiences of any saint with the pope (like St. Francis's initial and subsequent meetings, for example, and St. Bonaventure's and St. Thomas Aquinas's theological presentations) would have taken place at St. John Lateran. Pope Innocent III agreed to grant audience to St. Francis in the early days of the friars partly because of a dream he had of the Lateran Palace falling down and being held up solely by a beggar in a brown tunic.

There's a magnificent bronze monument to the east of the building in **Piazza di Porta S. Giovanni** portraying St. Francis and his early companions as they arrived in Rome. The inscription in translation reads "St. Francis of Assisi, Rome, Italy, and the World."

St. John's is still linked with the present pope as it has remained the official church of the Bishop of Rome, a title the pope assumes on his coronation. A place that has witnessed the progression of the papacy from the fourth century to the present day, St. John Lateran is the perfect place to visit prior to St. Peter's as it links the chronology of the official papal residences. It was—and still is—the first official Christian shrine in the western world.

The facade of the church is similar to that of St. Peter's with its papal insignias in stone outside. **The obelisk** in its square is the oldest in Rome (and the tallest in the world), dating as far back as the fifteenth century BC. It stood originally at the Temple of Anon in Thebes and was brought to Rome by Emperor Constantine's son, Constantius II, in AD 357, who had a long ship especially built to transport it. Many of the authentic decorations on its surface were destroyed during the last century.

On entering the front part of the church, there's a **statue of Emperor Constantine** to your left in the portico. The twelve apostles in stone circle the church with Sts. Peter and Paul flanking the papal altar, as well as portrayed in gold over the altar. Underneath is a statue of St. John the Baptist in his own chapel, which is almost Byzantine in design. The Bishop of Rome's throne is behind the altar, where all the popes have sat. The magnificent mosaic dome over the throne reminds every pilgrim of the central blessings of Christ and the heritage of the popes as the "Vicars of Christ." The side altar now reserved for private prayer is perfect in its classical proportions. **The ancient cloister** is also worth a visit. It is the only surviving evidence of the medieval structure after St. John's many fires and destruction. Over the gift shop is an image of **Pope Innocent III,** who was the pope who gave St. Francis official permission to preach.

Bl. John XXIII recalled his many times visiting St. John Lateran, including at the age of twenty-one when he celebrated what he called a solemn ceremony on entering the deaconate. On the eve of his ordination as a priest, he went with his seminarian teacher to the basilica for prayer, and when as pope he assumed the bishopric of Rome, he recalled taking possession of this basilica, the heart of his diocese, as "one of the most wonderful days of my life."

Scala Santa and Sancta Sanctorum (Holy Steps and Holy of Holies Sanctuary)

Across from the basilica are the surviving buildings of the old Lateran palace, among them the one that houses the Holy Steps. The Holy Steps are believed to be the ones that Jesus ascended in Pontius Pilate's house during his trial and were brought back from Jerusalem by Emperor Constantine's mother, St. Helena. Considered sacred, they have been covered in wood, and pilgrims ascend them on their knees in silent prayer. At the top of the staircase is the pope's private chapel, the Sancta Sanctorum, which contains many relics, including an image of Jesus Christ believed to be the work of St. Luke. It had been used many times in the past as a protective icon against the devastation of plagues.

S. Croce in Gerusalemme (The Holy Cross of Jerusalem)

From the St. John Lateran, walk down the Viale Carlo Felice to the Piazza of S. Croce in Gerusalemme where there are ancient brick remains of the palace of Emperor Constantine's mother, St. Helena.

This church was founded by St. Helena in AD 320 on the grounds of her private home to house the relics of the true cross, the cross that Jesus Christ was crucified upon. This church was therefore central to any Roman pilgrimage establishing its link with Jerusalem. Among the number of statues on its exterior roof is St. Helena herself with the cross. The present church was redesigned in the nineteenth century, and **St. Helen's Chapel** to the right of the main altar is full of stunning mosaics.

The Santuario della Croce (the Sanctuary of the Cross) was built especially for veneration of the three pieces of the true cross, which are encased in glass. There's also a nail from Jesus' crucifixion, two thorns from his crown, and pieces of the pillar to which he was tied and scourged.

DAY THREE

Morning: S. Maria Sopra Minerva, the Pantheon, and Basilica di S. Pietro (St. Peter's)
Afternoon: Musei Vaticani (Vatican museums, including the Sistine Chapel)

S. Maria Sopra Minerva (Holy Mary Over Minerva)

Begin your day at Piazza della Minerva, 42.

The jewel of the Church of S. Maria Sopra Minerva has a history as far back as ancient Rome. It was built in the eighth century over the ruins of the original temple to the goddess Minerva (Athena in Greek). Minerva was revered as the protector of Rome, especially in times of battle, and was patron of the military providing victory, peace, and abundance. Also recognized as the goddess patron of arts, of physicians, and of all humanity, she was referred to as "she who thinks ahead," the source of all practical wisdom. It is no coincidence then that this Christian church is dedicated to the Madonna, to the heritage of feminine wisdom, and its greatest treasure lies under the high altar, the body of St. Catherine of Siena, she "who thought ahead." In its early days the place was home to religious women, beginning with Basilian nuns who moved to Rome from the East, and in the thirteenth century Benedictine nuns had a convent on its site. They passed it on to the Dominicans who have cared for the church ever since.

The sixth-century BC **Egyptian obelisk** at its entrance was originally discovered in the garden of the old monastery and is supported by a marble elephant (sculpted by Bernini), representing the Christian virtues of intelligence and piety.

The interior of the church is a celebration of the feminine in its gothic architecture, its atmosphere of prayer, and the very holy presence of **St. Catherine's tomb.** Having died in a house close to her local Dominican church, St. Catherine (without her head, which was returned to St. Dominic's Church in Siena) originally lay in the **Capella del Rosario (Chapel of the Rosary)** for 350 years. During St. Catherine's funeral in this church, the residing priest could not be heard above the din of the crowds' petitionary prayers. The pictures that hung in the original room in which St. Catherine died were moved from their original location on Via Chiara, to just off the sacristy. The paintings include frescoes of many saints including Augustine, the Sicilian martyr Jerome, Lucy, and Appolinarius, and a pietà with John the Baptist.

Just beside the main altar of the church is a statue by **Michelangelo** of the Risen Christ.

Teatro Rossini

On exiting the church, the Via Santa Chiara (St. Clare Street) is straight ahead and number 14 is the house in which St. Catherine lived with her spiritual family during the last year of her life. It is now a theater.

In the theater is the **Capella del Transito** (a chapel erected in the room in which St. Catherine died). It's usually locked. However, on certain days of the month you can visit it, but this being Rome, there are no standard times!

The Pantheon

At the other side of the Church of S. Maria Sopra Minerva, there's the imposing Pantheon, the oldest and largest standing Roman temple, believed to have been built over two thousand years ago. When Rome became Christianized, the Pantheon became a church, although when the popes were in Avignon, it was used as a fortress and a poultry market. The Renaissance artist Raphael (who died in Rome in 1520) is buried in the Pantheon, at his request. His tomb lies below a Madonna by Lorenzetto (1524) and beside it is a memorial to his fiancée, Maria Bibbiena. His last unfinished painting, *The Transfiguration of Christ,* was placed at the head of his bier until it was moved for safekeeping to the Vatican museum.

Basilica di S. Pietro (St. Peter's Basilica)

From the Pantheon walk to Vatican City along the back streets of the older part of Rome over Ponte Umberto I (the Bridge of Umberto the First), down the Lungotevere Castello past the Castel S. Angelo (once the papal fort), and into Via Conciliazione.

At the beginning of Via Conciliazione is a magnificent statue of **St. Catherine of Siena** (Santa Catharina), honoring her contribution to bringing the papacy back to Rome. Near the end of her life, she journeyed daily to pray at St. Peter's and advise the pope on the ways of making peace with the curia and the Roman governors.

St. Peter's Basilica stands over the original cemetery and burial grounds for persecuted and martyred Christians, which included St. Peter himself (who was crucified upside down at his request, as he felt unworthy to suffer the same death as Jesus). A temple was erected to St. Peter and the martyrs on this site by Emperor Constantine in 349, but the only structure surviving from that time is the **obelisk** in the piazza, which is the second largest in Rome after the one outside St. John Lateran. It was brought to Rome in AD 37 by the then Emperor Caligula to embellish the grounds of the nearby circus (where it was believed that those buried next to it could still enjoy its spectacles in the afterlife). Now the obelisk stands in the center of the extraordinary circular piazza designed by Bernini and erected between 1656 and 1667, and it houses an urn with relics of the true cross.

Bernini's entrance to the basilica is composed of 284 columns and 88 pillars embracing huge statues of St. Peter and St. Paul. Pope Julius II had commissioned a new church in 1506 to replace the older one, which was collapsing. It took over a hundred years to complete and many Renaissance artists were involved in its design. Michelangelo, who had already completed work on the Sistine Chapel, designed the magnificent dome, considered the tallest in the world (450 feet high), offering his services for free in contrition for his sins. He died before its completion.

St. Peter's is now the official residence of the papacy and headquarters of the Roman Catholic Church, the center of the independent state of the Vatican, which was awarded its sovereignty in 1929. The **papal apartments** are to the right of the church and behind it is the museum and the gardens. In a high window from the papal apartments, the pope addresses his parishioners and visitors to Rome each week. In the center of the facade of St. Peter's above the main doors is the **Benediction loggia**, the middle balcony where the pope traditionally blesses and presides over official outside ceremonies. It was here that St. Pius X and Bl. John XXIII addressed the crowds after they were voted pope.

The basilica is entered by many steps to its vast portico. The famous **Porta Santa** (Holy Door) is to the right, the one which was opened at the turn of the millennium by Pope John Paul II, keeping with the traditional ritual of the Jubilee. Inside to the right is the famous **Pietà** sculpted by the young Michelangelo in his mid-twenties between 1497 and 1500, and further on the same side is the **tomb of Bl. John XXIII**—inscribed in Latin as *Joannes XXIII*. Originally entombed in the crypt with most of the other popes, he was placed in this glass sarcophagus after his beatification. Showing hardly any decomposition, his body is dressed in his favorite papal attire—the medieval red velvet with white fur border cape and hat (which probably influenced the traditional dress of the present-day Father Christmas).

The high altar's canopy (designed by Bernini) is suspended in perfect symmetry under Michelangelo's dome. The throne above the tomb of St. Peter in the crypt below is the **Chair of the Popes.**

St. Peter's tomb is the most highly venerated martyr's shrine in western Christendom. The bronze statue of him to the right of the high altar, sitting in the original seat, establishes his place in the heritage of the seat of popes at the Vatican.

St. Pius X's tomb is to the left of the high altar with a bronze plaque that shows him giving communion. To the left of the statue and door, surrounded by images of angels, is his body in its own side chapel. His hand with its papal ring has been mummified, and he wears a brass death mask. To the right of this side altar, adorned with angels, is a large bronze of Bl. John XXIII blessing a family.

The Vatican Museums and the Sistine Chapel

The Via Porta Angelica from St. Peter's leads to the Vatican museums.

These rooms originally made up the papal palace but after the papacy had amassed so much fine art, they were turned into museums. The most prominent patron of the arts was Pope Julius II (1503–13) who had a knack of recognizing—and supporting—artistic genius. **The four Raphael Rooms** in the museum were originally Pope Julius II's private apartments, which took Raphael sixteen years to decorate, and he died before finishing.

Michelangelo was lured from Florence later in his life to design Pope Julius II's tomb (see San Pietro in Vincoli, p. 306). When he was assigned the ceiling of the **Sistine Chapel,** he reluctantly undertook the task to appease Pope Julius, although Michelangelo had suggested Raphael as more suitable for the job. It took Michelangelo four years of uninterrupted, back-breaking work to paint over three hundred figures on a surface of a thousand square meters. The ceiling became a model for later Roman masterpieces, especially reflected in the work of Caravaggio and Bernini. It took another twenty-five years for Michelangelo to be commissioned to paint *The Last Judgment* on the wall behind the Sistine Chapel altar. When completed, just a year before Michelangelo was to die, the Council of Trent (1545–63) set strict new guidelines for piety in devotional paintings. This naturally excluded nudity, and a decision was quickly made by the curia to conceal the genitals of Michelangelo's already-painted figures. In what was probably the bigger insult to Michelangelo, the Vatican employed another painter to do the job—Da Volterra, who was nicknamed *Il Braghettone* ("the pant-maker")—of painting cloths over all the exposed genitals.

The Sistine Chapel became the place where the pope granted audiences, where the ballots for a new pope took place (and still does), and where many Vatican II sessions were held.

In the museums are **St. Helena's sarcophagus** and that of her daughter Constantia, and the painting of **St. Francis** that is considered most like him. Among its many other treasures, including an impressive Egyptian collection, is the library, containing the most comprehensive collection of writings in the history of Christendom. The library is viewed by written appointment only.

DAY FOUR

Morning: S. Maria del Popolo, S. Maria in Montesanto, and Sant'Andrea al Quirinale
Afternoon: S. Marcello al Corso and the Gesu (The Church of Jesus)

The special churches of many of the saints, most particularly Bl. John XXIII, along with some outstanding devotional art, make up this last day of Roman pilgrimage.

S. Maria del Popolo (Holy Mary of the People)

Begin your last day at the imposing Piazza del Popolo, number 12. This square has witnessed the course of Christianity from persecution to reform to reconciliation.

This great church is dedicated to the Holy Mother of Christ as patron and helper in liberating the Holy Sepulcher Church in Jerusalem to the Christians after the First Crusade in 1099. There was an older church on the site that was erected by Pope Paschal II after the death of the notorious persecutor of the Christians, Emperor Nero. Evidently a chestnut tree grew on the spot where Nero's ashes had been laid in this grand piazza, and as black ravens would squawk in its branches all day long, locals swore that it was haunted by Nero himself. After the tree was cut down and the earlier church erected over the spot, the ghost of Nero was no more.

In the **Cerasi Chapel** is Caravaggio's (1517–1610) famous paintings of the *Conversion of St. Paul* and the *Crucifixion of St. Peter.* The **Chigi Chapel** was designed by Raphael.

The cluster of buildings around the church also formed the Augustinian community of Rome, which **Martin Luther** (an Augustinian priest) visited on retreat in 1511, offering Mass at its main altar. Disgusted by the corruption and wealth he witnessed (including the power-mongering of the papacy and the sale of indulgences), Luther returned to Germany to lead the counter-Catholic movement called the Reformation.

S. Maria in Montesanto

At the foot of the piazza are two churches that share similar architecture. Go to the one on the left.

S. Maria in Montesanto is the church where Bl. John XXIII was ordained to the priesthood. When swearing his oath of eternal fidelity at its altar, he looked up at the painting of the Madonna, which is still hanging, and wrote in his diary, "She seemed to smile at me from the altar, and her look gave me a feeling of sweet peace in my soul and a generous and confident spirit." "Our Lady" told him that she was pleased with the young priest and would watch over him all his life. Bl. John XXIII said that he never forgot the feeling he experienced from her on that day.

Sant'Andrea al Quirinale

From the Piazza del Popolo, walk down the Via del Babuino through the Piazza di Spagna into the Via Due Macelli and around the Quirinale to 29 Via del Quirinale and the Church of St. Andrew.

Bl. John XXIII would frequently visit this church as a young priest when he lived and worked in the Vatican before being posted abroad. He chose this church for prayer and contemplation. It is called "the pearl of the Baroque" because of its architecture. Its impressive interior was designed by Bernini and built by his assistants between 1658 and 1670.

S. Marcello al Corso

From Piazza del Quirinale, wind through the back streets to the Piazza San Marcello, 5, and the Church of S. Marcello.

Built on one of the earliest sites of Christian worship in Rome, the original Romanesque building was burned down in 1519 and replaced by the present structure. One of Raphael's students began the work on the ceiling frescoes, but it was completed by others due to the student fleeing Rome during the Great Sack of 1527. One of the most powerful paintings of the crucifixion hangs on the sacristy wall, painted by the seventeenth-century Dutch master Van Dyck.

The Gesu (Church of Jesus)

Walk from the San Marcello to the Piazza del Gesu and the first Jesuit church.

Built between 1568 and 1584, this church honors the founder of the Society of Jesus, St. Ignatius of Loyola (1491–1556), who came from Spain to Rome in 1537. He is buried in the side chapel dedicated to him. The imposing high altar in gold almost shimmers with the many prayers said in this church. Its ceiling has a painting that resembles sculpture, an outstanding example of how Renaissance painters attempted to outsmart sculptors in the race for artistic superiority.

This church was also one of Bl. John XXIII's favorites. He said that through praying here he was given solutions to most of his problems.

It is fitting to end this day at the side altar where a simple and beautiful crucifix hangs, a reminder of the focus of any Christian pilgrimage. As the saints guide us in prayer, they usually steer us toward the source of their faith, into the embrace of Jesus Christ.

IV

Pilgrimages in Southern Italy

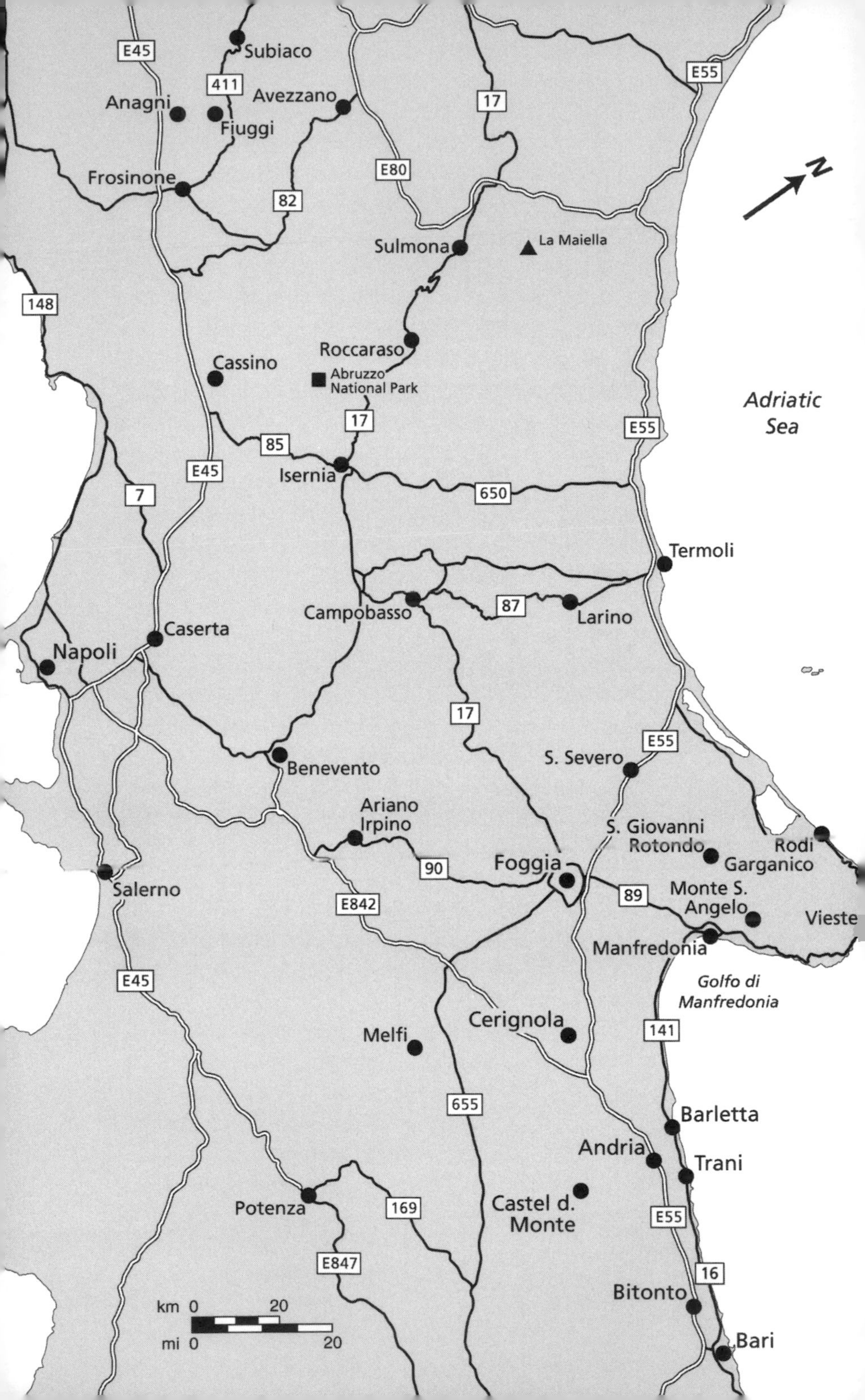

Subiaco
E45
411
Anagni
Fiuggi
Avezzano
17
E55
Frosinone
E80
82
Sulmona
La Maiella
N
148
Roccaraso
Cassino
Abruzzo National Park
Adriatic Sea
17
E55
85
Isernia
E45
650
7
Termoli
Campobasso
87
Larino
Caserta
Napoli
17
E55
Benevento
S. Severo
Ariano Irpino
S. Giovanni Rotondo
Rodi Garganico
Foggia
90
89
Monte S. Angelo
Vieste
Salerno
E842
Manfredonia
Golfo di Manfredonia
E45
Cerignola
141
Melfi
655
Barletta
Andria
Trani
Potenza
169
Castel d. Monte
E55
E847
16
Bitonto
km 0 20
mi 0 20
Bari

ST. BENEDICT
The Pioneer Monastic

"St. Benedict shifted the whole impact of asceticism to the interior—from the flesh to the will....One of St. Benedict's secrets was to purify the hearts of men by acts that were outwardly ordinary, simple, insignificant...."

Thomas Merton, *The Waters of Siloe*

His Life

Benedict was born into a well-to-do family in Norcia in the province of Perugia in AD 480. He had a twin sister, Scholastica, who was called to religious life at a young age and entered a nearby convent. Benedict left home in his teens, sent to Rome by his family to further his studies in Greek, Latin, law, and writing. His nurse, Cyrillia, accompanied him. At the age of seventeen, he fled the corruption he witnessed in Rome, searching for an escape somewhere remote and pastoral. He probably knew of Subiaco, which inherited its name from Nero's villa, Sublaqueum, which the emperor had built by a series of artificial lakes between the years 54 and 68. Originally it was a region inhabited by the Aequi who, as an independent race, were invaded and defeated by the Romans in 304 BC. After the victory, the Romans constructed aqueducts in the area to supply water to Rome, and Emperor Nero used the banks of these lakes to build his summer home. Thereafter, the valley was called Nero's Valley. A constant supply of fresh water continued to attract migrants, but many of these were not seeking summer sojourns as much as simple places in which to contemplate God. There was already a Christian community at Subiaco and a parish church dedicated to St. Lawrence with a priest in residence called Florentius. There was also a grassroots monastic community (with monks scattered among the caves in the hills) under a superior called Adeodatus.

On their way southeast of Rome, Benedict and Cyrillia stopped at a Christian community called St. Peter Affili. After experiencing a miracle there, Cyrillia considered it the best place to settle, but Benedict slipped away on his own, abandoning his nurse and continuing his search for solitude and isolation. On his arrival in the valley of the Anio River, Benedict met a monk called Romanus, who lived in a small monastery at Subiaco under the prior Adeodatus and who told him of a cave in the hills above the ruins of Nero's villa where Benedict might want to spend time. Romanus supplied young Benedict's daily bread from his own food ration, lowering a basket into the cave by a rope with a bell attached to announce its arrival.

The life Benedict had chosen was not easy: he was open to the elements, exposed to the cold and damp, and faced with his own desires, which went unmet—all without the usual comforts of a home. But during the next three years as a hermit, he was transformed through prayer, and his reputation for wisdom and holiness began to spread through the valley.

The local common people began to visit him, and he became their teacher not only in the ways of God but in basic literacy, as Benedict taught them how to read and write. This caused some problems for Romanus, who was finding it harder to preserve Benedict's anonymity; at an advancing age, he also found it difficult to continue to climb the hill each day and to share his food. One day during Lent, when Benedict was twenty, no bell was heard, no rope lowered, and no food delivered. After three years practicing the life of a hermit with his daily sustenance provided, Benedict then had to surrender his dietary needs to the elements, eating herbs and wild berries, which made him physically weak. But just as Easter came, a new visitor arrived. A local priest had been told in a dream to bring provisions to a hermit cave dweller and he arrived laden with meat and good food for Benedict's Easter feast. On meeting the solitary monk, the priest was touched by Benedict's gentle nature and the purity of his soul.

A few days later some monks arrived to visit Benedict. They came from a monastery about eighteen miles away at Vicovaro and had learned of this young man of prayer and discipline who was educating the locals, and they asked him if he would be their abbot since theirs had passed away. Benedict accepted the appointment and began establishing a few basic rules for the small community, including the essential practice of the cardinal virtues of humility and obedience. Benedict's preliminary Rule for monastic life was, however, too stringent for this clutch of monks, who then tried to poison him. Benedict was saved from dying when his goblet of wine broke in two after he had blessed his meal before eating. Discovering their plot to kill him, Benedict rebuked them. He returned to his familiar cave in Subiaco and resumed his solitary practice.

The local peasants, happy that Benedict had returned, renewed their regular visits to him. They sat at his feet as he passionately told them stories about the early monastics in Egypt and about their contemplative life (which Benedict must have studied in Rome). Many of the locals converted, desiring to serve God beyond their common class, but there were no opportunities to free them from enslavement to wealthy landlords. Benedict saw the need for community and appointed twelve monks (the same number as Christ's apostles). He taught them the ways of prayer and solitude as well as study and work. He moved out of his cave into the ruins of Nero's Sublaqueum—a symbolic act in itself of creating light over darkness, by providing a holy place of Christian prayer in the home of one of Christianity's prime persecutors, whose regime had killed St. Peter and St. Paul. It was as if Benedict had single-handedly blotted out this huge transgression by establishing the first roots of Western Christian monasticism within the walls of Nero's imperial villa. Benedict named the place St. Clement's, after the third pope in succession to St. Peter, martyred in the year 100. Apart from the clear message that Benedict wanted to establish—of the healing of the heritage of St. Peter—the choice of name could also have been due to St. Clement's life, including his exile in the Crimea, where he worked in the mines and by a miracle opened a continuous supply of water to the community. As a preacher St. Clement converted many and established up to seventy-five churches before his martyrdom by being thrown into the sea with an anchor around his neck. Benedict was certainly prophetic by his choice of name and place. Nero's villa, with its permanent water supply, stood almost directly beneath his cave, as if it had been waiting for this healing transformation, and the naming of St. Clement as patron married the sacred and secular requirements for prayer, rest, and labor.

The first monks busily set about erecting the hermitage of St. Clement's out of Nero's stones, and they cleared the surrounding land and planted crops so as to be able to feed themselves as well as have enough to provide for the local poor. Benedict's fame spread, especially among the intellectuals from Roman society, as he proved that the ideal and example of the early Egyptian hermitage settlements could also successfully be put into practice in Nero's Valley. As the monastic life provided an alternative to other religious life at the time, many traveled to Subiaco to witness what the community was doing in its simple and clear directive of *Ora et Labora* (Prayer and Work). It wasn't long before more hermitages were called for. Benedict continued with the same composition for each house: as in Egypt, a superior and twelve monks, with the superior as the spiritual director for his own monks, but still under the supervision of Benedict, who was the abbot for all. Nero's Valley was slowly transformed, and before too long was renamed the Holy Valley.

Children were included in the early monastic communities and were called *oblates*—offerings to God. They followed the monastic Rule as well as attended school, which was called the "School of the Lord's Service." Roman noble families sent their children to be educated by the Subiaco monks, and many of these boys stayed and became monks themselves. Two such boys were the brothers Maurus (aged twelve when he arrived) and Placid (aged seven), who both played an important role in the future expansion of the Benedictine heritage. On their arrival they immediately learned about humility and obedience, prayer and work. They also learned about the power of God's presence through two personal miracles. One was when Placid accompanied Benedict one night to the top of a mountain to pray for those monks who complained of the difficulties of obtaining water for their hermitages. After Placid's Father Abbot had prayed at this spot, a spring burst forth from some stones to supply the much-needed water. The other was when Benedict told

Maurus to go immediately to the nearby lake because he knew that Placid was in trouble. When Maurus arrived, he found Placid in the middle of the lake at the point of drowning and fighting for his life. Maurus went to his rescue—not once questioning why he was able to walk on the water. Pulling his brother to rescue, he marveled that his Father Abbot could both know from afar about Placid's danger and, at the same time, enable him to rescue him. But Placid's experience of the near-drowning was different: he told Maurus that it wasn't he who had saved him but the Father Abbot himself who had pulled Placid out of the water.

THE ROOTS OF MONASTICISM

The solitary quest for God in an ascetic life is a common, long-established spiritual discipline. To persevere in prayer and fasting, relying solely on the elements and renouncing the desires and needs of the material world to purge and purify the body, mind, and soul in order to achieve union with God–this was considered one of the highest calls of religious life, the experience of a hermit considered the most transcendent.

In the East, the Buddha attained enlightenment by his particular practice of asceticism, which enabled him to reach total detachment from ordinary everyday things and to live in infinite time and space. In the West, biblical prophets like Elias, Hosea, and John the Baptist lived out their ascetic search for God in the desert.

In early Christianity, after hundreds of years of widespread persecution, colonies of hermits sprung up in the early fourth century at the Nile Delta in Egypt. Presumably evolved from the ascetic practices of the Essenes in Qumran on the shores of the Dead Sea (where John the Baptist mastered his life as a hermit in the desert), these colonies became widespread in the wilderness of Judea.

The seeds of Christian monasticism were first planted in Egyptian, Syrian, and Palestinian soil toward the end of the third century where the term *monk* (taken from the Greek word *monos,* meaning "alone") established the official description of a hermit. One of the first well-known monks (also called a founding Desert Father) was a man from Alexandria called Antony, now St. Antony (AD 251–356), who lived in a hut in the desert practicing the rigors of solitary discipline and prayer. Toward the end of his life there were hundreds of hermits following his example, and they would gather at weekends for common prayer and Eucharist.

The tradition of a more formal, organized community, which became the "hermitage," began in the upper Nile region in AD 320 under the leadership of St. Pachomius (292–346), a Coptic-speaking Egyptian who converted to Christianity while serving in the Roman army. This community was known as a *coenobium,* meaning "common," where the following of a basic rule of religious life was agreed upon, and committed to, by each member, who also worked for his or her livelihood. This work included the weaving of baskets, ropes, and linen that served their needs or could be sold to outside communities and traveling traders.

Highly educated in the schools of rhetoric in Constantinople and Athens, St. Basil of Caesarea took to searching the hermitages in Palestine and Egypt for a spiritual director. The solitary life of a hermit did not suit his temperament, so instead he founded a monastic community based on the *coenobium* formula in his hometown of Caesarea. After being appointed bishop, St. Basil brought the monastic movement under the control of the hierarchy of the Church. The laity then no longer practiced their faith in isolated communities, but were now under ecclesiastical guidance. St. Basil recorded the essential principles of monastic life using the language of the Pachomian colony as its foundation, which was that the one spiritual body was made up of its many members, a concept enthusiastically adopted and incorporated into the teachings of the institutional Church. The virtue of obedience as the foundation of living in the spiritual family aided the entrenchment of the Church's dogmatic control of its members; being part of the one body of the Church required unquestioned adherence to the authority of its leaders. The Eastern Orthodox Churches adopted variants on these communities but, unlike the Roman Church, permitted the independent life of the anchorite or hermit as a deserving vocation.

Into Europe

Fascination with monks and the monastic life wound its way into Europe through pilgrims' tales and the circulation of books. Lives of the Desert Fathers and Rules of their communities were published in Greek and Latin and were widely read in Rome, Milan, and parts of France. This led to a flood of converts setting out for Egypt and Syria to take up life in these communities. One such man was St. Cassian who, in 385, left his monastery in Bethlehem to tour the settlements in Egypt, but settled in south Gaul (now France). Defining the role of abbot (leader of the overall community), he published a number of discourses he had had with Egyptian abbots, and these works became spiritual classics, essential reading for anyone considering or living the contemplative life.

St. Martin of Tours (315–97) is considered to have founded the first formal monastery. Born in Hungary, he had pursued the company and teachings of St. Hilary, a married Frenchman in Poitiers who had, after converting to Christianity, been exiled in 356 to the East by the emperor on advice of Arian bishops. St. Martin followed St. Hilary there and became devoted to the monastic vocation. On his return to France, St. Martin was made bishop of Tours in 370 and is regarded as the protagonist of the Gaulist monastic movement in the fourth century. Even as bishop, St. Martin embraced the anchorite lifestyle of the Desert Fathers, which included fasting to overcome the desire for food, and lacerating the flesh to transform the physical senses. After founding a monastery in Gaul (based upon the principles of the desert Christian communities), St. Martin formalized the European version of the original Eastern monasteries. Books on St. Martin's life were widely read, along with those on St. Cassian and St. Antony, but it wasn't until St. Benedict's time that the monastic Rule (including all the elements of what went before) was written in a form that could be lived and understood. It was compiled in Italy in the fifth century and became the "bible" on which all monasteries were formed. The life of St. Benedict was also documented by St. Gregory the Great (c. 540–604) and was published fifty years after St. Benedict's death. St. Gregory wrote, "The holy man could not teach otherwise than he lived." St. Benedict's call to monasticism was surely influenced by his study of the texts of his predecessors. From the seeds of the Desert Fathers, St. Benedict planted the foundation of all future mendicant religious orders, which included not only the Benedictines but the Cistercians, Dominicans, Franciscans, Carmelites, and many others over the centuries succeeding him.

After years of applying his monastic Rule to the way of life of his monks and the people in Subiaco, Benedict, now in his forties, became the target of envy and jealousy. During Benedict's flourishing ministry, the old parish priest, Florentius, had watched his parish community dwindle, as his congregation turned to the great Benedict for guidance and the flood of visitors from Rome ignored him. In Florentius's old age, his heart was eaten up with hatred, and all he desired was to rid himself of his religious rival. He arranged to send Benedict a loaf of poisoned bread instead of the *eulogia*—the eucharistic bread used in the ceremony of the Mass. Benedict was suspicious of the loaf and placed it on the window ledge where his tamed raven would come for its daily ration of corn. The bird was disturbed by the bread and flapped and squawked. Benedict asked it to fly off with the loaf as far away from the monastery as possible so it could do no one harm. The raven, assured of more than its ration of corn on return, took the poisoned loaf in his beak and flew away from Subiaco.

Florentius did not stop here, however. He began to spread more perfidious poison among the monastic oblates through untrue gossip and provided opportunities to tempt oblates to break the Rule. On learning of all this, Benedict, in his anxiety, prayed for the security and protection of his young monks' faith and vocations. In the end, it seemed better for the future of the community that Benedict depart. There was much sorrow and consternation among the monks at Benedict's decision, but he was steadfast in his resolve to turn from evil always toward the good. Appointing Maurus to succeed him as abbot, he left with a group of monks, including Maurus's brother, Placid, to where God was calling him next. A few days after his departure, as Florentius gloated over his victory, the wooden beams of his outside balcony gave way beneath him, and Florentius fell to his death, crushed by their weight as he hit the ground.

Benedict was forty-seven when he left Subiaco for Rome. He made his journey a pilgrimage of peace, spreading the news of the monastic way of life among all he met.

From Rome, he and his companions ventured south toward Naples, probably because Maurus and Placid's father owned the enormous mountain of Cassino (then called Casinum), and there was a possibility that, if Benedict felt called, it could be the perfect place to build a new hermitage. The village of Casinum was very poor; its people had suffered constant invasions by barbarians due to its vulnerable situation as a direct point from Sicily northward on the main thoroughfare between Naples and Rome. The mountain itself already had quite a history; it was once a Roman military fortress because of its clear view of the surrounding valley, and ruins of the temples of the gods were scattered around its summit. In even more ancient times, it had been a place for devil worship, but this sinister history didn't prevent Benedict who, after meditating on the mountain to discern God's will, cleared the land of all pagan effigies and the energy of the devil and erected a place of prayer. The monks cleared roads up the mountain and transformed the pagan temples into chapels. Benedict dedicated the temple of Apollo to St. Martin of Tours (linking the early monastics) and erected an oratory to St. John the Baptist, possibly because of his personal affiliation with this early desert prophet, who dressed in animal skins and lived off berries and locusts, as Benedict had done as a young man while in his cave at Subiaco.

It took courage and enormous faith to survive the physical and spiritual challenges of building the new hermitage. The battle of good and evil raged as each stone was placed on top of the other. Many of the monks found the stones too heavy to lift, but after Benedict interceded with prayer and the Sign of the Cross they became lighter. The devil frequently appeared to Benedict in horrible forms, such as black snarling dogs and evil-smelling smoke, and called him "*Maledict*"—meaning "cursed"—instead of his own name Benedetto—meaning "blessed, holy." Benedict ignored the evil games, although the monks frequently heard demonic voices. At one time a young boy, Severus, son of a Roman senator, was crushed, as the wall he'd been working on collapsed on top of him. He died instantly, but through Benedict's prayers was brought miraculously back to life. Benedict taught the monks not to fear the devil, and even when the devil set fire to the kitchen, he made the brothers place a Sign of the Cross over their eyes and look again to see the fire extinguished.

When the building at Cassino was complete, there were three hundred men and boys living at the monastery, with their own Father Abbot's cell in the once-fortified lookout of the Roman fortress—*La Torretta* (the tower). Benedict taught the monks the subtle fineries of the Rule through practicing humility and obedience, and overcoming pride and temptations. He also loved to tell the monks stories of other saints—especially monastic founders such as St. Martin in France and St. Patrick in Ireland.

People began to climb the mountain to witness the monks' practice of *Ora et Labora* and to be baptized. Montecassino became a community, attracting many to its walls and its surroundings. Before long, other land was offered to Benedict, and new monasteries were built. One of these was Terracina where Benedict appeared in the abbot's dream to give him the design and plans for its erection. Placid and Maurus's father, who had already donated Montecassino, gave the monks eighteen farms in Sicily, and Benedict sent Placid, now twenty-one years old, to erect a monastery in a land ravaged by Saracens and pirates. On Placid's departure, his older brother Maurus left his position as abbot at Subiaco and came to Montecassino as Benedict's personal assistant, a service he rendered for about two years before being sent to France to open a monastery there.

Benedict's twin sister, Scholastica, moved to be nearer her brother, establishing the Monastery of St. Mary in the valley below at a place called Plombariola. This was the first community of monastic women who followed the Rule of Benedict, wearing similar habits of black tunics with the added black veil.

Visitors and pilgrims arrived at the mountain in search of spiritual solace, prayer, and education, but more often basic shelter and food, and knowledge of herbal remedies and potions, which the monasteries could offer from their libraries and their gardens. The sick would also come for care and healing, and many came to die at Montecassino, where the peaceful environment was the only haven they could find in their war-torn, tormented lives. The monks' practice of hospitality was to welcome everyone as if it was Christ himself. During times of famine, the monks gave as much as they could to the local people from their own labor on the land, and many miracles were witnessed in the multiplying of supplies, healings, and more raising from the dead through the prayers and blessings of the holy Abbot Benedict.

In the Fall of 540, when Benedict was sixty years old, he heard the sad news of the murder of Abbot Placid and most of his monks in Sicily. The monastery had been prospering, as had the one at Terracina, but Placid's monastery had suffered the fate that Benedict had initially feared: the community was invaded by pirates and his monks tortured and killed. One monk had survived to tell the tale, and Maurus wanted to go and take his brother's place as abbot, but Benedict prevented him. By now Rome was a shadow of its former self—there was war and famine across the land—and traveling was not only unsafe but plainly stupid for a defenseless monk.

Amid the sea of violence, however, the calm, caring, disciplined community of the monastery of Montecassino flourished. Montecassino offered an embrace of poverty and exemplified the perfect Christian society of the prayer-filled monastic life where monks labored alongside the common people on the land and then translated and copied manuscripts in the library.

There were many examples of Benedict's ability to prophesy and see the future, and most of these prophecies were handed down by monks in whom he confided. For instance, Benedict foresaw the downfall of Rome. He also saw the coming destruction of the Montecassino monastery, predicting the exact year (577 by the Lombards), and he told of its rebuilding afterwards. He predicted the extent of the Rule and its power in the future, and he predicted his own death. But it was his twin sister, Scholastica, who intuited the timing of their parting. Benedict visited her just once a year due to the restrictions of visits outside the monastery and the necessity for the segregation of gender. During one annual visit where they dined together (always in three rooms, they in one, the monks accompanying Benedict in one by themselves, and the nuns in the other), his sister took the liberty of requesting him to stay longer and not leave after dinner, as usual. Adamant at adhering to the Rule, Benedict refused her request, but she prayed to God to be able to spend more time with her wise brother so that they could talk about "the joys of heaven." On a clear star-filled night there suddenly appeared a thunderstorm and torrential rain that prevented the monks from returning up the mountain, so her prayer was answered. Brother and sister in blood and faith spent the whole night speaking of God and sharing their prayer. This was to be Scholastica's last request on earth as she died peacefully two days later. Benedict, who had seen her soul depart her body in a vision, brought her corpse to Montecassino for burial and placed it in the tomb that had been prepared for him in the chapel of St. John the Baptist. The monks were alarmed at the abnormal request, but buried her as instructed out of obedience to their abbot.

It was not long after this, at the age of sixty-seven, that Benedict joined Scholastica in their shared grave. He had prophesied the exact day of his death—March 21. The monks took him to the oratory choir at dawn on that day, and after receiving the Eucharist, Benedict blessed his weeping monks and told them in a faint voice not to be unhappy, as he would always be with them. He died standing on his feet with his arms outstretched, in the same physical posture as his beloved Christ crucified. He had served Christ with all the gifts given to him, the gift of solitary prayer, of leadership, of wisdom and intellect, of passion for the monastic life, and of love for his brothers and sisters and the world. Following his own heroic ideal, he had changed the religious environment forever. Founding a community based on spiritual virtue, he had established an alternative way of life in which holiness could be perfected, not isolated from the fullness of human experience, but transformed by the practice of love, respect, obedience, and humility. He founded a way to serve God and be happy. And his legacy lives on.

CHRONOLOGY

480	Born a twin (sister Scholastica) in Norcia, Perugia.
495/6	Sent to Rome for further education.
497	Leaves Rome for a cave in Subiaco.
500	Appointed abbot to monks of Vicavaro. Discovers plot to poison him. Returns to solitary life.
501–26	Establishes and presides over numerous monastic communities in the valley.
526	Departs Subiaco for Montecassino.
546	Dies at Montecassino March 21.
1964	Proclaimed Patron of Europe by Pope Paul VI.

OFFICIAL FEAST DAY: July 11

Spiritual Essentials

St. Benedict's prime teaching was of the necessity of a life of balance between contemplation and action, work and prayer.

COMMUNITY

Solitude and silence in a person's prayer life needs to be nourished within community. Everyone is equal in his or her needs for quiet, as well as belonging and sharing.

LIVING PRAYER

A life of simplicity requires constant, disciplined, and reverent prayer. Avoiding sloth and mindless speech is part of teaching our physical selves to be more aware of our imperfections and of our wasted energy and wasted talk. Humility is the key to growth.

SURRENDER AND FAITH

We need to seek God in the poverty of not knowing how God will care for each of us. In doing this we grow in faith and reliance on God's will. We need to trust in God's goodness and to be flexible and obedient when called. By trusting in God's wisdom we can overcome infirmities and darkness.

A PURE HEART

In desiring eternal life, our soul progresses to deeper unity with God. In practicing daily silence, we are able to live purely in the joy and love of the Divine's heart.

THE BENEDICTINE LEGACY: THE RULE AND GROWTH OF MONASTIC LIFE

There's no firm evidence of how St. Benedict's Rule of monastic life circulated Europe, but the common belief is that Theodemar, the abbot of Montecassino in the mid-ninth century, sent a copy of the original to Charlemagne. A much earlier version turned up in England (in AD 750) and was presumed to have been brought there by Augustine of Canterbury (this Rule's text is presently kept in the Bodleian Library in Oxford).

The original Benedictine Rule consisted of a prologue and seventy-three chapters that comprised a summary of spiritual and practical organization of a monastic community. It detailed the ascetical life and its aims and virtues, as well as the divine office of prayers, readings, and psalmody, and instructions on the daily disciplines of every monk. Included are constitutional details, the elections and rank of the abbot, the order of the day, codes of conduct (with instructions on how to deal with those who break the codes), as well as definitions of the behavior of the monks toward the abbot and vice versa. Obedience and humility were the keys to an orderly sacred community, and studies have revealed the influence that Roman and military culture had upon St. Benedict at the time. For instance, the formulaic order of power from the superior down to the basic training of perfect obedience and humility in the common ranks of monk (including the expectation that, when joining a community, a monk must not only renounce all individual wealth to be true to the Rule but also the proprietorship of his own body) was, like the army, a necessity for being able to conquer the enemy. The enemy, however, from a monastic understanding, was the evil lures of the world and the devil itself. On the other hand, unlike the army, the underlying Benedictine's quest was to love God above all, and to be in the joy of surrendering to the grace of divine union.

All monks were expected to rise at 2 a.m. (3 a.m. in the summer) to sing the Vigils (or Matins). In Pachomius's community in Egypt, monks were awakened in the early hours by trumpeters. St. Benedict adopted a more gentle approach—that one monk would rouse the others with a bell or knock at their doors. Lauds was sung at first light and then every three hours monks gathered for common prayer. This prayer was central to the community. In between prayer times, monks did manual work, read, cared for each other and the sick, greeted visitors, and so on. There was no talking during meals and other assigned periods of silence. St. Benedict listed "Seventy-two Instruments of Good Works," which the monks would study to discern their behavior—idleness was referred to as an "enemy of the soul"—and for interior purification and practice of virtue he formed a twelve-step program (using the ladder as a metaphor.

The strength of St. Benedict's Rule was its common sense and its underlying love and respect for each individual as well as the community. "Let no one do what is best for himself, but rather what is best for another," St. Benedict taught, and he summarized a monk's life as being one that should be lived as if always in "Lenten observance." He concluded what he called "this little Rule" with the advice that it was for beginners, and that if practiced over time, a monk could arrive at "the heights of doctrine and virtue under God's guidance."

St. Benedict's Rule was also studied and practiced in the wider Church communities—St. Gregory (the Great), when pope, introduced the Rule into his own house in Rome in the late sixth century, which led to its influence on the organization of the future institutional Church. And in the secular environment, the Rule provided a blueprint for developing a more democratic and open society. As a result, it is commonly believed that the Benedictine Rule was one of the greatest influences on the development of Western civilization during its time.

The Spread of the Rule's Influence

The Rule and the way of monastic life perfectly complemented that of the nobility and higher ranks of secular society. The Benedictine Monastery was similar in organization to the great aristocratic residence, where its estate lands were tilled by dependent laborers. Writer Georges Duby explains the correlation in his book *Art and Society in the Middle Ages*—"Rooted in rural prosperity, and like the rustic villas to which senatorial nobility had withdrawn, [the Benedictine monastery] preserved the memory of the abandoned city. Of this, the Benedictine monastery was a smaller copy, closed in on itself, but provided with every convenience: springs, thermal baths, a collection of solid buildings arranged round a central space, the cloister, its porticoes decorated with capitals like those of the forum."

Duby further explains that a community of men "entrenched like warriors" against evil and in prayer all day became important mediators between the people and divine power, and as a result grew extremely influential within the society.

In addition to the spiritual and material composition of the monasteries, the Benedictine communities also became custodians of the arts—through the support of painting and literature, and development of sacred music and Gregorian chant. All were interwoven in the excellent education that was offered to anyone who had thirst for knowledge. Because the Benedictine monastery was an obvious refuge from the corruption of the world, many people supported the communities through fees for educating their children, or through gifts of land or monetary donations.

From Montecassino and the earlier communities in Gaul, the monastic life spread quickly throughout Europe, and St. Benedict's Rule was fine-tuned by different cultures: The growth of monastic life in England and Ireland enabled the Rule to be practiced within the Celtic traditions. And by the seventh and eighth centuries, monasteries formed a vast fraternity throughout the whole of Europe, linked by their location on popular pilgrim routes. As sick pilgrims required care, many monasteries founded hospitals within their walls and had apothecaries of medicinal herbal potions.

It was in the tenth and eleventh centuries, in the great Abbey of Cluny in France, that monks were called to spend more time in focused prayer and study than in manual labor and education and care of the sick. This heralded a reform movement, out of which sprang offshoot communities. The Cistercian Order is one example, and it was followed closely by other cloistered communities that practiced silence and kept apart from the world. In 1012 St. Romuald (who came from a noble family in Ravenna) founded the Camaldolese Benedictines, which combined community life with the more ascetic life of a hermit, therefore returning the Benedictine life to its original roots.

In the twelfth century, most members of society could not survive without the Benedictine monasteries. Yet there also rose a movement away from what was perceived as too powerful an establishment, which is why St. Francis of Assisi achieved such a following. As a young man, St. Francis found solace in the Benedictine monastery on Mount Subasio near Assisi, and it was the Benedictines who, after the rise in popularity of the Franciscans, gave them use of their many hermitages. St. Francis's own Rule for the Franciscans adopted many of St. Benedict's principles with the exception of a radical interpretation of poverty and humility, with no ownership of land or goods, and with no regular provisions.

Over time, the Benedictine influence spread to the New World. In 1846 four monks from Bavaria landed in New York and created the first Benedictine monastery to serve immigrants in Pennsylvania.

As if proof of St. Benedict's genius, his Rule has been the backbone of communal religious life for centuries. Changing, reforming, returning, and refining, it lives on and provides a framework for the expression of sacramental life. Today its oblates are not only young children in its monastic schools nor young men and women called to the order, but also men and women in the secular world living the Benedictine ideal in daily life. Some of the more famous of them are the American religious activist and writer Dorothy Day, and French theologian Jacques Maritain and his wife, Raïssa Maritain. The first woman to be awarded a doctorate was a Benedictine Oblate–Elena Piscopia in the seventeenth century.

Like St. Francis, St. Benedict had an influence on the world far greater than just religious heritage. Western monasticism has influenced many forms of community and organizations, including democratic governments and universities; it has also helped ensure the longevity of artistic expression with patronage and publishing.

A Pilgrim's Prayer to St. Benedict

Glorious St. Benedict
As we walk in your footsteps
And learn of your heritage,
May we be filled with the grace of contemplation,
silence, and listening,
Which your blessed hermitages
Afford every pilgrim.
May we hear the word of God
As we listen in the stillness.
May we know the virtue of obedience
As we say "yes' to whatever God calls us to do.
May we have the discipline to undertake our daily work
in prayerful peace and security,
And may we consecrate all that we do
To the greatness and glory of God.

The Pilgrimage

Destinations: Subiaco, Abruzzo National Park at La Maiella, and Montecassino
Suggested length: Three to four days

This pilgrimage begins in Rome and can take three days ending in Montecassino, but four days would leave more space for prayer and contemplation and time to take in the stunning scenery in the mountains.

DAY ONE: Subiaco

The drive from Rome to Subiaco is approximately 76 kilometers and takes about 1 hour and 30 minutes in total. At Uscita #14 on the ring road, exit onto the A24 to L'Aquila. After 35 kilometers exit at sign for Vicovaro and Mandela, taking the south turning. After the toll station, turn left and follow the signs to Subiaco.

On the outskirts of the town of Subiaco there's an imposing stone statue of St. Benedict, Patron of Europe, with a welcome sign to the "Birthplace of Western Monasticism." The bridge over the river to the right, just before the archway into the town, is dedicated to St. Francis who had visited Subiaco, presumably entering over this bridge.

Follow the signs to "Monasteri" and "Monasteri di S. Scolastica" and "Sacro Speco di S. Benedetto," which means "Sacred Cave of St. Benedict." Continue on Via dei Monasteri winding out of town for at least 30 to 40 minutes until you reach a parking area opposite the ruins of Nero's Villa, where St. Benedict built his first monastery.

There is little left but columns and some stones as it was destroyed in an earthquake in the thirteenth century.

Continue by foot up the cobbled pathway, or you can drive up to the gates of St. Benedict's monastery.

N.B. There are two monasteries at Subiaco—St. Scholastica, which is in the valley below, and St. Benedict, which is in the caves above. It is recommended that you visit St. Benedict first followed by St. Scholastica.

The Monastery of St. Benedict/Sacro Speco di S. Benedetto (Holy Grotto)

The present monastery was built in the thirteenth century around St. Benedict's original cave, which has been a place for pilgrimage and devotion since his death. High up and jutting out of the rock, the monastery affords a magnificent view of the mountains and the large crucifix on the hill opposite. Its terraced gardens fall away into the valley below, where, in the silence, all that can be heard is the wind in the firs. Over the door of the entrance courtyard is a painting of St. Benedict writing his Rule. There's also an inscription in Latin, which in translation reads:

> "If you searched for the light, Benedict, why did you choose a dark cave? A cave doesn't offer the light you desire. Why have you gone to darkness to seek radiant light?"

and the answer is inscribed:

> "Only in a profoundly dark night do the stars brightly shine."

There are stunning frescoes on the way to the upper church—images of St. Benedict, St. Scholastica, St. Francis, and the Evangelists. **The church** is one of the most ancient and beautifully preserved places of prayer that can be found in the whole of Italy. The highly colored, mostly fifteenth-century frescoes that cover the walls and ceilings (depicting stories of St. Benedict's life, of the first monks who joined him, and also of scriptural scenes) give the impression of entering an inner sanctum of the finest treasures.

The pulpit adorned with roses and an eagle are the remains of the thirteenth-century church, and there are images of the four early Doctors of the Church—Gregory, Jerome, Augustine, and Ambrose—on thrones immersed in books. Here would be an excellent place to begin your pilgrimage and offer your intent.

In the second part of the upper church there are many more frescoes depicting scenes from the life of Benedict, including the attempts at poisoning him by the monks of Vicovaro. Through a hole in the wall the devil peeps in—a reminder that evil always lurks nearby.

The stairwell to the left of the altar leads down to the caves and the lower church.

Among the many frescoes there's one of Pope Innocent III holding the bull that was presented to the monks with revenue for their welfare in 1205, and another of St. Benedict meeting Romanus who is showing him to the cave. There are images of St. Benedict and St. Scholastica and some of the miracles—for example, Placid's life being saved from drowning in the nearby lake and the poisonous bread being given to the raven.

The Original Cave

St. Benedict's original cave, where he lived undisturbed for three years, has been a place of high veneration from the earliest times. The twelve lamps represent the twelve monks that began the first monastery, and the white marble statue of the young Benedict was sculpted by Raggi (1657), a student of Bernini. On the wall is a fresco depicting Romanus lowering the basket of food.

St. Gregory's Chapel

From the lower church, take the spiral stairway that leads to this tiny chapel named after St. Gregory the Great, biographer of St. Benedict.

On the wall is a fresco that the monks believe is the greatest likeness of **St. Francis.** It was painted during the saint's life, probably after his visit to Subiaco. The Latin inscription reads Fr. Franciscus and shows no evidence of the stigmata, another proof that it was drawn in the middle of his life. The other image is of Cardinal Ugolino (later Pope Gregory IX), a great friend and supporter of St. Francis who personally consecrated the chapel. It was probably this event that drew St. Francis to Subiaco. A beautifully simple picture of the Risen Christ is by Antoniazzo Romano, and the other painting is of St. Gregory the Great studying the book of Job.

Our Lady's Chapel

The steps downward lead to Our Lady's Chapel where the walls adorn frescoes of her life, death, and assumption into heaven.

Grotto of the Shepherds

Further down from Our Lady's Chapel is the Grotto of the Shepherds. This is the cave in which St. Benedict instructed the neighboring shepherds in reading, writing, and praying. Walking further on, there's the little **terrace garden of the roses.** Here it is believed that the young St. Benedict threw himself into the thorns to overcome temptation—something that St. Francis did at La Porziuncola. The image on the wall is of St. Francis grafting roses on the thorns. The view from this vantage shows how the original caves were placed and where Romanus would have had to stand to let the rope down with food for St. Benedict.

The Transept

Return to the transept by the high altar in the upper church.

In the transept are paintings of St. Benedict and St. Scholastica's last supper together where they spent the night speaking of divine things, and also a painting of the miracle of St. Peter and St. John healing the lame man outside the Temple, along with a beautiful image of the martyr St. Agnes, with the familiar lamb. There's also a painting of the martyrdom of Abbot Placid at the hands of pirates in Sicily.

The courtyard beyond leads to the monks' residences and the Garden of the Ravens.

Garden of the Ravens

In memory of the tamed raven in St. Benedict's time, ravens still gather here around the statue of St. Benedict, which is inscribed, "Stay there, O Rock, and do not hurt my sons." This is St. Benedict's blessing of protection of the great cliff behind—as security of the peace and contemplation in the birthplace of Western monasticism.

L'abbazia di S. Scolastica (The Abbey of St. Scholastica)

Although the lower abbey in the valley is named after St. Benedict's twin sister, St. Scholastica, it is not the convent where she lived with her nuns, which is near Montecassino. This building was actually built at the time of St. Benedict and probably was one of the earliest monasteries after the original at Nero's Villa. It was dedicated to Pope St. Silvester and gradually became the main monastery at Subiaco, till at least the twelfth century. It has always been a dwelling for the monks and, with some restoration, has survived Saracen attacks, earthquakes, the plagues, and the Napoleonic wars, right through to being bombed by the Allied Forces in World War II. It is also the home of many "firsts." Between 1463 and 1464, two German printers arrived from Mainz and established the first printing press in Italy. During the year of their stay, they printed over a thousand copies of a few titles—a Latin grammar book for children, *De Oratore* by Cicero, three works of Lactantius, and St. Augustine's *City of God*. The monks still print material on a press set up in 1907.

The bell tower was built under the direction of Abbot Humbert between the years 1052–55 and is the oldest in central Italy. This tower has been the inspiration for most of the bell towers on churches ever since.

In the main entrance is **the monks' store.** Products sold here are locally produced and include honey and herbal remedies. Visitors' purchases support the community. In return, a guided tour to the interior cloisters and church is available.

The Three Cloisters

The first cloister is in a Renaissance style and was completed in the seventeenth century. There are many photographs on its walls, including some of Bl. John XXIII on his visit in 1960 where he said Mass in the church. Copies of ancient documents, examples of early printing, and images of the formation of the early monastic communities are also on the walls. Over 100,000 books and 580 ancient manuscripts are housed in St. Scholastica. The library and archives can be visited only by special appointment.

The second cloister is more Gothic and is much older, dating back to the eighth century—there are some urns in evidence from the remains of Nero's villa. On the eastern side of the cloister is the facade of the ancient church built toward the end of the twelfth century. And above it looms Humbert's famous bell tower.

The third cloister is called the Cosmatan Cloister. It has many thirteenth- and fourteenth-century frescoes, and much of its white marble was taken from the ruins of St. Benedict's first monastery after it was destroyed by an earthquake.

Over the course of time there have been five churches in this monastery. Three of these have disappeared, leaving only the others in ruins. The Gothic church has been merged into the neoclassical one that exists today. The facade of the Gothic church with its ancient doors is on the east side of the Gothic cloister. The newest church is eighteenth century by Bergamese architect Giacomo Quarenghi who was inspired by the designs of Palladio. Images of Benedictine life abound—on the ceiling St. Scholastica is in the heavens—and on a side altar is the mummified body of St. Chelidonia, who is the co-patron of the town of Subiaco.

St. Scholastica is still a working monastery. There is a local farm and a thriving pilgrim community.

The newly restored "Foresteria del Monastero" is a lodge for visiting pilgrims and because of Subiaco's remoteness is an excellent place to stay. For further information, visit www.benedettini-subiaco.it or e-mail foresteria@benedettini-subiaco.it. The phone number is 0774–85569.

St. Benedict's Medal

There is much devotion around the St. Benedict medal, which bears the Sign of the Cross. With the Sign of the Cross,

Benedict cast out demons and saved lives—including his own from poisonous deaths, so the St. Benedict medal is considered a special symbol of connection to him and to the sacredness of the power of Christ. The medals have been distributed for centuries and have been associated with miraculous healings and other material and spiritual favors granted through St. Benedict's intercession.

The circular medal shows St. Benedict himself on one side, holding the cross and the book of his Rule. On the other side of the medal is a cross. In the space outside the cross, at the four angles in the center, are the letters CSPB—*Crux Sancti Patris Benedicti,* or the Cross of Holy Father Benedict. The other letters on the cross and around the edge of the medal are shortened forms of Latin prayers of protection against the powers of darkness and the poisons of evil.

DAY TWO: The Hermits' Caves in Abruzzo

This part of the pilgrimage seems like a detour away from Montecassino, but it is, in fact, a perfect way to experience the early elements of Benedictine spirituality through visiting the dwellings of religious hermits. One monk, who became pope for a short while, was the most famous hermit of this area, and he is now a recognized saint, St. Peter Celestine.

ST. PETER CELESTINE (1215–96)

Peter Morrone was the eleventh child in a peasant farming family. His father was much older than his mother, who was partly paralyzed, so his birth was considered miraculous. Peter's intelligence and zeal for God were recognized early by his mother, and she encouraged him to pursue religious life. At the age of sixteen he became a novice at the local Benedictine monastery of Santa Maria in Faifoli, but four years later he felt called to a life of solitude, almost at the same age St. Benedict was called to his cave eight hundred years previously.

Peter's abbot sent him to Rome to gain approval to leave the community. The journey took him three years. Traveling by foot through mountainous terrain, he arrived in Rome in 1238 and spent a further three years in the city as he was to complete his education and be ordained. In Rome, Peter learned the elements of leadership, which served him well in his future work, and in 1241, at the age of twenty-six, he finally left the city to begin his hermit's life. He chose for his dwelling a cave on Mount Marrone in the Abruzzo, perhaps familiar with the area from his travels to Rome. Before long, local shepherds and woodcutters in the region helped spread news about Peter, and people began to flock to him, some to witness the solitary monk and others to gain spiritual wisdom from him.

Five years later, life became unbearable for Peter, who had thirsted for the solitary life and was now surrounded by crowds of disciples. So he left his original cave in the spring of 1246 and headed to the mountain region of La Maiella, named after the pagan female warrior and fertility goddess Maja, because of the womblike cells and caves in its ravines and rock cliffs. Peter chose to dwell on a rock pinnacle of the "Great Mother Mountain," as it was then referred to, where the Romans had, in ancient times, erected a temple to Mithras, the male god of light (originally an Eastern deity from Iran who conquered the sun and became originator of life).

The place was perfect for prayer. It was named Santo Spirito (Holy Spirit) by the Benedictines, who owned the land as part of the extended holdings of the great monastery of Montecassino. Hermit monks had moved there in the eleventh century to live in a series of interconnected caves. One of the monks, Desiderius, later became the abbot of Montecassino in 1086 and then pope (Victor III) within the year. But at the time Peter came to Santo Spirito, it had been abandoned for a long time and had suffered the ravages of time and neglect. Peter set about renovating the caves and rebuilding the church, and as he did so, he envisioned a spiritual utopia, which Santo Spirito represented. He had a dream that the Kingdom of the Holy Spirit could be experienced here and spread throughout the world. As if by Divine Providence, other like-minded monks joined him to share this vision and the practice of solitary prayer and silent penance. At Santo Spirito, high up in the caves of the rocks, all the monks could hear was the voice of the Spirit in the wind that whipped through the gorge, and the songs of the birds that flew below them.

It didn't take long for Peter to agree to assume the role of abbot to the few hermits on the mountain. They followed the Rule of St. Benedict but with the additional understanding that the pursuit of the solitary life was central to the community. Peter's clutch of hermits survived and thrived for over forty years, gaining fame and respect—but also suspicion—from religious authorities. The suspicion was due to Peter's outright support of the Franciscan Spirituals (the group closest to the poverty ideals of St. Francis, which was striving for survival against ecclesiastical pressure after St. Francis's death). Peter's group was also under suspicion for the belief and reality of a spiritual utopia experienced among his cave-dwelling hermits. Both positions placed Peter and his followers uncomfortably close to the rank of heretics, a damaging prospect as his communities began to spread throughout the region and further afield, and as lay groups became associated with the monks in taking care of the poor and the sick. Peter knew that, with the spread of popularity, he would have to gain permission from the pope to establish an official order independent of the Benedictines.

Pope Gregory X had called a Church council in France, which was to occur in Lyons in 1274, so Peter once again set off on foot, on one of the longest, and most vital trips of his life. Unbeknownst to him, two other important religious figures were also making their way to Lyons—the Dominican St. Thomas Aquinas and the Franciscan St. Bonaventure. Aquinas died on the way, and Bonaventure died at the council and was buried at Lyons. Peter survived not only the trip but the outcome. He had to apply personally for permission to found an order as there was a papal decree that emphatically stated that there would be no more new orders. This was partly due to the extreme problems the papacy was experiencing due to the growth of the Franciscans and Dominicans, and due to the continuing battle with the forces of heresy. But Peter must have made an impression because an exception was made for him, and official permission was given to form the Celestines on March 21, 1274.

Almost two decades later, in 1293, at the age of seventy-eight, Peter announced at a chapter of his twenty-monastery congregation at Santo Spirito that he required further solitude at the end of his life and was handing over the role of abbot to retire to an isolated cell in Sant'Onofrio (still in existence today above the town of Sulmona at Morrone). His solitary sojourn did not last long, however, because a year later he was summoned to Rome. The Vatican had been held in deadlock over the decision of a papal successor to Nicholas IV, and Peter had written to the cardinals pleading with them to make a decision so as to keep the Church from vulnerability and confusion. To his surprise, the cardinals appointed Peter himself as pope, and reluctantly he set off on a donkey to the Basilica of S. Maria del Colle (or Collemaggio) in L'Aquila (a church he had built himself to Mary, the holy mother, for her protection of him in France). At this church so close to his heart, he was crowned Pope Celestine V on August 29, 1292, in the presence of the kings of Hungary and Naples.

Peter was ill-equipped for the role of pope. A seasoned hermit with little or no experience of politics was seen as an advantage by "the spirituals" (who longed for reform in the papacy) and who supported him wholeheartedly, but they were outnumbered by the powerful monarchies of Europe (led by the king of Naples) who took advantage of Peter to their benefit. With no ability to discern the political climate and his disinterest in material wealth—which resulted in his giving away much of the Vatican's possessions—Peter was rendered powerless, which only contributed to the already existing confusion in Church governance and direction. After a few months in office, Peter abdicated in Naples (the first pope to do so), citing his need to return to the life of a hermit and to live in his cell at Sant'Onofrio for his remaining years. His resignation, having only aggravated the further threat of schism in the institutional Church, caused his successor, Pope Boniface VIII, to imprison him for his own safety and the future of the papacy. Ordered to return to Rome to serve out his imprisonment, Peter became elusive, dodging the papal soldiers sent to accompany him and hiding out in hermitages and monasteries until it became too dangerous for him to stay in Italy. He made arrangements to escape to the East by boat, but as he was awaiting for the ship to arrive, he was discovered, arrested on the beach at Vieste, and brought to the papal palace. It was decided that Peter's prison would be a fortress in Fumone, isolated from the world and protected from invaders. He died a year later in a dark and damp cell where he never heard, or felt, the wind of his beloved Maiella, nor saw the clouds crossing the sky that seemed so close to heaven. This forced isolation—and the suspicion that he might have been assassinated—made a case for canonization, which happened just a few years later in 1313 in the papal court of Avignon.

St. Peter Celestine's remains, after being placed in various locations, were finally entombed in his beloved church in L'Aquila, the Basilica of Collemaggio, where he had, from his papal throne, bequeathed a special indulgence of "La Perdonanza" (The Pardon). This "Pardon" brings pilgrims to Santo Spirito each year beginning on August 29 (the date of Peter's papal coronation where he made the proclamation) through the first week of October (the date of St. Francis's feast day, in recognition of the "Pardon" granted to La Porziuncola in Assisi). Pilgrims come mostly on Saturdays by foot to Santo Spirito, which is locally known as "the landscape of the soul," where they sleep on the ground in and around the little church and return to their homes by Sunday evening.

Leave Subiaco the way you came to the A24, but turn in the easterly direction toward L'Aquila. Take the fork (when the two main roads intercept) onto the A25 toward Chieti and Pescara. At Popoli take the No. 5 side road (signed Tocco da Casauria), which runs parallel to the A25, and turn off at S. Valentino going southward. Follow signs for Roccamorice.

Roccamorice

In the fifteenth century, Roccamorice was called Rocco di Maurizio, and although an unassuming town, it holds considerable history. Its main street is named after St. Peter Celestine, and there's a seventeenth-century inscription on the house that was acquired by him in 1270, presumably as a central point in town to trade farm goods (produced at the nearby Grange of San Giorgio, a previous Cistercian monastery and farm later acquired by St. Peter in 1271). Since 1995, the whole area has been a national park and the hermitages are slowly being restored by the state. The ancient Tholos shelters (circular, igloo-like rock shepherd huts frequently utilized by hermits in the past) still dot the landscape.

On the outskirts of the town going south there is a statue of an immigrant with a suitcase—a reminder that Roccamorice was a place so poor during the World Wars that most of its inhabitants emigrated to the Americas.

Take the No. 614 route to Santo Spirito—there are signs by the side of the road.

Eremo di Santo Spirito (Hermitage of the Holy Spirit)

This is the place where St. Peter restored the abandoned Benedictine monastery, which was built over the Temple of Mithras on the Maiella mountain. The church has "Porta Celi" inscribed over its door, which in local dialect could mean "Heavenly Door," the "Door to the Heavens," or the door to the paradise of the cells beyond, the place where St. Peter planned to—and did for nearly forty years—establish the Kingdom of the Holy Spirit. After his imprisonment and death in 1296, the hermitage suffered decay and neglect. At the beginning of the fifteenth century, it became a shelter for shepherds, but in 1586 some Celestine friars moved back in and restored the original church and some caves. At the end of the seventeenth century, the addition at the back of the church was built by the Marquis of Bucchianico, Don Marino Caracciolo, also known as the Prince of Santo Buono. The residence was named Casa del Principe (the home of the prince), and Don Marino built it to escape the worldliness of the kingdom of Naples as a retreat for himself and other intellectuals and artists to meet and converse. From the seventeenth to the twentieth centuries, there were periods of renewal followed by neglect and vandalism. Waves of destruction came upon the hermitage around 1806 when the Celestine Congregation were threatened with suppression, and in 1820 it was set on fire.

Nowadays, it seems that no particular religious order claims ownership, so people longing for a contemplative life of solitude still come and set up in the caves and in the Casa del Principe, and then move on. There are stories of strangers who come and go—a man calling himself Fra Pio, dressed like an army officer, moved into St. Peter's final cave Sant'Onofrio (near Salmona) for ten years between 1940 and 1950. And there were also female hermits in the Abruzzo—the most famous being St. Colomba, who spent her life in a hermitage on Mount Infornace. Most recently a small band of nondenominational friars under the leadership of Brother Cesare moved into Santo Spirito, but on last visit it appeared as if they'd moved on.

Whatever you find at Santo Spirito you find, and if the door of the church is open, there's a side altar dedicated to St. Peter Celestine and some preserved paintings originally placed there by the Prince of Santa Buono. Behind the church are the corridors carved into the rock, the drainage pipes the hermits used, as well as some small gardens where vegetables would have been cultivated. To the right of the church are the **Scala Santa (Holy Steps),** which wind up the rock face to the "Maddalena." Built in the overhang of the jutting rock, this simple chapel is dedicated to **St. Mary Magdalen.** Surrounding the chapel are tiny monks' cells, some with evidence of the bare essentials of the solitary life.

Eremo di San Bartolomeo di Legio (Hermitage of St. Bartholomew)

Leaving Santo Spirito back toward Roccamorice, it might be necessary to ask directions to find the track road to "San Bartolomeo," as it is not clearly defined on the maps, but it is not a long drive. There are occasional signs on the way, and there's no car access to its footpath.

Cut into the stunning gorgelike range, *the footpath* was walked from as early as the sixth century by locals on pilgrimage. While there is a chapel erected in honor of St. Peter Celestine, patron of Roccamorice, the cells predate St. Peter and his monks and were a well-known place for early hermits who migrated from Sicily after the Arab occupation. Recent cave excavations revealed twelve-thousand-year-old tools from presumed Stone Age hunters. The altar in the oratory to St. Bartholomew is still tended by locals, and pilgrims' prayers are said on knees up the ancient steps. Others visit the site for the miraculous spring water that originally burst from a door latch after a desperate and thirsty monk, in the heat of the summer, hurled a rock at it. It is believed that the water heals wounds to newborn babies, and eradicates a particular mold that kills vineyard grapes.

DAYS THREE AND FOUR: Abbazio di Montecassino (The Abbey of Montecassino)

For a more rural route to Montecassino, take the SS263 through San Leonardo south toward Roccaraso, then the SS83 to Sora and the SS509 into Cassino. A more direct route is to take the SS17 to Isernia south of Roccaraso and the SS85 through to the lower part of Cassino.

The structure of the Abbey of Montecassino has been completely rebuilt after its destruction in World War II. It has been restored mostly to its fourteenth-century layout and design, proving again that resurrection is possible after numerous defeats. Although destroyed four times, no monks have been killed at its site as St. Benedict predicted. The Lombards burned Montecassino to a cinder in 577, and after its restoration in the eighth century, one of the monks there, who was a historian called Paolo Diacono, was the first to set aside a room to use as a "scriptorium," a place where monks transcribed poetry, grammar, math, geometry, and history. As a result, most of the world's classics were saved from extinction, including the works of Ovid, Plato, Horace, and Virgil. The library today contains over forty thousand parchments. In the tenth century a local judge from Cassino, involved in transcribing testimony over a land deal with the Benedictines, wrote down, for the first time, the vulgate Italian language.

In AD 960, Saracens destroyed the abbey, and three hundred years later Emperor Frederick II sacked the monastery, robbing it of its many treasures. In 1349, it was seriously damaged by an earthquake, where again no monks were killed. It suffered its most severe destruction, however, in February of 1944. Because of its geographical situation at the highest point in the valley, Montecassino became the front line between the German and Allied forces. Through Abbot Gregorio Diamare's diary at the time, we have a record of the monks' and local civilians' days leading up to the bombing. Again, no Benedictines were killed, but false evidence of German occupation and misunderstandings on the Germans' military position at Montecassino led to what American colonel Mark Clark called "a tragic error"—a full-scale air artillery assault. Most of the buildings of the monastery were destroyed with the exception of La Torretta (the turret in which St. Benedict had lived), which miraculously remained standing. The Germans, aware of the vulnerability of the abbey to attack, had previously exported most of Montecassino's valuable art (as well as St. Benedict's remains) to the safety of the Vatican in Rome.

To prove again that it was invincible, Montecassino was raised from its ashes, rebuilt over ten years, and reconsecrated in 1964 by Pope Paul VI.

Porter's Lodge and Entrance Cloister

At the entrance gate the word PAX ("peace") is inscribed over the door, which was the original entrance to the site of St. Benedict's cell. The cloister that, in St. Benedict's time, was the temple of Apollo is where the original oratory of St. Martin of Tours stood. The monks gathered for prayer and liturgy in this oratory, and it was where

St. Benedict died. The imposing eighteenth-century statues of St. Benedict (the original, still standing and untouched by bombs and tremors) and St. Scholastica (a copy of the original) flank the great staircase.

The Bramante Cloister

Built in 1595 in the more familiar Renaissance style, this cloister has some special mosaics on the exterior walls and a bronze statue of St. Benedict in its center, arms outstretched—similar to the position in which he died.

War Cemetery

The war cemetery on the slopes of the monastery's surrounding hill serves as a tomb for more than a thousand Polish soldiers who lost their lives in the 1944 battle to liberate the mountain.

Upper Cloister

At the top of the staircase there's the Benefactors' Cloister, composed of a selection of statues representing the many popes and kings who, at some time or other, supported Montecassino. Beyond the central well in the cloister is the basilica.

The Basilica (Cathedral)

Its bronze doors are of particular interest as some date from the eleventh century when Abbot Desiderius (who later became Pope Victor III) was resident at Montecassino. The inscriptions list the holdings that the monastery had at the time, as well as give depictions of the history of Montecassino—St. Benedict's arrival, the building, and incidents and miracles that happened, as well as scenes of subsequent attacks on the abbey. The cathedral was completely rebuilt in the 1950s, almost as an exact replica of the seventeenth-to-eighteenth-century church that was destroyed in 1944. Much of the marble that survived has been incorporated into the restoration, but sadly the original frescoes are lost forever (although sketches can be seen in the museum). The paintings by L. Giordano depict the consecration of the original basilica in 1071, and *The Glory of St. Benedict* features the saint flanked by St. Gregory the Great, Pope Paul

VI, and Victor III. The prophets Abraham and Moses link the heritage of monastic life begun in the desert.

The **side chapels** are dedicated to St. Gregory the Great, St. Joseph, the Blessed Sacrament, and Abbot Bertarius, who was killed in the Saracen invasion in 883.

The **Chapel of the Relics** (of numerous saints) can be entered through the imposing sacristy. Opposite the monument chapel to Piero de Medici (Pope Leo X's brother) is the **Chapel of the Pietà.**

At the high altar is a sculpture of St. Benedict and St. Scholastica, united in the spirit of the next life, and the bronze urn contains their mortal remains. Even during the extensive bombings in 1944, this venerable site was saved from destruction. An artillery shell that got wedged between the steps of the altar never exploded.

The choir is where the monks still celebrate the Holy Hours by following the Benedictine Rule of the psalms and Gregorian chant. On the walls of the choir are eighteenth-century paintings of scenes from St. Benedict's life. Especially worth noting is his receiving Maurus and Placid from their parents as Benedictine Oblates.

The crypt was originally built in 1544 and hewn out of the mountain rocks. Restored in 1913 due to damp erosion, the chapels are dedicated to the brothers Maurus and Placid, the latter being martyred in Sicily. Below the windows on the wall, among others, is a bas-relief of St. Peter Celestine. Bronze statues of St. Benedict and St. Scholastic adorn the altar.

End your pilgrimage with prayer at the high altar of the basilica in the presence of the remains of St. Benedict and St. Scholastica.

The Museum

Of special interest are the eleventh- to fifteenth-century illuminated manuscripts and designs and illustrated prayer books in precious bindings.

ST. PIO OF PIETRELCINA
(Padre Pio)
Jesus' Alchemist

"For gold is tested in the fire,
and those found acceptable, in the furnace of humiliation.
Trust in God and God will help you:
make your ways straight and hope in God."
Sirach 2:5–6

"To souls loved by God, tribulations are more precious than gold or rest."
St. Pio of Pietrelcina

His Life

Mystics commonly experience an interior alchemy, attaining an advanced spiritual state in which they live both in the celestial, otherworldly realms of heaven, and in the everyday finite world at the same time. A lifetime of persevering in the practice of virtue and purification of the soul with all its dilemmas, darknesses, temptations, joys, and sufferings leads eventually to the glorious bliss of unity with the Divine.

The life and teachings of a Franciscan Capuchin monk from a small rural town in southern Italy have vastly contributed to what English mystic, writer, and teacher Evelyn Underhill described as the "Upper School," the place where the "Science of Ultimates and the Science of Union" are comprehended and lived in the absorption of self in harmony with the transcendent. Padre Pio's life—through his example, his teachings, and especially the wounds of the stigmata that accompanied him for fifty years—not only has all the elements of an advanced mystic in our contemporary world, but also sheds light on those who would follow, love, and unite with Jesus. Many Christian mystics have written about this before: St. Teresa of Avila's *Interior Castle* charts the course of the inner work of the soul as it moves toward union with God. St. Catherine of Siena's theology of divine conversation in her *Dialogue* and St. John of the Cross's *Dark Night of the Soul* both explain the hidden gift of love; Blessed Angela of Foligno was one of the earliest mystics to write on the inner alchemy; from her experience as a Franciscan tertiary, she developed major teachings that not only reflected the elements of Christian mysticism but also shed light on St. Francis's mysticism and the gift of his stigmata.

But above all—and beyond all—is the contemporary life of Padre Pio, who not only experienced the traditional elements of mysticism, but also brought an advanced understanding to the theology of suffering and mercy. Through Padre Pio's plummets into the darkest temptations and through his endurance in the interior battleground of good and evil, he rose in our midst as a light of truth and peace, of mercy and love; like Christ, belonging to this world, but being simultaneously not of this world. Padre Pio's mysticism and his experiences create a clear alchemy of the Christian soul, united in love with his Beloved, Jesus, and yet he did not claim anything as his own doing. Called to follow the Rule of St. Francis, Padre Pio exemplified the genius of its founder by revealing the way of poverty, obedience, service, humility, and love as the disciplines that guided him. But more than this, Padre Pio's life followed Jesus' on earth. The way of the cross was his, not at the end of his life but almost from the beginning. Padre Pio walked and talked the suffering Christ, worked miracles, bestowed mercy and forgiveness, and provided for the needs of his community—and eventually the world—with healing and hope, clarity and love. He brought people back to God, showing them the way; he suffered the curse of a celebrity; he practiced patience, acceptance, and humility in the face of suspicion and accusations; and he endured with joy everything for the will of God.

Like many saints before him, Padre Pio encompassed the two realms (finite and infinite in one body, one life) and, as a result, he could promise to continue his work in these two realms in his next life. There is much evidence of the truth of his promise with the hundreds of thousands of people today who continue to be touched by him.

Padre Pio was born on May 25, 1887, the second child of Grazio and Maria Giuseppa Forgione, and he was named Francesco (Francis). His parents and his older brother, Michele, provided a warm and loving home for him although they were peasant farmers with little material means. The Forgiones were lucky to have a few acres of land outside the town of Pietrelcina, at Piana Romana, where they cultivated grapes, grazed goats, kept a few ducks, and grew grain. Their home in Pietrelcina was composed of a couple of dwellings and a turret on a narrow lane in the older part of town. A few simple rooms with no plumbing, it was home nonetheless to Francesco and Michele and their eight siblings, of which two died in infancy and one in her twenties. Another of Francesco's sisters, Grazia, later became a nun in the Bridgettine Convent in Rome. Although unable to read or write, the Forgiones had a reputation for being good, honest people who not only displayed common sense, but hard work, a keen sense of humor, and deep, unwavering faith. Francesco remembered that his mother's common prayer was to live by the will of God, to look always to heaven first for everything, and to rely on the love and protection of the Holy Mother, especially as the Madonna of Liberatrix (liberty or freedom). Through the Madonna's intercession, the people of Pietrelcina survived an epidemic of cholera in 1854; the farmers also brought gifts to her shrine for answering their prayers for rain in the growing season. Francesco's father was devoted to Our Lady as well. At the young age of nineteen, Grazio had been made Master of her Feast, an honor he never forgot.

Francesco was a quiet, well-behaved child who preferred to stay at home than get tossed around in play with the other kids of the village. He displayed his dislike of foul language at an early age, never spoke about himself, and was quietly spending devotional time alone in his local parish church, aptly named S. Maria degli Angeli after St. Francis's favorite church. Francesco remembered receiving visions and ecstasies from as early as five years of age and was also visited regularly by an evil being in threatening grotesque forms. He recalled that he used to scourge himself "for Jesus" as a boy and continued to do so into his teens.

Francesco's health was always fragile. He began having what he called "mysterious illnesses" from the age of ten, although he would recover after spending time on the family farm in Piana Romana, which he loved. He longed for an education, but it was only when he was ten that his father granted him his wish, saying almost prophetically that his son had better become a monk with what he learned. Like many poor Italian farmers, Grazio traveled to the Americas to seek work, spending time in South America before ending up on a Pennsylvania farm. From there he sent home $9.00 a week to cover the family's expenses. He and his wife had wanted to grant their son his wish for schooling, but as he was too old for the state education system, private tutoring was the only alternative. Francesco's mother insisted on this as best for him, his father provided the money from his daily toil, and an ex-priest was found to do the task. Francesco was so frightened of this man that he frequently didn't turn up for class and preferred to spend time in his favorite place, the church, where he attended daily Mass and Benediction. His mother, though, did not give up on him and entrusted him to the tutelage of a respected local teacher called Angelo Caccavo, who guided his pupil through the rudiments of secondary education.

Even in his teens, Francesco remained apart from the other teenagers in town, passing his time studying, reading, or attending to his responsibilities as an altar boy.

With his father still in the United States, he found an alternative father figure in a Franciscan Capuchin friar called Brother Camillo, who frequented the town to request alms for the nearby friary at Sant'Elia. Brother Camillo was an imposing sight with his large, black, bushy beard, and Francesco liked him. Perhaps because of Brother Camillo, Francesco decided when he was sixteen to join the Capuchin Order. An uncle attempted to change his mind, suggesting that the Benedictines seemed to have a more healthy lifestyle; they had a bit more weight on them than the emaciated Franciscans and looked better nourished. But Francesco was clear that the Franciscan Capuchins (with their simple brown habit and full beards) was the right order for him.

Things were not easy for Francesco as he planned to enter the novitiate. For a start, his interior life was full of struggles and fights between what he called the "white and black clouds and the monster," and the exterior environment tested his endurance and faith as well. Falsely accused of flirting with the stationmaster's daughter (by another altar boy in jealousy), he was summoned by the religious community, which threatened not to accept him into the novitiate, as this behavior was immoral—and unsuitable—for a would-be monk. He protested his innocence, the charges were eventually dropped, and he entered the Capuchin Friary at Morcone, becoming Fra Pio of Pietrelcina (Brother Pio of Pietrelcina). It has never been confirmed who chose the name "Pio"—whether Francesco chose it himself, perhaps in honor of the sixteenth-century pope St. Pius V (some of whose relics were kept in Pietrelcina)—or it was bestowed upon him by his Capuchin superiors. On taking his new name, he also received the tonsure (the shaving of the middle part of his upper head as a sign of obedience). Clothed in the brown habit of a Franciscan, he began his four-year novitiate.

He was first sent to study philosophy at Sant'Elia and there he forged a vital relationship with one of his professors, Padre Benedetto—another black-bearded friar who was to be one of the most important influences on Pio's soul formation when he became his spiritual director. Life at the friary had its challenges. Pio's fragile health made him prone to frequent fevers and weaknesses, although he never complained of the few blankets provided the young friars at night (too few to keep out the numbing cold), and the scarce, sometimes overcooked food, which most of the monks complained about. Pio, however, received the reputation of being a model friar, humble, approachable, not prone to mindless talk. Many of his early friends in the community recalled how much time he gave to prayer, and how frequently he entered an exalted state. But this model friar was not to lead a model life as a novitiate in the Capuchin community because of his almost permanent ill health. He wished to be sent to the missions as a philosophy student, but his health prevented it, and even staying in the friary only made him worse. Sent home to Pietrelcina to recover, he repeatedly attempted to return and became so ill that it was as if he was being prevented from the life he was preparing for. After several trips home and back, he ended up living full-time in his parental home, taking up residence in his old boyhood bedroom in La Torretta (the turret in the old town) or, when he could in the summers, in his family's beloved farm in Piana Romana where the environment, the pure air, and the rest accelerated his healing. Pio's mysterious illness always dumbfounded the doctors. The symptoms of coughing, chest pains, and high fevers gave the impression he had tuberculosis, although this was never confirmed. But the condition fits into the progress of a soul in early mystical life, as illness is commonly a method of physical and spiritual purification; many saints took to their beds for years with illnesses that no one could fathom. But what we do know about Fra Pio was the enormity of the interior purification he was going through, as he later recorded the experience in letters to Padre Benedetto, his teacher and spiritual director, correspondence that took place between 1910 and 1922.

GOD'S GAME OF LOVE

In one of Fra Pio's early visions as he was entering religious life, Christ showed him a huge beast whom he had to fight to win what Pio called "The Battle of Belief." It was to become the course of his interior life, not only the inward struggle of good and evil, but the very real physical assaults and fights that he had to endure against the powers of darkness (which he would refer to as Cossacks) and the devil (which he frequently called Bluebeard). Together the inward and the outward struggles were a method of strengthening and purifying himself against evil. Temptations he documented as "impure imaginings" or "despair" were referred to as "obstacles" on his path. He said that tricks were played on him, with the devil appearing as St. Francis at one time and the Holy Mother the next. The physical assaults he suffered at the hands of the powers of darkness were as real as any adverse acts of violence. They were armed with clubs and iron weapons, and he was frequently beaten by them in his bed, stripped naked, punched, and dragged around his room. He wrote once to his superior Padre Agostino that the demons suggested he burn a letter from Agostino without reading it. When he refused, they attacked his body, which became "bruised all over from the blows." When the assault ceased, he said that everything was cold in his body, and after they left, he spit up blood.

This was not the only attack. The sounds of banging and crashing coming from "La torretta" were heard by many of Pio's neighbors, and some of his Capuchin brothers would help him off the floor in the friary, as he bled from physical wounds. After his ordination, Padre Pio became an expert at advising others of temptations, illustrating his comprehension of the course of the battle. In a letter dated September 13, 1920, addressed to one of his spiritual daughters, Antonietta Vona, he warned her not to let temptations frighten her. He said they were "trials of the souls whom God wants to test when God sees they have the necessary strength to sustain the struggle, thus weaving the crown of glory with their own hands." He also reminded many that the devil "has only one door by which to enter the soul" and that is the person's own will. Pio won this spiritual combat by handing over his personal will to be wholly surrendered to the great will of God without reservation. Peace always followed the battle, he described, and each time a greater sense of peace, and therefore a greater absorption of God's will into the self. But in Fra Pio's life, the battle raged on many fronts. Besides the physical sickness and the torments of evil, he faced the growing attitude of his superiors that he was unfit to be a Franciscan Capuchin, that he might be allergic to friary life, and that God might wish him to be in exile but in the world, perhaps living like a hermit. There were no easy solutions to the matter, except that Pio was finally ordained a priest in the cathedral at Benevento on August 10, 1910. Joyfully, the following Sunday, he said High Mass at his own parish at Pietrelcina surrounded by his family, with a luncheon afterward lovingly prepared by his mother in their simple kitchen.

THE DOUBLE EXILE

Padre Pio, not yet twenty-five-years old with an advanced prayer life, living in what he termed "the double exile" in Pietrelcina, was becoming who he was meant to be. He knew it, and yet he was tormented. Writing to Padre Benedetto, he catalogued his struggles with his spiritual and physical health, his interior "diabolical temptations," and his realization that suffering might be his vocation and path. He asked his director if he might offer himself as a victim for suffering souls and was given permission to do so. His physical health deterred him from the possibility of hearing confessions, which he sorely wished to do, and from aiding the local priest with the distribution of the sacraments. His responsibilities then as a priest were greatly curtailed.

In the autumn of 1911 Padre Pio wrote to Padre Benedetto about something that had happened to him while praying at his favorite elm tree on the land at Piana Romana. "In the middle of my palms there appeared a spot of red almost in the shape of a penny, accompanied by a sharp and strong pain in the spot's center." He added that the pain was more perceptible in his left hand, that it hadn't gone away, and that he had pain on the soles of his feet too. This first sign of the wounds of Christ came and went over the course of that year. A doctor's examination revealed a possible connection with tuberculosis, but Padre Benedetto knew that this young priest's vocation was getting serious—so serious, in fact, that Padre Pio's superior, Padre Agostino, became more actively involved in corresponding with Padre Pio, concerned that he be kept on a tight rein and not fall into possible fanaticism, or let his obvious ecstatic prayer life get out of hand. The Capuchin Provincial, also concerned about the special case of Padre Pio, suggested that he be called back into the community, but no sooner had he arrived than he fell dreadfully ill and was returned to Pietrelcina after five days. A special grant was then afforded him by Pope Benedict XV (who later became a strong supporter of Pio) to remain a

Franciscan friar *outside* the community, officially allowing him to continue to wear the habit of a Capuchin monk.

Even though Padre Pio's ministry was limited, he began to teach local laborers to read and write, and he formed a choir at the church. His Masses became famous for being unusually long—they lasted up to two hours as he was transported into the mystical experience of unity with Christ. Every aspect of Padre Pio's Mass was experiential, including the profound silences and meditations that occurred within it. Witnesses said that he became physically radiant and almost translucent during the service. He would sometimes weep, and his body shook over the suffering of Christ. In the little parish church of S. Maria degli Angeli, however, all this caused a problem, as most of the farm workers expected a fifty-minute service before going to work—a sort of "in and out" Mass to start their day, so they stopped attending, which left only the local women in the pews. This was a sign of what was to come because it was predominantly women who made up his congregation, who were his faithful followers and loyal supporters, and who were his major pupils in the spiritual life.

In 1916 toward the end of World War I, Padre Pio was called to the Medical Corps in Naples, and he changed his brown Franciscan tunic for a military uniform. Like young Angelo Roncalli (later Pope John XXIII), Padre Pio suffered the life of the barracks, which was certainly an unsuitable place for him. As if rewarded by God for his endurance, he found his permanent home at the end of the war. After a visit to Rome for his sister's entrance into the convent (which was to be the last trip of his life), he breathed a sigh of belonging when he came to rest at the S. Maria delle Grazie (Our Lady of Grace) Friary on the outskirts of the town of San Giovanni Rotondo, nestled in mountains close to the sea. Before being a friary, it had been a home for the local poor. Still a plain structure, it housed seven resident monks in their cell-like rooms attached to a small church. This Capuchin community was recognized for its austerity, which made the place more than suitable for Padre Pio. The townsfolk numbered around twelve thousand when Pio arrived; little did anyone know how famous this out-of-the-way place would become in the future.

Even though the external environment was more conducive for Padre Pio's physical health, he still continued to suffer from insomnia and constant headaches, and his interior struggles and temptations heightened. His correspondence at the time was full of the mystical language of the soul: an interior fire burned him up—his heart as if pierced with an arrow causing him to "blaze up more and more with exceeding love of God"—and he had an interior wound in his side which, he explained, was "always open and causes me continual agony." He feared that this "excess of suffering" would kill him, but almost at the same time he added that "my ever-open wound enrages me against my will, it makes me no longer myself and drives me delirious. And I am powerless to resist." Padre Benedetto recognized the link with the passion of Christ and wrote, "The fact of the wound completes your passion just as it completed the Passion of your Beloved on the cross."

Beginning June 4, 1918, Padre Pio experienced the deeper suffering that accompanied the crucifixion, that of the absence of God, what is known as 'the dark night of the soul." He described the total "unspeakable torments" of being abandoned, of losing God, of going astray, of being alone with nothing, of being confined in a "harsh prison" (similar to Christ's last night in the high priest Caiphas's house), of hanging on—almost grasping—to the virtue of "holy obedience" to carry on. Padre Pio wrote that he did not understand "anything anymore," that he doubted that his prayers were prayers at all, that in the "forsaken" and empty place in which he was immersed, he believed himself in "a state of fatal lukewarmness," and because of it, he felt God pushing him further and further away from the divine heart. "I see that my ruin is irreparable, because I can see no way out. Alas! I have lost every path, every means, every support, every rule." Padre Benedetto understood this dark night as the ultimate prelude to the gifts of transformation in God's love. He wrote to the young priest to reassure him, but during the month of August Pio was silent and did not answer back until two months later. At that time he wrote to Padre Benedetto against his will, he said, but under the virtue of holy obedience, and described something shameful and embarrassing—the extraordinary experience of September 20, 1918, which was to change his life forever.

"MY CRUCIFIXION"

The incident happened in the church of the friary after Padre Pio had celebrated Mass. He was meditating in a place of "peacefulness," a sort of "sweet sleep" of the soul. His internal and external senses and "the very faculties of [his] soul were immersed in an indescribable stillness." He felt an "absolute silence" around him, a respite for all the turmoil of his interior suffering, and then "all this happened in a flash." He described seeing a "mysterious person" with his "hands and feet and side" dripping blood. Padre Pio was frightened at this sight and thought that he was going to die, as his heart was "about to burst out of my chest." When the vision disappeared, he noticed that his own hands, feet, and side were dripping with blood. He thought that he was bleeding to death as the wounds and the pain hadn't ceased. He also expressed his embarrassment at the exterior signs of what he was suffering interiorly. The interior signs he could tolerate, he said, as he wished to be "inebriated with pain" for the love of Christ and for his vocation. But this, this "unbearable humiliation," a prominent exterior expression, was something he thought he couldn't bear. Later, he wrote that Jesus had said to him, "Would you have abandoned me, if I hadn't crucified you? Under the Cross one learns to love, and I do not give it to all, only to those souls that are dearest to me." But just as Padre Pio was grappling with what sort of gift of love the stigmata would be to his "mission" as he called it, he became the central attraction among the Capuchins, and a cause of suspicion in his Church.

Because of the rarity of stigmata and because it happened in the age of developing science and technology, Padre Pio's wounds had to be examined by medical professionals. The first examinations were undertaken by a chief surgeon from a hospital near Bari and took place between May 1919 and July 1920. In the reports, the doctor described the wounds as of "an ordinary nature," a cut about two inches long in Padre Pio's side with no signs of festering or of healing, wounds that remained unchanged with time. He also mentioned that there was a smell from the wounds similar to "an inebriating perfume."

A university doctor from Rome reported that Padre Pio was using iodine to disinfect his wounds and to help stop the bleeding. The doctor suggested that the wounds could be self-inflicted or could be evidence of a physical disease. The other friars from Our Lady of Grace were invited to participate in further tests. They were told to keep all medicines away from Padre Pio and to monitor attempts at self-infliction. This eight-day test ended with the bandages being removed to reveal that the bleeding had not ceased, that no scabs had formed, and that the wounds were the same as before. The edges of the half-inch deep wounds on the back of his hands were clean, but the inner parts on his palms were covered with scabs. Padre Pio always winced when his wounds were touched, and the pains in his feet made it difficult for him to walk. As blood from his wounds seem to stream more profusely during his saying of Mass, he began wearing woolen gloves to stop the bleeding and hide his stained bandages.

In October 1919, another medical doctor was called to the friary to examine Padre Pio's emotional state. He wanted to confirm whether or not Padre Pio was prone to hysteria (as some in the Church had suspected).This doctor reported that, even though Padre Pio didn't eat much food, he had a grounded, healthy personality with obvious intelligence, a generous and sincere character, and a sense of humor. As none of the suspicions of "hysteria" stood ground, the Franciscan community thought everything was best left alone. But it wasn't, and it couldn't be left alone, because already people were noticing the woolen gloves and smelling the sweet aroma (described like roses and violets) that exuded from their local friar. Padre Pio had at one time in his correspondence mentioned being "drowned in the heavenly perfumes" at the foot of the cross, where, he wrote, "we will be without doubt reinvigorated." When questioned about his perfume, he replied that it was "sweets for the children."

It didn't take long for the medical evidence of the stigmatized Franciscan to leak from the walls of Our Lady of Grace. Stories of Padre Pio, the emerging religious celebrity, began appearing in the international press. It was a time of despair after World War I and people grabbed at this sign of hope, of God's presence, a phenomenon rarely experienced, a chosen priest. With San Giovanni Rotondo turned into a center for pilgrimage and healing, Padre Pio and his fellow monks found themselves working full time in the confessionals as crowds descended on the town. As there was a scarcity of housing, pilgrims waited for absolution for sometimes up to two weeks while camping in the surrounding fields.

The sick began to attend Padre Pio's early morning Mass. The church was packed and could hardly house the growing crowds. The local laundry service, which used to wash Padre Pio's bloodstained undergarments, turned itself into a reliquary, with pieces of soiled cloth cut up and sold to hungry pilgrims. The monks, aware of what was happening, stopped sending out Padre Pio's laundry, but this didn't prevent desperate entrepreneurs from selling pieces of cloth stained with chicken blood. The police were brought in to protect Padre Pio as he was intermittently grabbed and jostled while people snipped at his habit. Droves of devout women flocked to the sacristy after morning Mass to kiss Padre Pio's hands and to push envelopes of prayer requests at him.

The superior of the friary complained about the disruption, the local parish clergy complained to the Vatican, and Padre Pio complained to no one. All he asked was forgiveness for bringing such suffering to his community. But what could be done?—Nothing except to accept the extraordinary phenomenon that was at work in him. But this was just the beginning. It was like a floodgate had been opened, and there was no way to force it back.

THE MISSION

Padre Pio's "mission" became clearer and more concise after the stigmata. When he was younger, he had undergone—and survived—the pain and suffering of interior purification, including temptations and assaults, and his reward was the exterior revelation of the wounds of Christ. As Padre Pio's mystical life proceeded in the service of others, his will—that door where he said the devil can enter—was entirely rent from him in the service of God's will. In his novitiate he had vowed never to refuse anything that God asked of him, that he had been instructed "to become holy and make others holy," and that suffering was the place in which he would accomplish this. He once said that he was aware of suffering even in his mother's womb, and that as a man he was "happier than ever" when he was suffering. "Jesus is well aware that my entire life, my whole heart, is consecrated to Him and His sufferings." He explained that the only "proof of love" is to be found in that suffering. Padre Pio's fame spread not so much because of his endurance of his own wounds, but for the relief he brought to others. He lifted people from their own miseries into the light, joyous, glorious place of spiritual liberty and truth.

He began this mission in the service of God's will to become holy and bring others to this holiness in the confessional, where he would sit sometimes up to eighteen hours a day. Mornings were set aside for women in the confessional booths, and afternoons were reserved for men in the sacristy. Padre Pio wasn't always a gentle confessor. He occasionally upset those who came to him, reprimanding them for being devious, unclear, and without remorse. But many welcomed this honesty. Not a man to mince his words, Padre Pio was known to be able, in a few minutes, to transform the soul who sat with him. He was given the gift to search each soul to its depths, knowing its needs, its secrets, its revelations. He shook up complacency in the sacrament of mercy and forgiveness, reading people's hearts with a clarity that made many uncomfortable. But he was only interested in holiness, in wholeness, and he knew that God wished it through him. "Better to be reprimanded by me in this world than by God in the next," he once said. And he sometimes refused absolution on the grounds there was no true contrition, angering those who had come to him. When they realized that he was right, they would invariably return humbled and honest.

But there was more than the conferring of mercy going on in Padre Pio's presence. People began to experience other extraordinary things. For instance, those who came to Padre Pio speaking languages other than Italian found themselves to be understood by him and to understand his advice even though he spoke to them only in his own language. There were many incidences of "other tongues" that Padre Pio was known to utter, without any education or background or direct experience. When questioned about this ability, he replied that his guardian angel always did the interpreting. Then there were the gifts of healing. Like Christ, Padre Pio would always begin with the state of the soul before healing the body. Forgiveness and mercy first, healing afterwards. People came out of the confessional able to walk when paralyzed before, to see when blind, to hear when deaf, and when they rushed to thank him, he always answered, "Don't thank me, thank God."

His other extraordinary gift was prophecy—he could see not only into the future but also into the states of souls in the afterlife; people would ask him about their dead loved ones and he would tell them. He also foretold the election of some future popes, as well as the coming of war and other dark things that brought his countenance to an ashen gray. His most visible spiritual ability was bilocation (being in two or more places at the same time). Yet what Padre Pio observed with the thousands who converged upon the friary was that many were spiritual thrill-seekers who didn't want to live by faith but sought only the extraordinary. Among them were the skeptics who came to see for themselves if what they had heard about him was true. One atheist said to him, "I don't believe in God!" to which Padre Pio replied "But God believes in you...."

The infinite gifts that poured through Padre Pio's presence were explained by him in letters not only to his own director but to his directees. One of the many women who corresponded with him, seeking guidance in her spiritual life, was instructed about the stages of becoming holy and receiving the rewards. First, he wrote, that she needed to master her passions, to rise above herself, to have "contempt for ourselves and for the things of the world," preferring "humiliation rather than glory, suffering rather than pleasure." Expounding on Christ's teachings, he added that loving our neighbor "as ourselves for love of God" was vital, but more tantamount was "loving those who curse us, who hate and persecute us, and even doing good to them." The virtues of holiness he listed as humility and detachment, prudence and patience, justice and kindness, chastity and diligence, and the willingness to carry out one's responsibilities "for no other reason than that of pleasing God and receiving from God alone the reward we deserve...." In this way we receive the power of transformation from our humanity into God. Pio mentioned how a person cannot at all become proud "on account of the gifts he recognizes in himself." If anything, that person is even more humbled before God, "for the Lord's gifts increase," and as they do so, the recipient realizes that they can "never fully repay the giver of all good things."

And so it was that Padre Pio shared the paradox of the stigmata, an infinite gift of God's love through the thirst for the suffering Christ, accompanied by the finite world's suspicion and misunderstandings, which plagued him within his own religion and caused him much humiliation and isolation throughout all his life.

Forced to surrender to whatever God's will was for him, in 1922 he was suddenly forbidden contact of any kind with his beloved director Padre Benedetto; this exile from such deep friendship and understanding continued for the rest of their lives and ended their correspondence. Twenty years later, at Padre Benedetto's deathbed, a friar asked him if he wished to send for Padre Pio, to which Padre Benedetto replied that there was no need, that Pio was already beside him.

Pio's further challenge of loving one's neighbor was living with the unremitting "pious women"—a group of local women who became like a band of defenders, not necessarily of Padre Pio's mission but of their right to first access, the place of preference and prominence to their very own saint. These women were reported to chain their pews in the church for daily Mass, and attack strangers with their nails, hairpins, and any other pointed instrument at their disposal, especially if these strangers wrongly placed themselves in the line-ups for either Mass or confession or both. And these "pious women" were even known to break out into fistfights in the church to gain their rightful place. All this uproar before Padre Pio's early morning Mass turned the other friars into guardians of decorum, and they took turns to stand in the gallery and call out for silence, order, and respect. Padre Agostino, who had taken on the prime task of keeping order, would lose his temper on a number of occasions. The older he got, the more he cursed, using obscene language with the congregation, and he had to be gently removed from these duties.

Reports of the continual obsessive behavior of the pious women spread to the powers-that-be, not only in the Franciscan Order but also at the Vatican, and Padre Pio's even greater cross was to singularly bear the brunt of these women's fanaticism, which would later deny and restrict his ministry. Unbeknownst to him, Padre Pio was now assigned the role of scapegoat for all the disorder, because without his stigmata, prophecies, miracles, and healings, the whole community would not have been turned upside down and inside out, making the town into a circus. But other lights were shining in the darkness. Not all Padre Pio's "spiritual daughters" were as excessive as "the pious women." Many of the women who came to him for spiritual direction were Franciscan tertiaries (members of the Third Order) who supported and prayed for him and whose prayers in the past had helped him recover from his mysterious illnesses. In fact, the groups that surrounded him in his prayer circles (where they met to say the Rosary) were responsible for much of the care of the community on his behalf.

One day, in 1923, an American woman arrived in San Giovanni Rotondo who, on meeting Padre Pio, changed her life—and his—for the better. Mary Pyle was to spearhead the growing missionary and community projects and become Padre Pio's most loyal and loving disciple.

Adelia McAlpin Pyle was born in New Jersey in 1888 (a year after Pio) into an upper-class Presbyterian family. A somewhat bossy socialite, she hit the New York scene at the age of twenty-four, although she became introspective after her father's sudden death of a heart attack at the age of fifty-six. Employed as an interpreter by famous children's educator Dr. Maria Montessori, Adelia had a skill with languages that frequently brought her to Europe. There she converted to Catholicism (in Barcelona in 1921), taking Mary as her baptismal name. Having heard of Padre Pio and his miraculous prayers, Mary wrote a letter to him about her ongoing lethargy and her suffering over her unclear life direction.

It took two years for her to personally arrive at his door. When their eyes met, she fell on her knees and murmured, "Father," and as he reached for her, he called her "my child." It was an obvious connection that never faltered. They both knew they were meant to be near each other; he told her to stop traveling and searching and to take up residence in San Giovanni Rotondo. After some rearranging of her life, she rented a room and began attending Padre Pio's daily Mass. Her family, especially her mother and brother, thought she had gone quite mad and made their own way from New York to the Italian town, from Foggia traveling by way of donkey cart. Not an easy pilgrimage, it became more than worth it when, on meeting Padre Pio, Mary's mother became his friend as well, and the family accepted her newfound vocation. Mary became a member of the Third Order, a Franciscan tertiary, and was given special dispensation to wear the Capuchin habit, the brown tunic with white rope around her waist and sandals on her feet. She sold all her jewelry and belongings and gave the money to Padre Pio. Instead of being referred to as *"l'americana"* ("the American"), the locals began calling her "Brother Mary." Mary built a pink house near the friary with her family's money and made it her home, sharing it with many others.

In 1925, Padre Pio helped open a small hospital in town as the locals, especially the poor, were dying from lack of proper medical care. The nearest medical establishment was in Foggia, which if you had the money could be reached in a few days; otherwise there was nothing closer. The twenty-bed hospital was named after St. Francis. It was a sign of the early stirrings of Padre Pio's work to come—the loving aid of healing to the sick residents of his town.

Having taken up residence next to the friary and becoming not only Padre Pio's confidante but also his assistant, Mary met with visitors, interpreted, translated, and responded to the ever-mounting English correspondence. This further tormented the pious women. Complaints about Mary were added to the complaints about nearly everyone new in town. The Capuchin superiors felt the only solution was to transfer Padre Pio—perhaps to Ancona—but this suggestion nearly caused a town riot, which had to be suppressed by the mayor and police. So Padre Pio stayed, but with limitations imposed by Pope Pius XI, who had little sympathy for the disruptions, the notoriety, and the shift of pilgrimage power from Rome to the celebrity at San Giovanni Rotondo! In 1931 Padre Pio was forbidden by the Holy See from saying public Mass or hearing confessions. When this order was officially read to him by his superior in the choir, Padre Pio whispered, "God's will be done," although he cried with Padre Agostino afterwards, who said, "You must remain on the cross and men continue to drive the nails in. All will be for God's glory and the good of souls." Padre Pio spent his time—"the imprisonment," he called it—in prayer and contemplation in the friary. This "imprisonment" lasted two years and was officially lifted in 1934 with no apology, just a statement that further investigations had revealed that there had been a "misunderstanding."

"THIS WAR WILL MAKE THE MOST BEAUTIFUL FLOWERS"

In 1938 the town of San Giovanni Rotondo was rattled with an earthquake, which irreparably damaged St. Francis's hospital. It was like an early warning of the winds of change blowing off the sea. The people turned to Padre Pio for prophetic insights, and he spoke of his soul "gripped in terror and desolation." He said that Italy "didn't want to listen to the voice of love," but he offered hope, saying that faith would "reawaken in the Italian heart" and that "this war will make the most beautiful flowers blossom in the church of God, in a land most entirely arid and dry." But he also mentioned the cloud of thick darkness that the world would have to undergo before this time arrived. Brother Mary (now known as "Mamma") had set up an informal school for local children, while helping the poor and organizing the prayer groups and the choir. But now, because of her American citizenship, she had become an enemy of the state. Her immediate future looked bleak as it was expected that she would be imprisoned in one of the camps. But through the Capuchins' intercession with government officials in Rome, Mary was interned instead, confined in Padre Pio's brother's house in Pietrelcina, where she took care of his aging father, Grazio.

It was in January 1940, in a discussion with three friends in his cell at the friary, that the future "work of God" became clear to Pio. From his experience with the thousands who came to the friary for healing—of body and soul—a new hospital, a large, fully equipped place of healing, was urgently needed in the town. This place was to be special in that it was to be built on prayer and the virtues of faith and generosity, and that it was to be called a home, not a hospital—*Casa Sollievo della Sofferenza,* "Home for the Relief of Suffering." A foundation was instantly formed, guided by Padre Pio and his three friends, one of them a medical doctor called Guglielmo Sanguinetti.

Padre Pio saw the building of the new hospital as his "earthly work," something he was to do for the material world that combined the infinite love of God with the faith of the doctors and nurses who were to provide service for no fixed salary, just from the goodness of their hearts. The inclusion of a chapel, his fellow Capuchin monks taking care of the spiritual side of cure, would complete the vision. But apart from a gold coin that a poor woman had given Padre Pio, funds were slow coming in, largely due to the accelerating war and the advancing of the Allied forces into Italy. Nearby Foggia was where the biggest Italian air force base was located, serving the entire central and southern part of the country, and British General Montgomery, along with American Mark Clark, knew their only way forward was to capture and control Foggia's air base. This occurred in late 1943 (prior to the fatal bombing of Benedictine Abbey Montecassino), which made the surrounding towns—including San Giovanni Rotondo—particularly vulnerable to attack. But Padre Pio interceded on the town's behalf. For example, one day two American servicemen—who were neither particularly religious nor in tune with the goings on in a local friary—allegedly took off on a bombing mission from Foggia in the direction of the coast. On nearing the skies over San Giovanni Rotondo, they saw a man with gray hair and beard in a brown tunic and sandals, *flying beside their plane,* and signaling them not to go in that direction. They were so spooked that they automatically switched their flight path. Back at the air base, they both spoke of this extraordinary experience in the clouds. They were shown a photograph of Padre Pio and confirmed that it was indeed he who had flown beside them to warn them away from his beloved people and the community in which he carried out his ministry. It also confirmed Padre Pio's prediction that San Giovanni Rotondo would be spared bombing as it was a blessed place.

This was not the only story of Padre Pio's influence during that period, but what the war accomplished—which was, perhaps, one of the "beautiful flowers" he had mentioned—was to bring Pio and his mission to the British and American people. Unlike his father, Grazio, who had journeyed to the United States to labor for his family, Padre Pio labored for his community by physically staying in one place, but, through prayer, extending his soul in bodily form to the far reaches of the world. This resulted in more pilgrims arriving in San Giovanni Rotondo than ever before, and along with them came the benefactors for the new hospital, La Casa.

"I AM ALWAYS WHERE I AM"

Padre Pio's appearances all round Europe—to those he knew and had requested his prayers, and also to those he had never met—astounded his followers all their lives. He turned up by bedsides of the sick and the dying to offer consolation, prayers, and healings; he offered advice and spiritual directives to many of his devotees in their homes without leaving the friary; he sometimes appeared in answer to letter writers, and he even appeared to his medical doctor for a few hours after his own death. These appearances came in a variety of forms, the more commonplace being as he physically was, the more unusual accompanied by a flowery fragrance or, at one time, a handprint on a windowpane. A brother friar recalled seeing him appear in two places on a social occasion when Padre Pio had forgotten about the other commitment, which was to take place at the same time. Pio went off quietly, closed his eyes in meditation, performed the other duty, and then returned to the room without ever leaving it.

When quizzed about this ability, Padre Pio spoke of an "extension of his soul and body" and said that his angel would invariably take on his bodily appearance on his behalf, although he was well aware what was going on. When asked whether he remembered the surroundings, like the rooms in which he visited, he answered that he only remembered the personal encounter. He acknowledged that it was God "who sends me. I do not know whether I am there with my soul or body or both, but I always remain attached to the thread of His will. For this reason I am always where I am." Throughout his life, Padre Pio appeared as far away as Uruguay and Hawaii, in answer to requested prayers.

As the war came to an end, members of the Allied forces streamed into San Giovanni Rotondo to attend Mass, confess to Padre Pio, request prayers, and experience what was referred to as "the only piece of heaven on earth." They would listen attentively to Mary Pyle's experiences, which she loved to share with her fellow countrymen. Padre Pio always encouraged foreign visitors from the richer Western nations to contribute to the poor and needy in their community by adopting a local family. He encouraged others to spread the news of La Casa and of the funds needed to erect the hospital as he did not want to borrow from the banks. He urged visitors to tell others about the project when they returned home and to form prayer groups to say the Rosary for the cause.

As the seeds were spread abroad, the work began to sprout in San Giovanni Rotondo. On hearing about La Casa, a Turin woman who owned some land next to the friary donated it for the hospital. In turn, an Englishwoman called Barbara Ward—who had visited Padre Pio to pray for the conversion of her titled husband-to-be, and returned to London to discover that he had been baptized in her absence—began a serious fundraising drive in London, contributing enough funds to get the first stage off the ground. Meanwhile, Dr. Sanguinetti, appointed by Padre Pio as its director, was concerned about his own means to carry out his duties. He wondered whether he could afford to move from his home in another town and take up the work full time without income, but Padre Pio only reminded him that "the Lord will provide." Sanguinetti immediately won enough money in a local lottery to take care of himself, build a house in San Giovanni, and get on with the work. Sanguinetti appointed an erratic but brilliant architect called Angelo

Lupi to design the structure, and volunteer builders began lining up. In 1954, the outpatient clinic was officially opened, which included a place for the prayer group meetings, of which Dr. Sanguinetti was also very much a part. Thus, in him was Padre Pio's wished-for perfect combination of science and prayer, physical and spiritual care, being present in equal balance throughout the work.

All seemed to be going well until a tragedy befell the progress, due to Sanguinetti's sudden death of a heart attack at the age of sixty. Sanguinetti had not lived to see La Casa completed, and Padre Pio mourned for his friend; in fact, he suffered such grief that he was unable to work, was absent even to his duties as a confessor, and would burst into tears at the mention of Sanguinetti's name. As soon as Sanguinetti was no longer at the helm, the architect Lupi began upsetting both the team and the flow of construction, but he, too, died prematurely. The work proceeded anyway, and in May 1956, with fifteen thousand people present, Padre Pio officially opened the best-equipped and most beautiful of hospitals in the entire peninsula of Italy with the words "This is what Providence created with your help." The hospital was not only able to serve the sick, but also was a leading-edge disease research center complete with air-conditioning in each room (though Pio had refused the gift of an air-conditioner in his own cell from a grateful follower) and a helicopter pad on the roof, alongside a monumental bronze statue of St. Francis surrounded by birds. When answering accusations of overspending on these details, he said, "Nothing is too good or too beautiful for the sick and suffering." This included no one's being turned away from help; even those who couldn't pay were provided care through others' generosity. However, Pio's original concept of the hospital being a "clinic for souls," staffed only with volunteers, Pio's "spiritual children," became unworkable. Sanguinetti's successor, a doctor called Luigi Ghisleri, needed to pay salaries to enable leading medical professionals to work there and so, over time, La Casa became more like a traditionally run hospital.

At the time of the hospital's opening, a new church for Padre Pio's friary, Our Lady of Grace, was also being built and was opened in 1959 to be able to hold the crowds, but all these signs of growth and stability were curtailed a year later. After Pope Pius XII's death, a new era was celebrated in Rome by the coronation of Pope John XXIII. An official investigation was ordered through the curia into what was perceived as religious fanaticism, largely due to the extreme behavior of the pious ladies, now getting older and more zealous than ever. There had been accusations from other local clergy that sexual impropriety had taken place between Padre Pio and some of these women. The selling of Padre Pio's bloodstained bandages was once again becoming big business. Also, the talking in tongues, the bilocations, and the hysteria that accompanied this—never mind the construction, which included new hotels and souvenir shops—all this was again getting out of control. In addition, the regular pandemonium prior to Padre Pio's early morning Mass, with the fighting and shouting, was also of grave concern, so a Vatican representative was dispatched to San Giovanni Rotondo. By this time, Padre Pio was seventy-three years old. Yet he would be subjected to humiliation, which included some younger friars bugging his confessional and the sacristy to record his conversations and other private encounters with women. To add further insults, the cardinal in charge of the investigation interviewed everybody in the community before talking to Padre Pio himself, and when they had an agreement to meet, stood him up as being "too busy" at that time. The placement of the hospital was also a concern—why couldn't Padre Pio have had it built in Rome where it would have been easier to serve the country? After the eventual face-to-face meeting with the cardinal, Padre Pio emerged silent and stunned, ready for another test of obedience. This time the measures were harsh. There were rules issued about keeping order in the church, numbered tickets to be gained for access to Padre Pio's confessional, and iron bars to be erected around it. Also, his new superior at the friary was to lock him in his cell at night to prevent him from being kidnapped. Padre Pio's only comment was that he felt like "a prisoner" in his own community. Along with disparaging remarks appearing in the national and international press, Padre Pio's final insult was to have La Casa taken away from his and the Franciscan tertiaries' control. The Vatican became its new proprietor.

All this took its toll on Padre Pio's already delicate health. He suffered chest pains and asthma and succumbed to frequent bronchitis. His stigmatized feet became very swollen and, unable to walk, he spent most of his days in a wheelchair. Even though the bars were eventually lifted from around the confessional and unenforced order returned, Padre Pio never regained his energy.

The Second Vatican Council opened the doors on a world that Padre Pio didn't recognize, although he accepted the changes to religious life. Mary Pyle reported that when bishops and cardinals came down to visit Padre Pio from Rome, it was as if the Council was happening at San Giovanni Rotondo, there were so many of them. They came with requests for prayers and blessings. Among them was the future Pope John Paul II (Karol Wojtyla from Poland), who early in his priesthood had received from Padre Pio an answer to his request for prayers for a camp survivor with cancer, who was then cured. Padre Pio had asked his correspondence assistant to save the letters from Wojtyla, saying that one day they would be important. When meeting Cardinal Montini, the future Pope Paul VI, Padre Pio rightly predicted his papacy.

One of the somberest moments of Padre Pio's life was when his sister visited him to announce that she was leaving her order, as she couldn't tolerate the more liberal ways now enforced on religious life. Padre Pio became angry with her, and evidently the visit ended without their being reconciled. After this he stopped speaking, having said that he couldn't bear his cross any longer. His closest friends were old, and most of them had died. Padre Agostino passed away of dementia after being nursed at La Casa. Padre Pio would weep every time he walked by Agostino's old cell door. His first superior, Padre Paolino, had also died, as had his older brother, Michele, nursed to the end by Mary Pyle in her home, which had been turned into a center for Franciscan missionary work. And Mary Pyle herself—who had once said to her beloved Padre, "What am I going to do when God calls you?" to which he replied, "You're going to greet me"—died in her seventies, having lived nearly forty years in San Giovanni Rotondo.

Padre Pio turned down the opportunity for a radio broadcast, saying he preferred to talk directly to God. He was obviously upset by the fast-changing fashions of the day with its miniskirts, rock idolatry, sexual liberation, and movies, which he spoke strongly against. It was at the time when the town was planning a celebration of his Golden Jubilee (fifty years as a priest) that Padre Pio weakened. Unable to sleep—he had always slept only a few hours each night all his life, as well as eating only morsels of food instead of full meals, saying that his field was already fertile—he suffered a severe kidney disorder and chest pains. On top of this, he was again plagued with visits from the devil, and the fear on his face frightened the younger monks who cared for him.

During the year of 1968, as if to herald the end of his earthly ministry, Padre Pio's stigmata wounds slowly disappeared. He had lived with the pain of them for fifty years, and now the bleeding had stopped. The fiftieth anniversary of Padre Pio's stigmata took place on September 20th with a candlelit procession and fireworks, but he slept through it and didn't appear at his window. However, on the morning of his death, he said Mass, and when the crowd called for him, his last words were "my children, my children." They shouted, "Viva Padre Pio, viva Padre Pio!" but he was already slipping over to the other side, finally going home. He had prophesied that he would die when the tomb his brothers were building for him in the crypt of the new church was finished, and so it came to pass. In much pain he turned to one friar and said, "I belong more to the other world than this one. Pray to Our Lord that I might die." Crying in the night, asking for forgiveness of his community for all the trouble he had caused, unable to breathe at times, he muttered only "Jesus, Mary, Jesus, Mary" as his parting mantra. One hundred thousand people flocked to the town at the news of his death. The friars laid his body in an open coffin in the church, placing gloves on his hands so as not to arouse further suspicion about his stigmata—how could anyone explain the fully fleshed hands with no sign of any fifty-year puncture or wound?

A single man gifted with an extraordinary sign of God's love passed into the heart of his Beloved, a man who had once said to a local teacher that from the time he was born, he knew that God favored him "in a most special manner." God had been not only Padre Pio's "savior and supreme benefactor" but also his most devoted, "sincere and faithful friend, the friend of my heart, my infinite love and consolation, my joy and comfort, my entire wealth." Padre Pio had said that his heart had always been on fire with love of God all his life, that the love of God, and God's love through him, made everyone who came to him transformed. People called Padre Pio the "heart of the world." He would probably answer, "Not mine, only God's."

CHRONOLOGY

1887	Born May 25 to Maria Giuseppa di Nunzio and Grazio Forgione and baptized Francesco Forgione.
1903	Enters the Franciscan Capuchin Order.
1910	Ordained a priest on August 10.
1911	Receives invisible stigmata.
1916	In medical corps in Naples; September 4 transferred to Our Lady of Grace friary in San Giovanni Rotondo.
1918	Receives the visible stigmata in the chapel of the friary on September 20.
1919	News spreads outside the friary. Pilgrims begin arriving.
1922	Officially forbidden contact with Padre Benedetto, his spiritual director.

1923	Mary Pyle's first visit.
1925	Establishes St. Francis's hospital, the first in the town.
1931–33	Banned from saying public Mass or hearing confessions.
1934	Ban lifted.
1938	St. Francis's hospital irreparably damaged in earthquake.
1940	Decides to build La Casa Solievo della Sofferenza.
1956	La Casa officially opens.
1959	The new church opens its doors at Our Lady of Grace.
1960–64	Vatican investigation and restrictions.
1965	His sister, Grazia, leaves the convent.
1968	Dies on September 23.
1999	Beatified by Pope John Paul II (who knew him) on May 2nd.
2002	Canonized by Pope John Paul II on June 16.

OFFICIAL FEAST DAY: September 23

Spiritual Essentials

THE ALCHEMY OF LOVE-MYSTICISM

The theology of the stigmata in its relationship to the life of an advanced mystic continues to be studied and written about. Many of the early teachings naturally came from Franciscans, since St. Francis was the first known stigmatic. One notable contribution was from St. Bonaventure, who delved into the mystery and wrote of the stigmatic's prayer, the very real demonic attacks and temptations, the purging of all the bodily senses (including sense of self), a burning up of the heart with divine love, and finally the absolute immersion of the soul into the likeness of the Beloved. These specifics on the journey of the stigmatic are not always similar, or occur in sequence, but what they do reflect is a commonality of experience. The mystic's experiences are beyond gender; the soul's absorption into the Beloved (sometimes interpreted as a "spiritual marriage") is not just reserved for women. Mystics who have recorded their reality in writing, and we can include St. Pio among them, always shed more light on and introduce a new element or two into the existing teachings.

In summarizing the love-mysticism of St. Pio, we can use the wisdom of medieval Franciscan tertiary and mystic Blessed Angela of Foligno. Her sequential instruction, which she documented and which influenced St. Teresa of Avila hundreds of years later, provides an outline for our better understanding Padre Pio. She called the "Sign of True Love," as a "carrying out of the will of the beloved," and she charted it in three stages:

1) Submission

When beginning on the route of love-mysticism, the place to start is in the submission of will, and this was evident in St. Pio's early life. Even at home the family's prayer was for "God's will" to be understood and followed above all else. Pio wrote in a letter that "it is always necessary to go forward, never backward in the spiritual life." He used the analogy of a boat that, if it does not forge ahead on a rough sea, is undoubtedly blown backward by the wind.

St. Pio made it clear that surrendering to God's will could not be done without love. "You must love, love, love above all else," he insisted. If your soul is longing to love God, he wrote once, then it is important to realize that God is already with you, already loving you, even if you only have the desire to love in return. When there is no desire to love God, God is not present to the person in the heart and soul. St. Pio taught this desire and attitude as already being an answer to prayer, already a fulfilled desire. He said that if you are afraid that you are not loving God enough or afraid that you are offending God in some way, you are already loving and no longer offending God. Pio spoke this way about the confessional and the sacrament of reconciliation, that many sins are forgiven because a person has loved much. With this teaching St. Pio illustrates the delicacies of building a relationship with the Divine in the early stages.

Included in the early submission to the will of God is the necessary acceptance of the internal marriage with the outer reality. Angela wrote, "If the loved one is poor, one strives to become poor, and if scorned, to be scorned." Certainly this was evident not only in St. Pio's beginnings but also throughout his life. The absolute acceptance of the circumstance of one's life as God's will is not a passive non-doing or non-striving, but an active embrace of the love of God within the circumstance. In the case of St. Pio, his circumstances included his quiet humility as a boy, the gift from his parents of an education that led directly into religious life, the ongoing torment of temptations in his novitiate, which he knew was strengthening his soul even as it sickened his body, and finally the stigmata that made him vulnerable to scorn, shame, and embarrassment. Instead of attempting to find ways to escape what was happening to him, he looked as deeply as he was able into his interior to see what God's will was within these experiences, and because of this alacrity and his ability to endure, he was given the gift of revelation: that suffering was the path chosen for him by God. He embraced it not only as a way of life, but as a mission of generosity, a vocation to relieve the suffering of others.

With this active clarity, Padre Pio advanced to being able to surpass his own sufferings by being happy and joyful *in the suffering*, at the same time warning himself to avoid selfishness by instead thirsting for the better part of the suffering. Later in his life he wrote that he did not have the strength to deprive himself of suffering, that he was simply unable to do so. He knew he was "a chosen soul" for Christ's ministry, and what accompanied Christ's path was little—or no—comfort from the suffering. In this deprivation St. Pio would derive only joy. He said later in life that his long experience of physical and spiritual suffering brought him to this realization of joy—providing, he added, "one does not cease to cry out to [Jesus]." This alchemy of joy and suffering was "a happiness tasted only in the moments of affliction." St. Pio said that if he wished only for his own joys and went in search of them, he would be denying himself the opportunities to comfort his beloved Lord. And in providing the particulars of physical crucifixion, St. Pio said that Jesus was in the habit of "using repeated blows with a salutary chisel" to clean and prepare the stones "that must form part of the eternal edifice." This was St. Pio's understanding of his interior and exterior role in the building of Christ's kingdom, of his doing Christ's work in the world.

2) Abandonment

The second part of the journey of the mystic lover is to leave anything and anyone behind contrary to God's will or to the opening of one's heart. In St. Pio's early life, he seesawed between leaving home for the friary and leaving the friary for home until it became clear what God's will was for him in his mysterious illnesses. He received the early experiences of the stigmata at his favorite oak tree at Piana Romana, and the full-fledged wounds in the chapel of Our Lady of Grace in San Giovanni Rotondo, where he spent the rest of his life. In his not belonging to either home or community, he belonged solely to his Beloved. And in this nonattachment to exterior place, his preparation in his interior advanced him to such heights that he could, in the end, belong to the entire world. It was as if the enormity of his mission could not be limited to "either/or" of the status quo. During the time of discernment, he said he gained "a wonderful knowledge of God and his incomparable greatness...a great knowledge of myself, and a profound sense of humility...a great contempt for all the things of the earth and a great love for God and virtue." He wrote to one of his spiritual daughters, "[You must] allow your divine Spouse to act in you and to lead you by the paths he chooses."

St. Pio taught that "doubt and worry" were great insults to the Divine. He explained that worrying showed a lack of humility and pure intention. Doubting and worrying, he wrote, were clear signs "that the person concerned has not entrusted the success of his action to the divine assistance but has depended too much on his own strength."

St. Pio likened the struggles in accepting the will of God to a violinist's relationship with the violin. If the instrument is out of tune, you don't give up playing it; you listen to hear the source of the discord and tighten or loosen the string lovingly with patience and perseverance. He advised that our hearts are like the instrument of the "heavenly musician"—we must either tighten or loosen the strings of them so that the divine conductor can perfect the orchestra. In using such similes, St. Pio illustrated the subtleties of soul perfection: that we are not soloists but a part of an orchestra, and that we have to practice to perfect ourselves so that we can vitally contribute to the whole.

3) Mutual Revelation of Secrets

In the third and highest action, Bl. Angela explains that nothing can be hidden from God and each other, that hearts are open and bound together in a mutual harmony of all the three stages—surrender, abandonment, and the openness of love and truth. This certainly was St. Pio's path. He combined all his experiences to become a confessor for souls, a prober of truth, a seeker of reconciliation, a man dispensing the mercy of God, pulling others toward holiness. He spoke of the necessity of breaking down one's "habitual imperfections"—those secrets in the soul, the places where darkest shames and impurities can dwell, and to bring them to light with the help of God's grace.

St. Pio was told by Christ that he was "infatuated" with his heart, which enabled Pio to be "devoured by the love of God and love of neighbor." Pio wrote of seeing himself incapable of "bearing the weight of this infinite love, of squeezing all of it into my small existence," and this he continually feared, that he was unable to contain the enormity of the divine love in "the narrow little house of my heart." But he would tell people to rely on Jesus for everything and all will be well, to not hurry with your tasks, your prayer, or your intentions, but to "spin a little every day, thread by thread weave your design until it is finished and you will infallibly succeed."

At what had St. Pio succeeded?—An interior purification of the light of suffering, a heart absorbed into God's, a very real example of linking oneself to Christ's passion, death, and resurrection through our everyday lives. With his love of and commitment to Jesus, St. Pio lived in the desert, was tempted by the devil, overcame evil, was led and led himself to crucifixion, spent his life in generosity bringing forgiveness and mercy to others, brought healing through the freedom and comfort of the spirit to those far and wide, and in dying lay down his life for his friends.

"I belong entirely to everyone," he said. "Everyone can say Padre Pio is mine."

He knew his mission was to continue "the work" after he died; in fact, he said he would be more effective after his death: "I will be able to do much more in heaven than I can do on earth."

Those who have been touched by the heart of St. Pio can vouch for the truth of this statement. A man in life who was "always where I am" is always where everyone else is who wishes his help, guidance, prayers, mercy, and blessings. And this is why the swell of his love and intercession continues to grow through the hundreds of thousands of devotees worldwide.

A Pilgrim's Prayer to St. Pio of Pietrelcina

St. Pio, Padre Pio,
Friend of the world, and a father to me,
As I visit the places you lived and worked,
And witness the faith of other pilgrims,
May I surrender all preconceptions, all notions of miracles,
And look only for your loving guidance
To lead my soul closer to God.
Padre Pio, walk beside me.
Welcome me to the places you knew.
Speak the words I need to hear.
Show me what I need to do.
Bless my journey homeward

Where you have promised you would be,
Waiting for all your spiritual children
At the gates of eternity.

The Pilgrimage

Destinations: Pietrelcina, Piana Romana, San Giovanni Rotondo, and Bari
Suggested Length: Two to four days

If beginning this pilgrimage from Rome, you will need to factor in a day of car travel to Pietrelcina; to visit Pietrelcina and nearby Piana Romana a further day; and to travel to and spend ample time at San Giovanni Rotondo another day. And if you wish to drive south to Bari afterward to visit the tomb of St. Nicholas (an optional, and highly suggested, add-on to the end of this pilgrimage), then this would total four days.

DAY ONE: Pietrelcina

Traveling from Rome (or continuing on from Montecassino if you have completed the St. Benedict pilgrimage), take the A1 south, and at the outskirts of Napoli exit at Caserta Sud. At Caserta take the No. 265 road to Benevento, which will take about an hour. At Benevento (where Padre Pio was ordained in the cathedral), follow the road to Campobasso. Exit off the ring road around Campobasso (the road that circles the outside of the town), following the signs for Pietrelcina (indicated No. 212).

The old town of Pietrelcina (meaning "Little Rock") is mostly composed of pedestrian lanes, so it is necessary to park outside the town in its many parking lots and walk in.

Convento "Padre Pio" Sacra Famiglia (Padre Pio Convent of the Holy Family)

This is the church of the 1955 seminary of Sacra Famiglia (Holy Family) of the Franciscan Friars Minor, built in honor of St. Pio in his hometown. Here you could light a candle and offer your prayer and intent for your pilgrimage.

S. Maria degli Angeli (St. Mary of the Angels)

Following the main street through the town you reach the parish church of Pietrelcina, where young Francesco Forgione would come and quietly pray, and where he began his ministry as a priest. He said his first Mass here and his confessional is to the right of the nave.

There is a particularly moving picture of him in the church near the altar. Other notables are the displays of some of his relics, including one of his gloves, some bones, and a bloodstained cloth. The image of St. Michael on the wall is typical, stamping out the power of the devil.

Family House and Turret, 27/28 Vico Storto Valla (Crooked Valley Lane)

Follow on the street to the right and down some steps arriving at "the big rock."

This rock was the landmark for all the Forgione children as they were nearing home. St. Pio would frequently request those from Pietrelcina to remember him to the big rock—the inscription on it reads just that—"Salutatemi la morgia."

The house in which St. Pio was born and lived his childhood is composed of two simple buildings together on the south side of the lane. The kitchen, with its fireplace for cooking and heating the rooms, and the parents' bedroom (where he was born) are preserved as they were. Across the lane is "La Torretta" (the turret), which was St. Pio and Michele's bedroom as boys. It later became St. Pio's private cell while living his exile from community as a Capuchin novice. It was from this turret that neighbors heard the noises of the beatings and battles that St. Pio experienced while he struggled with the powers of darkness.

Chiesetta di S. Anna (Little Church of St. Ann)

Up some steps at the end of the lane is the small church where St. Pio was baptized, where he made his first communion and confirmation, and where he often said Mass. His stone baptismal font is on the left, and also his confessional is displayed.

Casa Materna di P. Pio (St. Pio's mother's house)

This was the first house that his parents lived in when married and was probably St. Pio's mother's original family home. This small abode was where she prepared the celebration lunch for him after his ordination and his first Mass in their hometown on Sunday, August 14, 1910.

Casa Zio Michele (Michele's House)

Nearby is his brother Michele's house where St. Pio lived as a young priest between 1912 and 1916. His bedroom there is preserved as it was. This is also where Mary Pyle lived in exile during World War II.

Piana Romana

Leave the town of Pietrelcina, following the signs for "Piana Romana," which is a fifteen minute drive.

The first place to visit would be the **"masseria"** (the Forgiones' family farmhouse). This rustic spot was St. Pio's favorite, particularly during summer, and he would always receive healing for his physical ailments here. The park behind the house was the family's farm where a few goats and ducks were kept and vegetables and vines cultivated. The **well** was built by his father. The **chapel** in the park with its picture on its outside wall of Christ descending to St. Pio was built in the 1950s while Pio was still alive. It was constructed around **the oak tree** where St. Pio first experienced the invisible signs of the stigmata in 1910. The oak is still behind the altar. In the park behind the chapel protected by a cage is **the rock** on which St. Pio loved to pray and meditate.

The contemporary church opposite the park, which was constructed in the millennium Jubilee year to honor St. Pio, does not have many architectural or devotional qualities, but it is worth a visit just the same before departing this holy hamlet.

DAY TWO: San Giovanni Rotondo

Retrace your drive, returning via Pietrelcina and Campobasso, and take the exit to Foggia on the S645. Foggia can be avoided by turning off just before Lucera on the S160 toward S. Severo, and then take the S272 to San Giovanni Rotondo, following the signs thereafter. You can also reach San Giovanni Rotondo from Foggia via the S89 toward Manfredonia, turning off onto the S273 on the way. The road to San Giovanni Rotondo will curve up and over the mountain range that surrounds it. At the summit there's a shrine to St. Michael the Archangel, the protector against evil. Drive straight in to the town or park outside and walk in. The highest street on the mountain is the one that leads to Our Lady of Grace Church and Friary, as well as the hospital.

Casa Sollievo della Sofferenza (The Home for the Relief of Suffering)

St. Pio's vision and accomplishment is like a light on the hill. It is still a working hospital, not only serving the community with over a thousand beds, but serving as a medical research center that's considered the best in Italy. The quote on the outside wall is from the "Canticle of the Creatures" by St. Francis: "Praise and blessing to my Lord for Sister Charity, and give thanks and service to God with great humility." The two words in the stars on the brick are *Amor* (Love) and *Caritas* (Charity). The magnificent statue of St. Francis surrounded by flying birds is perched on its roof. The St. Pio International Prayer Groups' central office has its own entrance in the front.

S. Maria delle Grazie (Our Lady of Grace) Church and Friary

The new church was built in the 1950s to house the crowds of pilgrims who flocked to Padre Pio's Mass and confessional. There are many relics and mementos including one of his tunics. The side door leads to the friary, the old church, and his tomb. His cell is No. 5, an eight-by-ten-foot bedroom and study with a sink. Over his desk is an image of the Holy Mother (Our Lady Liberatrix from Pietrelcina), who, he said, never left his cell and guarded and guided him all his life; there are also images of St. Michael and the pope, for whom St. Pio always prayed. St. Pio died in this room.

The old church in the friary is where, as a young priest, St. Pio received the bleeding stigmata that he lived with all his life, and it was in this church that he spent hours of ecstatic prayer. When he was not permitted to say public Mass or to hear confessions, this church became his private chapel for prayer as he waited out his "imprisonment."

The crypt is where his remains are entombed in marble. He died within a day or two of its completion. This is the perfect place to end your pilgrimage.

Via Crucis

To the left of the friary, sandwiched between the hospital and the church up on the mountain, is a park where the Way of the Cross is depicted with St. Pio as Simon of Cyrene, helping Christ with his cross on his way to his crucifixion. St. Pio had always said that his suffering was given to him to relieve Christ's suffering.

The Lottery

You might notice a statue or photo of St. Pio at ticket counters of lottery offices, especially in southern Italy. He is often called upon for luck when buying lottery tickets due to what befell Dr. Sanguinetti (the first director of the hospital) who, when St. Pio told him that "the Lord will provide," immediately won a lottery windfall.

A VISIT TO BARI AND ST. NICHOLAS

The following visit to Bari is suggested as a final destination to the St. Pio pilgrimage because St. Nicholas, although not of Italian descent, was also a man of generosity and kindness, whose loving acts for the people of his community spread to the entire world in the model of Father Christmas, bestower of cheer, lover of children and families, and bringer of hope.

St. Nicholas

Nicholas was born in Patara, a town in the province of Lycia in the region of Asia Minor (now Turkey) in the late third century. His family recognized his special gifts at a young age—he was intelligent and big-hearted, with a strong belief in God. Educated in the Greek language and philosophy (as he lived in the Eastern Roman Empire), he found the teachings of the early Christian Church the most stimulating. With his newfound study of theology, he followed his calling to become a priest and joined the Church. He threw himself into building up his parish community and rigorously practiced the Christian virtues of giving to those in need; protecting the Christian families in his care from poverty, despair, and persecution; and upholding justice and righteousness. Because of this, and especially because of his generosity and wisdom, Nicholas had many devotees.

One incident handed down by tradition formed the basis of the ritual and manner of Father Christmas's gift-giving. A destitute family that had suffered from famine and had no hope of income were intent on selling their children to slavery until they received a sack of coins tossed anonymously through their window. The second time this happened, one member of the family recognized the donor as Father Nicholas as he disappeared, a lone figure, into the darkness of the night.

Nicholas's popularity in Patara spread to Myra, the capital of Lycia, and in AD 305 Nicholas was voted by the people to become their bishop. With deacons and others in his diocese at Myra, he continued to serve those in need. But it was certainly not a safe environment to openly practice Christianity. The Roman Empire was still persecuting Christians, and Nicholas and many of his companions were not spared. It was the Hellenists, however, who imprisoned him for his Christianity and probably destroyed his church with its rich library of books and objects. While in prison, Nicholas led his fellow prisoners to live with hope and courage in a climate of destruction amid dismal conditions. He surprisingly survived the many years of incarceration, and on his release (due to Emperor Constantine's conversion), he began tirelessly to build up his community again, working also in the hospices to care for victims of persecution and those who had become sick in prison. He eventually restored the community. He must have been an extraordinary man as he touched so many people's hearts by championing their needs and listening to their souls. There is some evidence from Byzantine documents that as bishop, Nicholas would have attended the Council of Nicaea in AD 325. He died on December 6 in an unknown year.

Nicholas's body was venerated by thousands throughout the East, as he had become a patron for Greeks and Russians, as well as a prominent saint in the Eastern Orthodox Church. His fame spread posthumously throughout Europe as Christmas rituals emerged out of pagan traditions. For instance, offering gifts during the winter festival of Equinox became gifts to the Christ-child at the nativity, and this in turn became the gift of St. Nicholas delivered by him in a sack secretly on the eve of Christ's birth, a tradition that evolved from being tossed through a window to delivered down the chimney.

Always a time for love and wonderment, the Christmas traditions of sharing fruits and nuts with friends, and feasting with family, grew out of these old traditions. But in the Eastern Church, St. Nicholas was never forgotten in his own right as a dispenser of care and provider of needs throughout the year. Myra became a vital stop for anyone traveling west or east, and was revered as a special place of pilgrimage to pray and view the miraculous "holy liquid"—sometimes called the oil or "manna" of St. Nicholas—that exudes, even to this day, from his remains. Sadly, however, the saint was not to lie long in peace in his special church at Myra. He had become so popular that a plot was hatched, and successfully accomplished, by a group of Italian mariners returning from Antioch in 1087. They decided that trade could be stimulated in their hometown, the great port of Bari on the eastern coast of Italy, if they possessed St. Nicholas's remains, so they attacked the caretakers of the church and smashed the sarcophagus with hammers and swords. They transported the bones of St. Nicholas in a silk cloth, sailing speedily out of port as the locals threw themselves into the sea after them, crying and petitioning for the return of their saint. After a month at sea, the crew arrived in Bari and presented St. Nicholas's shroud to the local bishop, who had it placed for safety in a nearby Benedictine monastery. Further violence ensued—this time in the streets of Bari—as locals argued over where he was to be entombed among them. There was so much commotion in the streets that two people were killed in the skirmishes.

The solution was a new church, which the presiding Norman king—and ruler of Bari—Roger Guiscard gave permission to build. It was consecrated on October 1, 1089, by Pope Urban II, and, almost as predicted, pilgrims began to arrive from all over Europe, and of course, the East. Apart from being the co-patron of Russia and Norway, of children and prisoners, and latterly patron of Bari, St. Nicholas was also proclaimed patron and protector of sailors—surely a bitter irony! The anniversary of his arrival at Bari (May 9) is celebrated each year with special festivities by the townspeople, including taking his remains out to sea for a few hours. The church that carries his name and houses his tomb is one of the most magnificent examples of early Norman-influenced architecture, constructed mostly by Muslim artisans who left their cultural and religious mark upon its walls.

Basilica di San Nicola (The Basilica of St. Nicholas) at Bari

From San Giovanni Rotondo drive south along the coastline on the S159. From anywhere else it is easy to find roads into the great port town. A city made up of myriads of tiny streets, white-washed houses, and clotheslines, it is recommended you keep a close eye on your valuables and park your car in a secure lot.

The Church of St. Nicholas is easy to find as it is on the outskirts of town as you enter from the north. As the streets are narrow and everyone is friendly, ask directions on coming into the city.

The church was built on the land of the Court of Capatano, which already housed five churches when St. Nicholas's remains arrived. The churches of St. Basil, St. Sophia, St. Demetrius, and St. Eustatius all were destroyed to prepare for the large basilica, but St. Gregory remained and can be visited today. The Dominicans became St. Nicholas's custodian in 1951, and many monks can be seen in the church and the buildings around.

As if St. Nicholas's influence lives on, breeding hope in pilgrims, there are few places like this in Europe where Western Christians and Eastern Orthodox pilgrims come together in joint worship, and there is also hardly a church that will not, quite literally, take your breath away.

Everywhere you walk, and everywhere you look, reveals a masterpiece of architecture. With its placement of stone and use of space, the church attempts to create an encasement of the heavenly mysteries.

The main nave is surrounded by the Matrons' Galleries, which were places reserved for noblewomen so that they could follow the religious ceremonies protected and without disturbance. The main altar was built between 1123–25 and there Muslim influence is evident. The mosaic floor is from the emperor's original Byzantine palace, and the decorations in the apse have been identified by some scholars as monograms of Allah. The stone throne is Norman. Behind the altar is a more modern use of black marble to complement the ancient altar. Everything is in perfect symmetry, with a surprising array of different pillars from different ages. The images of St. Nicholas on its walls reveal his Turkish ancestry with his dark skin and beard.

And with its Orthodox-style icons, Byzantine décor, Norman architecture, and Arabic influence, St. Nicholas is certainly one of the most unique churches on earth. Perhaps it is not just historic circumstance that has created such a place, but the very real presence of a saint who is, beyond all the saints in this book, the most famous in the world.

The Crypt

The tomb of St. Nicholas is central in this underground masterpiece. Two angels hold bottles at the front opening, which is believed to hold the "holy liquid" that exudes from his bones.

To the left of the crypt is the Eastern Orthodox chapel where Christians from both Churches pray, and in between them is an image of the great Dominican saint Thomas Aquinas. St. Nicholas's Basilica is now the home of the Institute of Ecumenical Theology, where both Catholic and Orthodox teachers and students come together to study each other's traditions in the common faith of the salvation of Jesus Christ.

Suggestions for Pilgrimage Intentions

Animals, pets: St. Francis

Faith and Spirituality
Deeper faith and belief: St. Anthony, St. Pius X, St. Apollinare
Deeper love of God: St. Clare
Developing a pure heart: St. Anthony, St. Clare
Discovering God's call: St. Francis, St. Catherine
For finding clarity: St. Anthony, St. Pius X
Forgiveness and purification: St. Anthony, St. Benedict, St. Pio
Journey of the soul: Bl. John XXIII
Opening of heart and soul: St. Catherine, St. Veronica
For richer and healthier interior life: St. Pio
Spiritual guidance: St. Pio, St. Pius X
Wisdom: St. Pius X, St. Bonaventure

Family
Family healing: Bl. John XXIII
Fertility and birth: Bl. John XXIII
Forgiveness and purification: St. Anthony, St. Benedict, St. Pio
Help with study: St. Bonaventure, St. Pius X, St. Anthony, St. Benedict
Interfaith: St. Catherine, Bl. John XXIII
Meeting your life partner: St. Francis, St. Clare, St. Anthony
Patience and perseverance: St. Catherine, Bl. Margaret
Pets, animals: St. Francis

Lay and Religious Vocations
Blessings on ordination: Bl. John XXIII
Church renewal: Bl. John XXIII, St. Pius X
Clarity on work and vocation: St. Clare, St. Anthony, Bl. John XXIII, St. Bonaventure, St. Pio
Developing personal talents: St. Bonaventure

Discovering God's call: St. Francis, St. Catherine
Gratitude for partnership: St. Francis, St. Clare
Help with community: St. Clare
Help in leadership: St. Pius X, Bl. John XXIII, St. Bonaventure
Help in prayerful action: St. Pio, St. Francis
Help with study: St. Bonaventure, St. Pius X, St. Anthony, St. Benedict
Meeting your life partner: St. Francis, St. Clare, St. Anthony
Religious equality, reform, and unity: Bl. John XXIII
Spiritual guidance: St. Pio, St. Pius X

Peace
For personal or world peace: St. Francis, St. Catherine, St. Anthony, St. Pius X, Bl. John XXIII
Interfaith: St. Catherine, Bl. John XXIII

Personal Challenges
Courage in life changes: St. Anthony, St. Vitale
Humility: St. Bonaventure, St. Benedict, St. Francis
Overcoming fear: St. Clare, Bl. Margaret
Preparing for change: St. Catherine
Finding a simpler life: St. Francis, St. Clare, St. Pius X, St. Benedict

Suffering
Comfort for the dying: St. Pio
Healing from illness: St. Anthony, Bl. Margaret, St. Pio
For patience and perseverance: St. Catherine, Bl. Margaret
For strength: St. Clare, Bl. Margaret, St. Pius X
Revelation in suffering: St. Pio

Women
A balanced life: St. Francis, St. Benedict
Fertility and birth: Bl. John XXIII
Guidance on feminine principles: St. Clare, St. Veronica
Honoring the sacred feminine: Holy Women of Tuscany and Umbria and individually, St. Catherine, St. Veronica
Religious equality, reform, and unity: Bl. John XXIII

Acknowledgments

My editor, Jan-Erik Guerth, suggested in a phone call that I write a spiritual travel book to Italy. I was overcome by the prospect, but grateful when he agreed that a book of pilgrimage following Italy's more prominent saints would suffice. My beloved husband and partner in work and prayer, John Dalla Costa, agreed to do the driving and navigating, and to be by my side as we tackled the idiosyncratic Italian road systems. Then he translated Italian texts, shared his vast knowledge (and library) of history and theology, scribbled words of advice on yellow stick-it notes throughout drafts of the manuscript, and celebrated all stages of progress. Without him this book would never have made it to print. My gratitude overflows.

My dear friend and literary agent, Linda McKnight, cheered me on and cheered me up as we tackled the publishing of a spiritual book in dry and parched lands. Jane Gelfman's friendship and support are a continued blessing in my life. Grace and John Bozzo generously helped unravel some of the puzzling details of the Abruzzo caves and chapels. And last, but not least, I am grateful for the enormous opportunity for soul growth that studying these saints has afforded me. Their examples, lives, and teachings shine in the golden sunlight of Italy, reflecting the beauty of spiritual achievement and the depth of the love of God.

Thank you, Jan-Erik, for this opportunity to discover more about them and to travel to places I might never have been.

Lucinda Vardey

The author is grateful to those who have kindly granted her permission to reproduce in this book the images as listed below.

Blessed Margaret of Castello, The National Shrine of Blessed Margaret of Castello, St. Louis Bertrand Church, Louisville, Kentucky, U.S.A.

Blessed Pope John XXIII, Pontificio Istituto Missioni Estere, Sotto Il Monte Giovanni XXIII, Italy.

Sant'Appolinare by Stefania Salti (artist).

San Vitale by Renata Augusta Venturini (artist and sculptor).

St. Anthony, Basilica di Sant'Antonio, Padua, Italy.

St. Benedict, P. D. Mauro Meacci, Abbot of Subiaco (RM), Italy.

St. Catherine of Siena *(a particular from the painting "Il Vecchietta" by Lorenzo di Pietro)* Ministero per i Beni e le Attività Culturale. Foto Sopritendenza PSAD Siena e Grosetto.

St. Clare, Provincia Serafica S. Francesco D'Assisi, O.F.M., Italy.

St. Francis and Jesus Christ, Eremo di Montecasale, Sansepolcro (AR) Italy.

St. Pio of Pietrelcina, La Bottega dell'Arte Sacra, San Giovanni Rotondo, Italy.

St. Pius X, author's photo from Our Lady of the Rosary Church in Lourdes, France.

St. Veronica Giuliani, Monastero "S. Cuore" Clarissa Cappuccine, Mercatello sul Metauro, Italy.

"L'incredulità di San Tomaso" (front cover image), La Chiesa S. Nicolo, Treviso, Italy.

Bibliographical References

Author's Note: References have been arranged in the order in which they appear or were used in the book.

St. Francis of Assisi: Christ's Work of Art

God's Fool: The Life and Times of Francis of Assisi by Julien Green, translated by Peter Heinegg (San Francisco: Harper SanFrancisco, 1987).

Art and Society in the Middle Ages by Georges Duby, translated by Jean Birrell (Oxford: Polity Press, in association with Blackwell Publishers Ltd., 2000).

Francis of Assisi by Arnaldo Fortini, translated by Helen Moak (New York: Crossroad, 1992).

A Short History of the Franciscan Family by Damien Vorreux, OFM, and Aaron Pembleton, OFM (Chicago: Franciscan Herald Press, 1989).

The Writings of St. Francis of Assisi, edited by Halcyon Backhouse (London: Hodder and Stoughton, 1994).

St. Francis and the Third Order by Raffaele Pazzelli, TOR (Chicago: Franciscan Herald Press, 1982).

The Life of St. Francis of Assisi by St. Bonaventure, from the original *Legenda Sancti Francisci* (Rockford, IL: Tan Books and Publishers, Inc., 1867).

The Land of Saint Francis: Umbria and Surroundings by Luciano Canonici (Terni, Italy: Plurigraf, 1987).

The Little Flowers of Saint Francis, translated by Leo Sherley-Price (Harmondsworth, Middlesex: Penguin Books Ltd., 1959).

The New Jerusalem Bible, Reader's Edition (London: Dartman, Longman & Todd Ltd., 1985).

ART & SOUL: SANSEPOLCRO AND CAPRESE MICHELANGELO

Piero Della Francesca by Marco Bussagli (Florence: Guinti Gruppo Editoriale, 1998).

Michelangelo by Marco Bussagli (Florence: Guinti Gruppo Editoriale, 2000).

Holy Women of Tuscany and Umbria

St. Catherine of Siena: Light of Truth

Saint Catherine of Siena by Alice Curtayne (1929; reprint Rockford, IL: Tan Books and Publishers Inc., 1980).

My Nature Is Fire: Saint Catherine of Siena by Catherine M. Meade, CSJ (New York: Alba House, 1991).

Catherine of Siena: Passion for the Truth, Compassion for Humanity: Selected Spiritual Writings, edited by Mary O'Driscoll, OP (Hyde Park, NY: New City Press, 1993).

Praying with Catherine of Siena by Patricia Mary Vinje (Winona, MN: Saint Mary's Press, 1990).

Catherine of Siena by Mary O'Driscoll, OP (Strasbourg, Cedex, France: Editions du Signe, 1994).

Catherine of Siena: The Dialogue, translated and introduced by Suzanne Noffke, OP (New York/Mahwah, NJ: Paulist Press, 1980).

The Letters of Catherine of Siena, vol. 1, translated with introduction and notes by Suzanne Noffke, OP, Medieval and Renaissance Texts and Studies (Ithaca, NY: Cornell University Press, 2000).

A Life of Total Prayer: Selected Writings of Catherine of Siena, edited and introduced by Keith Beasley-Topliffe (Nashville: Upper Room Books, 2000).

St. Clare of Assisi: The First Flower

St. Clare of Assisi by Nesta de Robeck (Chicago: Franciscan Herald Press, 1980).

Clare of Assisi: A Biographical Study by Ingrid J. Peterson, OSF (Quincy, IL: Franciscan Press, 1993).

In the Footsteps of Saint Clare: A Pilgrim's Guide Book by Ramona Miller, OSF (St. Bonaventure, NY: The Franciscan Institute, St. Bonaventure University, 1993).

Praying with Clare of Assisi by Ramona Miller and Ingrid Peterson (Winona, MN: Saint Mary's Press, 1994).

Clare of Assisi by Marco Bartoli, translated by Frances Teresa, OSC (London: Darton, Longman and Todd Ltd., 1993).

Francis and Clare: The Complete Works, translated by Regis J. Armstrong, OFM Cap, and Ignatius C. Brady, OFM (New York: Paulist Press, 1982).

Clare of Assisi: Light for the Way, no author (Strasbourg, France: Editions du Signe, 1991).

ART & SOUL: URBINO

Urbino: A Historical and Artistic Guide, edited by by Giuseppe Cucco (Villa Verucchio, Italy: Edizioni Lithos, 1996).

Raphael by Carlo Pedretti, translated by Paula Boomsliter (Florence: Guinti Gruppo Editoriale, 1998).

The Story of Civilization: The Renaissance by Will Durant (New York: Simon & Schuster, 1953).

The Italian Renaissance by J. H. Plumb (Boston/New York: American Heritage Inc., Houghton Mifflin Company, 1989).

Personal contributions from art historian Professor Thomas Martone.

St. Veronica Giuliani: Love's Mediator

Santa Veronica Giuliani: Il centenario delle stimmate, 1697–1997 (Città di Castello, Italy: Monastero Cappuccine S. Veronica Giuliani, 1997).

Saint Veronica Giuliani, Capuchin Poor Clare by John Leonardi, OFM Cap (Mercatello, Italy: Monastery of St. Veronica, 1986).

Saint Veronica Giuliani: The Purgatory of Love, translated by Dr. Oliver Knox (Città di Castello, Italy: Centro Studi Veronichiano, 1983).

Un incontro con Santa Veronica Giuliani by Remo Bistoni (Perugia: Edizioni Francescane Italiane, 1995).

Blessed Margaret of Castello: Unheralded Survivor

The Life of Blessed Margaret of Castello, 1287–1320 by William R. Bonniwell, OP (Rockford, IL: Tan Books and Publishers Inc., 1983).

Beata Margherita de la Metola: Una Sfida alla Emarginazione (Città di Castello, Italy: Petruzzi Editore, 1988).

St. Bonaventure: Prince of Wisdom

Bonaventure: Selected Spiritual Writings, edited by Timothy Johnson (New York: New City Press, 1999).

Bonaventure: Mystical Writings by Zachary Hayes (New York: Crossroad Publishing Company, 1999).

A History of the Franciscan Order: From Its Origins to the Year 1517 by John R. H. Moorman (London: Oxford University Press; Chicago: Franciscan Herald Press, 1988).

New Jerusalem Bible Saints, edited by Henry Wansbrough (London: Darton, Longman & Todd, 2002).

St. Anthony: The Miracle Worker

Benignitas, 1316, a legendary biography.

Legenda Assidua, 1232, the first biography of St. Anthony, written at the time of his canonization, less than a year after his death.

St. Anthony: The Wonder-Worker of Padua by Charles Warren Stoddard (1896; reprint, Rockford, IL: Tan Books & Publishers Inc., 1971).

St. Anthony, Doctor of the Church by Sophronius Clasen, OFM (Chicago: Franciscan Herald Press, 1961).

Anthony of Padua: Proclaimer of the Gospel by Lothar Hardick, OFM (Strasbourg, France: Editions du Signe, 1994).

The New Jerusalem Bible, Reader's Edition (London: Dartman, Longman & Todd Ltd., 1985).

Sts. Apollinare & Vitale: Early Martyrs of Ravenna

Ravenna: Mosaics, Monuments and Environment by G. Mustachinni (Ravenna: Cartolibreria Salbaroli, 1989).

The Story of S. Apollinare: Patron of Ravenna by Stefania Salfi and Renata Venturini (Ravenna: Edizioni Stear, 2000).

The Story of St. Vitale: Holy Martyr of Ravenna by Stefania Salfi and Renata Venturini (Ravenna: Edizioni Stear, 2000).

St. Pius X: The Man in Between

"San Pio X: A centocinquant'anni dalla nascità," a supplement to *Famiglia Cristiana* (1835–2 giugno–1985), 1985.

La Terra di San Pio X, Parrochia di S. Matteo in Riese, 1997.

Se'ndava in Grappa, Comune di Crespano del Grappa, Biblioteca Comunale, L'Orsa Minore, Fogli di Cultura Locale, 1996.

Military Memorials of the First World War, Ministry of Defense, General Committee for the Honors to War Fallen, Rome, 2001.

Blessed John XXIII: Hero of the Sacred Mountain

Journal of a Soul, 1895–1962 by Pope John XXIII, translated by Dorothy White (London: Geoffrey Chapman Ltd., 1965).

John XXIII: Pope of the Century by Peter Hebblethwaite (London and New York: Continuum, 1984, 2000).

The Stories of Pope John XXIII: His Anecdotes & Legends by Louis Michaels (Springfield, IL: Templegate Publishers, 2000).

Casa del Beato Papa Giovanni (Bergamo, Italy: Editrice Edinord, 2000).

Contributions to Vatican II summary by John Dalla Costa, M.Div.

A Pilgrimage in Rome

Decline and Fall of the Roman Empire by Edward Gibbon (1776; reprint London: Bison Books Ltd., 1969).

Collins Concise Encyclopedia of Greek and Roman Mythology (Glasgow: Wm. Collins Sons & Co. Ltd.; Chicago: Follet Publishing, 1969).

The Oxford Dictionary of Saints by David Hugh Farmer (Oxford and New York: Oxford University Press, 1978).

The Twelve Caesars by Michael Grant (London: Phoenix Press, 1975, 1996).

The Geometry of Love by Margaret Visser (Toronto: HarperFlamingo, 2000).

Rome: A Guide to the Eternal City by Loretta Gerson, Silvia Mazzola, and Venetia Morrison (London: Napoleoni & Wakefield Ltd., 1999).

Rome, Eyewitness Travel Guides (London: Dorling Kindersley Limited, 1993).

The Catholic Encylopedia, Volumes 1, 3, and 11 (New York: Robert Appleton Company 1907/8/11).

St. Benedict: The Pioneer Monastic

Medieval Monasticism: Forms of Religious Life in Western Europe in the Middle Ages by C. H. Lawrence (Harlow, Essex: Longman Group UK Limited, 1984).

The Rule of St. Benedict, translated with introduction and notes by Anthony C. Meisel and M. L. del Mastro (New York: Image Books, 1975).

St. Benedict, Hero of the Hills by Mary Fabyan Windeatt (San Francisco: Ignatius Press, 1986).

Montecassino: The Story of the Most Controversial Battle of World War II by David Hapgood and David Richardson (Cambridge, MA: Da Capo Press, 1984).

The Abbey of Montecassino (Montecassino, Italy: Pubblicazioni Cassinesi, 1998).

The Shrine of the Holy Grotto, Subiaco by the Benedictine Fathers of Subiaco (Subiaco, Italy: The Monastery of St. Benedict, 2001).

Il Monastero di Santa Scolastica, Subiaco (Subiaco, Italy: Edizioni Monastero S. Scolastica, 1999).

Art and Society in the Middle Ages by Georges Duby, translated by Jean Birrell (Oxford: Polity Press, in association with Blackwell Publishers Ltd., 2000).

Gli Eremi di Roccamorice by Enrico Centofanti and Alberto Di Giovanni (L'Aquila, Italy: Gruppo Tipografico Editoriale, 2000).

St. Pio of Pietrelcina (Padre Pio): Jesus' Alchemist

Words of Light: An Anthology of Thoughts from Padre Pio's Letters, translated by Andrew Tulloch (London: St. Paul's Publishing, 1997).

Padre Pio: The True Story by C. Bernard Ruffin (Huntingdon, IN: Our Sunday Visitor Publishing Division, 1991).

Padre Pio: His Life and Mission by Mary F. Ingoldsby (Dublin: Veritas Publications, 1978).

Padre Pio: In My Own Words, compiled by Anthony F. Chiffolo (London: Hodder & Stoughton, 2001).

La Casa Sollievo della Sofferenza 2002, official organ of the Padre Pio prayer groups for La Casa Sollievo della Sofferenza (House for the Relief of Suffering).

Angela of Foligno: Complete Works, compiled and translated by Paul Lachance, OFM (Mahwah, NJ: Paulist Press, 1993).

A VISIT TO BARI AND ST. NICHOLAS

Saint Nicholas, Bishop of Myra by D. L. Cann (Toronto: Novalis, 2002).

The Basilica of Saint Nicholas by Gerardo Gioffari, OP (Bari, Italy: The Dominican Fathers of Saint Nicholas's Basilica, 1997).

Index